Stratification and Mobility

Stratification

and Mobility

Mark Abrahamson
Syracuse University

Ephraim H. Mizruchi
Syracuse University

Carlton A. Hornung
University of Maryland

Macmillan Publishing Co., Inc.
New York

Collier Macmillan Publishers
London

To our wives, Marlene, Ruth, Gail

Macmillan Publishing Co., Inc.
866 Third Avenue, New York, New York 10022

Collier Macmillan Canada, Ltd.

Library of Congress Cataloging in Publication Data

Abrahamson, Mark.
    Stratification and mobility.

    Includes index.
    1. Social classes. 2. Social mobility. 3. Social
classes—United States. 4. Social mobility—United
States. I. Mizruchi, Ephraim Harold, joint author.
II. Hornung, Carlton A., joint author. III. Title.
HT609.A24   301.44   75-11830
ISBN 0-02-300201-8

Printing: 1 2 3 4 5 6 7 8   Year: 6 7 8 9 0 1 2

Preface

The proliferation of research directed to aspects of American social stratification and social mobility, especially since the 1950s, has clearly established that social inequality is a matter of concern to both sociologist and layman. In more recent years certain issues have been articulated that have led to ideological, theoretical, or methodological controversies. These, for the most part, have resulted in substantial contributions to both the breadth and depth of understanding of the structures and processes by which social inequalities emerge, persist, and are transformed.

In this book we attack what we feel are some of the most important theoretical and methodological issues associated with the study of social stratification and social mobility. Ideological issues, as such, are not a central concern but, when appropriate, we attempt to point out how they make a difference in directing and interpreting research in this area.

Our major concern is with social mobility both in American and cross-national perspective. Our broad perspective is classical and we rely a great deal on insights and hypotheses derived from the works of Max Weber, Karl Marx, Georg Simmel, Henri de Saint-Simon, Auguste Comte, and the Scottish Moralists, to name but a handful of those whose contributions warrant recognition as classical writers. In this respect we pay homage to the late C. Wright Mills, who tried to stimulate a whole generation of sociologists to pursue this course.[1]

What we examine and emphasize are issues of conceptual, theoretical, and methodological concern. We are not "abstract empiricists," nor are we "armchair sociologists." [2] We are primarily interested in the interplay between sociological theories of stratification and mobility and the empirical realities of everyday life. Although most of the hypotheses with which we deal can be assessed by reference to systematically gathered empirical data,

[1] C. Wright Mills, *Images of Man* (New York: George Braziller, 1960).
[2] C. Wright Mills, *The Sociological Imagination* (New York: Oxford U. P., 1959).

some are based on more informal intuitive methods. Thus, some generalizations in this book will be more solidly supported than others. Every effort is made to clarify the degree of tentativeness associated with the hypotheses and theories presented.

The book is organized into four parts. In Part One we provide some of the broad perspectives that underlie our approach and some novel ways of conceptualizing stratification processes. For example, Simmel's emphasis on the significance of numbers in quality of social interaction is used to hypothesize the structuring of inequality. The same idea is used to contrast local community stratification with national stratification. In Part Two we attempt to place the study of social stratification and social mobility into the broader context of sociological theory and its antecedents. Some of the sources of contemporary controversy are dealt with, but our concern is with the common denominators rather than the diversities in perspective. In Part Three we review the emergence of empirical approaches to social stratification in contrast with the more classical approaches. Stratification research is viewed against the background of the ecological schools of the 1920s and 1930s and the gradual shift to variables other than ecological position, including education and occupation. Occupation emerges, in our view, as the most important indicator of social position and concomitant life-styles and life-chances. The increasing conceptual and methodological precision that emerges from the processes described in the first three parts of the book leads to the increasing capacity of sociologists to measure and assess hypotheses about social mobility in the United States and cross-nationally. In Part Four we demonstrate what contemporary analysts of social stratification and social mobility are doing; how they go about their work; and the status of hypotheses and generalizations about opportunities for social mobility in the United States. The nature of the obstacles to social mobility standing in the way of people in ascribed categories is probed in Chapter 9. We close the book with an analysis of comparative stratification and mobility, the directions that mobility may be expected to take both in the United States and in the other industrialized societies, and an assessment of the hypothesis that stratification patterns are converging in these societies.

Because so much is dealt with in such a limited amount of space we have been unable to provide an equal amount of depth on each issue. We have chosen to emphasize those aspects of an almost infinite variety of conceptual and methodological issues that we feel are most salient at this point in history. Thus, this is not a book on conflict theory, nor is it a book on functional theory or any other single theory. We have reviewed aspects of the conflict and functional approaches—as well as others—to provide an overview of the major perspectives in this area of sociological study. Ultimately, however, we have had to treat in depth some matters that receive relatively less attention in general books on social stratification. There is much that is original here and some that is not. The reader is the best judge of our effort.

A number of colleagues have made various contributions by reading parts of the manuscript and making suggestions, among them John Pease and George Ritzer. Mark Mizruchi, then an undergraduate student in sociology, provided the student's perspective. Robert Perrucci contributed by intensively discussing several of these concepts in the context of work on another book dealing with somewhat similar matters. While we acknowledge, with appreciation, their help we alone bear the responsibility for the final product.

M. A.

E. H. M.

C. A. H.

Syracuse, N.Y.

Contents

Part Three

Empirical Perspectives

Part Four

Social Mobility

Part One

Introduction

1 Perspectives and Concepts in the Study of Social Stratification and Social Mobility

Social Inequality in Historical and Contemporary Contexts

Social inequality is a basic fact of life in all known societies and has been described in song and story from as far back as man's earliest excursions into the realm of linguistic expression. The chroniclers of man's experience in antiquity and in more recent history apparently could not avoid noting that some men possessed more than others: more wealth, more prestige, more influence over others, or more of something else that was highly valued and relatively scarce in a given society. Hierarchical distinctions between social categories are described, for example, in the early literature of ancient China[1] and in the Old Testament and the extensive literary, historical, and political tracts of the ancient Greeks.[2] The pervasiveness of an elaborate conception of a hierarchic society in France during the Middle Ages, even if exag-

[1] Cf., Max Weber, *The Religion of China*, trans. H. Gerth (New York: Free Press, 1951), Chaps. 1 and 2.
[2] Cf., Alvin W. Gouldner, *Enter Plato* (New York: Basic Books, 1965), pp. 9–13.

gerated,[3] and the political realism of Machiavelli describing aspects of Italian society during the early Renaissance are testimony to the concern with ranked groups that characterized Western life in those periods.[4] The proliferation of rank-linked behavior into a wide variety of social settings in England and Europe has become a subject of interest to a number of contemporary historians. They have been investigating aspects of social stratification from the sixteenth century to the present,[5] encompassing a period of dramatic social upheavals that includes revolutions that markedly transformed all of the stratification systems in the West.

The differential distribution of highly valued goods and social capacities and opportunities is everywhere associated with hierarchies of individuals and groups that sociologists call *strata*. These strata are more or less organized into systems of social stratification that order relationships between members of various groups as they interact in a variety of social contexts. Associated with a given system of social stratification is a set of implicit or explicit values that legitimate the persistent inequalities in some societies or which, in others, challenge the very existence of unequal distribution of scarce goods and opportunities. These values play an important role in the process of placing individuals and groups in relatively high or low positions and in the judgments that are made regarding the performance of those who possess differential quantities of the criteria that determine placement.

Who possesses these criteria, and in what amounts, varies from place to place and from time to time. In the contemporary United States, blacks and women feel—and they are supported by many others who share their perceptions—that they possess fewer goods and opportunities than they legitimately deserve. In the Soviet Union and Poland, it is the Jews and political nonconformists who feel that their opportunities are circumscribed. And in South Africa and Rhodesia, it is, again, the blacks who share this understandable dissatisfaction.

The variation in societal contexts within which inequality is perceived as both legitimate and illegitimate is equalled by the great variety in form that we observe in the pattern or structure of social inequality across known societies. The relative value of prestige as a criterion for placement in a hierarchy, for example, varies in different societies. So does political power and wealth. What social factors are responsible for this variation and what their differential influences are for the life-chances of individuals are the fundamental issues we address in this book.

---

[3] J. Huizinga, *The Waning of the Middle Ages* (New York: Doubleday Anchor Books, 1956), pp. 56–57.

[4] Cf., Niccolo Machiavelli, *The Prince and the Discourses* (New York: *The Modern Library*, 1940). The Introduction is by M. Lerner.

[5] Bernard and Elinor Barber, eds., *European Social Class* (New York: Macmillan, 1965).

A scholarly and, sometimes, practical concern with how people are differentiated stems from some of the earliest known commentaries on man. These descriptions of social inequalities in the behavior of men are useful because they provide historical insight into the nature of stratification in different epochs. In addition they help us formulate hypotheses that shape both the layman's conceptions of stratification and the empirically oriented theories of contemporary sociologists. The following description of the display of wealth and influence in ancient Sicily, which apparently played a role in a slave rebellion, suggests a recurrent theme that exemplifies a basic concern of stratification analysts, *conspicuous consumption.*

> The actual outbreak of the revolt was due to Damophilus of Enna, a particularly arrogant multimillionaire. . . . He farmed a vast number of acres, owned immense herds of stock, and tried to outbid the Italian settlers in the island not only in luxury but in the quantity of his slaves and the inhuman harshness with which he treated them. He traveled round his estates in a four-wheeled carriage with thoroughbred horses and a retinue of armed slaves. He also made a point of having round him a troupe of pretty boys and a bevy of ill-bred hangers-on. . . . In his town and country residences he made an elaborate display of plate and purple, and gave banquets of a royal arrogance and of a profusion which put the proverbial luxury of Persia into the shade. Indeed, he was more than Persian not only in his extravagance but in his arrogance. It was the old story of an ill-bred and uncultivated character finding itself in possession of irresponsible power and unearned riches, and the chain of excess and pride duly terminated in the destruction of Damophilus himself and in a great disaster for his country.[6]

Diodorus' description suggests even more than the concept of conspicuous consumption and thus exemplifies an awareness of aspects of social stratification akin to the seventeenth- and eighteenth-century analysts of society. The criteria for placement in strata in terms of wealth and power are clear. Implicit, however, is the view that power and wealth require responsible use; that ostentatiousness is behavior unbecoming to a man of means; and that it is only legitimate for those who have been "properly" socialized to possess wealth and power. The idea of noblesse oblige, in short, appears to have been well developed among the ancient Greeks.

Numerous examples of the variety of stratification forms also appear in the Old Testament, in the works of Homer and in *The Shu King,* the historical classic describing society and culture in China between 2355 and

---

[6] Arnold J. Toynbee, "Diodorus of Agyrium," *Greek Civilization and Character* (New York: New American Library, 1953), p. 76. In this context cf. Gouldner, *Enter Plato* (New York: Basic Books, 1965).

719 B.C.,[7] to name but a few sources. The historical data, thus, provide ample evidence to support our assumption that patterned social inequalities are a ubiquitous phenomenon.

Social description, however, is not necessarily sociological analysis, and it is the latter that is our primary concern here. Much of the substance of the presociological tracts that deal with social stratification is *ideological* rather than analytical. One of the most elaborate statements on inequality and one that, probably more than any other, had a substantial impact on social relationships within Western societies for many centuries was put forward by St. Thomas Aquinas during the thirteenth century. In his idea of patriarchalism, Aquinas enjoined the good Christian to voluntary acceptance of and submission to the inequalities that characterize society.

> By the ruling classes they [the inequalities] are to be utilized as an opportunity for the exercise of charity and devotion toward their less fortunate brethren; and by others as occasions for displaying the virtues of trust, patience and humility to those above them. All social relationships are modeled on the family, with its patriarchal domination of the husband over the wife and children, and the corresponding willing subordination of those patriarchally ruled . . . patriarchalism explicitly recognized the existing social hierarchy and emphasized the duty of every man to remain within his own class and to be content with his present position.[8]

Thus, a careful reading of early documents not only indicates a search on the sociologist's part for important analytical concepts but perhaps, equally important, through them we can discover how universal are the behavior patterns under investigation. With respect to the quotation from St. Thomas Aquinas, furthermore, a little reflection suggests that this explication of what were earlier, scattered ideas, provided the undergirding for the ideologies supporting the various estate systems in Europe and slavery in America.[9] This provides an increment of understanding with respect to the interplay between behavior patterns associated with social stratification and the values that legitimize them.

Our focus on social description is not intended to suggest that analyt-

---

[7] *The Shu King,* trans. W. G. Old (London: The Theosophical Publishing Society, 1904). With commentary. Cf. also, Max Weber, *The Religion of China,* trans., H. Gerth (New York: Free Press, 1951), Chaps. 1 and 2.

[8] H. E. Barnes and H. Becker, *Social Thought from Lore to Science* (Boston: Heath, 1938), pp. 248–249.

[9] The virtue of holding one's place is also an important implication of the concepts of order that are integral to the functionalist approach in sociology. Émile Durkheim's analysis of anomie, for example, implies that the moral integration of a society requires limits on the aspirations of its members. Durkheim, the nineteenth and twentieth century pioneer of sociology, did not hold that a society should be static, however, but that overweening ambition can be a threat to stability. Cf. Mizruchi (1964, pp. 104–106) for a discussion of Durkheim's perspective with respect to stratification and anomie.

ically significant sociological ideas are only a product of recent history. The relentless march of secularism following the period referred to as the Middle Ages produced numerous writers whose proposals for the establishment of new social forms as well as those that would maintain the status quo included many presociological concepts that must have influenced later analysts of society. The works of Niccolo Machiavelli,[10] Thomas More, Francis Bacon, and others writing in the sixteenth century[11] clearly influenced the nineteenth-century sociology of Henri de Saint-Simon, Karl Marx, and Vilfredo Pareto, to name but a few. Even William Shakespeare, whose clear perception of stratification and the behavior it entailed is evident in his plays, must have influenced the later analysts of social stratification. His influence on Marx's assumptions regarding the relationship between wealth and power is reflected in the latter's use of the play *Timon of Athens* to illustrate the effects of money.[12] Awareness of the sources of influence on the sociological analysts of social stratification provides a clearer perception of the implications of the particular theoretical perspectives that characterize contemporary approaches.

Studying social stratification thus means focusing on (1) the processes underlying the vertical placement of group and individuals; (2) the variations in existing and emerging structures of social inequality; (3) the strategies for maintaining and changing positions within these structures; (4) the processes by which these structures are changed; and (5) the consequences of these processes for various groups in society, particularly their life-styles and life-chances.

Group Size, Interaction, and Stratification

In virtually every social situation involving two or more individuals, there is some degree of *social differentiation;* that is, differences between individuals, groups, or social positions become defined in the course of social interaction. These differences may be based on sex, age, skin color, or another ascribed characteristic of participants, or they may be defined on the basis of achievement factors such as skill, expertise, or training. The differences that evolve may take the form of a "functional differentiation"—or division of labor—according to which the occupants of social positions are expected to make distinct contributions to the perpetuation of the group or, at the same time, a "rank differentiation" according to which there is an unequal distribution of rewards to occupants of social positions.

---

[10] Cf., Machiavelli, loc. cit.

[11] Cf., Barnes and Becker, op. cit., Chap. 8.

[12] Karl Marx, "Money," in *Early Writings,* ed. and trans. by T. B. Bottomore (New York: McGraw-Hill, 1964), pp. 189–194. Shakespeare's interest in the topic was primarily a reflection of the concerns of his own period of history.

We begin with the assumption that as size of the group increases, the nature of the social interaction in a given context changes in the direction of relative rigidification of rank and role expectations. Furthermore, we hypothesize that stratification systems emerge out of and are reinforced by this process of patterning.

In two-person groups, that is, *dyads,* there is the greatest opportunity for actors to attain pure equality in their interactions.[13] These relationships may be formal and impersonality may be a dominant mode, but the probability that actors will treat one another in an informal and personal manner is greatest because they see one another as persons rather than objects. As persons, there is the lowest probability that social structural constraints will obscure the fundamental human qualities that each actor possesses. Simmel holds that the need of each to maintain the dyad—withdrawal of one of the actors can terminate the existence of the group—leads to strong sentiments that bind the partners.[14] In formal organizations such as the United States Army, for example, officers and enlisted men will interact on a first-name basis from time to time so long as the context is defined as informal and the relationship is dyadic. This involves mutual recognition that the parties are fundamentally men, tied to one another, and that although organizational formalities are necessary for accomplishing specific goals, they should not be thought of as legitimate in their intrusion into the more basic social bonds that hold people together.

When another actor is added to the context, making the relationship *triadic,* the quality of the interaction changes. The third person, when added, increases the probability that the relationship will be more formal and impersonal. It will be more formal because he may symbolize for the others the authority of external group constraints on interaction through its norms and role expectations. It will be more impersonal because each actor must now take into account the reaction of two others to their performance rather than one. In short, the common denominator changes from a shared awareness of individuality and difference, as Simmel suggests, to an awareness of what the members of the triad share in common as subordinate to social rules.[15]

What is of most direct concern with respect to social stratification, however, is not the dyad or triad as such but the role of increasing imperson-

---

[13] Georg Simmel, *The Sociology of Georg Simmel,* ed. and trans. by Kurt Wolff (New York: Free Press, 1950).

[14] Ibid., p. 124.

[15] Ibid., pp. 122–128. It is also interesting to note Simmel's hypothesis that the equitable distribution of group "benefits" becomes increasingly difficult as the size of the group increases. In other words, "distributive injustice" is directly related to group size. At a very macroscopic level, Simmel viewed this as posing a serious problem for communistic societies, and it suggests a reason why some form of stratification may be universally expected to occur.

ality as a concomitant of increasing size. Stratification systems, according to our hypothesis, grow out of the depersonalization process that is an aspect of the categorization of actors into ranks based on selected values. Mandeville observed aspects of the process more than two centuries ago (1714).[16]

As size increases, people begin to sort others not on *personal* characteristics—which, due to limited intimacy they cannot know—but in terms of *social* characteristics—which are ranked implicitly according to the degree of desirability of this or that characteristic. This sorting process is a process of discrimination[17] and exclusion and it involves determination of who will interact with whom and at what levels of intimacy or impersonality. In sum, as size increases so does *social distance*.

Social-Distance Strategies

Social distance implicitly involves some notion of *social space* to which entree will be relatively more open or closed, depending on the social characteristics—including rank—of those conceived of as occupying this space. Thus, the degree of intimacy that actors will share with others is guarded by a whole array of sentinels whose major characteristics are social and whose incidental qualities are personal. For example, if we select marriage as symbolizing the greatest degree of intimacy between actors and we examine the sorting out process which is enhanced by rules determining the degree of eligibility of partners in the United States, we can describe the degree of social distance between actors sharing certain social characteristics.[18]

Beshers, Mizruchi, and Perrucci, in a paper dealing with social-class and mate-selection strategies, focus on the behavior of families with given social-class characteristics and their efforts to have their children marry upward. Avoidance of marriage to someone of a lower-ranked group is their second concern.

Parents attempt to manipulate the social relationships of their offspring to arrange the desired result. They classify all young males into eligible and ineligible mates for their daughters. "Sons' status may be taken as fixed or

---

[16] In Louis Schneider, "Mandeville As Forerunner of Modern Sociology," *Journal of the History of the Behavioral Sciences*, **6**:221 (1970). See quotation in chapter 2.

[17] In this context cf. David Matza, *Becoming Deviant* (Englewood Cliffs, N.J.: Prentice-Hall, 1969), Chap. 7.

[18] The discussion closely follows the article by James Beshers, Ephraim H. Mizruchi, and Robert Perrucci, "Social Distance Strategies and Status Symbols," *Sociological Quarterly*, **4**:311–324 (Winter 1963). The significance of spatial relations, literally, in status and other arrangements is dealt with by a number of researchers. Cf., for example, Robert Sommer, *Personal Space* (Englewood Cliffs, N.J.: Prentice-Hall, 1969).

determined by actions independent of marriage choice, such as occupation, but under patrilineal status rules the daughter's status is solely assigned by marriage." [19]

Within the pool of eligibles daughter is presumably given a free choice. In order to control this mate-selection process parents must perform two acts. First, they must be able to discriminate between eligible and ineligible mates in terms of their awareness and perception of the status-symbol distribution. Secondly, they must be able to prevent the daughter from making an independent choice—for example, running off with an ineligible mate. For the latter they exert some control over the daughter's behavior—attained, in part, through careful socialization—and some degree of control over contact with ineligibles.

There are several alternative ways in which the parents can exert control over the mate-selection process. (1) They can, through socialization, insure that the daughter will "naturally" engage in the process of "sorting out" eligible and ineligible mates. This socialization includes the development, explicitly, of the ability and the desire of the daughter to recognize the distribution of status symbols. (2) Where the socialization process has been defective, or merely to complement and reinforce the socialization process, the parents may engage in more active control over the daughter's likelihood of being *exposed to or having contact with* ineligible males. Thus, imperfect socialization may be mitigated by controlling the *opportunities for contact* between the daughter and potential mates. This may be done through the selection of area of residence, college attended, vacation spots, or by direct threats of sanctions.[20] (3) The status symbols of a particular class may be arranged in such a way as to ensure that the pool of potential suitors will *sort themselves* into categories of eligibles and ineligibles. This strategy does not require the active participation of the daughter, nor does it require the use of visible power strategies.[21] What it requires are shared cognitive, evaluative, and cathectic definitions of status symbols *within* classes and nonshared definitions *between* classes. This system is effective despite the fact that there is a rather rapid diffusion of status symbols down the class structure. With diffusion, all that is required is that the "upper" groups either change their symbols or change their evaluative and cathectic defini-

[19] Beshers, Mizruchi, and Perrucci, op. cit., p. 315.

[20] See, for example, August B. Hollingshead, "Cultural Factors in the Selection of Marriage Mates," *American Sociological Review*, **15**:619–627 (Dec. 1950); and Marvin B. Sussman, "Parental Participation in Mate Selection and Its Effect upon Family Continuity," *Social Forces*, **32**:76–81 (1953). Note that social distance and spatial distance tend to reinforce the stratification arrangements described here.

[21] The very invisibility of the control leads to a more effective rigging of the mate-selection game within a cultural ethos of democratic social relationships and romantic love. In connection with the consequences of visible and invisible control in another setting, see Alvin W. Gouldner, *Patterns of Industrial Bureaucracy* (New York: Free Press, 1954), p. 161.

tions of the symbols. The parents of a particular class, then, must fend off males with lower status symbols but must attract males with higher status symbols. The phenomenon of class segregation, then, may be regarded as a system of social relationships including status symbols, social distance, and sanctions such that the daughters of higher classes are protected from the sons of lower classes. Thus, the norms governing segregation are expected to be most restrictive for the following kinds of contact situations: (1) As the daughter approaches marriageable age, segregation tightens; (2) as the types of contact tend to symbolize equality of status (for example, eating meals together), segregation tightens; (3) as the difference of rank increases, segregation tightens.[22]

Thus, as we shift our perspective from the dyad, with its greater equality and intimacy to interaction between categorized persons and groups it is possible for us to observe how organized social inequalities have emerged to intervene between persons who might relate to one another as such.

A concrete illustration of the hypothesis of Beshers et al. is afforded by John F. Scott, a sociologist, in a study of the role of sororities in courtship. Because "love is a potentially random factor, with no regard for class boundaries," Scott proposes that college sororities have evolved as a way for parents to cope with these dangers. He notes, as do Beshers et al., that the problems are particularly acute for the parents of girls because marriage is a more important determinant of their social position than it is for males. Thus, we see that the degree to which alumnae control entrance into the sorority and on-going sorority activities is greater than among fraternities. For example, Scott points out that sororities are more likely to require the recommendations of former members before a girl is allowed to pledge. The pledges are then kept busy, studying and making homecoming displays and other activities within the house. Their potentially external social life is also handled within the sorority through exchanges with the "right" fraternities, "fixer-uppers," and the like. Finally, through a variety of rituals—such as pinning ceremonies—the sorority helps to insure that dating the right boys will lead to formal courtship and marriage. Thus, through sororities, parents exert a continuing remote control influence over endogamy and thus intervene, symbolically and empirically, in the process of intimacy and equality of interaction.[23]

At a more macroscopic level restrictiveness also varies, both within and between societies, on the wealth dimension. E. Adamson Hoebel, an anthropologist, describes similarities in primitive societies where there is generally great premarital freedom both in sexual expression and mate

---

[22] Beshers, et al., op. cit., pp. 315–316.
[23] John F. Scott, "Sororities and the Husband Game," *Transaction,* **2** (1965).

selection. Because chance marriages could terminate the intergenerational continuity of family standing for the families with wealth in these societies mate selection is, correspondingly, more closely regulated. Among the Ifugaos of the Philippines, for example, there is great freedom to select a mate for all except the offspring of the wealthiest families. Their marriages are arranged in infancy, or even before birth. "To have a scion find a compatible but propertyless bride in the damsel's dormitory is for the upper-class Ifugao a greater calamity than for an American blue blood to marry a chorus girl." [24]

The formulation by Beshers et al. and the examples taken from Scott and Hoebel illustrate how social distance and impersonality are outcomes of organized social activities and enhance the persistence of social inequalities. In sharp contrast to Simmel's dyadic relationship, characterized by greater intimacy and egalitarianism, these impersonal processes reinforce *structured* social inequalities by treating persons as objects rather than subjects. This, we assume is, at least in part, an outcome of increasing size and the management of social space through choice of intimates. Thus, in the real world people interact with others through choices they make as well as those that are forced on them by the social constraints imposed by their relative position in the social structure.

Roles, Interaction, and Stratification

The interplay between interactional processes and social structural prescriptions and constraints are the phenomena out of which an understandable and predictable stratification relationship between student X and professor Y can be used as a meaningful illustration. One might, for example, begin by examining the educational institution: its relationship to economic, religious, and other institutions and the definitions of appropriate role behavior associated with it. With this type of (macroscopic) approach, attention is drawn away from the concrete, situational factors influencing interaction between the specific student and professor. If a more microscopic view were followed, relatively greater emphasis would be placed on situationally relevant considerations, such as the effects of other students being able to observe the interaction, the impact of the student's standing in the class, and so on.

As we argued at the outset, some degree of social differentiation evolves in virtually every social context. Although it is possible in many cases to associate the contribution made by an individual with the personal qualities

---

[24] E. Adamson Hoebel, *Man in the Primitive World* (New York: McGraw-Hill, 1958), p. 189.

of that individual, it is still best to view that contribution as a social role, linked to a specialized position, for these reasons:

1. Specific individuals enter and leave a group, but there tends to be a succession of persons who make the same contribution, despite differences in their personal styles. In other words, groups have "careers," apart from the individuals who happen to be members at any given time.

2. In groups of the general type there is a consistent tendency for the same specialized contributions to be associated with particular positions.

Within any small group it is reasonable to expect to find some degree of role differentiation in response to the functional problems of group maintenance, survival in a competitive environment, or the like. However, there may be little overlap or compatibility between role differentiations in different groups. For example, the same roles do not occur, nor would the same contributions be similarly evaluated, in a youth gang as in a bridge club. Thus, a microscopic approach to stratification, even though it initially focuses on differentiation, cannot begin with broad assumptions about the specific differentiations associated with concrete groups. However, the ways in which differentiation occurs, and its effects on interaction, can be studied in a way that transcends the uniqueness of particular groups.

We have been implying that social stratification is a dynamic process inextricably bound up with our most fundamental social relationships. That is, stratification permeates our motives, choices, and actions in virtually all social situations: from the most formal to the most informal; from what would appear to be the most commonplace to the most esoteric; and even from the most individualistic and romantic to the most social and instrumental.

Principal Types of Stratification Systems: Caste, Estate, and Class

Because we have argued that stratification systems grow out of, and are reinforced by, interaction and that varying degrees of rigidification of strata is the outcome, it is well to view types of stratification along a continuum from the most rigid, conceptually, to the most fluid. Rigidity and fluidity are conceptualized as the poles of a single dimension, varying in terms of the probability that a person's entire life will be spent in the same stratum into which he was born.

It is important to point out that there is no society in which the extreme degrees of either rigidity or fluidity have been observed. Thus, following

Weber, they are "ideal types," or caricatures of reality that are highly exaggerated. Their value is in illuminating tendencies within any society.

CASTE. The most rigid of stratification systems is the caste system. Although it is found in a number of societies in Africa and even among the ancient Israelites, the best known caste system in recent history has been India's.

In many preindustrial cities, ethnic groups are strongly associated with distinct occupations. Therefore, castelike stratification simultaneously involves ethnicity and occupation, as persons are physically segregated, often in locked residential areas. These separated areas are known locally by the distinguishing ethnicity or occupation of its residents; however, both are involved. It is common to find in modern Afghanistan, for example, segregated blocks such as the "Street of the Goldsmiths." [25]

Probably originally based on a division of labor,[26] castes are categories of families who are segregated from other categories in marriage and interaction. In India, in spite of official government efforts to abolish them, there remain four major castes based on color and numerous subcastes numbering in the thousands. Their activities today diverge from what they were a century ago when three of the major castes were designated as rulers and the fourth, the Sudras—also known as the Pariahs—were designated to serve the superordinate castes. Of the rulers, the Brahmans were priests, the Kshatriyas warriors, and the Vaisyas merchants and peasants. Status awareness remains strong in India to this day, particularly in relation to the lowest strata who are regarded as unclean.

In the United States, the closest approximation to a caste system has been the stratification of whites and blacks, particularly in the Old South where intermarriage was a violation of state law in most states. Although physical segregation and social distance between whites and blacks have been diminishing in recent decades, the behavior between those categorized more closely approximates the caste model than the estate or class models.

What is interesting in comparing the Indian context with that of the United States is the nature of the norms that influence outcomes in these spheres. In India, where caste arrangements have permeated the whole society for centuries, the system has been supported by a great deal of consensus regarding the desirability and rightness of these arrangements. In the United States, castelike relationships between blacks and whites always have been surrounded by some degree of controversy regarding their desirability, even in those states where laws were passed to support these arrangements.

[25] Gideon Sjoberg, *The Pre-Industrial City* (New York: Free Press, 1960).
[26] For an elaborate treatment of caste in India, see Kingsley Davis, *The Populations of India and Pakistan* (Princeton: Princeton U. Press, 1951); cf. also, Max Weber, *The Religion of India* (New York: Free Press, 1958).

In India, the degree of consensus supporting caste has been high,[27] and in the United States, taken as a whole, the degree of consensus generally has been low. Today, the governments of both countries have been making systematic efforts to abolish the patterns.

It is also well to note that, in reality, there always has been some degree of mobility in India and in the United States. Female hypergamy, or upward marriage, always has been possible in relationships between some castes, and an entire caste has been known to alter its position upward by developing an occupational specialty and enforcing boundaries between itself and other castes by rigid adherence to endogamy.

In sum, caste systems are organized into hierarchies made up of closed groups that share similar rank in relation to other castes but that may rank one another within the caste. Rank is normatively *ascribed* by birth, rather than *achieved,* and endogamy is the major means for reinforcing the system. However, unlike other types of stratification systems, mobility by a whole caste may legitimately occur.

ESTATE. Estates, on the other hand, are somewhat less rigid than castes. Upward and downward mobility do occur and marriages between strata, although frowned on, may occur. Although caste systems appear to be supported more by fundamental belief systems than by formalized rules, estate systems usually are legally constituted systems with specific rules for the placement of families and persons in the hierarchy; the fulfillment of obligations of possessors of rank determine their specific position at any point in time. Thus, like the warrior castes who were obligated to serve during periods of external threats to a society, the aristocracy is traditionally expected to train its male offspring to serve in time of national or local emergency.

Estate systems ordinarily were associated with feudal societies in which one's relationship to land determined his position. Thus serfs, as contrasted with slaves, could not be sold but changed masters when the land that they worked was sold. Aristocrats were given land, and land was also taken away, on condition of military support to a given ruler; similarly, outstanding deeds in the service of a ruler often were rewarded with land and title.

The best-known systems and their archaic remnants were found in Europe as recently as five decades ago. The English system, which began to erode during the eighteenth century, and the German and Russian systems, which were strongly in evidence only a century ago, are excellent examples. At the top of the hierarchy was a king, a kaiser, or czar, supported by a

---

[27] Indeed, adherence to caste-linked behavior patterns and acceptance of the status quo is mandated by religious precepts. A rather thorough, elementary discussion of this dimension may be found in Egon Bergel, *Social Stratification* (New York: McGraw-Hill, 1962).

hereditary military-landowning class. At an almost equally ranked position in relation to the military aristocracy was a priesthood, which provided a channel for mobility that did not require high rank at birth or wealth. Just below the priesthood were the merchants and craftsmen, followed by peasants who held their own land, and, at the bottom, the serfs.

Although there were some variations from the ideal type among these three systems, the general outlines were approximately the same. The major emphasis among the nobility was on the maintenance of a style of life that was dignified and appropriate for one's position and on endogamy. Status consciousness was characteristic of all estates but mobility through marriage, when it did occur, was more likely in the lower estates. With respect to occupation, however, sons were expected to follow in the footsteps of their fathers except when the military or priesthood were selected as lifetime pursuits.

It must be pointed out, however, that the intergenerational continuity of occupational pursuits was often more normatively ideal than real. A variety of circumstances and customs often prevented the actualization of the ideal. In many agrarian societies, for example, there was an explicit rule of primogeniture (all inheritance goes to the first-born male). Later-born males were then (often) precluded from following in their father's agricultural footsteps. Even without rules of primogeniture, many sons in a single family sometimes presented a situation in which—if all were to follow their father—the land was fragmented into unworkably small plots.[28] In all of these situations some youngsters were forced off the farm. Thus, even in highly traditional, agrarian societies, where cultural values emphasize continuity, other norms and conventions often resulted in many offspring not following their family's "occupational heritage."

Remnants of estate systems are still noticeable in the West. Although titles of nobility are officially relinquished as a price for citizenship in the United States, and the French, Germans, and Russians no longer officially recognize the titled, the nobility do continue to recognize one another. Those whose means allow them to continue to maintain life-styles that set them off from "commoners" continue also to marry either among themselves or among the wealthy. In England, titles are recognized formally and the existence of the House of Lords, politically weak though it is, provides a clear image of continuity between the older stratification forms and the new. However, events of recent history are eroding the system to the point where it is more meaningful to describe Great Britain as having a class system rather than a system of estates.

CLASS.   Class systems are our primary concern in this book. They represent the greatest degree of fluidity with respect to mobility; exogamous marriage is

[28] Joseph A. Kahl, "The Social Concomitants of Urbanization and Industrialization," *Human Organization,* **3**: 63–73 (1960).

most common in this type of system. Conceptions of the nature of class vary and they are a source of stimulating controversy not only among sociologists but among other social scientists as well. Because so much attention is devoted to social class and social mobility, we must limit our discussion to a general level, unfolding the more specific and penetrating ideas in the chapters that follow. Our focus here is primarily on the United States.

Community and National Class Structures: Ascribed and Achieved Status

We suggested at the outset that all social interactional contexts are stratified and that as size increases, the consequent impersonality leads to the categorization of groups. This assumption is supported by the observation of the nature of class stratification in local communities when they are compared with stratification in American society as a whole.

In the relatively small American community it is possible for most members to know and interact at some level with others in the same community. The smaller the number of people the greater the probability of knowledge of one another and participation with each other in work, church, school, or voluntary associations, to select a few contexts. At the very least, peers have the opportunity to interact with each other. As size of community increases, the proportion of those in the population with whom members can interact decreases. At first there is the tendency to make distinctions between members of families and to assess their standing as unique persons. In time, a family name or section of town in which one resides becomes the classification principle for placement within strata. Thus, in their studies of American communities, which are described elaborately in later chapters, Warner, the social anthropologist, and his associates will establish that units in the various communities are families rather than individuals. Family rank, then, became the rank of the offspring on the local level—in short, it was ascribed.

As communities became larger and as heterogeneity proliferated, it became difficult to rank others residing in the same general context. Because ranking functions as a precipitant to anticipated responses in interactional contexts, members intuitively sought means by which to categorize others and to sort them into manageable response classifications. This sizing-up process is central to intraclass and interclass interactions and triggers the actions of those relating to each other in an impersonal setting. Knowledge of families and residence provided sufficient information for categorization when the number of units were small and when physical mobility was limited.

Increasing impersonality called for impersonal criteria for ranking one another. At the same time, American values shifted from an emphasis on ascriptive factors—that is, "who you are at birth"—to an emphasis on *achievement* factors—that is, "what you can do"—in stratification.[29] This coincided with a relative decline in the importance of family activities in America and an increase in the importance of work activities. Physical mobility proliferated as occupational opportunities increased and this, in turn, weakened ties to kin groups in communities of origin. One's occupation became severed from one's family and it was by the former activity rather than the latter that one's exploits became known. Thus, one's occupational rank became the index to one's style of life, wealth, and influence.

As a direct result of this process, we assume that Americans now rank one another primarily on *impersonal* criteria that are sufficiently conspicuous to be recognized as indicators of organizational or institutional positions and as capable of providing cues that call for subordinate, egalitarian, or super-ordinate responses. Thus, houses, clothing, automobiles, and other concrete and impersonal goods function as status symbols that stand for, and are appropriate to, given positions in a social-class hierarchy. In addition to concrete possessions as symbols of position, conspicuous behavior patterns also serve as indicators.

One of the best-known analyses of conspicuous consumption was offered, late in the nineteenth century, by Thorstein Veblen. In the following excerpt, Veblen analyzes the origins of conspicuous consumption, which he related to the emergence of a leisure class.

Conspicuous Consumption and Leisure*

Thorstein Veblen

So soon as the possession of property becomes the basis of popular esteem, therefore, it becomes also a requisite to that complacency which we call self-respect. In any community where goods are held in severalty it is necessary, in order to keep his own peace of mind, that an individual should possess as large a portion of goods as others with whom he is accustomed to class himself; and it is extremely gratifying to possess something more than others. But as fast as a person makes new acquisitions, and becomes accustomed to the resulting new standard of wealth, the new standard forthwith ceases to afford appreciably greater satisfaction than the earlier standard did.[1]

---

[29] Cf., Talcott Parsons, *The Social System* (New York: Free Press, 1951).

* Thorstein Veblen, *The Theory of the Leisure Class* (New York: Macmillan, 1899), pp. 31–32; 35; 41; 43; 49–50.

The tendency in any case is constantly to make the present pecuniary standard the point of departure for a fresh increase of wealth; and this in turn gives rise to a new standard of sufficiency and a new pecuniary classification of one's self as compared with one's neighbours. So far as concerns the present question, the end sought by accumulation is to rank high in comparison with the rest of the community in point of pecuniary strength. So long as the comparison is distinctly unfavourable to himself, the normal, average individual will live in chronic dissatisfaction with his present lot; and when he has reached what may be called the normal pecuniary standard of the community, or of his class in the community, this chronic dissatisfaction will give place to a restless straining to place a wider and ever-widening pecuniary interval between himself and this average standard. The invidious comparison can never become so favourable to the individual making it that he would not gladly rate himself still higher relatively to his competitors in the struggle for pecuniary reputability.

In the nature of the case, the desire for wealth can scarcely be satiated in any individual instance, and evidently a satiation of the average or general desire for wealth is out of the question. However widely, or equally, or "fairly," it may be distributed, no general increase of the community's wealth can make any approach to satiating this need, the ground of which is the desire of every one to excell every one else in the accumulation of goods. If, as is sometimes assumed, the incentive to accumulation were the want of subsistence or of physical comfort, then the aggregate economic wants of a community might conceivably be satisfied at some point in the advance of industrial efficiency; but since the struggle is substantially a race for reputability on the basis of an invidious comparison, no approach to a definitive attainment is possible.

If its working were not disturbed by other economic forces or other features of the emulative process, the immediate effect of such a pecuniary struggle as has just been described in outline would be to make men industrious and frugal. This result actually follows, in some measure, so far as regards the lower classes, whose ordinary means of acquiring goods is productive labour.

But it is otherwise with the superior pecuniary class, with which we are here immediately concerned. For this class also the incentive to diligence and thrift is not absent; but its action is so greatly qualified by the secondary demands of pecuniary emulation, that any inclination in this direction is practically overborne and any incentive to diligence tends to be of no effect. The most imperative of these secondary demands of emulation, as well as the one of widest scope, is the requirement of abstention from productive work.

Abstention from labour is not only an honorific or meritorious act, but it presently comes to be a requisite of decency. The insistence on property as the basis of reputability is very naive and very imperious during the early stages of the accumulation of wealth. Abstention from labour is the conventional evidence of wealth and is therefore the conventional mark of social standing; and this insistence on the meritoriousness of wealth leads to a more strenuous insistence on leisure. *Nota notae est nota rei ipsius.* According to well-established laws of human nature, prescription presently seizes upon this conventional evidence of wealth and fixes it in men's habits of thought as something that is in itself substantially meritorious and ennobling; while productive labour at the same time and by a like process becomes in a double sense intrinsically unworth. Prescription ends by making labour not only disreputable in the eyes of the community, but morally impossible to the noble, free-born man, and incompatible with a worthy life.

It has already been remarked that the term "leisure," as here used, does not connote indolence or quiescence. What it connotes is non-productive consumption of time. Time is consumed non-productively (1) from a sense of the unworthiness of productive work, and (2) as an evidence of pecuniary ability to afford a life of idleness. But the whole of the life of the gentleman of leisure is not spent before the eyes of the spectators who are to be impressed with that spectacle of honorific leisure which in the ideal scheme makes up his life.

So much of the honourable life of leisure as is not spent in the sight of spectators can serve the purposes of reputability only in so far as it leaves a tangible, visible result that can be put in evidence and can be measured and compared with products of the same class exhibited by competing aspirants for repute. Some such effect, in the way of leisurely manners and carriage, etc., follows from simple persistent abstention from work, even where the subject does not take thought of the matter and studiously acquire an air of leisurely opulence and mastery. Especially does it seem to be true that a life of leisure in this way persisted in through several generations will leave a persistent, ascertainable effect in the conformation of the person, and still more in his habitual bearing and demeanor. But all the suggestions of a cumulative life of leisure, and all the proficiency in decorum that comes by the way of passive habituation, may be further improved upon by taking thought and assiduously acquiring the marks of honourable leisure, and then carrying the exhibition of these adventitious marks of exemption from employment out in a strenuous and systematic discipline. Plainly, this is a point at which a diligent application of effort and expenditure may materially further the attainment of a decent proficiency in the leisure-class properties. Conversely, the greater the degree of proficiency and the more patent the evidence of a high degree of habituation to observances which serve no lucrative or other directly useful purpose, the greater the consumption of time and substance impliedly involved in their acquisition, and the greater the resultant good repute. Hence, under the competitive struggle for proficiency in good manners, it comes about that much pain is taken with the cultivation of habits of decorum; and hence the details of decorum develop into a comprehensive discipline, conformity to which is required of all who would be held blameless in point of repute. And hence, on the other hand, this conspicuous leisure of which decorum is a ramification grows gradually into a laborious drill in deportment and an education in taste and discrimination as to what articles of consumption are decorous and what are the decorous methods of consuming them.

NOTE

1. The similarity between Veblen's observation here and Durkheim's analysis of the causes of anomic suicide is striking. (Ed.)

Part Two
Theoretical Perspectives

2 The Early Classicists and the Transition from Romanticism

Mandeville and "The Fable of the Bees"

Sociological interest in stratification as an aspect of life to be systematically explored is, like the field itself, a relatively recent phenomenon. Although it is always difficult to single out the scholar or group of thinkers who stands closest to the beginning, it appears that Bernard Mandeville, an early eighteenth century Dutch physician, and a small group, described as the Scottish Moralists, were among the first to perceive the significance of behaviors associated with stratification in their general—rather than unique —aspects.

Mandeville's classic, *The Fable of the Bees* (1714) has several times led scholars to compare his ideas with those of Thorstein Veblen, particularly those embodied in the latter's *The Theory of the Leisure Class* (1899).[1] Of particular interest to stratification analysts is the similarity between Veblen's conception and description of conspicuous consumption,

[1] New York: Macmillan, 1899. In this context see Louis Schneider, "Mandeville As Forerunner of Modern Sociology," *Journal of the History of the Behavioral Sciences*, **6**:219–230 (1970).

and the perceptions of seemingly identical processes by Mandeville reflected
here:

> People, where they are not known, are generally honour'd according to their
> Clothese and other Accoutrements they have about them; from the richness
> of them we judge of their Wealth, and by their ordering of them we guess at
> their Understanding. It is this which encourages every Body, who is con-
> scious of his little Merit, if he is any ways able, to wear Clothes above his
> Rank, especially in the large and populous Cities, where obscure Men may
> hourly meet with fifty strangers to the Acquaintance, and consequently
> have the Pleasure of being esteem'd by a vast Majority, not as what they
> are, but what they appear to be: which is a greater Temptation than most
> People want to be vain.[2]

The Scottish Moralists

Mandeville was soon joined by others in the eighteenth-century thrust
toward the emergence of a generalizing sociology. The Scottish Moralists—
who were philosophers, historians, and, sometimes, theologians—reflected
seriously on the nature of man and the social organization of behavior.
Among them were such well-known scholars as Adam Smith (1723–1790),
David Hume (1711–1776), and Adam Ferguson (1723–1816).

In addition to their concern with more general sociological, philosophical, and economic questions, some of the moralists commented on rights
and obligations (Ferguson), ambition and distinctions among ranks
(Smith), and the three different orders of people (Smith).[3]

In *The Theory of Moral Sentiments,* for example, Adam Smith asks,
"to what purpose is all of the toil and bustle of this world? What is the end
of avarice and ambition, of the pursuit of wealth, of power, and pre-
eminence?" [4] His reply is in the form of a descriptive statement on vanity,
esteem, and—in more contemporary terms—status.

Later, Smith, writing on social mobility, asks: How does one of lower
rank hope to distinguish himself?" he must acquire superior knowledge in
his professions and superior industry in the exercise of it. . . . These talents
he must bring into public view. . . ." [5]

And, finally, with respect to this best-known Scot, in his essay entitled
"The Three Great Orders of Society," Smith deals with the interplay between
source of income and power in a manner that clearly anticipates aspects of
Marx's analysis of capitalism.[6]

[2] As quoted by Schneider, op. cit., p. 221.
[3] *The Scottish Moralists,* ed. by Louis Schneider. (Chicago: U. of Chicago, 1967).
With an Introduction by Schneider.
[4] Ibid., p. 223.
[5] Ibid., p. 229.
[6] Ibid., pp. 235–237.

Thus, by the eighteenth century both the field of sociology in general and the study of social stratification in particular began to emerge as disciplines that would be characterized by efforts to extrapolate what characterized societies generally from those occurrences that appeared to be unique. By the end of the eighteenth century the fundamental influences that determined the character of contemporary sociology had been formulated by Mandeville, the Scottish Moralists, Montesquieu, and Rousseau.[7]

Saint-Simon and Comte

Henri de Saint-Simon was one of the many utopian socialists who influenced every aspect of literary and scientific activity in England and Western Europe during the early part of the nineteenth century. The intellectual and artistic life of the times was dominated by a romantic vision of man in society, particularly with respect to the distant past and the anticipated future. With the passing of feudalism and the emergence of scientifically based industrial-urbanized societies, man became the rootless pawn in the game of resettlement and adaptation to (perceived) economic needs. The utopian socialists focused on the need for a new basis of morality and moral integration as a means of stabilizing industrial society.

Although the eighteenth and nineteenth-century forerunners of contemporary sociology did not ignore the influence of hierarchical differences on the total life-situations of diverse groups in society, except for Marx and Weber, they contributed little to the systematic use of stratification as a significant sociological variable. Saint-Simon and Comte, regarded as the direct fathers of contemporary sociological science, were interested in social stratification primarily as a phenomenon that was to be dealt with in creating new forms of society.

Saint-Simon, concerned with the creation of a new social order to simulate the unity of the old social organization of the Middle Ages, placed his faith in an elite system. A spiritual elite made up of scientists and a temporal elite including "industrialists and other 'productive' property owners"[8] would jointly rule the new society. Conflict over the power to control land and men had been a characteristic of the old regime, the new would be known for its harmony. As Frank Manuel describes the newly envisioned society, the regimentation by superiors of the feudal order would be replaced by occupational ties; the commands of the old would give way to the directives of the new; the role of subject would be replaced by the role of member; and all would be collaborators. The force of the old would yield to the cooperation of the new, and class conflicts would disappear, because

[7] *Émile Durkheim, Montesquieu* and *Rousseau*, trans. R. Mannheim (Ann Arbor: University of Michigan Press, 1960).

[8] I. Zeitlin, *Ideology and the Development of Sociological Theory* (Englewood Cliffs, N.J.: Prentice-Hall, 1968), p. 58.

positions of power would be eliminated and the basis for antagonism abolished.[9]

But a stratification system of some sort would also be part of the new society. The elites referred to earlier, however, would not hold their positions because of birth, as in the feudal order. Merit alone, as expressed in one's performance as a scientist, artist, or industrialist, would place men in the hierarchy, and the activities that warranted their placement would contribute to the regeneration of the society in decline.[10] While seeking new alignments among old classes of "haves and have-nots," Saint-Simon actually left the class structure and the institution of private property intact.[11] And, according to Manuel, he was naive about the nature of power. Note the following in which Manuel emphasizes the romantic similarity in outlook of Saint-Simon and Marx, with whom we will deal subsequently.

> However much Marx differed from Saint-Simon in analyzing the historical process, there was agreement between them that the new society emerging from the last conflict of systems or classes would witness the twilight of power and the cessation of power conflicts among men. Both saw power and aggressiveness not as ineradicable characteristics of man but as transient historical manifestations generated by previous, imperfect social systems and destined to perish with them. Their optimism was a corollary to their analysis of the classes designated as the agents of the last revolution. The "industrials" were by definition productive entrepreneurs to whom the spirit of war and conflict was alien; it would be contrary to their nature to become intoxicated with power. The proletarians were in their nature men who worked, not men who exploited, hence they could not engineer a proletarian revolution and thereafter exploit others. The simplicity with which socialist theory turned its head away from the realities of power was the great blind spot of its outlook.[12]

August Comte, whose relationship to his mentor Saint-Simon has led to much controversy,[13] did not question the idea of a society with divisions between the haves and have-nots because, in his new society, rivalry would give way to increasing love. Man the individual, the owner of property, and the

---

[9] Frank Manuel, *The Prophets of Paris* (New York: Harper Torchbooks, 1965), p. 134.

[10] The emphasis on one's deeds contrasted with one's birthright as a basis for determination of one's position anticipates the contemporary sociological and anthropological distinction between achieved and ascribed status.

[11] Zeitlin, op. cit., p. 61.

[12] Manuel, loc. cit.

[13] Comte, some years the junior of Saint-Simon, worked with him, but was loathe to credit Saint-Simon with his own intellectual development. There is, however, an interplay between the ideas of Comte and those expressed earlier by Saint-Simon.

One of Comte's clear contributions is the offering of the term, *sociology*; Saint-Simon called the new field social physics rather than sociology. He chose this name because the field was to be to social behavior what physics was to physical phenomena. Cf. Alvin W. Gouldner, *Socialism and Saint-Simon* (Yellow Springs, Ohio: The Antioch Press, 1958).

toiler in the factory, would subordinate his personal impulses for the unity of humanity. Primarily embroiled with planning and creating a society based on social scientific principles and organized along medieval lines with himself as the high priest, Comte remained aloof from the class struggles associated with the mid-nineteenth-century period and thus failed to influence the varied conceptions of social stratification that were emerging on all sides.

Marx and Sociological Romanticism

The first major systematic analysis of social stratification was contributed by Karl Marx. We will begin here by briefly discussing Marx's approach.

The controversies surrounding Karl Marx as both an analyst of societies and as a revolutionary are complex and multifaceted. Marx was a systematic analyst in whose writings are a number of implicit hypotheses about social organization and human behavior. The empirical support that can be brought to bear on these hypotheses, outside of Marx's ideological framework, further affirms the importance of distinguishing between Marx as prophet and Marx as social scientist.[14] Further complications result from distinctions between the young Marx and Marx during the second half of the nineteenth century, the period of intensive efforts to organize politically the workers of Western Europe, England, and the United States. But, the Marx who described the alienation of the worker and who, with Engels, contributed a stirring portrait of the class structures associated with industrialized societies during the nineteenth century was clearly a romanticist.

The romanticism that influenced Marx was similar to the visions of life that pervaded the literary activities of a large segment of the social commentators of the period. The adherents of the rapidly proliferating social-scientific activities of this period could not avoid contamination. Most relevant to sociology and the conceptions of social stratification and integration that influenced the scientific observers of the scene was what has been called German sociological romanticism.

> This perspective . . . had at the very center of its conception of the world, a picture of a pre-modern peasant society in which all men lived in harmonious mutual respect of authority and subordinate, in which all felt themselves integral parts of a community which in its turn lived in continuous and inspiring contact with its own past. Traditions were stable, the kinship group was bound together in unquestioned solidarity. No one was alienated from himself or isolated from his territorial community and kin. Beliefs were firm and universally shared.[15]

[14] Cf., for example, Mark Abrahamson et al., "The Self or the Collectivity: Simulation of a Marxian Hypothesis," *Social Forces,* **3**: 299–305 (March, 1969).

[15] Edward Shils, "Daydreams and Nightmares; Reflections on the Criticism of Mass Culture," *Sewanee Review*: 599 (Autumn 1957).

This specific form of romanticism, a variant of the many perspectives classified under this rubric, is even better understood when we see it as part of a larger framework of ideas. H. G. Schenk, in a recent book, has described the romantic mind as one characterized by "Utopian dreams for the future side by side with nostalgia for the past. . . ." [16]

Aspects of Marx's perspective are influenced by a romantic conception of the nature of alienation and a vague vision of a communalistic society devoid of class antagonism. His approach to social stratification, however, is clearly of another stamp, as reflected in this widely known quotation from the *Communist Manifesto* by Marx and Friedrick Engels (1848): "The history of all hitherto existing society is the history of class struggles."

The Marxian Analysis of Social Stratification

Marx died prior to completing an explicit definition of social class.[17] However, in the *Communist Manifesto*, an excerpt which is reprinted here, there appears the clearest and most concise statement of the Marxian approach to social stratification in particular, and societal processes in general. Although it was primarily intended as a political document, it is at once a theoretical statement on the nature of European history, on the emergence of economic systems and human rights, and a presumed prophecy of the elimination of political power and class antagonism. In it Marx and Engels briefly describe the various role of "oppressor and oppressed," the stratification systems of ancient Rome, feudal Europe, and emergent capitalism, as well as the economic and sociological processes that created the conditions of perceived oppressions.

On the Emergence of Social Classes*

Karl Marx and Friedrich Engels

The East-Indian and Chinese Markets, the colonisation of America, trade with the colonies, the increase in the means of exchange and in commodities generally, gave to commerce, to navigation, to industry, an impulse never

[16] F. G. Schenk, *The Mind of European Romantics* (New York: Doubleday Anchor Books, 1969), p. xxii.

[17] Ralf Dahrendorf has brought together the central ideas on class that were dispersed throughout many of Marx's works. See Dahrendorf's *Class and Class Conflict in Industrial Society* (Stanford, Calif.: Stanford University Press, 1959), pp. 8–27.

* pp. 10–18 of the Samuel Moore translation, London, 1888.

before known, and thereby, to the revolutionary element in the tottering feudal society, a rapid development.

The feudal system of industry, in which industrial production was monopolised by closed guilds, now no longer sufficed for the growing wants of the new markets. The manufacturing system took its place. The guild-masters were pushed aside by the manufacturing middle class; division of labour between the different corporate guilds vanished in the face of division of labour in each single workshop.

Meantime the markets kept ever growing, the demand ever rising. Even manufacture no longer sufficed. Thereupon, steam and machinery revolutionised industrial production. The place of manufacture was taken by the giant, modern industry, the place of the industrial middle class, by industrial millionaires—the leaders of whole industrial armies, the modern bourgeois.

Modern industry has established the world market, for which the discovery of America paved the way. This market has given an immense development to commerce, to navigation, to communication by land. This development has, in its turn, reacted on the extension of industry; and in proportion as industry, commerce, navigation, railways extended, in the same proportion the bourgeoisie developed, increased its capital, and pushed into the background every class handed down from the Middle Ages.

We see, therefore, how the modern bourgeoisie itself the product of a long course of development, of a series of revolutions in the modes of production and of exchange.

Each step in the development of the bourgeoisie was accompanied by a corresponding political advance of that class. An oppressed class under the sway of the feudal nobility, it became an armed and self-governing association in the mediæval commune; here independent urban republic (as in Italy and Germany), there taxable "third estate" of the monarchy (as in France); afterwards, in the period of manufacture proper, serving either the semi-feudal or the absolute monarchy as a counterpoise against the nobility, and, in fact, corner-stone of the great monarchies in general—the bourgeoisie has at last, since the establishment of modern industry and of the world market, conquered for itself, in the modern representative state, exclusive political sway. The executive of the modern state is but a committee for managing the common affairs of the whole bourgeoisie.

The bourgeoisie has played a most revolutionary rôle in history.

The bourgeoisie, wherever it has got the upper hand, has put an end to all feudal, patriarchal, idyllic relations. It has pitilessly torn asunder the motley feudal ties that bound man to his "natural superiors," and has left no other bond between man and man than naked self-interest, than callous "cash payment." It has drowned the most heavenly ecstasies of religious fervour, of chivalrous enthusiasm, of philistine sentimentalism, in the icy water of egotistical calculation. It has resolved personal worth into exchange value, and in place of the numberless indefeasible chartered freedoms, has set up that single, unconscionable freedom—Free Trade. In one word, for exploitation, veiled by religious and political illusions, it has substituted naked, shameless, direct, brutal exploitation.

The bourgeoisie has stripped of its halo every occupation hitherto honoured and looked up to with reverent awe. It has converted the physician, the lawyer, the priest, the poet, the man of science, into its paid wage-labourers.

The bourgeoisie has torn away from the family its sentimental veil, and has reduced the family relation to a mere money relation.

The bourgeoisie has disclosed how it came to pass that the brutal display of vigour in the Middle Ages, which reactionaries so much admire, found its fitting complement in the most slothful indolence. It has been the first to show what man's activity can bring about. It has accomplished wonders far surpassing Egyptian pyramids, Roman aqueducts, and Gothic cathedrals; it has conducted expeditions that put in the shade all former migrations of nations and crusades.

The bourgeoisie cannot exist without constantly revolutionising the instruments of production, and thereby the relations of production, and with them the whole relations of society. Conservation of the old modes of production in unaltered form, was, on the contrary, the first condition of existence for all earlier industrial classes. Constant revolutionising of production, uninterrupted disturbance of all social conditions, everlasting uncertainty and agitation distinguish the bourgeois epoch from all earlier ones. All fixed, fast-frozen relations, with their train of ancient and venerable prejudices and opinions, are swept away, all new-formed ones become antiquated before they can ossify. All that is solid melts into air, all that is holy is profaned, and man is at last compelled to face with sober senses his real conditions of life and his relations with his kind.

The need of a constantly expanding market for its products chases the bourgeoisie over the whole surface of the globe. It must nestle everywhere, settle everywhere, establish connctions verywhere.

The bourgeoisie has through its exploitation of the world market given a cosmopolitan character to production and consumption in every country. To the great chagrin of reactionaries, it has drawn from under the feet of industry the national ground on which it stood. All old-established national industries have been destroyed or are daily being destroyed. They are dislodged by new industries, whose introduction becomes a life and death question for all civilised nations, by industries that no longer work up indigenous raw material, but raw material drawn from the remotest zones; industries whose products are consumed, not only at home, but in every quarter of the globe. In place of the old wants, satisfied by the production of the country, we find new wants, requiring for their satisfaction the products of distant lands and climes. In place of the old local and national seclusion and self-sufficiency, we have intercourse in every direction, universal inter-dependence of nations. And as in material, so also in intellectual production. The intellectual creations of individual nations become common property. National one-sidedness and narrow-mindedness become more and more impossible, and from the numerous national and local literatures there arises a world literature.

The bourgeoisie, by the rapid improvement of all instruments of production, by the immensely facilitated means of communication, draws all nations, even the most barbarian, into civilisation. The cheap prices of its commodities are the heavy artillery with which it batters down all Chinese walls, with which it forces the barbarians' intensely obstinate hatred of foreigners to capitulate. It compels all nations, on pain of extinction, to adopt the bourgeois mode of production; it compels them to introduce what it calls civilisation into their midst, that is, to become bourgeois themselves. In a word, it creates a world after its own image.

The bourgeoisie has subjected the country to the rule of the towns. It has created enormous cities, has greatly increased the urban population as compared with the rural, and has thus rescued a considerable part of the population from the idiocy of rural life. Just as it has made the country dependent on the towns, so it has made barbarian and semi-barbarian countries dependent on the civilised ones, nations of peasants on nations of bourgeois, the East on the West.

More and more the bourgeoisie keeps doing away with the scattered state of the population, of the means of production, and of property. It has agglomerated population, centralised means of production, and has concentrated property in a few hands. The necessary consequence of this was political centralisation. Independent, or but loosely connected provinces, with separate interests, laws, governments and systems of taxation, became lumped together into one nation, with one government, one code of laws, one national class interest, one frontier and one customs tariff.

The bourgeoisie, during its rule of scarce one hundred years, has created more massive and more colossal productive forces than have all preceding generations together. Subjection of nature's forces to man, machinery, application of chemistry to industry and agriculture, steam-navigation, railways, electric telegraphs, clearing of whole continents for cultivation, canalisation of rivers, whole populations conjured out of the ground—what earlier century had even a presentiment that such productive forces slumbered in the lap of social labour?

We see then that the means of production and of exchange, which served as the foundation for the growth of the bourgeoisie, were generated in feudal society. At a certain stage in the development of these means of production and of exchange, the conditions under which feudal society produced and exchanged, the feudal organisation of agriculture and manufacturing industry, in a word, the feudal relations of property became no longer compatible with the already developed productive forces; they became so many fetters. They had to be burst asunder; they were burst asunder.

Into their place stepped free competition, accompanied by a social and political constitution adapted to it, and by the economic and political sway of the bourgeois class.

A similar movement is going on before our own eyes. Modern bourgeois society with its relations of production, of exchange and of property, a society that has conjured up such gigantic means of production and of exchange, is like the sorcerer who is no longer able to control the powers of the nether world whom he has called up by his spells. For many a decade past the history of industry and commerce is but the history of the revolt of modern productive forces against modern conditions of production, against the property relations that are the conditions for the existence of the bourgeoisie and of its rule. It is enough to mention the commercial crises that by their periodical return put the existence of the entire bourgeois society on trial, each time more threateningly. In these crises a great part not only of the existing products, but also of the previously created productive forces, are periodically destroyed. In these crises there breaks out an epidemic that, in all earlier epochs, would have seemed an absurdity—the epidemic of over-production. Society suddenly finds itself put back into a state of momentary barbarism; it appears as if a famine, a universal war of devastation had cut off the supply of every means of subsistence; industry and commerce seem to be destroyed. And why? Because there is too much civilisation, too much means of subsistence, too much industry, too much commerce. The productive forces at the disposal of society no longer tend to further the development of the conditions of bourgeois property; on the contrary, they have become too powerful for these conditions, by which they are fettered, and no sooner do they overcome these fetters than they bring disorder into the whole of bourgeois society, endanger the existence of bourgeois property. The conditions of bourgeois society are too narrow to comprise the wealth created by them. And how does the bourgeoisie get over these crises? On the one hand by enforced destruction of a mass of productive forces; on the other, by the conquest of new markets, and by the more thorough exploitation of the old ones. That is to say, by paving the way for more extensive and more destructive crises, and by diminishing the means whereby crises are prevented.

The weapons with which the bourgeoisie felled feudalism to the ground are now turned against the bourgeoisie itself.

But not only has the bourgeoisie forged the weapons that bring death to itself; it has also called into existence the men who are to wield those weapons —the modern working class—the proletarians.

In proportion as the bourgeoisie, that is, capital, is developed, in the same proportion is the proletariat, the modern working class, developed—a class of labourers, who live only so long as they find work, and who find work only so long as their labour increases capital. These labourers, who must sell themselves piecemeal, are a commodity, like every other article of commerce, and are consequently exposed to all the vicissitudes of competition, to all the fluctuations of the market.

Owing to the extensive use of machinery and to division of labour, the work of the proletarians has lost all individual character, and, consequently, all charm for the workman. He becomes an appendage of the machine, and it is only the most simple, most monotonous, and most easily acquired knack, that is required of him. Hence, the cost of production of a workman is restricted, almost entirely, to the means of subsistence that he requires for his maintenance, and for the propagation of his race. But the price of a commodity, and therefore also of labour, is equal to its cost of production. In proportion, therefore, as the repulsiveness of the work increases, the wage decreases. Nay more, in proportion as the use of machinery and division of labour increases, in the same proportion the burden of toil also increases, whether by prolongation of the working hours, by increase of the work exacted in a given time, or by increased speed of the machinery, etc.

Modern industry has converted the little workshop of the patriarchal master into the great factory of the industrial capitalist. Masses of labourers, crowded into the factory, are organised like soldiers. As privates of the industrial army they are placed under the command of a perfect hierarchy of officers and sergeants. Not only are they slaves of the bourgeois class, and of the bourgeois state; they are daily and hourly enslaved by the machine, by the overlooker, and, above all, by the individual bourgeois manufacturer himself. The more openly this despotism proclaims gain to be its end and aim, the more petty, the more hateful and the more embittering it is.

The less the skill and exertion of strength implied in manual labour, in other words, the more modern industry develops, the more is the labour of men superseded by that of women. Differences of age and sex have no longer any distinctive social validity for the working class. All are instruments of labour, more or less expensive to use, according to their age and sex.

No sooner has the labourer received his wages in cash for the moment escaping exploitation by the manufacturer, than he is set upon by the other portions of the bourgeoisie, the landlord, the shopkeeper, the pawnbroker, etc.

The lower strata of the middle class—the small tradespeople, shopkeepers, and retired tradesmen generally, the handicraftsmen and peasants—all these sink gradually into the proletariat, partly because their diminutive capital does not suffice for the scale on which modern industry is carried on, and is swamped in the competition with the large capitalist, partly because their specialised skill is rendered worthless by new methods of production. Thus the proletariat is recruited from all classes of the population.

The proletariat goes through various stages of development. With its birth begins its struggle with the bourgeoisie. At first the contest is carried on by individual labourers, then by the work people of a factory, then by the operatives of one trade, in one locality, against the individual bourgeois who directly exploits them. They direct their attacks not against the bourgeois conditions of production, but against the instruments of production themselves; they destroy imported wares that compete with their labor, they smash machinery to pieces, they set factories ablaze, they seek to restore by force the vanished status of the workman of the Middle Ages.

At this stage the labourers still form an incoherent mass scattered over the whole country, and broken up by their mutual competition. If anywhere they unite to form compact bodies, this is not yet the consequence of their own active union, but of the union of the bourgeoisie, which class, in order to attain its own political ends, is compelled to set the whole proletariat in motion, and is moreover still able to do so for a time. At this stage, therefore, the proletarians do not fight their enemies, but the enemies of their enemies, the remnants of absolute monarchy, the landowners, the non-industrial bourgeois, the petty bourgeoisie. Thus the whole historical movement is concentrated in the hands of the bourgeoisie; every victory so obtained is a victory for the bourgeoisie.

But with the development of industry the proletariat not only increases in number; it becomes concentrated in great masses, its strength grows, and it feels that strength more. The various interests and conditions of life within the ranks of the proletariat are more and more equalised, in proportion as machinery obliterates all distinctions of labour and nearly everywhere reduces wages to the same low level. The growing competition among the bourgeois, and the resulting commercial crises, make the wages of the workers ever more fluctuating. The unceasing improvement of machinery, ever more rapidly developing, makes their livelihood more and more precarious; the collisions between individual workmen and individual bourgeois take more and more the character of collisions between two classes. Thereupon the workers begin to form combinations (trade unions) against the bourgeoisie; they club together in order to keep up the rate of wages; they found permanent associations in order to make provision beforehand for these occasional revolts. Here and there the contest breaks out into riots.

Now and then the workers are victorious, but only for a time. The real fruit of their battle lies, not in the immediate result, but in the ever expanding union of the workers. This union is furthered by the improved means of communication which are created by modern industry, and which place the workers of different localities in contact with one another. It was just this contact that was needed to centralise the numerous local struggles, all of the same character, into one national struggle between classes. But every class struggle is a political struggle. And that union, to attain which the burghers of the Middle Ages, with their miserable highways, required centuries, the modern proletarians, thanks to railways, achieve in a few years.

This organisation of the proletarians into a class, and consequently into a political party, is continually being upset again by the competition between the workers themselves. But it ever rises up again, stronger, firmer mightier.

Holding that class antagonism and class conflict have characterized all known societies, Marx and Engels, to summarize here, suggest that from complex arrangements of various strata in past societies has emerged a relatively simple set of relations between two classes, the *bourgeoisie* and the *proletariat*.

The bourgeoisie, formerly serfs, grew out of the burghers of the earliest towns and grew in importance as a concomitant of the decline of feudalism and the guild system and the simultaneous increase in commercial activity associated with the rapid expansion of new markets. As demand for goods increased, markets expanded, the single workshop replaced the guild, and the bourgeoisie increased in size and importance. Finally, industrial activity was revolutionized by the use of steam and expensive machinery and the result was a concentration of ownership of the means of production and exchange by this new industrial class holding a position of power in the world market.

Accompanying the transformation of economic activity and the emergence of the bourgeoisie as the new leaders of industry was the growth of their political power. From an oppressed class, subordinate to the feudal nobility (that is, the landed aristocracy), they advanced through a series of stages to a position of dominance over the affairs of the modern state.

The *proletariat,* on the other hand, originally emerged out of the laboring classes of the modern state. Recruited from all classes of the population, including elements of the ruling classes and the bourgeoisie, the proletariat is now the revolutionary class, in contrast to the bourgeoisie during the decline of feudalism. All of the proletarian's social relations have been altered by the fact that he is now without property. Being without property, his major thrust is toward abolishing individual property. Finally, the processes of change are seen as inevitable, resulting in the transformation of bourgeois society. The consequent "victory of the proletariat" is the outcome of historical forces associated with the flow of commerce and the revolution in industry.

Although it is clear that Marx and Engels prophesied the concentration of the mass of society into two large social classes, it is equally clear that their sociological view of the stratification systems of the nineteenth century was more complex. The *aristocracy* still exists, if only to do battle with the proletariat. The *lower middle class*, the small manufacturer, the shopkeeper, the artisan, the peasant, fights the bourgeoisie to save itself from extinction. And "that passively rotting mass thrown off by the lower layers of old society," the *Lumpenproletariat,* represents still another stratum.[18] Marx and Engels, then, recognized at least five social strata that eventually would merge into the two antagonistic classes distinguished from one another by property relations: (1) the remnants of a well-integrated aristocracy; (2) a middle class, which controlled the industrial, commercial, and political life of Western Europe and the United States; (3) a lower middle class; (4) a laboring class; and (5) the *Lumpenproletariat.* As we will show subsequently, Marx and Engels were far superior in their analysis and description of the European social strata of their time than in their prognostications about stratification arrangements and the nature of societies to come.

Their conception of stratification was, and indeed remains, sociologically significant for at least two reasons. First of all, it is clearly a sociological theory in the most fundamental sense. Man's social position, rather than his innate, personal qualities is conceived of as *the* major influence on his total life situation. Furthermore, it is not an abstract position but a concrete one that is critical here. In striking out against the utopians for appealing to society at large rather than to the interests of particular classes, they imply that the Saint-Simonians, the Fourierists, and the Owenites have not grasped the essential relationship between man and society.

Secondly, Marx and Engels hold that not only are man's social actions and power determined by his position in a social structure, but the mental states—his very *consciousness of life*—surrounding him in general and class consciousness, particularly, are determined by where he stands in relation

[18] *The Communist Manifesto,* op. cit., p. 22.

to an industrial and exchange system. It was the manifestation of this consciousness of one's connection with the economic basis of social relationships that in part provided the drift to association and identification with the proletariat. The significance of class consciousness as a potentially fruitful idea in the analysis of social stratification is reflected in both philosophical debate and empirical research in social science.[19]

What is most crucial to an understanding of Marx's concept of class is that in order for classes to exist in any real sense the awareness of similar life circumstances must be transformed into class opposition and conflict. The mere existence of objective differences between categories and strata is, in itself, not sufficient for us to describe—from a Marxian perspective—classes as existing. It is plausible, however, that objective differences between strata suggest a greater probability that conflict—and its consequence, classes—will emerge.[20] Thus, a critical area of stratification analysis, if we are to appreciate Marx's contribution, is the process by which objective differences lead to class conflict and consciousness. Louis Kriesberg, a sociologist, in a paper prepared especially for this volume, provides us with a perceptive analysis of the dynamics of class conflict. The fact that this is not a Marxist analysis per se is important because it demonstrates that Marx's contribution to sociological analysis fits clearly into the broader perspectives of conflict theory.

Class Conflicts*

Louis Kriesberg

Objective differences in class interests do not always emerge into class struggles. For a manifest conflict to arise, at least one class of people must (1) become conscious of themselves as a group, (2) come to perceive that they have grievances, and (3) formulate goals which would lessen their dissatisfaction, at the apparent expense of another party. Actually, these three aspects of

---

[19] See Dahrendorf, ibid; Abrahamson, op. cit; Ephraim H. Mizruchi, *Success and Opportunity* (New York: The Free Press, 1964); and Richard Centers, *The Psychology of Social Classes* (Princeton: Princeton University Press, 1949).

[20] It is important to bear in mind the potential controversy that might arise from suggesting a given sequence of events leading to class consciousness and conflict. From a rigorously sociological perspective, and Marx's must be so characterized, mental states occur in response to social action. Thus, class consciousness would be conceptualized as a *consequence* of conflict or some other set of social events rather than a precursor to conflict. In the real world, as Kriesberg suggests, understanding conflict may require a slightly different analysis.

---

* For further corroboration of the perspective expressed in this paper, see Louis Kriesberg, *The Sociology of Social Conflicts* (Englewood Cliffs, N.J.: Prentice-Hall, 1973).

a manifest conflict are highly interdependent. Who we are, what we have to complain about, and who is to blame for it are all related and help determine each other. For example, if capitalists are in charge and we are underpaid, we are proletarians.

In studying these aspects of manifest conflict we are interested in accounting for basic variations in these subjective states. If we want to account for the intensity and extensiveness of class conflict, we must consider: the characteristics of the classes, the relations between them, and their social environment. In this article we will consider only how characteristics of each class or stratum affect their group consciousness, grievance, and goal.

It might be argued that whether or not a stratum enters into conflict with another depends entirely on the relationship between them. Alternatively, it might be contended that some strata are basically aggressive or hostile and such characteristics account for class conflicts. Generally, I would emphasize between parties as the explanation for their disputes. But we also need to examine the role of internal or domestic factors which affect the emergence of conflict groups. That is what I do here.

Collective Identity

We begin by examining how characteristics of the people in a given stratum affect the likelihood that they (or some of them) come to view themselves as having a collective identity. We ask what about them makes them think that they share a common fate, that they have more in common with each other than they have with members of other strata?

A prerequisite for a sense of common identity is communication within the stratum. Insofar as communication among members is hindered or handicapped relative to nonmembers, so is the likelihood that a sense of commonness and collective identity will develop. Many factors affect the ease of communication. The proximity and density of the members of a class, their absolute number, the social and non-social barriers between them, and the social and technical skills the members possess all affect the rate of communication.

Thus, factors which bring persons of a social stratum into large concentrations facilitate their communication with each other and the development of common perspectives. Industrial employment in large factories provides such opportunities for workers.

Communication, of course, does not depend entirely on physical distance. Access to the technology of communication and the possession of the social skills for communication are more critical. Social strata which have members with such resources more readily develop collective self-consciousness and express this in some organizational form. One of the factors which accounts for the order in which trade unions have been established is the ability of the workers to communicate and organize: printers, shoemakers, and other skilled craftsmen were the first to form trade unions.

Significantly, those who have more status, power, or material wealth are also most likely to have more of the requisite skills and resources for communication (Parkin 1971). Furthermore, those with more power, if they have enough, may use their power to limit the possession and development of the skills needed for communication among the groups with less power. For example, education has been forbidden or limited for slaves, and ever since slavery, American blacks have not had equal access to education.

The availability of the means of extensive communication also favors the dominant groups. Thus, the mass media generally convey the perspectives of whites, of males, and of upper-white-collar occupations (for example, Johnson, Sears, and McConahay 1971). Members of sub-dominant categories, then, have less opportunity to develop a collective identity.

Homogeneity of the members in a social category tends to facilitate communication and the growth of a sense of solidarity and common fate. For example, Landecker (1963) found that class consciousness was more frequent among persons with high status crystallization than among those with low status crystallization. One of the frequently observed difficulties in the formation of worker solidarity in the form of trade union membership or of class consciousness in America has been the extensive immigration and ethnic heterogeneity of the American workers (Perlman 1928, pp. 162–169; Bok and Dunlop 1970, p. 30).

Finally, the boundedness and degree of organization of a stratum affect the growth of group solidarity. The more clear and unchanging are the boundaries of a stratum, the more likely are the members to develop a sense of common fate. Members of a caste are more likely (everything else being equal) to think of themselves as a collective group with a common interest than are members of a social class.

The more highly interdependent and integrated are the members of a category, the more likely they are to see themslves as a collectivity with common interests. This may be observed in the variations in solidarity among different occupations (for example, L. Kriesberg 1953; Seidman, London, Karsh, and Tagliacozzo 1958). Miners, for example, are vitally inter-dependent in their work activities and historically have had a high sense of solidarity compared to other occupational groups (Gouldner 1954). Of course, the solidarity of the miners is reenforced by many factors, such as isolation and concentration.

Sense of Grievance

The aspect of class conflict which has received the most attention is the degree of discontent or dissatisfaction within the working class. This is understandable. Seeing a group pursue an aim which is incompatible with another group's desired position, it seems natural to ask what is making them do that and answer in terms of their dissatisfaction. Even if that cannot provide a comprehensive explanation for the emergence of social conflicts, it is an essential element.

The sense of grievance must reside in the relations between the classes, in their environment, or in the characteristics of the members themselves. We will consider only the third here. Dissatisfaction, discontent, or a sense of grievance means that people have less than they think they should and could have.

We will discuss three approaches to the sources of discontent. These approaches might be viewed as competing or supplementary. The first approach emphasizes the absolute magnitude of the deprivation the members of a stratum endure and the number of spheres in which the people are deprived (Dahrendorf 1959). The second emphasizes the inconsistent levels which people have in different rankings (Lenski 1954; Goffman 1957). The third approach emphasizes the changes over time in what people have or what they think they should have (Gurr 1970; Davies 1962).

Deprivation.   The idea is that the more deprived people are, the worse they feel. They do not need any particular insight to know that they are deprived. In any case, other groups of people are readily available for comparison; reference groups can always be found. The important corollary of the idea is that people who are low ranking in several dimensions are more deprived, and feel that they are, than are persons who are high in some ways even if they are low in others.

There are additional reasons why we might expect that insofar as people are deprived, and uniformly so, they will be dissatisfied. First, the homogeneity of the members of the stratum facilitates their interaction and the likelihood that they view themselves as a collective entity.

In addition, if members of a stratum do not share positions with persons in other classes, conflict lines will be superimposed. Instead of being bound together by crosscutting ties they will find each conflict issue reenforces the other. Feelings of dissatisfaction will not be muted. Suppose all poor people lived in one region of the country, were of the same low status ethnicity, and had little political power. Then, in the event that a conflict along income lines arises, all the other bases of cleavage would be drawn into the struggle. If these various categories were not superimposed, then people of low income might be of a different ethnic, regional, or political position and have ties of friendship or calculative interest which see them as allies at another time, on another issue.

Furthermore, we might expect that people who are deprived in one sphere, without satisfactory redress, will generalize their dissatisfaction from one area of discontent to another. They have fewer compensating satisfactions. In short, the more deprived people are, the more likely are they to feel frustrated.

There is much evidence supporting these arguments. Inkeles (1960) reviewed data from many societies and found that persons of lower occupational or economic levels tend to be dissatisfied, as indicated by responses to several different kinds of questions. Similarly, occupational studies report that the lower the prestige, income, or work autonomy of an occupation, the more likely are its members to be dissatisfied with it (for example, Friedmann and Havighurst 1954; Blauner 1964).

We also expect that the more spheres in which people are ranked low, the more likely are they to feel dissatisfied. Thus, findings indicate that education and income each are directly related to being happy and to having a higher ratio of positive to negative feeling (Bradburn and Caplovitz 1965, pp. 10–11; Bradburn 1969, p. 95). Furthermore, these two variables generally have cumulative effects.

There are other reasons, however, to expect that greater deprivation is not directly related to greater sense of grievance and dissatisfaction. First, people who rank low on a consensually valued dimension tend to think poorly of themselves and wish to avoid identifying themselves in terms of that dimention. This means that they avoid interacting with others similarly placed or at least avoid making any collective identification. The absence of solidarity then interferes with collectively recognized and experienced dissatisfaction.

If deprivation is severe, persons will be preoccupied with the day-to-day private efforts at coping rather than develop collectively shared discontent. Even moderate deprivation can be mentally restricting. Buchanan and Cantril (1953, pp. 20–22) in a public opinion study in nine countries found that workers were less likely to identify with persons of their nation not of their own class and less likely to identify with persons of their own class in other countries, compared to middle class respondents. Related to this, is the fact that the deprived tend to accommodate to the deprivation. This may take the form of suppression and denial of hostile feelings and of placating and in-gratiating behavior (Karon 1958; Parker and Kleiner 1970). These reactions do not aid in the development of a collective sense of grievance. Another, related point deserves notice. Severe deprivation may make people despair of changing the conditions. As an accommodation to such despair, even the self-recognition of collective discontent may not occur. (See Mizruchi 1967.)

Rank Disequilibrium. Another major theme in contemporary discussions of sources of discontent is rank disequilibrium, status inconsistency, or rank in-congruence. The idea is that persons who are high in some rank dimensions and low in others will be particularly dissatisfied. There are several alleged reasons for this. First, it is argued that there is a tendency within social systems for people to have approximately equivalent ranks in different ranking systems; therefore, a person who is high on some ranks and low on others is odd, is treated as odd, and feels so himself. Social interaction is uncomfortable and this discomfort is communicated to the persons with inconsistent ranks (Lenski 1954; Hughes 1944). Consequently, rank disequilibrium is experienced as a source of strain.

This strain is compounded by the tendency of others to try to relate to people in disequilibrium in terms of their low ranks and the persons in dis-equilibrium themselves trying to interact with others in terms of their high ranks (Galtung 1964). This might be seen in a male worker "putting down" a woman supervisor as "just a woman" and the supervisor treating the worker as just that. Relations among workers in restaurants abound in such problems (Whyte 1948).

The third major reason that status inconsistency is a source of grievance is that it makes people feel that their low rank is particularly objectionable. This is partly because other people treat them in terms of the low rank when that is not the major way they see themselves. It is also the case because if they use the high ranks as a reference or comparison level, the low rank is more objectionable than if they used a lower rank as the reference level. The low rank is particularly grievous, in addition, because the high rank provides a claim for an equal level on the other ranks. Moreover, the high rank makes it credible that the same level be attained on other ranking dimensions. As observed earlier, having less than you would like is not enough to make a grievance; you must also think that it is possible to have what you think you should have.

A final consideration deserves noting. If people have high ranks along some dimensions, they are likely to have resources and skills which give them reason to think that they might alter their circumstances, at least compared to those who are uniformly deprived. The sense of competence or possible efficacy would make it easier for persons to admit, recognize, and collectively acknowledge their dissatisfaction.

Changes in Attainments and Expectations.   The third major source of grievance arises from a decline in what people have or an increase in what they expect. This gap or discrepancy is argued to be the fundamental basis for revolts and other kinds of turmoil and violence (for example, Gurr 1970; Feierabend, Feierabend, and Nesvold 1969; Davies 1962; Tanter and Midlarsky 1967).

Changes in either expectations or attainments can increase an unwanted discrepancy between them. Members of a society or class may have decreasing amounts of what they previously possessed. This might be due to a poor harvest or it might be due to another group reducing the autonomy, income, or honor of these people. The expectations persist, at least for a while. Having attained a certain level, that level is felt to be appropriate, desirable, and certainly attainable. A fall in actual attainments, then, would produce dissatisfaction and a sense of grievance.

Another kind of change is stressed in many studies of revolutions (for example, Davies 1962; Brinton 1955). It accounts for revolutions occurring when conditions improve. Improving conditions which cease to improve or deteriorate create a sense of grievance. Expectations continue to advance at the rate which past experience dictates. Even a leveling off of progress and certainly a fall in attainments is experienced as deprivation.

The third major type of discrepancy arising from changes in expectations and attainments is of rising expectations. For a variety of reasons, people may raise their expectations about what they could and should have and hence discover that what they have is intolerably inadequate. The phrase "revolution of rising expectations" refers to this idea particularly in regard to the economically underdeveloped countries. The peoples in these societies are increasingly dissatisfied with their conditions as they become familiar with what there is to have and what people in economically advanced societies already have. Within every society leaders sometimes promise gains and even begin programs which raise expectations that are unmet. For example, in the United States, the expectations of the blacks and of the poor were raised in regard to racial equality and to the ending of poverty by federal governmental actions and words in the early 1960s.

We can try to integrate the explanations of dissatisfaction by specifying the effects for different aspects of discontent. It may be that simple deprivation is the best predictor of the intensity of dissatisfaction. But the expression of such dissatisfaction depends on the belief that some alteration is possible. It is in this regard that status inconsistency, relative deprivation, and changes in expectations and actual conditions have particular pertinence.

Goals

For a class conflict to emerge, classes must believe that they hold incompatible goals. Not all aims to redress grievances are oppositional and incompatible with those of a potential adversary. A working-class goal of other-worldly salvation, for example, may be compatible with managerial goals, although an observer might regard the two groups as being in a potential conflict relationship. In this section we will examine group characteristics which affect the formulation of incompatible aims.

Any discussion of goals and ideology must include some reference to leadership. The spokesmen of a conflict group play a primary role in the formulation of aims. Discontent may be dormant and fester; unhappiness may appear to be a necessary part of the human condition. Often, it is. But leaders can also point to possible changes and future conditions in which the grievances lessen or disappear.

For a conflict organization to mobilize support and sustain itself, let alone expand, the succession of goals must be closely related to the group's capacities. An appropriate balance must exist between the aims to be attained and the effort needed to attain them.

Particularly for newly emerging conflict organizations, the choice of immediate goals is important in building support for the organization (Haggstrom 1968).

In organizing the poor in community action programs during the 1960s organization building was more successful if demands were met with initial resistance and later yielding by the opposition. Resistance is important because it seems to confirm the validity of the analysis which claims that a conflict organization is necessary. Yet failure to attain any benefits would also reveal the invalidity of the diagnosis of the problem or the way of solving it.

Leaders also play an important role in the articulation and integration of diverse interests. For example, George Wallace, like Barry Goldwater, in 1964, may have appealed to white fears about racial integration and "crime in the streets." But Wallace combined this with expressions of concern about the welfare of the working man and of the little people. Wallace received a larger measure of support from workers and trade union members than Goldwater (Lipset and Raab 1970, pp. 362–367).

In the case of the labor movement one can trace a variety of formulas that leaders constructed to build a viable conflict organization. During the nineteenth century in the United States, many national trade unions began but did not survive: the Knights of Labor, the National Labor Union, and the Industrial Workers of the World (Perlman 1928). The "pure and simple trade unionism" of the American Federation of Labor provided a set of immediate and long-term goals which were always partially attainable. Thus, when the founder-leader, Samuel Gompers, was asked what the workers wanted, he answered, "More, more, more, and more."

In elaborating goals, beliefs about the past as well as the present and the future are promulgated. Certain beliefs about the past can make ends seem more legitimate and attainable. Leaders can argue that the desired future position is attainable because such a position once existed; for example, land and other property were once communally owned.

Leaders agitate not only by trying to increase the sense of grievance or discontent, but also by offering a better and attainable future. To depict how exploited and victimized people are seems to contradict the possibility that such a weak group can better itself against the desires of the victimizing group. One way out of the paradox is to use the power of weakness. People who really have nothing are invulnerable from threats and coercion. Having nothing, they can lose nothing. The *Communist Manifesto* so exhorted the workers to unite in struggle, "you have nothing to lose but your chains." (Blau 1964, pp. 230–231).

The nature and direction of the goal is strongly shaped by the grievance underlying it. Considering how the sources of discontent affect aims will help to integrate the apparent contradictions in the discussion about the sources.

People who are deprived or whose conditions have deteriorated are more likely to support radical goals and large changes in their relationship to the presumed adversary than people with status inconsistency or improved conditions. For example, during periods of severe economic depression in the United States relatively radical aims have been voiced by some, albeit small, groups within the labor movement; but during the economic upswing after the Depression trade union organizations, with much more reformist goals, expanded (Dunlop 1951). Or, we might consider blacks in the United States during the 1960s. Blacks with higher education and income tended to be conventional militants while those who were more uniformly worse-off tended to be disproportionately in support of black separatist objectives (Marx 1969, pp. 57, 117).

The direction of goals, whether to the left or right, toward increasing or decreasing inequalities, also depends on the nature of the discontent. Deteriorating conditions for the formerly high ranking persons, even if the deterioration is only relative to those lower than themselves, makes them favor aims which restore previous inequalities. It is from such groups that reactionary political movements have drawn disproportional support. We also expect status inconsistents with ascribed or investment statuses lower than achieved or reward statuses to support goals which would be conservative or reactionary compared to persons with over-rewarded kinds of inconsistencies, who would support more liberal or equalitarian aims (Schmitt 1965; Broom and Jones 1970).

The pattern of status inconsistency also affects the content of the goal. People will try to raise themselves along the dimensions in which they have relatively low status. Hence they will be challenging those who are above them on that dimension. This helps determine the goal and the adversary. Thus, persons with low ethnic status and high occupational and income levels might try to raise the status of their ethnic category and challenge those who presume to have higher ethnic status, or individuals may try to "pass" and deny their ethnicity.

Fundamentally, the content of the grievance determines the goal. If economic deprivation is experienced, then efforts usually will be directed at improving those conditions. But how that is to be done and who is the opponent to those efforts depends in part on the leaders' ideas as well as the prevailing ideas among the members of the class. This requires bringing the relations between the conflicting parties and their environment into the analysis.

Many class characteristics, in addition to those discussed here, interact to affect the ends to be pursued. Goals however, are not merely the expression of the inner desires of the members of one class. The relations between the classes with which they interact must also be taken into account.

In this paper we have reviewed the important attributes of social classes which affect the emergence of class struggle. We have considered how those attributes shape the sense of solidarity, of grievance, and of objectives. These elements of thought and feeling are essential if a class struggle is to arise.

REFERENCES

Blau, Peter M., *Exchange and Power in Social Life* (New York: John Wiley & Sons, Inc., 1964).
Blauner, Robert, *Alienation and Freedom: The Factory Worker and His Industry* (Chicago: The University of Chicago Press, 1964).
Bok, Derek C. and John T. Dunlop, *Labor and the American Community* (New York: Simon and Schuster, Inc., 1970).
Bradburn, Norman M., *The Structure of Psychological Well-Being* (Chicago: Aldine Publishing Co., 1969).
———, and David Caplovitz, *Reports on Happiness* (Chicago: Aldine Publishing Co., 1969).
Brinton, Crane, *The Anatomy of Revolution* (New York: Vintage Books, 1955). Originally published in 1938.
Broom, Leonard and F. Lancaster Jones, "Status Consistency and Political Preference: The Australian Case," *American Sociological Review*, **35**:989–1001 (December, 1970).
Buchanan, William and Hadley Cantril, *How Nations See Each Other* (Urbana: University of Illinois Press, 1953).
Dahrendorf, Ralf, *Class and Class Conflict in Industrial Society* (Stanford: Stanford University Press, 1959).
Davies, James C., "Toward a Theory of Revolution," *American Sociological Review*, **27**:5–19 (February, 1962).
Dunlop, John T., "The Development of Labor Organization," in Joseph Shister (ed.), *Labor Economics and Industrial Relations* (Chicago: J. B. Lippincott Co., 1951), pp. 48–56.
Feierabend, Ivo K., Rosalind L. Feierabend, and Betty A. Nesvold, "Social Change and Political Violence: Cross-National Patterns," in Hugh Davis Graham and Ted Robert Gurr (eds.), *Violence in America* (New York: Bantam Books, 1969), pp. 632–687.
Friedman, Eugene and Robert J. Havighurst, *The Meaning of Work and Retirement* (Chicago: University of Chicago Press, 1954).
Galtung, Johan, "A Structural Theory of Aggression," *Journal of Peace Research*, **2**:95–119 1964).
Goffman, Irwin W., "Status Consistency and Preference for Change in Power Distribution," *American Sociological Review*, **22**:275–281 (June, 1957).
Gouldner, Alvin W., *Patterns of Industrial Bureaucracy* (New York: The Free Press, 1954).
Gurr, Ted Robert, *Why Men Rebel* (Princeton, N.J.: Princeton University Press, 1970).
Haggstrom, Warren C., "Can the Poor Transform the World?" in Irwin Deutscher and Elizabeth J. Thompson (eds.), *Among the People* (New York: Basic Books, Inc., 1968), pp. 67–110.
Hughes, Everett C., "Dilemmas and Contradictions of Status," *American Journal of Sociology*, **50**:353–359 (March, 1944).
Inkeles, Alex, "Industrial Man: The Relation of Status to Experience, Perception, and Value," *The American Journal of Sociology*, **66**:1–31 (July, 1960).

Johnson, Paula B., David O. Sears, and John B. McConahay, "Black Invisibility, the Press, and the Los Angeles Riot," *The American Journal of Sociology*, **76**:698–721 (January, 1971).

Karon, Bertram P., *The Negro Personality* (New York: Springer Publishing Co., 1958).

Kriesberg, Louis, "Customer versus Colleague Ties among Retail Furriers," *Journal of Retailing*, **29**:173–176 (Winter, 1953–54).

Landecker, Werner S., "Class Crystallization and Class Consciousness," *American Sociological Review*, **28**:219–229 (April, 1963).

Lenski, Gerhard E., "Status Crystallization: A Non-Vertical Dimension of Social Status," *American Sociological Review*, **19**:405–413 (August, 1954).

Lipset, Seymour Martin and Earl Raab, *The Politics of Unreason: Right Wing Extremism in America, 1790–1970* (New York: Harper & Row, Publishers, Inc., 1970).

Marx, Gary T., *Protest and Prejudice* (New York: Harper & Row, Publishers, Inc., 1969).

Mizruchi, Ephraim H., "Aspiration and Poverty," *Sociological Quarterly*, **8**:439–466 (Autumn, 1967).

Parker, Seymour and Robert J. Kleiner, "The Culture of Poverty," *American Anthropologist*, **72**:516–527 (June, 1970).

Parkin, Frank, *Class Inequality and Political Order* (New York: Frederick A. Praeger, Inc., 1971).

Perlman, Selig, *A Theory of the Labor Movement* (New York: Augustus M. Kelley, 1928).

Schmitt, David R., "An Attitudinal Correlate of the Status Congruency of Married Women," *Social Forces*, **44**:190–195 (December, 1965).

Seidman, Joel, Jack London, Bernard Karsh, and Daisy L. Tagliacozzo, *The Worker Views His Union* (Chicago: The University of Chicago Press, 1958).

Tanter, Raymond and Manus Midlarsky, "A Theory of Revolution," *The Journal of Conflict Resolution*, **11**:264–280 (September, 1967).

Whyte, William F., *Human Relations in Industry* (New York: McGraw-Hill Book Co., 1948).

3 Class, Status, and Power

Max Weber

Whereas Marx attributed primary importance to economic forces in historical and societal change, Max Weber (1864–1920) articulated an argument that, although it acknowledged the significance of economic factors, placed greater emphasis on the role of ideas in societal process.[1] In taking issue with the "economic determinism" that characterized the Marxian approach to stratification, Weber noted that although China, India, and ancient Israel had attained economic and organizational capacities that were necessary (economic) conditions for capitalism to emerge, the absence of a set of *values* comparable to those that characterized Protestantism explained why rational capitalism emerged as a distinct and pervasive structure only in the West. Weber's focus was, thus, on "rationality" as a pervasive norm in Western societies and on the consequences of rationality for social behavior in general and, in particular, for the rise of capitalism and the growth of structured activities culminating in bureaucracy as a dominant social form.

[1] Max Weber, *The Theory of Social and Economic Organization* (New York: Oxford, 1947).

Weber is credited with introducing a multidimensional approach to stratification in which he places a greater emphasis than Marx on non-economic considerations. Specifically, Weber called attention to three dimensions, or hierarchies, of stratification: *class, status,* and *power,* which he linked to the economic, the social, and the legal-political aspects of societal structure. Furthermore, Weber noted that each of these hierarchies had collective referents that he termed *classes, status groups,* and *parties.* These hierarchies, according to Weber, are interrelated in such a way that behavior in one sphere has implications for outcomes in the other spheres. Thus, for example, in a relatively well-integrated system, one whose class rank was high could reasonably be expected to rank high on the status and power dimensions. Nevertheless, each sphere, or hierarchy, may be viewed, for analytical purposes, as independent of each other. The core of Weber's ideas on these matters is contained in the following excerpt.

Class, Status, and Power*

Max Weber

According to our terminology, the factor that creates "class" is unambiguously economic interest, and indeed, only those interests involved in the existence of the "market." Nevertheless, the concept of "class interest" is an ambiguous one: even as an empirical concept it is ambiguous as soon as one understands by it something other than the factual direction of interests following with a certain probability from the class situation for a certain "average" of those people subjected to the class situation. The class situation and other circumstances remaining the same, the direction in which the individual worker, for instance, is likely to pursue his interests may vary widely, according to whether he is constitutionally qualified for the task at hand to a high, to an average, or to a low degree. In the same way, the direction of interests may vary according to whether or not a *communal* action of a larger or smaller portion of those commonly affected by the "class situation," or even an association among them, for example, a "trade union," has grown out of the class situation from which the individual may or may not expect promising results. [Communal action refers to that action which is oriented to the feeling of the actors that they belong together. Societal action, on the other hand, is oriented to a rationally motivated adjustment of interests.] The rise of societal or even of communal action from a common class situation is by no means a universal phenomenon.

The class situation may be restricted in its effects to the generation of

---

* *Essays in Sociology,* trans. H. Gerth and C. Wright Mills (London: Routledge, 1952), p. 181.

essentially *similar* reactions, that is to say, within our terminology, of "mass actions." However, it may not have even this result. Furthermore, often merely an amorphous communal action emerges. For example, the "murmuring" of the workers known in ancient oriental ethics: the moral disapproval of the work-masters' conduct, which in its practical significance was probably equivalent to an increasingly typical phenomenon of precisely the latest industrial development, namely, the "slow down" (the deliberate limiting of work effort) of laborers by virtue of tacit agreement. The degree in which "communal action," and possibly "societal action," emerges from the "mass actions" of the members of a class is linked to general cultural conditions, especially to those of an intellectual sort. It is also linked to the extent of the contrasts that have already evolved, and is especially linked to the *transparency* of the connections between the causes and the consequences of the "class situation." For however different life chances may be, this fact in itself, according to all experience, by no means gives birth to "class action" (communal action by the members of a class). The fact of being conditioned and the results of the class situation must be distinctly recognizable. For only then the contrast of life chances can be felt not as an absolutely given fact to be accepted, but as a resultant from either (1) the given distribution of property, or (2) the structure of the concrete economic order. It is only then that people may react against the class structure not only through acts of an intermittent and irrational protest, but in the form of rational association. These have been "class situations" of the first category, (1) of a specifically naked and transparent sort, in the urban centers of Antiquity and during the Middle Ages; especially then, when great fortunes were accumulated by factually monopolized trading in industrial products of these localities or in foodstuffs. Furthermore, under certain circumstances, in the rural economy of the most diverse periods, when agriculture was increasingly exploited in a profit-making manner. The most important historical example of the second category (2) is the class situation of the modern "proletariat."

Types of "Class Struggle"

Thus every class may be the carrier of any one of the possibly innumerable forms of "class action," but this is not necessarily so. In any case, a class does not in itself constitute a community. To treat "class" conceptually as having the same value as "community" leads to distortion. That men in the same class situation regularly react in mass actions to such tangible situations as economic ones in the direction of those interests that are most adequate to their average number is an important and after all simple fact for the understanding of historical events. Above all, this fact must not lead to that kind of pseudo-scientific operation with the concepts of "class" and "class interests" so frequently found these days, and which has found its most classic expression in the statement of a talented author, that the individual may be in error concerning his interests but that the "class" is "infallible" about its interests. Yet, if classes as such are not communities, nevertheless class situations emerge only on the basis of communalization. The communal action that brings forth class situations, however, is not basically action between members of the identical class; it is an action between members of different classes. Communal actions that directly determine the class situation of the worker and the entrepreneur are the labor market, the commodities market, and the capitalistic enterprise. But, in its turn, the existence of a capitalistic enterprise presupposes that a very specific communal action exists and that it is specifically structured to protect the possession of goods *per se*, and especially the power of individuals to dispose, in principle freely, over the means of production. The existence of a capitalistic enterprise is preconditioned by a specific kind of "legal order." Each kind of class situation, and above all when it rests upon the power of property *per se*, will become most clearly efficacious when all other determinants of reciprocal relations are, as far as possible, eliminated in their significance. It is in this way that the utilization of the power of property in the market obtains its most sovereign importance.

Now "status groups" hinder the strict carrying through of the sheer market principle.

.   .   .

In content, status honor is normally expressed by the fact that above all else a specific *style of life* can be expected from all those who wish to belong to the circle. Linked with this expectation are restrictions on "social" intercourse (that is, intercourse which is not subservient to economic or any other of business's "functional" purposes). These restrictions may confine normal marriages to within the status circle and may lead to complete endogamous closure. As soon as there is not a mere individual and socially irrelevant imitation of another style of life, but an agreed-upon communal action of this closing character, the "status" development is under way.

In its characteristic form, stratification by "status groups" on the basis of conventional styles of life evolves at the present time in the United States out of the traditional democracy. For example, only the resident of a certain street ("the street") is considered as belonging to "society," is qualified for social intercourse, and is visited and invited. Above all, this differentiation evolves in such a way as to make for strict submission to the fashion that is dominant at a given time in society. This submission to fashion also exists among men in America to a degree unknown in Germany. Such submission is considered to be an indication of the fact that a given man *pretends* to qualify as a gentleman. This submission decides, at least *prima facie*, that he will be treated as such. And this recognition becomes just as important for his employment chances in "swank" establishments, and above all, for social intercourse and marriage with "esteemed" families, as the qualification for dueling among Germans in the Kaiser's day. As for the rest: certain families resident for a long time, and, of course, correspondingly wealthy, for example, "FFV, that is, First Families of Virginia," or the actual or alleged descendants of the "Indian Princess" Pocahontas, or the Pilgrim fathers, or of the Knickerbockers, the members of almost inaccessible sects and all sorts of circles setting themselves apart by means of any other characteristics and badges . . . all these elements usurp "status" honor.

.   .   .

For all practical purposes, stratification by status goes hand in hand with a monopolization of ideal and material goods or opportunities, in a manner we have come to know as typical. Besides the specific status honor, which always rests upon distance and exclusiveness, we find all sorts of material monopolies. Such honorific preferences may consist of the privilege of wearing special costumes, of eating special dishes taboo to others, of carrying arms— which is most obvious in its consequences—the right to pursue certain non-professional dilettante artistic practices, for example, to play certain musical instruments. Of course, material monopolies provide the most effective motives for the exclusiveness of a status group, although, in themselves, they are rarely sufficient, almost always they come into play to some extent. Within a status circle there is the question of intermarriage: the interest of the families in the monopolization of potential bridegrooms is at least of equal importance and is parallel to the interest in the monopolization of daughters. The daughters of the circle must be provided for. With an increased enclosure of the status group, the conventional preferential opportunities for special employment grow into a legal monopoly of special offices for the members. Certain goods become objects for monopolization by status groups. In the typical fashion these include "entailed estates" and frequently also the possessions of serfs or bondsmen and, finally, special trades. This monopolization occurs positively when the status group is exclusively entitled to own and to manage them; and negatively when, in order to maintain its specific way of life, the status group must *not* own and manage them.

The decisive role of a "style of life" in status "honor" means that status groups are the specific bearers of all "conventions." In whatever way it may manifest, all "stylization" of life either originates in status groups or is at least conserved by them. Even if the principles of status conventions differ greatly, they reveal certain typical traits, especially among those strata which are most privileged. Quite generally, among privileged status groups there is a status disqualification that operates against the performance of common physical labor. This disqualification is now "setting in" in America against the old tradition of esteem for labor. Very frequently every rational economic pursuit, and especially "entrepreneurial activity," is looked upon as a disqualification of status. Artistic and literary activity is also considered as degrading work as soon as it is exploited for income, or at least when it is connected with hard physical exertion. An example is the sculptor working like a mason in his dusty smock as over against the painter in his salon-like "studio" and those forms of musical practice that are acceptable to the status group.

Weber uses the term *class* in much the same way as the Marxians do; that is, to refer to any group of people in the same objective situation. According to Weber, members of a class share the same life chances with respect to "a supply of goods, external living conditions, and personal life experiences, in so far as this chance is determined by the amount and kind of power, or lack of such, to dispose of goods or skills for the sake of income in a given economic order." [2] Further reminiscent of Marx, Weber

2 Ibid.

holds that property and lack of property are the basic features determining one's *market situation* and that one's position in the market specifically determines one's life-chances. Thus, it is economic interest that creates classes.

But classes are not communities, although they may become bases for communal action.[3] As men perceive the similarities in their objective situation, they may indeed act collectively in pursuit of their common economic interests. The mere fact of awareness of class situation does not, however, lead to communal action.

An important hindrance to the strict carrying out of rational market principles in communal and societal actions are *status groups*. Status groups, in contrast to classes, *are* usually communities, if only of an amorphous kind. They often are maintained, Weber proposed, through intermarriage. In contrast to a rank situation determined primarily, and perhaps even solely, by a market situation, Weber formulated a concept that would emphasize "the impact of ideas upon the formation of groups without losing sight of economic conditions."[4] Weber held that there were important group dimensions involving degrees of cohesiveness, inclusiveness, and consciousness of rank that provided organizing principles for interaction among those who shared similar life-styles. Derived from the idea of *Stand* in German, Weber held that distinctions based on prestige, or *status honor,* reflected an awareness that aspects of rank systems were traditionally valued as ends in themselves and that some sense of community existed among rank groups in complex societies. This awareness of "one's own kind" represented a variant of the estate system of the Middle Ages,[5] and determined the degree of social intimacy and distance between those within a given status group and those aspiring for inclusion. In sum, what you own is distinguished from who you are, and even though there is an interplay between the two, there is a tendency to separate the two dimensions in our daily lives. Weber even suggests, by example, that in America a subordinate business associate could, and often did, attain social equality outside of the business context if he shared an "equal birthright."[6]

The third dimension in Weber's trilogy is *power*. Although power is organized into social structures that Weber called parties, it is diffused throughout all social structures. Efforts to influence communal actions reflect rational perspectives in society in contrast to those based on traditional values, which provide support for status groups. However, power is a

[3] Ibid., p. 180.
[4] Reinhard Bendix, *Max Weber* (New York: Doubleday Anchor Books, 1962), p. 86.
[5] Cf. Chap. 2.
[6] Gerth and Mills, op. cit., p. 187.

factor in the thrust toward increased rank position in both the class and status spheres because it is an aspect of all social relationships.

"In general, we understand by 'power' the chance of a man or a number of men to realize their own will in a communal action even against the resistance of others who are participating in the action." [7] Power may be sought as a means toward increased status honor or position in the market or it may be pursued as an end in itself. The higher one's rank with respect to a class or status group, the greater the probability that one's capacity to influence others also will be high.

Two types of power can be delineated, corresponding to Weber's concern with both the social and economic factor in social structures. Power derived from traditional authority that is based on the desire to rule and agreement to obey involves legitimate domination supported by a legal order. Thus, one's position in a hierarchy may be determined by an election or by birth, as in an estate system.[8]

To quote Weber:

> The manifested will of the ruler or rulers is meant to influence the conduct of one or more others and actually does influence it in such a way that their conduct to a socially relevant degree occurs as if the ruled had made the content of the command the maxim of their conduct for its very own sake.[9]

Thus, the organization of legally supported power relationships, with respect to the authority of a ruler over those ruled, influences conduct quite apart from economic and status interests. And it may, indeed, be the basic organizing principle for a total societal structure.

The second type of power is that derived primarily from economic interests. Although status honor may be attached to the attainment of economic power, conspicuous situations occur in which the desire for status honor is clearly relinquished in favor of appeal to "common man" symbols. For example, the typical American boss may deliberately relinquish claims to social honor.[10]

But the rank structure of power that is most relevant to the study of social stratification in its three dimensions is the *party*. Existing within larger social frameworks, like societies and communities, or as cliques within smaller organized groups, its goal is the same; influencing the outcomes of ongoing activities. Parties are to be found in rationally organized communities where there are functionaries whose decisions can be influ-

---

[7] Ibid., p. 180.

[8] Cf. Chap. 2.

[9] M. Rheinstein and E. Shils trans., and Max Rheinstein, ed., *Max Weber on Law and Economy in Society* (Cambridge: Harvard U.P., 1954), p. 328.

[10] Gerth and Mills, op. cit., p. 180.

enced by party members. Their goal is always to attain power and their means vary under varied conditions, ranging from naked violence to canvassing for votes.[11] Thus, *the organization of political activity, the market and the allocation of status honor represent the primary rank systems that provide the focal point for the Weberian analyst of stratification.*

However, it is not the existence of three distinct dimensions that is of primary interest in understanding stratification. It is, rather, the interrelationships among the three. Traditional theories of social stratification, such as those espoused by Marx, are primarily concerned with the manner and extent to which the individual's actions and life-chances are determined by position in a single vertical social class or stratum hierarchy. In contrast to these traditional approaches, theories of status consistency and status integration have emerged that share a primary concern with the consequences of the configuration of positions occupied by individuals across a number of dimensions of social differentiation. Although distinct theories, status consistency and status integration both predict that an inconsistency or malintegration of positions occupied by individuals has important consequences for their actions as well as for the structure and stability of society.

Origins and Development of Status Consistency Theory

It is difficult, if not impossible, to isolate the exact origins of the status consistency idea in the history of sociological thought. However, the writings of Max Weber, Pitirim A. Sorokin, Emile Benoit-Smullyan, and Gerhard E. Lenski are particularly noteworthy in their ideas of the core of the theory of status consistency.

In general, the theory of status consistency has its origin in criticisms of unidimensional approaches to social stratification and the subsequent reconceptualization of stratification as a multidimensional phenomenon, which—as noted earlier—is generally cited as stemming from the work of Max Weber.

Germane to the development of the theory of status consistency was Weber's observation that an individual's position in the class or economic hierarchy did not unconditionally determine his position in either the social honor or power hierarchies. In other words, Weber suggested the possibility that an individual could occupy a high-ranking position in one of the principal dimensions or hierarchies of stratification while occupying a lower-rank position in either or both of the remaining hierarchies. Weber also noted that individuals who are differentially ranked across the major

11 Ibid., p. 194.

dimensions of social stratification find themselves aligned with different groups that possess potentially contradictory vested interests and that these competing allegiances have important implications for the behavior of individuals as well as for the structure and stability of society.

These observations by Weber concerning the imperfect correlation between the principal dimensions of social stratification; the competing and potentially contradictory allegiances faced by individuals who are differentially ranked across the hierarchies of class, status, and power; and the suggestion that these competing allegiances have implications for the behavior of individuals and the structure of society provided the initial catalyst for later scholars to focus their attention on the horizontal and interhierarchical characteristics of stratification systems.

The early writings of Sorokin, the second theorist important to the origin and development of status consistency theory, largely paralleled the insights of Weber. There was, however, a minor difference in that whereas Weber considered the economic, social honor, and power hierarchies to be the major dimensions of social stratification, Sorokin pointed to the economic, political, and occupational hierarchies.[12] Nevertheless, Sorokin, like Weber, recognized the multiple bases, or dimensions, of stratification and even stressed the horizontal structure of social bodies.

In later writings, Sorokin elaborated on the implications of individuals being differently ranked across the multiple status dimensions. He referred to aggregates of such dissimilarly ranked individuals as composing a "disaffine" or "innerly antagonistic" stratum and defined them as being

> made up of the mutually contradictory, uncongenial bond-values that make the social position of its members innerly contradictory. The members of such an innerly contradictory stratum are urged by the mutually uncongenial or contradictory bonds to self-contradictory behavior and mentality. Likewise, such a disaffine stratum appears as a self-contradictory stratum to the outsiders who are in contact with it.[13]

In many respects, this statement by Sorokin captures a central tenet of what was later to be developed under the heading of status consistency theory.

Even though the groundwork for status consistency theory was put forth independently by Weber and Sorokin, Mitchell notes that the "generally recognized locus of current thinking on this topic is Emile Benoit-Smullyan." [14]

---

[12] Pitirim A. Sorokin, *Social Mobility* (New York: Harper, 1927), p. 11.

[13] Pitirim A. Sorokin, *Society, Culture and Personality* (New York: Harper, 1947), p. 289.

[14] Robert Edward Mitchell, "Methodological Notes on a Theory of Status Crystallization," *Public Opinion Quarterly,* **28**: 315 (Summer 1964).

Benoit-Smullyan distinguished between status, which he defined as "a hierarchy . . . of individuals ordered on an inferiority-superiority scale"; situs, defined as "membership in a social group"; and locus, which he defined as a type of social position which "arises from the socially standardized function which an individual performs in an organized group." [15]

In his discussion of status hierarchies, Benoit-Smullyan reiterated Weber's thesis that the economic, power, and social-honor hierarchies are the central and analytically distinct dimensions of social stratification. Also, like Weber as well as Sorokin, Benoit-Smullyan argued that an individual's position in one hierarchy was only in part dependent on his position in the other hierarchies. He further contended, however, that there is a tendency for an individual's position in each of the three hierarchies to reach a common level. Specifically, he wrote that there is a tendency "for a man's position in the economic hierarchy to match his position in the political hierarchy and for the latter to accord with his position in the hierarchy of prestige." [16] He referred to such a tendency as "status equilibration" and noted that "when legal, customary, or other barriers seriously hamper the equilibrating tendency, social tensions of revolutionary magnitude are generated." [17]

Benoit-Smullyan's contribution to the development of status consistency theory is twofold. First, his discussion of status, situs, and locus adds clarity to the criteria of social classification as well as to the relationship between status hierarchies, which constitute the major dimensions of social stratification. Secondly, his concept of status equilibration suggests that the differential ranking of individuals across the multiple dimensions of stratification has implications for the social mobility of individuals and for the stability of society.

Gerhard E. Lenski is generally given credit for introducing the concept of status consistency into the sociological literature, even though Stuart Adams had used the concept prior to Lenski's pioneer work in 1954. However, Lenski's work is especially important in that it has served as the reference point and model for a considerable quantity of empirical research.

Status crystallization, a term Lenski employed as a synonym for status consistency, directs attention to a comparison of the ranks of the statuses concurrently occupied by the individual in a number of "paralleled vertical hierarchies which usually are imperfectly correlated with one another." [18]

[15] Emile Benoit-Smullyan, "Status, Status Types, and Status Interrelations," *American Sociological Review,* **9**:151 (April 1944).

[16] Ibid., p. 160.

[17] Ibid.

[18] Gerhard E. Lenski, "Status Crystallization: A Nonvertical Dimension of Social Status," *American Sociological Review,* **19**:405 (August 1954); Stuart Adams, "Status Congruency As a Variable in Small Group Performance," *Social Forces,* **32**:16–22 (Oct. 1953).

An individual occupies a highly crystallized or consistent status configuration if the component statuses are equally ranked in their respective hierarchies, regardless of whether they are all high, middle, or low. Conversely, a poorly crystallized or inconsistent status configuration consists of a set of statuses that are unequally ranked. For example, the college professor who holds a degree is "status consistent" at least in terms of his occupational and educational statuses because they both are accorded high prestige. In contrast, the black physician is "status inconsistent" because physician is a high-prestige occupation, but Negro is a low-prestige racial-ethnic category. It is important to note that, as formulated by Lenski, degree of status crystallization, or status consistency, is an attribute of the *individual* that is analytically distinct from his rank in a social class or stratum hierarchy.

The status consistency concept clearly rests on the assumption found in the writings of Weber, Sorokin, and Benoit-Smullyan that the major rank systems or dimensions of social stratification are interrelated in such a manner as to result in individuals typically occupying statuses that are equally ranked in their respective hierarchies and, furthermore, that individuals whose status configurations involve components that are unequally ranked deviate from an assumed norm of consistency.

Lenski wrote that the purpose of his first study was to

> discover whether an analysis employing this new (nonvertical) dimension would be capable of accounting for some of the variance in political behavior which is left unexplained by traditional methods of stratification analysis.[19]

Although Lenski's choice of political attitudes and behavior as dependent variables follows from the work of Weber, Sorokin, and Benoit-Smullyan, the analysis was not predicted on a well-articulated set of theoretical premises, as evidenced by the fact that he did not predict the direction of any differences in the political attitudes of status consistent and inconsistent individuals.

Lenski's first step in operationally defining the degree of the status crystallization variable was to assign each respondent a percentile rank in each of the prestige hierarchies of occupation, income, education, and racial-ethnic membership. The individual's mean percentile rank was then determined and the total variation around the mean computed. The square root of the variation was then subtracted from 100 (that is, $100 - \sqrt{\Sigma(X_i - \overline{X})^2}$) such that the higher the score, the higher the individual's degree of status crystallization (that is, the more consistent are the ranks of his statuses).

[19] Lenski, loc. cit.

Lenski found for his sample of residents of the Detroit metropolitan area that liberal political tendencies were associated with low degrees of status crystallization regardless of the relationship between political liberalism and each of the separate status variables. Lenski also observed that certain types, or patterns, of low status crystallization are more closely related to liberal political tendencies than other types. For instance, individuals whose score is low by virtue of their income status ranking higher than their ethnic status are most likely to be "strongly Democratic (Party)" and "strongly liberal," whereas individuals who are "occupation-high and income-low" are, with the exception of high scoring individuals, least likely to be "strongly Democratic."

In discussing these results, Lenski noted that an individual with a poorly crystallized status configuration is

> a particular type of marginal man, and is subject to certain pressures by the social order which are not felt (at least to the same degree) by individuals with a more highly crystallized status.[20]

Like Weber, Sorokin, and Benoit-Smullyan, Lenski saw the existence of large numbers of such marginal men as an unstable condition in which society generates its own pressures for change. Accordingly, he equated support for the Democratic party and liberal political attitudes with support for social change and a desire to alter the existing social order, which he interpreted as a consequence of, or reaction to, a condition of low status crystallization.

In a second study, Lenski extended, and at the same time refocused, the implications of status crystallization. Whereas in his initial study he had focused on the implications of status for the structure and stability of society, in his second study he focused on the consequences of crystallization for interpersonal behavior. Following Everett C. Hughes, Lenski argued that persons with poorly crystallized status configurations occupied ambiguous positions in society and, as a result of the conflicting role directives encumbent upon them,

> are more likely to be subjected to disturbing experiences in the interaction process and have greater difficulty in establishing rewarding patterns of social interaction than others.[21]

Lenski was thus led to reason that low status crystallized individuals would avoid those social situations in which the unpleasant consequences of incon-

[20] Ibid., p. 412.
[21] Gerhard E. Lenski, "Social Participation and Status Crystallization," *American Sociological Review*, 21:459 (Aug. 1956).

sistency were most likely to occur. This gave rise to a series of three hypotheses to the effect that low status crystallized individuals would have lower rates and different motivations for participating in voluntary associations than would individuals who scored high. Lenski reported that the results of his analysis indicated that (1) status inconsistents were more likely to be "social isolates" than were status consistent individuals; (2) status inconsistent individuals were more likely to become "inactive" members of voluntary associations than were status consistent individuals; and, (3) status inconsistent individuals who were active members of voluntary associations were much less likely to report "social motivations" (that is, expectations of pleasurable interaction with others) than individuals who were status consistent.

In many respects these two studies set the course for future status consistency research, which involves a number of efforts at replicating Lenski's findings; refining his interpretations; and articulating the theoretical premises that underlie the status consistency concept.

However, for the most part, the research stimulated by Lenski's pioneer efforts have yielded inconclusive results as far as the predictive ability and explanatory power of the status consistency concept is concerned. It is instructive to consider some of this research.

Following Lenski's initial investigation into the relationship between status inconsistency and political attitudes, Auber and Kenkel, using different status hierarchies and a different operational procedure to measure inconsistency, found no differences between the political attitudes of status consistent and inconsistent individuals.[22] Findings similar to Kenkel's were also obtained by Dennis K. Kelly and William J. Chambliss, who write that the results of their study indicate that

> social class membership and ethnic background of respondent are far more important determinants of political attitudes than the degree to which persons are status consistent or inconsistent.[23]

In apparent contradiction to Lenski's conclusion that status inconsistents are more liberal than status consistents, sociologists Gary B. Rush,[24] as well as Larry Leon Hunt and Robert Cushing,[25] found that status incon-

---

[22] John F. Auber and William F. Kenkel, *Social Stratification* (New York: Appleton-Century-Crofts, 1954).

[23] Dennis K. Kelly and William J. Chambliss, "Status Consistency and Political Attitudes," *American Sociological Review,* **31**:381 (June 1966).

[24] Gary B. Rush, "Status Consistency and Right-Wing Extremism," *American Sociological Review,* **32**:86–92 (Feb. 1967).

[25] Larry Leon Hunt and Robert Cushing, "Status Discrepancy, Interpersonal Attachment and Right-Wing Extremism," *Social Science Quarterly,* **51**:587–601 (Dec. 1970).

sistent individuals are more prone to support extremist right-wing organizations (that is, Ku Klux Klan and John Birch Society) than are status consistent individuals.

Irving W. Goffman, however, provided a more direct test of Lenski's interpretation that status inconsistents desire to alter the existing social order when he examined the relationship between status consistency and "preference for change in the distribution of power." Goffman asked respondents to rank different groups such as labor unions and big business according to how much influence they perceived each of them as having on "how things go in this country." Respondents were then asked to rerank them in terms of how much influence they would like to see each of them have. The difference between these two rankings was taken as a measure of the individual's preference for change in the distribution of power. Goffman found that, within the upper and middle strata, status inconsistent individuals preferred a greater change in the distribution of power than status consistent individuals; no difference in preferences for change was found between status consistent and inconsistent individuals in the lower stratum. Goffman interpreted these results as partial support for Lenski's arguments.[26]

The results of Lenski's second study indicated that status inconsistent individuals were more often nonmembers, or less active members, of voluntary associations than status consistent individuals. He interpreted this as suggesting that status inconsistent individuals experience dissatisfactions in "normal interactions." Karl E. Bauman focused specifically on this question when he examined the relationship between status consistency and "dissatisfaction with everyday social interaction." In analyzing his data, Bauman observed a statistically significant relationship for middle-class respondents, but in the direction opposite to that predicted. In other words, middle-class status inconsistent individuals were *less* dissatisfied with everyday social interaction than were middle-class status consistent individuals. For lower-class respondents, however, there was no difference between status consistent and inconsistent individuals in their level of dissatisfaction with everyday social interaction. Bauman also reasoned that if status inconsistent individuals were to experience dissatisfactions in everyday social interaction, then they ought to be dissatisfied with "the community as a place to live," because it is the community that is a major source of status definition. In analyzing his data with respect to this second hypothesis, Bauman obtained exactly the same results. That is, middle-class status inconsistents were *less* dissatisfied with the community than middle-class status consistents; there

---

[26] Irving W. Goffman, "Status Consistency and Preference for Change in Power Distribution," *American Sociological Review,* **22**:275–281 (June 1957).

was no difference between consistent and inconsistent individuals in the lower class.[27]

While a number of investigators were attempting to assess and catalogue a range of consequences of status inconsistency for society and interpersonal behavior, others, particularly Elton F. Jackson,[28] concentrated on specifying the psychological consequences for the individual that are assumed to intervene between the structural condition of status inconsistency and the individual's political attitudes, racial prejudice,[29] social unrest,[30] aspirations for mobility,[31] and so on. Jackson reasoned that the greater punishments and fewer rewards engendered by the conflicting role directives associated with inconsistent statuses would lead the individual to experience *uncertainty* in what to expect from others and *frustration* in being unable to satisfy the conflicting demands placed on him. Jackson also reasoned that this psychological stress presumably experienced by status inconsistent individuals would manifest itself in the form of psychophysiological illness. Thus, Jackson hypothesized a direct relationship between degree of status inconsistency and psychological stress, using as an indicator of stress the number and severity of psychosomatic symptoms reported by the individual.

Jackson constructed a measure of status inconsistency by trichotomizing each of the education, occupation, and racial-ethnic hierarchies into the categories of high, middle, and low. An individual whose ranks were equal in all three hierarchies (that is, HHH, MMM, or LLL) was defined as status consistent. An individual with two equivalent statuses, with the third deviating from these by only one step (that is, HHM, LML, and so on) was defined as moderately inconsistent. Finally, an individual with no two scores the same (that is, HML, MHL, and so on), or with two scores the same and the third deviating by two steps (that is, HLL, HLH, and so on) was defined as sharply inconsistent.

Jackson's analysis revealed that the symptom rate for the sharply

[27] Karl E. Bauman, "Status Inconsistency, Satisfactory Social Interaction, and Community Satisfaction in an Area of Rapid Growth," *Social Forces,* **47**:45–52 (Oct. 1968).

[28] Elton F. Jackson, "Status Inconsistency and Symptoms of Stress," *American Sociological Review,* **27**:469–480 (Aug. 1962); Elton F. Jackson and Peter J. Burke, "Status and Symptoms of Stress," *American Sociological Review,* **30**:556–564 (Aug. 1965).

[29] Donald J. Treiman, "Status Discrepancy and Prejudice," *American Journal of Sociology,* **71**:651–664 (May 1966); S. Joseph Fauman, "Status Crystallization and Interracial Attitudes," *Social Forces,* **47**:53–60 (Oct. 1968).

[30] James A. Geschwender, "Status Inconsistency, Social Isolation and Individual Unrest," *Social Forces,* **46**:477–483 (June 1968).

[31] G. H. Fenchel, J. H. Monderer, and E. L. Hartley, "Subjective Status and the Equilibration Hypothesis," *The Journal of Abnormal and Social Psychology,* **46**:476–479 (Oct. 1957).

inconsistent group was significantly higher than the symptom rate for the status consistent group, but that the difference between the moderately inconsistent group and the status consistent group was, although in the predicted direction, not statistically significant. When the symptom rates associated with the various patterns of status inconsistency were compared, Jackson found the highest rate of psychosomatic symptoms, and therefore presumably the greatest level of psychological stress, to occur among individual's whose achieved status was lower than their ascribed status (that is, their achieved occupational status was *lower* than their ascribed racial-ethnic status). Jackson noted that this finding contrasts with Lenski's observation that the largest percentage of the "strongly liberal" occurred among those individuals whose achieved occupational status was *higher* than their ascribed racial-ethnic status.

The often unanticipated and sometimes contradictory findings of status consistency research raise questions concerning the theoretical value of the consistency concept. However, these less-than-impressive results can, no doubt in part, be attributed to a number of factors. First, there are numerous conceptual and methodological differences between studies including those that are implied replications of Lenski's initial work. Among these differences are (1) the use of different status hierarchies across which the individual's degree of status consistency is determined; (2) the use of different operational procedures to locate the individual's position within status hierarchies; (3) the computation of the individual's degree of inconsistency by radically different procedures; and (4) the use of different indicators and index-construction techniques to measure what is "apparently" the same variable (that is, political attitudes). Second, many of the studies reported to date have utilized data-analysis strategies that are inappropriate for the task in that they have been shown to involve deficiencies that have only recently come to the attention of sociologists. One of the most important of these deficiencies is the statistical problem known as "identification," which involves the difficulty of empirically isolating the effects of an inconsistency between the individual's statuses while controlling for the effects of the statuses themselves. Third, and most important, to date, the "theory" of status consistency lacks a well-articulated set of propositions specifying the conditions under which various types of inconsistency between particular status hierarchies leads to specific attitudinal and behavioral consequences.

Origins and Development of Status Integration Theory

The theory of status integration, which was first introduced by Jack P. Gibbs and Walter T. Martin as a "macrosociological theory purporting to be capable of explaining variation in suicide rates," [32] is deeply rooted in the thinking of Émile Durkheim and reflects his concern with the integration of the social order as a constraining force on the behavior of individuals. Durkheim wrote that

> When society is strongly integrated, it holds individuals in its control, considers them at its service and thus forbids them to dispose willfully of themselves.[33]

Accordingly, Durkheim asserted that "Suicide varies inversely with the degree of integration of social groups." [34]

However, just as Marx never defined exactly what he meant by the concept social class, Durkheim never provided a connotative, much less an operational, definition of precisely what he meant by integration. As a result, the integration concept has taken on a very general meaning, with numerous scholars pointing out that there are several conceptually distinct types of integration. Werner S. Landecker, for example, described four types of integration:

> cultural (consistency among the standards of a culture); normative (conformity of the conduct of the group to cultural standards); communicative (exchange of meanings throughout group); and functional (interdependence among group members through the division of labor).[35]

Gibbs and Martin were keenly aware that the selection of a particular type of integration and the choice of indicators for its measurement are critical issues in using Durkheim's theory as a point of departure to explain variation in suicide rates. An examination of the theoretical implications and linkages between Landecker's types of integration and Durkheim's theory led Gibbs and Martin to conclude that the types of integration suggested by Landecker were ill-suited for the task at hand. For example, Landecker's normative type of integration, even though it reflects Durkheim's emphasis on the consensual nature of integration, was rejected on the grounds that suicide varies independently of other forms of deviant behavior and because of its apparent limitations in accounting for the different rates of suicide across age and sex groupings.[36]

---

[32] See, for example, Walter T. Martin, "Socially Induced Stress: Some Converging Theories," *Pacific Sociological Review*, **8**:65 (Fall 1965).

[33] Émile Durkheim, *Suicide*: trans. J. A. Spaulding and G. Simpson (New York: Free Press, 1951), p. 209.

[34] Ibid.

[35] Werner S. Landecker, "Types of Integration and Their Measurement," *American Journal of Sociology*, **56**: 219–229 (Jan. 1951), as quoted in Jack P. Gibbs and Walter T. Martin, *Status Integration and Suicide* (Eugene: University of Oregon Press, 1964), p. 15.

[36] Gibbs and Martin, ibid., p. 16.

However, in Durkheim's comments on integration is the recurring theme that integration pertains to the strength of the ties that bind individuals to social groups. Gibbs and Martin infer that the strength of these ties involves the degree of stability and durability of social relationships. Accordingly, they state the first postulate of status integration theory as

> Postulate 1: The suicide rate of a population varies inversely with the stability and durability of social relationships within that population.[37]

Weber's suggestion that the fundamental requirement for the maintenance of social relationships is conformity to the demands and expectations of others[38] provided the basis for the second postulate of the theory:

> Postulate 2: The stability and durability of social relationships within a population vary directly with the extent to which individuals in that population conform to the patterned and socially sanctioned demands and expectations placed upon them by others.[39]

From this postulate Gibbs and Martin reasoned that the individual's inability to conform to the demands and expectations of others is a consequence of his encountering role conflicts that, in turn, are engendered by occupying incompatible statuses. Hence:

> Postulate 3: The extent to which individuals in a population conform to patterned and socially sanctioned demands and expectations placed upon them by others varies inversely with the extent to which individuals in that population are confronted with role conflicts.
>
> Postulate 4: The extent to which individuals in a population are confronted with role conflicts varies directly with the extent to which individuals occupy incompatible statuses in that population.[40]

Gibbs and Martin then argued that combinations of statuses that are incompatible in the sense that they engender interrole conflicts are occupied less frequently in the population than combinations or configurations of statuses that do not engender interrole conflict. They offered three reasons to support this argument: first, the concurrent occupancy of statuses that are recognized to be incompatible often is socially discouraged; second, the difficulties experienced by an individual in attempting to conform to conflicting roles may lead him to abandon one or more of the incompatible

[37] Ibid., p. 17.
[38] Max Weber, *The Theory of Social and Economic Organization,* trans. A. M. Henderson and Talcott Parsons (New York: Free Press, 1947), pp. 118–126.
[39] Gibbs and Martin, op. cit., p. 18.
[40] Ibid., pp. 19–24.

statuses; and third, individuals sometimes are deprived of one or more of their statuses when compliance with the role directives associated with one status precludes compliance with the role directives associated with another status.

At this point the authors state that the relative frequency that a combination of statuses is simultaneously occupied in the population is the *degree of integration* among the component statuses; or simply, the degree of status integration. This leads to the fifth postulate and the subsequent deduction of a grand theorem.

Postulate 5:   To extent to which individuals occupy incompatible statuses in a population varies inversely with the degree of status integration in that population.

Grand Theorem: The suicide rate of a population varies inversely with the degree of status integration in that population.[41]

According to the theoretical definition of status integration given by the authors, a status configuration that occurs relatively frequently in the population is more integrated than less frequently occurring status configurations. Furthermore, a population, or any collective (that is, a society, city, organization, or group), has a high degree of status integration when its members are highly concentrated in a few status configurations, whereas collectives in which members are "scattered more or less haphazardly throughout a large number of such configurations" [42] are less integrated.

Gibbs and Martin provide two tables to illustrate their definition and the computation of three separate measure of status integration that are used to examine three types of hypotheses derived from the grand theorem. The first, Table 3.1, depicts a hypothetical society with a maximum degree

TABLE 3.1

The Integration of Marital Statuses with Selected Status Configurations in a Hypothetical Society where Marital Integration is at a Maximum*

Marital Status	All Occupied Status Configurations				
	R1–A1– Rel–01– S1–P1	R2–A2– Re2–02– S2–P2	R1–A3– Re3–03– S1–P1	R1–A4– Rel–04– S1–P3	R2–A5– Re3–05– S2–P2
Single	.00	.00	.00	1.00	.00
Married	.00	1.00	.00	.00	1.00
Widowed	1.00	.00	.00	.00	.00
Divorced	.00	.00	1.00	.00	.00
ΣX	1.00	1.00	1.00	1.00	1.00
$\Sigma(X^2)$	1.00	1.00	1.00	1.00	1.00
Proportion of population	.07	.43	.03	.15	.32

* Gibbs and Martin, op. cit., p. 37.

[41] Ibid., pp. 26–27.
[42] Martin, loc. cit.

of integration between marital status and various combinations of race (R); occupation (O); age (A); sex (S); religion (Re); and, parental status (P). The figures in the body of the table(s) indicate the proportion of individuals occupying each marital status and the combinations of statuses designated by the column headings. In comparison, Table 3.2 depicts

TABLE 3.2

The Integration of Marital Statuses with Selected Status Configurations in a Hypothetical Society where Marital Integration is Less than a Maximum*

Marital Status	All Occupied Status Configurations				
	R1–A1–Rel–01–S1–P1	R2–A2–Re3–02–S2–P2	R1–A3–Re3–03–S1–P1	R1–A4–Rel–04–S1–P3	R2–A5–Re3–05–S2–P2
Single	.15	.05	.00	.35	.05
Married	.05	.75	.05	.25	.90
Widowed	.60	.15	.25	.20	.05
Divorced	.20	.05	.70	.20	.00
ΣX	1.00	1.00	1.00	1.00	1.00
$\Sigma(X^2)$	.4250	.5900	.5550	.2650	.8150
Proportion of population	.1435	.3825	.0870	.1970	.1900

* Gibbs and Martin, op. cit., p. 38.

status integration is simply the proportion of cases occupying each marital a hypothetical society in which the degree of status integration between marital status and these same combinations of statuses is considerably lower, as indicated by the differences in marital status among individuals within the same columns.

The first of the three measures of status integration expresses the degree to which marital status is integrated with each of the various combinations of statuses designated by the column headings. This measure of status *within* each column. A type 1 hypothesis predicts an inverse relationship between this measure of status integration and suicide rates within columns. For example, in reference to the first column of Table 3.2, the highest suicide rate is predicted to be among married persons, whereas the lowest rate is predicted to be among widowed persons; furthermore, in terms of the second column of Table 3.2, the highest suicide rate is predicted to be among single and divorced persons, whereas the lowest rate is predicted for married individuals; and so on for each column of the table.

The second measure of status integration and the second type of hypothesis involves the degree of marital integration with a family of statuses. This measure of integration is the sum of the squares of the proportions in each column (that is, the ΣX^2 row). With reference to Table 3.2, a type 2 hypothesis predicts the highest rate of suicide to be associated with the combination of statuses designated as column 4 ($\Sigma X^2 = .2650$), and the lowest rate to be associated with the combination of statuses found in the last column ($\Sigma X^2 = .8150$).

The final measure expresses the status integration of collectives and is computed by adding the products of the proportion of the population in each column (that is, the bottom row) and the column sum of the squared proportions (that is ΣX^2). A type 3 hypothesis predicts an inverse relationship between this measure of status integration and the suicide rate of collectives.

Gibbs and Martin utilized vital statistics to compute rates of suicide and census data to compute measures of the degree to which marital and occupational status were integrated with either age, sex, race, or various combinations of these. An examination of inter- and intrasocietal data supported the predictions of the three types of hypotheses of an inverse relationship between degree of status integration and suicide rates.

Unlike Lenski's initial efforts involving the status consistency concept, Gibbs and Martin's work did not stimulate a large quantity of empirical research. However, research reported by Chambliss and Marion F. Steele; David L. Dodge; and Kenneth Berry is worthy of comment.

Chambliss and Steele criticized the logical structure and questioned the empirical validity of the status integration theory as stated by Gibbs and Martin. With reference to the theory as an explanation of suicide, they argued that Gibbs and Martin did not specify the *process* by which stable social relationships make suicide an unlikely event. Rather, they claim that Gibbs and Martin simply

> assume that a series of statements specifying correlated variables which have some intuitively attributed connection to one another constitutes a scientific explanation.[43]

In addition, they reanalyzed Gibbs and Martin's data as well as data from Seattle in order to assess the empirical validity of the theory. They noted that the observed relationship between degree of status integration and rate of suicide varies considerably, depending on the number of categories of the age status variable employed and whether the measure of status integration expresses the degree to which marital status is integrated with age or the degree to which age is integrated with marital status. For example, when the measure of status integration expresses the degree to which marital status is integrated with the four age groupings used by Gibbs and Martin, the results are congruent with the inverse relationship predicted by the theory. However, when ten age groupings are used, the results are inconsistent with the predictions. Furthermore, when the measure of status

---

[43] William J. Chambliss and Marion F. Steele, "Status Integration and Suicide: an Assessment," *American Sociological Review*, **31**:526 (Aug. 1966).

integration expresses the degree to which either four or ten age groupings are integrated with marital status, positive rank order correlations between degree of status integration and suicide rates are observed, whereas negative correlations are predicted. These results lead Chambliss and Steele to conclude that the supportive findings obtained by Gibbs and Martin are likely to be unique to their data and methodology.

In response to Chambliss and Steele's criticisms of the logical structure of the theory, Gibbs and Martin asserted that

> in formulating the theory of status integration and suicide, we attempt to state it formally and also to do what Durkheim did not do—create a theory that can be tested systematically.[44]

They also claimed that the direction of causation between status integration and suicide is not in doubt in the major theorem. Therefore, nothing would be gained by stating the theoretical relations expressed in the postulates in terms such as "X leads to Y" or "X brings about Y," as suggested by Chambliss and Steele in their comments to the effect that the theory does not specify the process through which suicide is linked to a low degree of status integration.

Furthermore, with respect to the empirical validity of the theory, Gibbs and Martin noted that the procedure utilized by Chambliss and Steele to measure degree of status integration that led to negative evidence violated an important assumption of the theory. Specifically, they pointed out that movement in and out of statuses was assumed by the theory and that in light of this assumption it was inappropriate to related rates of behavior and to measures of status integration that expressed the degree to which an ascribed status (that is, age) is integrated with an achieved status (that is, marital status).[45] Rather, the appropriate measure of status integration expresses the degree to which an achieved status is integrated with an ascribed status, and when such a measure is applied to the data used by Chambliss and Steele, the results support the theory.

In other research, Dodge extended the work of Gibbs and Martin by adding a sixth postulate to the theory.

> Postulate 6: The extent of stability and durability in social relationships is inversely related to the prevalence of social stress in the population.[46]

[44] Jack P. Gibbs and Walter T. Martin, "On Assessing the Theory of Status Integration and Suicide," *American Sociological Review,* **31**:533 (Aug. 1966).
    [45] Ibid.
    [46] David L. Dodge, "Social Stress, Integration, and Chronic Disease Morbidity and Mortality" (Ph.D. diss., University of Oregon, 1963).

The addition of this postulate enabled Dodge to deduce the hypothesis that the prevalence of social stress in a population varies inversely with the degree of status integration. To evaluate this hypothesis, Dodge used 1950 census data to measure status integration and chronic-disease (that is, heart disease, cancer, and cirrhosis, for example) and mortality rates computed from 1950 vital statistics as indirect measures of the prevalence of social stress in a population. Dodge, and later Dodge and Martin,[47] reported that the results of the analysis provided moderate support for the hypothesis (particularly among white males).

The postulate added by Dodge set the stage for Berry's[48] investigation into the relationship between status integration and morbidity. Berry's work is important in that he restated each of the six postulates of status integration theory in terms of characteristics of individuals, as opposed to characteristics of populations. Following Dodge, Berry hypothesized that the frequency of hospitalization would be inversely related to the degree to which the individual's marital, age, and occupational status were integrated. Data on members of a particular health insurance plan were analyzed with very few significant relationships between the measure of status integration and the per cent hospitalized that were observed. However, when these data were analyzed at the aggregate level the predicted, although modest, negative correlation was found between per cent "high" on the measure of status integration and per cent hospitalized.

The disappointing findings obtained by Berry at the individual level of analysis does not, however, provide for a final verdict on the theory's utility at that level. One can question whether hospitalization for physical maladies constitutes a reasonably adequate measure of psychological stress. Furthermore, because the theory has received considerable support at aggregate levels of analysis, it suggests that alternative measures of the dependent variable, perhaps coupled with measures of status integration involving statuses other than those employed by Berry, may prove fruitful at the individual level of analysis.

Status Consistency and Status Integration Compared

The preceding discussion concerning the origin and development of the theories of status consistency and status integration suggests several important differences between the two theories. To begin with, status inte-

[47] David L. Dodge and Walter T. Martin, *Social Stress and Chronic Illness: Mortality Patterns in Industrial Society* (Notre Dame, Ind.: University of Notre Dame Press, 1970).
[48] Berry, op. cit.

gration is a macrosociological theory purporting to explain rates of behavior in *populations* and is, therefore, only indirectly concerned with the behavior of individual members. In contrast, status consistency, although formulated in terms of macro-characteristics of societies (that is, their paralleled, but usually imperfectly correlated, status hierarchies) is directly concerned with explaining the actions of *individuals* and is only indirectly concerned with rates of behavior in populations.

A second difference between these two theories is that status integration, unlike status consistency, is not limited to a consideration of hierarchically ordered statuses but also can be applied to nominal statuses such as sex and marital status. In this respect, status integration constitutes a more general theory of status compatibility, subsumming status consistency as a special subtype.

Status consistency and status integration also differ with respect to the presumed source of conflicting role directives. Status consistency conceptualizes compatible role directives as being associated with statuses that are equally ranked in their respective hierarchies, whereas incompatible role directives are thought to be associated with unequally ranked statuses. Furthermore, the degree of interrole conflict confronting the status inconsistent individual is seen as a function of the size of the discrepancy between the ranks of his statuses. In contrast, status integration conceptualized compatible role directives as being associated with frequently occurring combinations of statuses regardless of their ranks, whereas infrequently occurring combinations of statuses are seen as having incompatible role directives associated with them. This difference in the source of incompatible role directives is important because, given the alternative definitions of compatible statuses, it is possible that the occupant of a "highly integrated" status configuration is simultaneously a "status inconsistent" individual.

Several authors have, however, called attention to important similarities between status consistency and status integration, as well as to commonalities between them and other theoretical perspectives. James A. Geschwender, for instance, has noted that when status hierarchies are conceptualized as investments (that is, education) and rewards (that is, income), status consistency theory parallels exchange theory with its concepts of distributive justice, social certitude, and relative deprivation.[49] Furthermore, Edward Sampson's theory of expectancy congruence integrates status consistency with the theory of cognitive dissonance.[50] Along

[49] James A. Geschwender, "Continuities in Theories of Status Consistency and Cognitive Dissonance," *Social Forces,* **46**:160–171 (Dec. 1967).

[50] Edward Sampson, "Status Congruence and Cognitive Consistency," *Sociometry,* **26**:146–162 (June 1963).

the same line, Martin[51] and Howard F. Taylor[52] have pointed out that status consistency and status integration converge in predicting that the (objective) condition of inconsistent or poorly integrated statuses is a condition of psychological stress for the individual involved, which presumably leads to some form of stress reducing behavior (Figure 3-1). According to Taylor,

Inconsistent
or Poorly   Psychological Stress
Integrated
Statuses

Stress Reducing
Behavior
(i.e., withdrawal
from voluntary
associations)

Figure 3–1

status consistency and status integration are theories of socially induced stress that are conceptually and mathematically parallel to the cognitive consistency theories of social psychology. Proceeding from this point, Carlton A. Hornung has accomplished a partial synthesis of status consistency and status integration by defining "integrated-consistent" status configurations as the most frequently occurring combination of education and income statuses for each occupational status.[53] These configurations were utilized as points of maximum consistency relative to which degree and type of status inconsistency were computed. Two hypotheses were examined: first, following Segal's assertion that individuals come to expect rewards appropriate for their highest ranked status while others prefer to reward them in accordance with their lowest ranked status, it was predicted that, when differences in vertical status were controlled, status inconsistent individuals would be dissatisfied with their lowest ranked status; and second, the level of psychological strain an individual experiences in his present status configuration was predicted to vary directly with the degree to which his statuses were inconsistent. The results of the analysis indicated that degree and type of status inconsistency were nearly as efficient predictors of each dependent variable as education, occupation, and income statuses combined. Moreover, both hypotheses received substantial support in that degree and type of status inconsistency were found to be related to status dissatisfaction and psychological strain in the predicted direction. In addition, however, the effects of each type of status inconsistency were observed to differ at

---

[51] Martin, loc. cit.

[52] Howard F. Taylor, "Linear Models of Consistency: Some Extensions of Blalock's Strategy," *American Journal of Sociology,* **78** (March, 1973); Hubert M. Blalock, Jr., "Status Inconsistency, Social Mobility, Status Integration and Structural Effects," *American Sociological Review,* **32**:790–801 (Oct. 1967).

[53] Carlton A. Hornung, "Status Consistency: A Method of Measurement and Empirical Examination" (Ph.D. diss., Syracuse University, 1972).

various points in the vertical stratification hierarchy. For example, un-skilled workers whose income was consistent but whose education was high relative to that of other unskilled workers scored low on the measure of psychological strain; business managers, officials, and proprietors who occupied the same type of inconsistent status configuration scored high on the strain measure. This finding suggests that the failure to consider type of inconsistency and vertical or stratum position simultaneously may lead to misleading results and conclusions. Vertical position in the stratification hierarchy may augment or suppress the consequences of various types of status inconsistency.

In conclusion, status consistency and status integration are theories of status compatibility. They share a concern with the behavior of individuals and the structure of society as a result of stress from role conflicts occurring between statuses concurrently occupied by individuals across a number of dimensions of social differentiation and stratification. In terms of this con-cern with the behavioral implications of psychological stress, status con-sistency and status integration incorporate a number of similarly focused theoretical perspectives including exchange theory, cognitive consistency theories, and the psychosomatic stress theory of disease; herein lies their potential and importance for sociological theory.

Marx and Weber Compared

As the following article by Reinhard Bendix suggests, a great deal of ideological controversy has been associated with discussions of the connec-tions between the ideas of Marx and Weber on societal structure. To our mind, Weber is best understood as an elaborator and elucidator of Marx's ideas on social stratification rather than simply as a rejector or antagonist of Marx.

Inequality and Social Structure*†

Reinhard Bendix

In our world, inequality among men is considered an aspect of social organization, not a divinely ordained attribute of the human condition. Few still believe in transcendental justifications of inequality. Goodness and talent too often go unrewarded and those who carry the burden of poverty too often also suffer the stigma of social discrimination. Inequalities have changed over time, and we can infer that particular inequalities are alterable. Yet this awareness of change does not console or guide us. Unlike the theologians of old or the pioneers of social thought in the nineteenth century, we do not have a theory of social structure and inequality.

In 1835, Alexis de Tocqueville (1805–1859) wrote that the growth of equality was providential. "It may be God's will," he suggested in a letter, "to spread a moderate amount of happiness over all men, instead of heaping a large sum upon a few by allowing only a small minority to approach perfection." In the aristocratic societies of the past this minority had enjoyed inherited privileges. The French revolution had destroyed this aspect of inequality by instituting an equality of legal rights. In de Tocqueville's eyes, the revolution was a further step in the great rise of equality which had characterized European history for centuries. He recognized that legal equality existed side by side with vast differences between rich and poor. But his attention was focussed on the contrast between the brilliant society of the past, based on inherited privilege, and the emerging society, based on equal rights, in which cultural achievements would be modest. On balance, he preferred the latter as long as order and morality were ensured. De Tocqueville feared the perpetuation of revolutionary conditions. For where equal rights are proclaimed, the lines dividing authority from tyranny and liberty from license could be so blurred that an "undisciplined and depraved democracy would result." De Tocqueville had no explanatory model. But by assessing sentiments and moral qualities he anticipated certain cultural aspects of democratic institutions.

As a younger contemporary of de Tocqueville's, Karl Marx (1818–1883) gave more emphasis to the scientific character of his materialist philosophy. Rejecting the tradition of German idealism, he held that in the long run, ideas and institutions are determined by the material conditions under which men work. He allowed that in the short run history was affected by "accidents" and by ideas. But this reservation did not diminish his confidence in predictions based on "scientific" analysis. An understanding of the organization of production would provide the major clue to the development of society. Hence Marx undertook an economic analysis of capitalism. For the economically most advanced countries, Marx predicted a polarization between capitalists

* *American Sociological Review,* **39**:149–161 (April 1974).

† Completion of this study was facilitated by Grant GS–31730X of the National Science Foundation, at the Institute for Advanced Study, Princeton, N.J. For critical and editorial suggestions, I am indebted to Erik Bendix.

and workers that would eventually lead to a proletarian revolution and a re-organization of society. And this prediction seemed buttressed by Marx's great insights into the culture of capitalist societies.

It is puzzling that de Tocqueville so often proved right although his methods were impressionistic, while Marx's central proposition proved wrong although his methods were scholarly. For the study of inequality and social structure it is useful to learn where these earlier analyses went right or wrong.

My discussion distinguishes between modern and pre-modern history (broadly defined by the transition of the sixteenth and seventeenth centuries) and will provide some warrant for making that distinction. Marx's theory dealt primarily with the organization of production as the basis of social classes in a capitalist society. I shall contrast his argument with that of Max Weber. Both writers studied inequality with a view to status-differences and organized collective action, though for reasons to be indicated below, Weber gave closer attention to these topics. In the second part, I deal with inequality as a force in pre-modern history. I do so to make clear, as Marx and Weber did, that the types of inequality most familiar to us do not pertain to that earlier period and hence are of limited historical applicability. The paper concludes with some programmatic guidelines for analyzing the transition between pre-modern and modern social structures.

A. Inequality As a Force in Modern History

Class and Status.   More than a century has passed since Marx and Engels predicted the revolutionary overthrow of capitalism. Marx presupposed a society adapted to the nation-state. Capitalists and workers would become nationwide classes; the dynamics of a capitalist economy would eradicate all social divisions that interfere with that development. The study of the emerging working class in England suggested the force of large and growing numbers. Through massive deprivations and the increasing intensity of class conflicts the workers would emerge as a major agent of historical change. Marx saw class conflicts under capitalism as the first opportunity for correct historical prediction. And he believed that the coming revolution would end the exploitation of man by man. Thus, analysis, or science, and the strength of numbers were on the side of equity and justice and would bring about the reorganization of society (Tucker 1961, passim).

Marx's approach may be seen as a theory of group-formation. In his view, ruling classes are aware of their common interests and have the organizational means to promote them, while oppressed classes still seek to achieve class consciousness and organizational cohesion. Classes such as feudal landlords and capitalist entrepreneurs, which own the means of production, control the peasants and workers who depend on them for employment. But the influence of an owner's class is not confined to such a private exercise of economic dominance. It spills over into virtual control of government and a hegemony in the world of ideas and social institutions. The assumption is that ownership prompts the ruling classes to think alike and act in common, wherever the interests of property are at stake. Thus, in all spheres of society ownership of property is the basis for the exercise of rule.

Yet the ownership is only one basis of class and power. The other basis is deprivation. In the crowded factories of the early nineteenth century, lack of acquaintance and competing interests divided the workers amongst themselves. Although all of them lived a starkly deprived life, their common experience only engendered in each a dogged pursuit of his own interests. Marx knew that abject poverty makes men more selfish, not less. But he believed that the domination of capital created a common and bitter experience which would drive workers to develop common interests and a collective effort. Given sufficient ease of communication in the work place, classes would arise in collective reaction to a common opponent. In Marx's view, a politically conscious labor movement could only develop if workers would realize the futility of mere union activity. Capitalists could not grant enough concessions on wages and working conditions, because they could not abandon the pursuit of their own interests. Marx's economic analysis sought to establish this scientifically; the workers, he thought, would arrive at the same conclusion through experience. Their mounting dissatisfactions would result first in the conviction that capitalism must be overthrown and eventually also in revolutionary political organization (Bendix and Lipset 1968, p. 8; Weber 1968, I, p. 305). This emergence of labor as a political force would be aided by "bourgeois ideologists" and Communists, who articulate the common experience of labor and represent the interests of the movement as a whole (Marx and Engels 1967, pp 91, 95). In sum, the situation which workers share both forms them as a class and drives them to make a collective bid for power.

In his early writings, Marx distinguished between class as a condition of social life and class as a cause of collective action, between the *fact* that classes are unequal in relation to the ownership of the means of production (*Klasse an sich*) and the *meaning* this inequality has for a class as a spur to organization and action (*Klasse für sich*). Individuals do not form a group capable of collective action merely because they have certain attributes in common (like income, occupation, etc.). Rather, groups form as individuals with common attributes, acquire a collective consciousness and become capable of organized action.[1] Marx's prediction of a proletarian revolution rested on the thesis that capitalist society would sweep aside all interests or social ties that could hinder the formation of the two main classes. The purpose of his economic analysis was to demonstrate that necessity for the long run. And since he believed that demonstration successful, he could neglect a more detailed examination of social differentiation such as that begun in the incomplete last chapter of *Capital*, vol. III. Marx believed that in the upper strata the bourgeoisie would submerge everything of human value in the "icy waters of egotistical calculation." For the workers, a parallel effect would be achieved by the constraints of factory production which reduced everything to a deadened uniformity. Abject degradation would destroy their family life, religious beliefs, and national characteristics (Marx and Engels 1967, pp. 82, 89, 92). It would be because workers had lost everything that they would rise to regain their humanity (Tucker 1961, pp. 113–118, and passim).

In Marx's view, this polarization of classes would lead to a revolution and usher in a new and more rational social order. The class struggle promotes "reason in history" to the extent that political class-interests override the "infinite fragmentation of interest and rank into which the division of labor splits labourers as well as capitalists" (Marx 1962, III, p. 863). For evidence that men's basic interests divide along class lines Marx scanned the limited experience of English social history. He was convinced that the widening gap between the achievements and the possibilities of social organization would push workers into accepting his doctrines. And he looked forward to a society born of revolution in which "the process of material production" would be "consciously regulated by freely associated men" (Marx 1936, p. 92).

Today the prospect of a proletarian revolution has receded before the reality of other, less expected revolutions. Occurring in predominantly agricultural countries, revolutions appear now as the prelude to industrialization rather than as the result of a fully developed capitalism. Marx's effort to locate the collective force through which reason advances in history unduly narrowed his conception of the inequalities which matter even in the long run. Nationalism and citizenship, religious beliefs and ethnic loyalties, regional associations and linguistic groups have often proved stronger than proletarian class consciousness. And movements of this kind arise from just that "fragmentation of interest and rank" which, according to Marx, would be obliterated by "egotistical calculation" and the constraints of factory production. Here is one reason de Tocqueville saw further than Marx. For de Tocqueville, the sentiments and opinions of people mattered and the future thus appeared impenetrable. For Marx, these opinions were often no more than a "false consciousness" that would be eradicated by the mounting intensity of the class struggle. Marx's approach to the study of class was too reductionist to be successful. Nonetheless, Marx's problem is important. Property ownership and the division of labor are certainly bases for the formation of classes. The question remains under what circumstances such classes become organized groups.

Max Weber approached this question from the baseline Marx had established. *Class situations* exist wherever men are similarly situated by their "relative control over goods and skills." This control produces income, procures other goods, gains them a social position, and leads to a certain style of life. Those in a common class situation are often led to similar sentiments and ideas, but not necessarily to concerted action (Weber 1968, I, p. 302). By contrast, *class organizations* occur only when an immediate economic opponent is involved, organization is technically easy (as in the factory), and clear goals are articulated by an intelligentsia (Weber 1968, I, p. 305). Weber accepted Marx's reasons for the success of such organizations.

Nevertheless, Weber's approach modifies Marx's analysis in three respects. First, he denies that a common class situation will give rise to association, pointing out that many such situations result only in amorphous mass reactions. For Marx, the connection between class situation and class organization is a necessary one, arising from the "laws" of capitalist development. For Weber the connection is problematic. He treats Marx's concept of class as an ideal type, a logical construct based on observed tendencies. Second, Weber broadens Marx's concept of the economic determination of class situations. Ownership of the means of production or dependence on wage labor are important but special cases. In fact, there are a variety of property classes, commercial classes, and social classes beyond the land-labor-capital trichotomy which Marx inherited from the classical economists. Weber accepts Marx's thesis that class situations are determined economically, but he points out that these situations display the same instability as the market. For Weber class situation is ultimately market situation; such situations vary with the common experiences of individuals in response to shifting economic constellations (Weber 1968, I, pp. 303–305; II, pp. 928–929). Third, Marx maintained that "bourgeois ideologists" would contribute to the political radicalization of the labor movement. He believed that the radicalizing experience of workers and the radicalizing beliefs of ideologists are responses to the same compelling structure of capitalism. By contrast, Weber sees the responses of the people at large and of a minority of culture-carriers as divergent. It is true that the class-conscious organizations of workers "succeed most easily if they are led towards readily understood goals." But these goals "are imposed and interpreted by men outside their class (intelligentsia)." [2]

Weber agrees that the economic and political solidarity of workers might overcome their initial fragmentation of interests. But solidarity of this kind is weakened by religious or ethnic differences. And successful class organizations create new interests, among them a new awareness of status. The very process of organizing a class creates inequalities of status which impede concerted action on a broader front. Prestige is at least as enduring a basis of group formation as a common situation in the market. Weber speaks of a social order in which status is an "effective claim to social esteem," founded upon lifestyle, formal education, heredity or occupation. Typically, the circle of social equals is defined by means of social discrimination. Marriage and hospitality are confined to that circle and only certain forms of acquisition and employment are considered socially acceptable (Weber 1968, I, pp. 305–306).

In discriminating against "outsiders," status groups curtail the free operation of the market. For centuries, aristocracies prevented commoners from acquiring land. On occasion this practice required aristocrats to retain their land when it would have been more profitable to sell it to some wealthy bourgeois. Land was bound up with the aristocratic way of life and remained a symbol of status long after its economic profitability had declined. Analogous considerations apply to status-groups based on race, language, locality, or religion. Status groups endure as long as social honor is preferred to economic advantage, when a choice between them has to be made.

The inequalities of class and of status may be summarized as follows. *Classes arise out of common economic interests.* Classes based on the ownership of property or on deprivation in a common workplace are obvious examples. Marx understood that status distinctions would hinder the solidarity of classes, but he examined such distinctions only in his historical writings. He was convinced that his economic analysis had laid bare the overriding constraints of the class struggle and hence of the "historical movement as a whole." By contrast, *status groups are rooted in family experience.* Before the individual reaches maturity, he has participated in his family's claim to social prestige, its occupational subculture and educational level. Even in the absence of concerted action, families share a style of life and similar attitudes. Classes without organization achieve nothing. But families in the same status-situation need not communicate and organize in order to discriminate against people they consider inferior. Weber understood that their solidarity against outsiders may remain intact even when they are divided by intensive rivalries.

The common element in classes and status-groups is not just the pursuit of self-interest. Both Marx and Weber saw that "self-interest" without ideas explains little. They were both concerned with man's quest for mastery, which unwittingly prompts *homo economicus* to be involved with ideas and *homo hierarchicus* (Dumont 1972) with gain. But Marx thought that in the long run ownership of the means of production would prove the decisive determinant, and Weber did not. The difference becomes manifest in the contrast between evolutionism and a cyclical theory of change. For analytical purposes Weber thought it convenient to define classes and status-groups in terms that are mutually exclusive. Where market mechanisms predominate, personal and familial distinctions of status are discounted. Where considerations of prestige predominate, economically advantageous activities are often stigmatized. This extrapolation of class- or status-oriented actions leads to a model of social change.

> When the bases of the acquisition and distribution of goods are rel-
> atively stable, stratification by status is favored. Every technological
> repercussion and economic transformation threatens stratification by
> status and pushes the class situation into the foreground. Epochs and
> countries in which the naked class situation is of predominant significance
> are regularly the periods of technical and economic transformations. And
> every slowing down of the change in economic stratification leads, in
> due course, to the growth of status structures and makes for a resuscita-
> tion of the important role of social honor (Weber 1968, II, p. 938).

But these tendencies are simple only to the degree that historical change approximates the logic of ideal types. Such approximation is seldom close. The stability of status-stratification is always exposed to the instabilities of eco-nomic change and social mobility; and men are always interested in arresting these instabilities by status distinctions which help them fortify the economic advantages they have won. By assuming that class- or status-oriented behavior prevails only for a time, Weber suggests a model of alternating tendencies without predicting a final outcome. Note the contrast with Marx, who con-sidered economic determinants decisive in the long run and on that basis predicted the final overthrow of capitalism.

In a sense, Weber systematizes de Tocqueville's impressionistic insights. By putting status-groups on a par with social classes, and by seeing every group as a part of both the social and the economic order, Weber eliminates Marx's reductionism. Groups are no longer seen as the inevitable by-product of economic organization. Rather, they are formed by common economic in-terests, a shared style of life, and an exclusion of outsiders meant to improve the group's life-chances. Individuals do not develop a consciousness of their community merely because they live under similar conditions. A common consciousness and collective organization must be developed deliberately. Indeed, in Weber's view, groups are formed as readily from common ideas leading to common economic interests, as they are the other way around.

This consideration goes beyond the comparison developed so far. Marx viewed all culture as a dependent variable, because his theory of human nature made the necessary conditions of existence the ultimate historical determinant. Accordingly, all ideas reflect and "refract" the interests of classes like capitalists or workers, not the interests of intellectuals themselves. But culture has material conditions of its own: a transformation of intellectual life occurred along with colonial expansion, industrialization, and the emergence of the modern state. The invention of printing, the bureaucratization of government, the increased importance of formal schooling, and the emergence of a market for intellectual products are aspects of that transformation. In modern societies, intellectuals constitute a social group attached to the "material conditions of cultural production"; and these conditions allow for an extraordinary degree of mental and artistic experimentation, both in free-lance work and in the universities (Shils 1972, Chaps. 4, 7, 8, 11, 17). But such freedom goes together with alienation. In the United States, one writer has complained that lack of interference with writers only indicates the official indifference to matters of literary interest. In the Soviet Union, Osip Mandelstam observed that where men are sent to labor camps merely for writing a poem, poetry is power. To be sure, the work of intellectuals may also be coopted by the "powers" (Shils) in universities and other organizations. But whether formally free or institutionalized, modern intellectual life tends to form cliques and schools of thought or style. And on that basis, distinctions of class and status are formed among intellectuals which are at some remove from analogous distinctions in the larger society.

Organized Action.   The distinction between classes and status-groups invites the question of how the two are related. One answer is that in practice economic interest and the quest for prestige tend to reinforce each other. And this statement applies at all levels of the social structure.

Both classes and status-groups endeavor to maintain or improve their opportunities in society. But equally, mere possession of goods satisfies no one. Everyone wants to be held in high regard by those whose judgment he values. Wealthy persons seek prestige for themselves and future generations. Those who have little or nothing still pride themselves on their good name in the community. Even deviants or outcasts want to be held in high regard in terms of their own standards. At the same time, prestige or a good name are not enough. At some social levels, wealth is needed to make prestige more secure and luxury becomes a manifestation of both. At other levels, possessions have the more modest function of confirming status and probity within the community. Also, conspicuous consumption goods may add to the prestige of an individual among those for whose judgment he cares. Although wealth and prestige may exist separately, there is a widespread desire to improve one's chances in life by combining them.

There is also a built-in limit to that improvement, at any rate in so far as wealth and prestige depend on qualifications of some kind. Once acquired, any qualification imposes a limit to further mobility by means of other qualifications. For learning, experience and skills represent an investment of resources which the individual will be loath to discount the older he gets. A forty-year-old carpenter will not readily abandon his skill for learning another trade which would require that he put himself at the bottom of another skill-hierarchy, even if that other trade promises higher rewards eventually. The same goes for qualifications of all kinds, including academic ones. Also, as we advance in age, we develop a more intense interest in preserving the social and economic value of the investment we have made in the skills acquired already. All qualifications thus represent cumulative and increasingly irreversible commitments to an occupational way of life with its rewards and liabilities—perhaps the most fundamental reason for the persistence of class- and status-differences.

Group-interests cluster around the defense of such "occupational investments" and facilitate organized actions. Probably, monopolistic organizations are the most common method of preserving or increasing the economic and social life-chances of any group.

> When the number of competitors increases in relation to the profit span, the participants become interested in curbing competition. Usually one group of competitors takes some externally identifiable characteristic of another group of (actual or potential) competitors—race, language, religion, local or social origin, descent, residence, etc.—as a pretext for attempting their exclusion. . . .
> The jointly acting competitors now form an "interest group" towards outsiders; there is a growing tendency to set up some kind of association with rational regulations; if the monopolistic interests persist, the time comes when the competitors establish a legal order that limits competition through formal monopolies. . . . Such closure, as we want to call it, is an ever-recurring process; it is the source of property in land as well as of all guild and other group monopolies (Weber 1968, I, pp. 341–342).

Such monopolization, or "closure," is perhaps the main reason why Marx's theory of the labor movement proved false. Marx assumed that unfettered exploitation would prompt the workers to organize to protect their common interests. But the successful formation of working class organizations was also the means by which the gains won through organization could be monopolized through closure against further competition.[3]

Monopolization of opportunities is always a precarious achievement. It requires defense against the interests of outsiders and depends on the solidarity of the group. Group membership may be voluntary. But a monopoly can be ensured by rules which restrict membership, just as the solidarity of the group can be supported by rules which control participation. The organization of groups thus involves closure against further competition and control by the organization over its own members. Both strategies can be made more enduring if the monopoly is anchored in law and its restrictions are enforced by the government.[4]

Conclusions.   From the preceding discussion, two conclusions follow for the study of inequality, one political, and the other historical. On the political side, Marx had interpreted all social and political associations as parts of a superstructure determined by the inequalities within the organization of production. Weber challenged such reductionism. He agreed that classes *tend* to form under the conditions Marx had specified. But he denied that association and organized action must result from this tendency, even in the long run. In each case, concerted action depends on a staff of persons administering the rules of the organized group and on the fluctuating relations between group-members and the administrative staff. The same consideration applies to government. Weber would have agreed with Raymond Aron's distinction between ruling classes and political classes. On the one hand, there are "privileged people who, without exercising actual political functions, influence those who govern and those who obey, either because of the moral authority which they hold, or because of the economic or financial power they possess." But there are also those who "actually exercise the political functions of government" (Aron 1966, p. 204; Weber 1968, I, p. 56). The officials constituting this political class have an administrative apparatus ready at hand. Economic classes, by contrast, must organize to be effective. Public employment also induces a common outlook. Officials are recruited on the basis of educational background and technical competence, to which administrative experience is then added. To an extent, they can interpose their judgment between any decision and its execution. Their ability to do so is a major organizational reason for the decision-making capacity of government, even when the pressure of interest-groups is great. Actions of government have a momentum of their own, they are more than mere enlargements of tendencies already existing in the society. The first conclusion is, therefore, that *organized* actions are only a possible outcome of classes or status-groups, but a necessary by-product of the exercise of public authority.

The second conclusion is historical and requires more explication. Although economic and social differences exist in all societies, the distinction between classes and status-groups, between experience in the workplace and in the family is peculiar to modern history. At one time, workplace and family life were part of the same household unit; ambition for gain and status were thus not readily distinguishable. The process of separation has occurred over long periods of time and in several different ways. Originally, aristocratic estates encompassed all aspects of social and economic life; but with the growth of court society, this unity weakened. At the highest levels of the aristocracy, law or custom precluded commercial pursuits; yet status-preoccupations at Court depended on the economic yield of estates, often managed by an agent hired for the purpose. Here status striving could so prevail over economic activities that aristocrats disdained to concern themselves with their own income. In the case of business enterprises, Weber has characterized a very different separation of functions:

> First, the household ceased to exist as a necessary basis of rational business association. Henceforth, the partner was not necessarily—or typically—a house member. Consequently, business assets had to be separated from the private property of the partners. Similarly, a distinction began to be made between the business employees and the domestic servants. Above all, the commercial debts had to be distinguished from the private debts of the partners, and joint responsibility had to be limited to the former. . . .
>
> What is crucial is the separation of household and business for accounting and legal purposes, and the development of a suitable body of laws, such as the commercial register, elimination of dependence of the association and the firm upon the family, separate property of the private firm or limited partnership, and appropriate laws of bankruptcy (Weber 1968, I, p. 379).

As Weber notes, this development was paralleled at higher and subsequently at lower levels of government administration by the separation of the "bureau" from the household and of official finances from private property. A comparable separation occurred when workers had to leave their households in order to go to their places of work. Such was the case in the factories of the early nineteenth century, when men, women, and children began to be separately employed in workplaces away from their homes. Even today, this separation from the home has not been carried through in many economic activities like farming, small-scale trading, or various artistic endeavors. Yet, places of work have become separated from family households so generally that the distinction between classes and status-groups has acquired institutional as well as analytical importance.

Equally characteristic of modern history is the institutional separation of society and the state, of socio-economic position and public office. In modern Western societies great wealth and high social rank are institutionally separated from governmental authority. Property ownership and family status may facilitate political influence, but they provide no basis for the exercise of official functions. Conversely, lack of property or status —while obviously a handicap—do not imply exclusion from political participation. This separation of society from the state conflicts with the older view which treated public office as an attribute of social rank and wealth, and which viewed society as a whole as a reservoir of resources at the disposal of an absolute ruler. The separation of state and society also conflicts with the modern, pluralist view which sees society as a composite of interest groups, and government as the handmaiden of these interest groups. Neither the old nor the new approach accounts adequately for state and society as closely related, but separable complexes of organized, collective action. I suggest that the institutional separations of class from status-group, and of society from the state broadly distinguish the modernizing from the "traditionalizing"[5] components of the social structure.

B. Inequality As a Force in Pre-Modern History

To distinguish modern from pre-modern history is to distinguish both between periods of history and between types of society. Such division into ideal types has its uses, but it is a starting point of analysis, not an end product. Much of what we consider typically modern can be found in societies of the remote past. Contract was a major feature of medieval feudalism and universal beliefs characterized medieval Catholicism. Much of what we consider typically traditional can be found in present day societies. Kinship continues to play a role in our experience despite the decline of extended families; status considerations are a major preoccupation even in the absence of most outward tokens of status. We must beware of the simplistic view that traditional societies become modern in any straightforward or inevitable manner (Bendix 1970, Chap. XI).

What grounds do we have then for distinguishing between tradition and modernity at all? In their answers to this question there is little difference between Marx and Weber. For that reason I dispense with further comparisons between them.

One answer was anticipated in the preceding discussion. If "modernity" is shorthand for the separation of class, status, and authority, then "tradition" stands for their fusion. Until the early modern period, economic activities were an aspect of the household. Status depended more on the individual's family ties than it does where modernizing tendencies prevail. In this sense, India is a striking example of a traditional society. Her social relations hinge on differences existing from birth. Individuals deal with one another as members of religious, ethnic, or linguistic communities. This communal membership is given an elaborate cultural rationale. Such ascendance of the group over the individual exists elsewhere as well: the prevalence of communal ties characterizes the traditional aspect of societies.

De Tocqueville pointed out that medieval households were solidary despite the enormous social distance between masters and servants. Superiority of rank and bearing, refinement of taste, great wealth and luxury lifted the world of masters to a sublime level in the eyes of their dependents. Servants necessarily lacked these qualities. Their status was inferior in their own eyes as much as in those of others. Yet de Tocqueville points out that a personal intimacy often existed between master and servant, especially where their relationship was hereditary. The master's standing was handed down to him through his family, just as his servants also looked back to the loyal service of their forebears. Ties of sentiment arose out of such shared family histories. De Tocqueville's picture of the master-servant relationship (de Tocqueville 1954, I, pp. 8–9; II, pp. 177–185) had its parallel in the relation between the king and his subordinates. At court, an elaborate etiquette allowed for degrees of intimacy with the supreme ruler, routinizing the competition for status among service-ranks and enabling the king to govern by distributing favors (Elias 1969, Chap. 5).

This combination of social distance and personal intimacy is not confined to aristocratic households. It recurs in relations between the master and other members of his household, between merchants and domestics, craftsmen and their apprentices, and landlords and peasants. It recurs also between the pater familias and his dependents in the ancient world, or in the family compounds of Far Eastern societies that were ruled by the head of the clan. The composition and organization of households has been exceedingly diverse. But they have in common that they are patriarchal, every member of the household being subordinate to the head or master. They encompass persons of several social ranks, who depend for their standing in the larger community both on their place within the household and on the status of the household in the larger society. Many such households are based on the yield of the land, supplemented by commercial transactions. Since the household is a unit of production as well as of consumption, all productive and managerial functions are divided among its members according to rank. Like a king on a smaller scale, the master carries out socio-political functions. Within his domain, he is concerned with maintaining traditional forms of behavior in order to assert his authority and keep the passions of his dependents within bounds. Within the larger society he seeks to enhance the social standing and political role of his house.

Thus, the study of inequality in traditional societies poses problems of its own. The household is a personally dominated community in which the economic wellbeing and the status of the individual depend entirely on the master's decision, and in which the members of the house compete for his favor. On these terms, households are solidary groups. Hence, we need not inquire under what conditions household members of different rank would join in concerted action (class), or by what means they define the circle of their social equals (status-group). This is not to argue for a benign conception of patriarchal relationships. Personal dominance and competition for status are often harsh. The intimacies of men and women living closely together may be cruelly manipulated, since the narrow confines of the household allow for little privacy (Bendix 1971, pp. 70–83). Instances of despotic rule and revolt abound in the pre-modern history of societies. But in these conditions, rebellions depend upon men breaking out of the confines of their household or estate to join forces and who then are forced back into subservience once their revolt is crushed. Except in periods of crises, the proliferation of little domains effectively insulates the inequalities within households (Marx 1969, pp. 88–95 and passim; Weber 1968, I, pp. 356–384).

The household is as typical of traditional societies as the enterprise and the market are typical of modern societies. The difference can be seen by comparing modern economics with the pre-modern literature of the "oikos," or household and estate, a literature which goes back to antiquity (Brunner 1949, Chaps. 2, 4; 1968, pp. 103–127). A central ideal of economics since the eighteenth century has been free market exchange. By contrast, the ideal household of the older literature was economically self-sufficient and required trade only to supplement its own production. Manuals were written on the management of household and estate, outlining the relations of husband and wife, parents and children, master and servants. A whole range of productive activities was described, from farming to mining or brickmaking. The wife's activities too were enumerated. Attention was given to vineyards and breweries, to the care of animals and pharmaceutical knowledge, to irrigation and fishing, to forestry and hunting. Trade remained an ancillary activity which was condemned if pursued for economic gain. Clearly, this older literature documents that the separation of economic activities from the family household is a modern development.

Status and authority were as inseparable from the household as production was. We saw earlier that in modern history the status of the individual depends on his family's prestige, its occupational subculture, its educational level, and its economic position. Admission to the circle of equals can be a matter of intense competition. All this is true of the pre-modern period, but with one crucial difference: the household was under the inherited authority of a master. Heads of households determined who may eat at table and in what rank-order, as well as who is obliged to eat with the servants. Again, within the master's house, no one may marry without his express permission. This practice was still common in nineteenth century Europe not only in the family but among army officers and public officials who needed such permission from their superiors. Similarly, decisions on occupational choice or appropriate level of education were in the hands of the master. By law, the master had the right to punish his dependents, but in theory he was also liable for their conduct. His domination protected the people composing his estate and their welfare depended on his success in asserting the rights of his house and advancing its prosperity.

This view of tradition at the level of the individual and his community may be carried over to the larger society. For the division of society into communities composed of households had important consequences for the internal constitution and the outer boundaries of political structures. Prior to the seventeenth century, nation-states in the sense of contiguous territories with clearly defined frontiers did not exist. Thus, England's loss of Calais in 1558 marked the end of her territorial claims on the Continent which had lasted for centuries. In societies ruled by kings who grant land and rights in return for services, the polity typically consisted of competing jurisdictions. Kings and princes looked upon conquests of what we would consider alien territories, or upon acquisitions through intermarriage, as a means of increasing their resources. Each additional territory or other resource could serve as grants to obtain additional services. At the same time, the ruler's authority was limited internally. Each jurisdiction was removed to some degree from the sway of central authority, since within his domain the grantee exercised his own authority. As a result, larger political structures could be united only with difficulty, and unity once achieved remained precarious.

Internally, the politics of pre-modern history were swayed by efforts to defend the rights of the household or estate. Such defense was often of a piece with efforts at aggrandizement, in the same way as seeking the protection of the master of an estate was often a mixture of the desire for security and the submission to brute force. As Marc Bloch put it with reference to the Merovingian period:

> Everywhere, the weak man felt the need to be sheltered by someone more powerful. The powerful man, in his turn, could not maintain his prestige or his fortune or even his own safety except by securing for himself, by persuasion or coercion, the support of subordinates bound to his

service. On the one hand, there was the urgent quest for a protector; on
the other, there were usurpations of authority, often by violent means.
And as notions of weakness and strength are always relative, in many cases
the same man occupied a dual role—as a dependent of a more powerful
man and a protector of humbler ones. Thus there began to be built up a
vast system of personal relationships whose intersecting threads ran from
one level of the social structure to another (Bloch 1961, p. 40).

Patriarchal jurisdictions tend to pose rather similar political problems. A ruler's
authority often depends for its effectiveness on implementation of his orders
by a subordinate jurisdiction. At the same time, each jurisdiction insists on its
rights. To an extent, the ruler must accept the autonomy of his dependents.
But since his own position requires the collection of taxes in money and kind,
he must also control their jurisdictions. This uncertainty of power lay at the
root of the protracted feuds which fill the annals of pre-modern history.

Externally, a traditional society which is rent by such uncertainties, is
threatened also by uncertain boundaries. For us this is a difficult point to grasp,
as we are used to nation-states with clearly defined frontiers. But frontiers are
not easily determined if territorial holdings are at the same time more or less
autonomous jurisdictions. The border-areas of a kingdom will use the bargaining advantages of their location to increase the rights they enjoy from the
king. These territories are a tempting prize for the king's rivals. As a result, the
king's rule over the area may be precarious. Moreover, territorial and jurisdictional units are often widely scattered owing to the vagaries of inheritance,
grants, and alliances, so that not only adjacent areas but even the same area
may enjoy a variety of rights and owe allegiance to different rulers. Under
these conditions it is often possible for territorial jurisdictions to break away
when this appears politically promising. There are many instances in which
the area between two rulers is not marked by a frontier line, but by a disputed
jurisdiction.

Where the fortunes of men wax and wane with the fortunes of the house
to which they belong, victory or defeat in jurisdictional feuds bears directly
on the well-being of the individual. That well-being depends in large part on
the size and productivity of landholdings and on the degree to which political
authorities can exact tributes in money or kind. Patriarchal jurisdictions are
engaged, therefore, in efforts to better their holding vis à vis their relatives and
neighbors as well as in contests with the ruler over the amount and kind of
tribute to be paid. In the absence of stable frontiers, this arena of internal
contest stands exposed to intrusions from the outside.

C. Concluding Considerations

The internal struggle over wealth, status, and authority was exposed to
foreign influences in new ways in the transition from pre-modern to modern
social structures. The social structure of the earlier period was characterized
not only by uncertain frontiers, but also by a firm subordination of intellectual
life to Church and State. Then frontiers became more clearly defined, national
consciousness increased, and the earlier world-view was challenged by men

of ideas who became a social force in their own right. In his interpretation of the origin of capitalism, Marx emphasized the "primitive accumulation of capital" through overseas expansion and land-enclosures at home. In these and related developments Weber emphasized the rise of "rational calculation" as the characteristic which distinguished modern from earlier types of capitalism. Both writers acknowledged, but did not focus attention on the material transformation of intellectual life itself. Yet, the invention of printing, the development of science, and the growth of secular learning brought about a cultural mobilization which had a direct bearing on the social structure of early modern societies.

This impact of cultural mobilization tended to be obscured in nineteenth century Europe. The modern study of inequality began with the Scotch Moralists, Saint-Simon, and Marx. From their vantage-point, and within clearly defined national frontiers, it was plausible to consider "society" in isolation from other societies, and thus ignore their international setting. Inequality could be interpreted largely in internal economic terms, when the societies involved looked back on centuries of expansion overseas and were in the forefront of the modern, industrial and democratic revolutions. Against this view, I maintain that change is not only internal to a society. The age of exploration and with still greater impact the industrial and political revolutions of the seventeenth and eighteenth centuries altered the international environment of most societies. Once any of these transformations had been initiated by a country, that country became an object of emulation elsewhere. Intellectuals and governments play a key role in this emulation and adaptation. With the model of another country before them, they seek to overcome the political and social backwardness of their own country, if not to rival the model itself. This demonstration effect of expansion and revolution did not exist in the earlier period and has gone far to break up pre-modern structures of inequality—even in countries which retained their political and economic independence.

I want to retain the question posed by the Marxian study of inequality, but I do not believe in the Marxian answers. As both Lenin and Weber pointed out, it is necessary to distinguish structural tendencies from the capacity to organize effectively.

I do not believe that social strata or classes are nation-wide phenomena. This would be the case only if all differences arising from familial affiliation were erased. We know that this has not been the case, and today there is no reason to assume that it is the wave of the future.

I do not believe that social classes and status-groups can be studied satisfactorily by attention to a single society, that such groups are unaffected by events beyond a country's frontiers. This assumption is unwarranted both because ties across national frontiers have developed out of common religious or ethnic affiliations, and because conquest, political control, and the diffusion of techniques and ideas have had a major impact on the social structure of many countries.

Marx assumed that the "infinite fragmentation of interest and rank" would give way to a polarization of classes in the course of capitalist development.

In this he relied on the homogenizing impact of exploitation and "egotistical calculation." Today we lack this capacity for strategic simplification, but we lack also its attendant illusions.[6]

Much modern social thought retains its umbilical cord to Marx. I do not think the study of inequality and social structure will advance much until this cord is cut and Marx's insights are used irrespective of their doctrinal and political involvements. This paper is an effort in this direction.

NOTES

1. Note that Marx saw the emergence of the bourgeoisie and of the proletariat in terms of a common process of class formation. Cf. Marx and Engels (1939:48–9) for a description of the rising bourgeoisie and Marx (n.d.: 145–6) for a description of the rising proletariat.
2. Weber's point (1968, I, p. 305) is already apparent in Marx and Engels, though it is rather awkward from the standpoint of Marxian theory. See Marx and Engels (1967, p. 91) where the authors refer to "bourgeois ideologists" who go over to the proletariat and comprehend the historical movement as a whole. The authors stress (1967, pp. 95–96) the role of communists as a vanguard of the proletariat, but their specification reads like a catalogue of differences between intellectual preoccupations and workday experience. Against Weber, Marx and Engels would have insisted that the intellectual articulation is already preformed in the common class experience.
3. Weber calls this "domination by virtue of a constellation of interest (in particular by virtue of a position of monopoly)" (1968, III, p. 943). Marx analyzed monopolizing tendencies of the "ruling class," but Weber emphasized that such tendencies exist at all levels.
4. Weber calls this "domination by virtue of authority" based on a shared belief in its legitimacy (1968, III, p. 943).
5. I regret the introduction of this neologism, but it is meant to make the reification of "tradition" more difficult. For much the same reason Weber wrote *Vergesellschaftung* for *Gesellschaft* and *Vergemeinschaftung* for *Gemeinschaft*. Perhaps the simple nouns are unavoidable, but it should be understood that they stand for tendencies rather than entities.
6. One reason why the "fragmentation of interest and rank" continues is that social structures "once they have come into being . . . perpetuate themselves, even when the social conditions that created them have disappeared" (Schumpeter 1951, pp. 144–145). Oddly enough, this historical perspective has also disappeared from the Marxist tradition (Loewenthal 1969, pp. 23–24).

REFERENCES

Aron, Raymond
　　1966　"Social class, political class, ruling class." Pp. 201–210 in Reinhard Bendix and Seymour M. Lipset (eds.), Class, Status and Power. 2nd ed. New York: The Free Press.

Bloch, Marc
　　1961　Feudal Society. Chicago: University of Chicago Press.

Bendix, Reinhard
　　1966　"Karl Marx's theory of social classes." Pp. 6–11 in Reinhard Bendix and Seymour M. Lipset (eds.), Class, Status, and Power. 2nd ed. New York: The Free Press.
　　1970　Embattled Reason. New York: Oxford University Press.
　　1971　"Ideological and scholarly approaches to industrialization." Pp. 70–83 in Reinhard Bendix and Guenther Roth, Scholarship and Partisanship. Berkeley: University of California Press.

Brunner, Otto
　　1949　Adeliges Landleben und Europäischer Geist. Salzburg: Otto Müller.
　　1968　"Das 'Ganze Haus' und die alteuropäischer Ökonomik," Pp. 103–127 in Otto

Brunner, Neue Wege der Verfassungs- und Sozialgeschichte. Goettingen: Vanden-
hoeck & Ruprecht.

Dumont, Louis
1972   Homo Hierarchicus. London: Paladin.

Elias, Norbert
1969   Die höfische gesellschaft. Neuwied: Hermann Luchterhand.

Loewenthal, Richard
1969   "Unreason and revolution," Encounter XXXIII (November): 23–34.

Marx, Karl
n.d.   The Poverty of Philosophy. New York: International Publishers.
1936   Capital. New York: The Modern Library.
1962   Capital. Moscow: Foreign Languages Publishing House.
1969   On Colonialism and Modernization. Garden City: Anchor Books, Doubleday &
Co.

Marx, Karl and Engels, Friedrich
1939   The German Ideology. New York: International Publishers.
1967   The Communist Manifesto. Baltimore: Penguin Books.

Schumpeter, Joseph
1951   Imperialism and Social Classes. New York: Augustus Kelley.

Tocqueville, Alexis de
1954   Democracy in America. New York: Vintage Books.

Tucker, Robert
1961   Philosophy and Myth in Karl Marx. New York: Cambridge University Press.

Weber, Max
1968   Economy and Society. Tr. and ed. by Guenther Roth and Claus Wittich. New York:
Bedminster Press.

The Antiromantics: Pareto, Mosca, and Michels

Vilfredo Pareto (1848–1923), in contrast to Marx and particularly
Weber for whom rationality was a central concern, rejected "reason" as a
relevant factor in understanding men's behavior and its outcomes. Whereas
Marx had viewed man as a rational and perfectable creature, Pareto viewed
him as essentially nonrational and unchanging.[54]

It is a difference in sentiment, in the form of what Pareto called residues, rather than in man's rationality or his adherence to tradition that
distinguishes the relatively higher classes from the lower. In distinguishing
between two large classes in society, the *elite,* and *nonelite,* Pareto holds
that the latter responds to its social conditions on the basis of nonrational
sentiments, whereas the former view the world in terms of rational self-
interest.[55] Sentiments change and are reflected in changes in historically
identifiable periods. As the ruling elite begins to succumb to humanitarian

---

[54] Irving M. Zeitlin, *Ideology and the Development of Sociological Theory,*
(Englewood Cliffs, N.J.: Prentice-Hall, 1968).

[55] With respect to rationality and logical and nonlogical action, see Talcott Parsons, "Pareto's Central Analytical Scheme," in J. Meisel (ed), *Pareto and Mosca,*
(Englewood Cliffs, N.J.: Prentice-Hall, 1965), pp. 71–78.

sentiments, for example, they degenerate and give way to new elite groups who are willing to use force to attain and hold the highest positions of power in society.

The idea of the replacement of the old elite with the new is known as *the circulation of elites*. Because it is primarily elites who compete for power in society, rather than the lower classes generally, stratification structures largely remain the same, despite the successions. The classless society, of which the romantic Marx wrote, can never come about because the struggle between ruler and ruled is inherent in the nature of society. Those who possess elite qualities become elites,[56] but elites are of two types: governing and nongoverning. Both have the capacity to govern but only one holds office.

All segments of society are dominated in their behavior by a set of nonlogical, instinctive sentiments called residues that are distinctive of various categories of rulers and ruled.[57] Most characteristic of the speculators among the governing elite is the *instinct for combinations* (class 1 residues) referring to capacities for ideas, reflection, imagination and innovation. The *rentiers,* however, are more conservative in character and are influenced by the instinct of the *persistence of aggregates* (class 2 residues). The essential significance of this distinction between speculators and rentiers —that is, between lions and foxes—is reflected in the capacity of the latter to slow circulation, in contrast to the former. Thus, the process of governing is constantly affected by the interchange between these two types of elites. But Pareto's view of stratification is a dual one, and the elites represent only one class. What of those who are ruled?

The ruled in society are dominated not only by the elites in the social sphere but also by their own self-subjugating sentiments as well. It is among the masses that nonrational impulses dominate the behavior of men. Exploited by the ruling elites through the manipulation of their unreflective sentiments, the ruled generally accept traditions blindly and their social positions as given. Domination by class 2 residues, which include nonrational beliefs and sentiments, assures the elite that the gap between the realities of experience and the ideals of the culture can be filled with ideologies that maintain the status quo.

In attempting to appraise Pareto's contribution to social stratification it is well to keep in mind the contrast between the approaches of Marx and Weber. We held earlier that Weber's approach more fully grasped the complexity of stratification than Marx's, seeing it as multi- rather than unidimensional. Pareto seemingly learned little from Weber in this respect, having not only failed to grasp and conceptualize the several sets of pro-

---

[56] Zeitlin, op. cit., p. 187.

[57] Associated with these were what Pareto called derivations, explanations and rationalizations for behavior that presumably reflected the residues.

cesses that are significant in understanding stratification, but in choosing *independent* variables, which reduced the ultimate explanation to psychological causes.

> Two types of social order emerge out of the activities of these two groups. One is conservative, military and religious, using force as the main method of government. The circulation of elites is slow; economic stimulus, weak. In the opposite case economic interests supersede military ones; the costs of government are high, but so is economic stimulus; the conservative virtues decline, and finally the leading class, degenerating into humanitarianism, proves unable to keep the political power. Revolution or defeat in war ensues and puts an end to this part of the cycle.[58]

Marx, as we noted, placed the ultimate causes of social action in the social structure itself. Man acted as he did by virtue of his position in society. Weber elaborated this view by indicating that a person holds different stratification structures and that these not only influence him generally but there are connections between them through the activities of those holding the positions. Pareto, in attempting to explain variations in group political performance by variations in the residues held by members of different groups and categories, thus limited substantially his contribution to the sociological study of social stratification.

Gaetano Mosca (1855–1941) like Pareto, rejected Marx's implicit romanticism and its faith in the capacity of man to create and sustain a classless society. Rulers and ruled is a pereptual relationship. Just as, according to the Bible, "the poor you shall always have," elites, also, always will be with you.

Mosca, in general, takes a theoretical position much like Pareto's and there is much controversy—not unlike that surrounding the Comte and Saint-Simon relationship—about priorities. However, unlike Pareto, Mosca's views were in a constant state of flux and—more important, from a scientific point of view—more responsive to observation and experience. Thus, although he originally shared with Pareto the idea that psychological processes were the bedrock of political behavior, he was far more aware of the role played by social structure in influencing political behavior. Similarly, he rejected single-factor explanations for social processes, particularly Marx's economic determinism.

Like Marx, however, Mosca agrees that the history of all societies is a history of class antagonism and conflict between the rulers and the ruled. Unlike Marx he rejected the idea that this kind of relationship could be altered because it was rooted in the psychological processes associated with fundamental human nature.

---

[58] Franz Borkenau, "A Manifesto of Our Time," in Meisel, op. cit., p. 112.

Sociologically, Mosca stresses the importance of the organization of activity in pursuing political goals. It is primarily because elites are an organized minority that they are able to influence the *unorganized* majority.

Anticipating what C. Wright Mills referred to as "the power elite," [59] Mosca held that political elites pursue their own interests as they come to dominate the majority and this leads to control of other spheres of social action. Like Weber, Mosca suggested that personal influence attained in one sphere carried over into other spheres, as exemplified in the accumulation of wealth by political and military leaders.

Thus, Mosca understood well the role of organization in the larger spectrum of human activity, as well as the interplay between organizations. It is this feature that marks his contribution to the sociological understanding of social stratification.[60]

Robert Michels (1876–1936) was still another antiromantic who lauded Marx and Engels for their contributions to social science. Following Pareto and Mosca, Michels held that elites were inherent in the societal process because the craving for power is inherent in man.

In spite of his efforts to reduce organizational processes to mere outcomes of tendencies associated with human nature, as did Pareto, Michels's explanation of the *oligarchical* tendencies in organizations, especially democratic organizations, is to be found in social structural conditions. Oligarchical tendencies involve the concentration of power in the hands of a few whose power is self-perpetuated.

Like Durkheim and Simmel, Michels noted that as size of group increased, the quality of social relationships was altered. Michels held that true democracy, in the sense that all members shared directly in the decision-making process, is only possible in relatively small groups. Commitment in the small group is widely shared and strong members accept responsibility, occupants of positions are rotated, and so on. As size increases so does complexity and its concomitants—specialization of tasks and a presumed need for experts to aid in the decision-making process. In time the specialists, through their organizational expertise, become separated from the bulk of the membership and become a distinguishable elite. Originally selected to serve the organization and its goals, the elite develops interests of its own and organizational goals become obscured. Seeking to maintain its position and to pursue its own ends the elite is transformed into an oligarchy. Thus, Michels grasps one of the *implicit* problems in Marx's perspective: How can democracy work in modern society? As a consequence, Marx's romantic idea

[59] C. Wright Mills, *The Power Elite* (New York: Oxford U. Press, 1959).

[60] For a fuller exposition of Mosca's ideas see Gaetano Mosca, *The Ruling Class*, ed. and trans. H. Kahn, ed. and rev. A. Livingston (New York: McGraw-Hill, 1965); J. Meisel, *The Myth of the Ruling Class* (Ann Arbor: University of Michigan Press, 1962); and Meisel's *Pareto and Mosca*, cited previously.

that communism, as a type of organized political system, might resolve the problem of creating and sustaining a democratic state is rejected.

Michels's "iron law," encapsulated in the statement, "Who says organization says oligarchy," represents the final elaborate speculative perspective derived from Pareto and his primary dependence on *residues* and *derivations* in attempting to explain the rise and rotation of elites. It is raised to a more clearly sociological level by Mosca, who grasps the significance of organizations of men as contrasted with similarly motivated individuals as primary cause. Michels penetrates the very nature of organization itself and describes in detail the social process by which elites emerge. In Michels's work we are able to observe the unfolding of a *sociological* approach to stratification problems when contrasted with other approaches.

However, Michels also represents another trend in the social science theory of the recent past. Whereas Pareto and Mosca seemed to be only little, if at all, influenced by the sociological literature of the period in which they wrote,[61] Michels's work is clearly influenced by both Weber and Durkheim. As such it has a more direct connection with the sociological traditions that have emerged in the twentieth century.

---

[61] Pareto's reason for this is probably a result of his relative imperviousness to the ideas of others; cf. Meisel, 1965. Mosca's failure to incorporate more than the result of his own observations and experiences is more acceptable in terms of scientific norms because he had assumed the role of politician at the time when we might have further developed his theoretical approach.

4 Contemporary Theory in Stratification: Functional and Conflict Perspectives

Parsons and Functionalism

Of the contemporary, general theories of stratification, the functional theory has probably been the most influential. Its most succinct statement was offered by Kingsley Davis and Wilbert E. Moore in 1945.[1] A brief article by Davis alone preceded the joint statement by a couple of years;[2] and Talcott Parsons's essays, at about the same time, provided further elaboration of the theoretical perspective.[3]

During the early 1940s, Davis and Moore had developed a rather lengthy manuscript presenting the functional theory. Unfortunately, in light of the ensuing debate, they condensed their ideas into a brief seven-page article in the 1945 presentation. Extensive criticisms and rejoinders followed

---

[1] Kingsley Davis and Wilbert E. Moore, "Some Principles of Stratification," *American Sociological Review,* **10**:242–249 (1945). See, also, Kingsley Davis, *Human Society* (New York: Macmillan, 1949).

[2] Kingsley Davis, "A Conceptual Analysis of Stratification," *American Sociological Review,* **7**:309–321 (1942).

[3] Talcott Parsons, "An Analytic Approach to the Theory of Stratification," *American Journal of Sociology,* **45**:841-862 (1940).

as the "unqualified and dogmatic" presentation was attacked and, as a result, articulated.

Parsons' theoretical scheme was dominant in the sociological theory of the 1940s (and 1950s), and even though Davis and Moore made few explicit references to Parsons, his influence is obvious. One major continuum along which Parsons differentiated societies was the ascribed–achieved dimension. The first type was seen as characteristic of nonliterate, kinship-oriented societies; modern societies were seen as achievement oriented. Within the stratification system, this typology refers to the difference between rewards that are assigned on the basis of birthright characteristics (such as family lineage, sex, or race) and positional rewards, which are attained by one's own efforts (such as education).

In achievement-oriented societies, Parsons argued that there must be a strong relationship between the division of labor (which he termed, "the instrumental structure") and the distribution of rewards. Those roles that involve the greatest degree of "responsibility for the affairs of the collectivity" will have more "facilities" at their disposal, and these facilities are "in themselves rewards." [4] In essence, if there is a division of labor and achievement values within a society, then there must be differential rewards for positions of varying competence and responsibility. These differences in reward are the basis of the stratification system. "The only way to avoid this," Parsons concludes, would be to deny "differences of competence or responsibility, including denial of their functional relevance." [5]

One of the fundamental arguments made by Parsons is that stratification is necessary, and also desirable, for a complex achievement-oriented society—necessary because it allocates rewards and "connections" to positions according to the amount of collective responsibility entrusted to them; and desirable because this arrangement permits the entire system to function effectively. Thus, Parsons noted that industrial managers in Russia were part of the "intelligentsia" and received more of all types of rewards than ordinary workers. Their greater rewards are not valued as legitimate within the Soviet system, and the same inequities in the United States would be considered "capitalistic." Nevertheless, unequal rewards accrue to managers in both societies, and "a sociologist is at least entitled to be skeptical" that any ideology could change this pattern given "the essential structural situation" in a complex society.[6]

This view of the indispensability and function of stratification was very pervasive in American sociology during the 1940s. It was not only the

----

[4] One of the clearest statements of Parsons' view is presented in his book, *The Social System* (New York: Free Press, 1951), pp. 157–161. The quotations here are from p. 159.

[5] Ibid.

[6] Ibid., p. 160.

position of major theories, such as Parsons', but the basic assumption taken by the most influential researchers, such as Warner. In heterogeneous and differentiated societies, Warner posited, there is a great need for coordination. Those positions most entrusted with the responsibilities of co-ordinating and directing activities within the society will be the best-rewarded, most prestigeful positions.[7] Thus, a status rank is understandable only by identifying "its place" in the larger society.[8]

The Davis–Moore View

This indispensable function of stratification view was at the heart of the Davis-Moore statement in 1945. It was, of course, a view that Davis, in particular, had helped to articulate. More than any other presentation, however, their 1945 statement offered the functional theory in systematic, pro-positional form. In part, for this reason, the names of Davis and Moore are associated with the theory. In addition, the critical response to their brief and dogmatic assertions was immediate and extensive, continuing to the present. Theoretically, the criticisms could as easily have been directed at Parsons, for example, but the Davis-Moore presentation was much clearer than Parsons'; it also was very conspicuous, so it attracted the lions' share of the debate. This also contributed to the historical connection between the functional theory and those authors' names in particular.

In the 1945 statement, Davis and Moore posed as the central question: "Why different positions carry different degrees of prestige."[9] It is a different question, they insisted, to ask how specific individuals obtain those positions. Much of the ensuing criticism failed to appreciate the difference, but before considering this, let us first consider how they answered their basic question.

Differing degrees of prestige (and other types of rewards) are universal, they began, because every society must place "the proper" people into "the proper" positions and then motivate them to perform the duties associated with the positions. Unlike Parsons, they did not limit these inferences to achievement-oriented societies. All societies, competitive or not, were seen as having to absorb people into positions and then motivate them by differential rewards. Like Parsons, they saw this distribution of rewards as giving rise to a stratification system. Also like Parsons, and Warner, they argued that the ranking of positions would be determined by the functional importance of a position "for the society." They were unsure how functional importance

---

[7] W. Lloyd Warner, *Social Classes in America* (Chicago: Science Research Associates, 1949). See, especially, p. 8.

[8] W. Lloyd Warner and P. S. Lunt, *The Status System of a Modern Community* (New Haven: Yale, 1947).

[9] Davis and Moore, op. cit., p. 242.

might be measured, though. To use the prestige of a position as an indicator of its importance was certainly circular reasoning they recognized, so they proposed two possible guides: the functional uniqueness of a position, and the degree to which other positions are dependent on it. (The latter can be seen to be quite similar to Warner's view.)

In addition to functional importance, however, Davis and Moore also argued that the ranking of a position was determined by the relative scarcity of personnel. If the obligations of a position require substantial amounts of innate talent or extensive training, then greater rewards will have to be associated with the position in order to induce a scarce pool of potential incumbents to seek the position. What they did not explicitly consider was how functional importance and scarcity *jointly* contributed to reward. On the one hand they imply independent effects; that is, either great functional importance or high scarcity is sufficient to ensure high rewards. On the other hand, they imply a multiplicative interaction between the two variables; that is, if either one is very low it can mitigate the effects of the other. Their example, modern physicians, does not help to clarify the situation either. They view the position of the medical doctor as functionally important, and the training as so rigorous that few can qualify. Thus, both functional importance and relative scarcity of qualified personnel have congruent consequences for the rewards of physicians. It is very unclear what Davis and Moore think would happen if the effects of both variables were not congruent.

Much to the credit of the theory, they did explicitly recognize that although stratification was universal, its specific form would vary in relation to "major societal functions." Here Parsons' influence is most apparent, as Davis and Moore begin by considering the universality of religion and how increasing secularization is related to changes in the ranking of religious practitioners. In Parsons' theory an extreme emphasis was placed on the role of religion, and moral values in general, in the integration of society;[10] a declining cultural emphasis on religion was seen as occurring in response to the "rationalizing" influence of "progressive forces." Thus, the initial concern of Davis and Moore with the effects of religion on stratification systems shows a clear Parsonian influence.

Specifically, they proposed, in medieval types of societies the organized priesthood is very high in prestige. This high rank is due to the functional importance of religion in societies of this type where an "unlettered" population is highly "credulous." Given the importance of religious ritual in such "sacred" societies, it may be surprising, they note, that priests' positions are

---

[10] See the discussion of Parsons' emphasis on religion and "moralistics" in Alvin W. Gouldner, *The Coming Crisis of Western Sociology* (New York: Basic Books, 1970). See, especially, Chap. 7.

not still more highly ranked. What tempers their status, Davis and Moore note, is the ease with which anyone can claim to be in communication with deities, without fear of rebuke. Thus, there is a limited pool of eligibles in such societies only if literacy is a prerequisite. Therefore, the highest ranking of priests occurs, they note, when the priestly guild itself rigidly controls access to the profession.

Similarly, Davis and Moore go on to describe other possible variations in ranking due to changes in government, relations to the means of production, and technical knowledge. They conclude that actual stratification systems can be of a number of polar types, varying in equalitarianism, opportunities for mobility, degrees of stratum solidarity, and so on. However, even though the form may vary, functional importance and relative scarcity are seen as the basic principles of stratification.

The Criticisms

Since it first was presented, the Davis-Moore theory has been the target of numerous criticisms. Some have been well founded, and the exchanges that followed have led to many clarifications. Some of the criticism, however, has been based on misunderstandings generated by the complexity of the theory and its overly brief presentation.

The most visible critic has been Melvin Tumin, who wrote about a dozen papers in the 1950s and 1960s on varied aspects of the Davis-Moore theory.[11] One of the first issues raised by Tumin involves "the calculus of functionality." That is, do nonsubjective criteria exist by which the functional importance of a position can be assessed? He argues that Davis and Moore utilize nondemonstrable values in claiming, for example, that engineers are functionally more important to a factory than are unskilled workers. In the long run, Tumin asks, must not everyone in an enterprise be adequately motivated? Davis agrees with this, but points out that engineers must receive more training, which would not occur unless their work were more important and, hence, better rewarded. However, the ambiguity raised by the notion of functional importance has continued to generate debate. Richard L. Simpson, for example, has argued that the prestige of garbage collectors is lower than what should be accorded to them in light of the serious problem that uncollected refuse would present to a society.[12] Further-

[11] Several of these papers are reproduced in Melvin M. Tumin, ed., *Readings on Social Stratification* (Englewood Cliffs, N.J.: Prentice-Hall, 1970). A listing of these papers is presented in Tumin's book on p. 405.

[12] Richard L. Simpson, "A Modification of the Functional Theory of Stratification," *Social Forces,* **35**:130–139 (1956).

more, the noxious aspects of garbage collecting also may serve to limit the potential supply of recruits.

In considering Simpson's criticism from the perspective of Davis and Moore, George A. Huaco points out that the functional theory proposes only a *tendency* for rewards to vary with functional importance; its correspondence with actual rewards need not be perfect.[13] In other words, garbage collectors may be an exception, but few theories can avoid any exceptions. This reply does not resolve the problem either, though. As long as functional importance is not operationally defined, people are free to disagree with each other's intuitive evaluations. Thus, there will be no basis for arguing about whether the number of exceptions is greater or smaller than the number of nonexceptions.

Davis and Moore, it will be recalled, offered two guides: the uniqueness of a position, and the number of other positions that are dependent on it. Consider a baseball team in this regard. The pitcher's position is more unique than a right fielder's, for example, and this could be demonstrated by showing greater interchangeability of positions. Specifically, more people who also play other positions (such as first base or left field) also play right field than also pitch. The dependence of other positions—including the dependence of the entire team—is also greater on the pitcher than on the right fielder. Based on these indications of functional importance,[14] the material and symbolic rewards of pitchers should exceed those of right fielders.[15]

Pursuing the same pattern of reasoning, the functional importance of quarterbacks could be differentiated from that of offensive linemen; soloists could be differentiated from members of symphony orchestras, and so on. However, note that in each case positions are ranked in functional importance relative to other positions within the same organization. Interorganizational comparisons also are demanded by the Davis-Moore theory—that is, offensive linesmen have to be compared to musicians in orchestras. This latter comparison requires a basis for evaluating the relative functional importance of different components of a society. It is the type of analysis Davis and Moore themselves attempted in examining the changing role of priests as the religious institution within societies changed.

Davis and Moore assumed that stratification was an "unconsciously

---

[13] George A. Huaco, "The Functionalist Theory of Stratification," *Inquiry*, **9**:215–240 (1966).

[14] There is also the matter of relative scarcity to be considered, but in these examples, the effects of scarcity are probably congruent.

[15] This example, and other contrasting illustrations, are analyzed in Mark Abrahamson, "Talent Complementarity and Organizational Stratification," *Administrative Science Quarterly*, **18**:186–193 (1973). See, also, Arthur L. Stinchcombe, "Some Empirical Consequences of the Davis-Moore Theory of Stratification," *American Sociological Review*, **28**:805–808 (1963).

evolved" mechanism through which *societies* went about assuring that the best-qualified people wound up in the most important jobs. In a very Durkheimian sense, society was seen as the sui generis with stratification linked to its (that is, the society's) needs. The methodological dilemma posed by this conceptualization is that it suggests no apparent way of measuring functional importance. Some sociologists have focused on consensus in rankings as an indicator of functional importance.[16] Strictly speaking, however, peoples' perceptions of importance do not necessarily bear a close relationship to the actual contribution of a position to a society.[17] In other words, how are people to know for sure?

Consensus is, therefore, a very problematic indicator of functional importance. Unfortunately, no other indicator is yet apparent. Until a better one is developed, the concept of functional importance will remain methodologically unclear. Thus, the theory may continue to be influential conceptually, but there necessarily will be different interpretations of its applicability and an absence of empirical support for the theory at a very crucial spot. It should also be noted, however, that the usefulness of a theory —any theory—also lies in its role as a source of testable hypotheses, even if all aspects of the theory are not amenable to empirical assessment. We will have more to say about the role of the Davis-Moore theory in this regard later in the chapter.

A second major criticism of Tumin's is directed at the presumed inevitability and desirability of stratification systems. The more stratified a society is, he claims, the more likely are talented, lower-standing persons to go "undiscovered." Because their access to mobility channels often is denied, they are not likely even to develop their talents. From the standpoint of the society, he concludes, this is hardly functional. Furthermore, Tumin questions, must rewards be viewed as the best, or the only, way of recruiting appropriate talent? What about intrinsic work satisfaction as an alternative?

These motivational assumptions are at the heart of the criticism offered by the Polish sociologist, Wlodzimierz Wesolowski. Davis's and Moore's view of the indispensability of rewards is based, he contends, on the assumption that human nature is characterized both by selfish, materialistic drives and by laziness.[18] Rewards are correspondingly viewed as the necessary energizing mechanisms. They have disregarded, he concludes, the impact of cultural values on motives of behavior. This leads them to be insensitive to the possibilities, in some cultures, of training people to fill important positions without their reckoning on future material advantages.

---

[16] See, for example, Joseph Lopreato and Lionel Lewis, "An Analysis of Variables in the Functional Theory of Stratification," *Sociological Quarterly,* **4**:312–320 (1963).

[17] See Huaco, loc. cit.

[18] Wlodzimierz Wesolowski, "Some Notes on the Functional Theory of Stratification," *Polish Sociological Bulletin,* **3–4**:581–591 (1962).

In response to this line of criticism, Davis and Moore did later confine their generalizations largely, but not exclusively, to competitive, achievement-oriented societies. (This, by the way, brought their perspective into closer accord with Parsons'.) Concerning the dysfunctional "strangulation of talent," however, they correctly pointed out that their theory was not primarily an attempt to account for how specific individuals came to occupy certain positions. Rather, it was an attempt to account for the differential ranking of those positions. In a caste system, for example, where their model only partially applied, it is one thing to ask why certain people are in certain castes; but, it is quite different to account for the relative standing of the castes themselves.

There have been a number of attempts theoretically to reconcile various criticisms with the basic theory. In this connection it should be emphasized that many of the critics were not claiming that the functional theory was without value. More typically they were concerned with certain—and sometimes very fundamental—aspects with which they were in disagreement. In the following excerpt, Huaco reviews some of the more recent criticisms and concludes with an assessment of the theory's insights and liabilities.

The Functionalist Theory of Stratification*

George A. Huaco

In December, 1959, Dennis H. Wrong's "The Functional Theory of Stratification: Some Neglected Considerations" attempted to mediate between theory and its critics:

> The functional theory of stratification advanced by Davis and Moore attempts to explain the universality and necessity of inequality in societies with a complex division of labor, a task that is independent of efforts to explain the division of labor itself or the intergenerational perpetuation of inequalities along family lines. The theory is so general, however, that it excludes none of the Utopian models of "classless societies" proposed by Western thinkers and, its critics to the contrary notwithstanding, says nothing whatsoever about the range of inequality and the determinants of that range in concrete societies. The theory appears to understate the degree to which positions are inherited by failing to view societies in long range historical perspective. In common with the arguments of its critics, it also ignores the possible disruptive consequences of mobility and equality of opportunity, a theme notably neglected by American sociologists.[1]

*   Reprinted with permission from *Inquiry*, **9**:228–232 and 236–240 (1966).

Here the opening formulation is incorrect. Davis and Moore do not attempt "to explain the universality and necessity of inequality," but attempt to explain the universality of inequality by its alleged necessity. This aspect of the Davis-Moore theory, in effect, exemplifies the typical functionalist maneuver of explaining a cultural universal by claiming that it is necessary for the preservation or survival of a system. The observation that the Davis and Moore theory neglects "the power element in stratification," and is "lacking a truly historical perspective," [2] is quite accurate.

In 1960, Tumin's "Competing Status Systems," a contribution to Arnold S. Feldman and Wilbert E. Moore's *Labor Commitment and Social Change in Developing Areas*, repeated Tumin's earlier contention that "there is nothing inevitable at all about the need for unequal rewards for unequal work." [3] The following year, in his book *Social Class and Social Change in Puerto Rico*, Tumin argued that:

> We must conclude that the actual shape of any reward system or any system of inducement and recruitment into tasks will be a function of the relevant powers of the sectors who hold differing judgments about the respective importance of tasks. Stratification, then, to the extent to which, as some have suggested, it can be defined by the system of unequal allocation of scarce, valued goods and services, is something very different from an unconsciously evolved device by which societies insure that the most competent persons will be induced to take on the tasks considered most functionally important to the society. It is rather an outcome, specified partly by social reward distributions, which is a function of the competition among variable definitions of what is important to the respective powers available to the competing sectors to implement their decision [the passage is italicized in the original]. [4]

Since "the actual shape of any reward system" refers to the range of inequality, Tumin is here suggesting that the actual configuration of power is a crucial determinant of the range of unequal rewards attached to different positions. He is also suggesting that the effective power of relevant sectors implements their evaluation of which positions are more important than others by the allocation of greater rewards to these positions.

> It seems quite possible, however, to account for the universal presence of ranking, and evaluation systems, and for the presence of inequalities in scarce, valued goods and services in nearly all societies, without relying upon some very restricted notion of the conditions under which actors will be induced to take up certain roles and perform them conscientiously. It would be equally reasonable to imagine an earlier historical condition where differences in age and strength made it possible for some members of groups to seize what they wanted when they wanted them, and to proceed to institutionalize their power over others by allocating the goods and services as they saw fit. Once in control of the socialization of the young, it is not much of a trick to teach certain patterns of deference which no longer require differences in physical strength to maintain. [5]

This formulation seems to involve some confusion. Tumin is unquestionably correct in taking power as a major determinant of role *ascription*; and a power explanation goes a long way in accounting for why the present incumbents of high-reward positions are who they are. But can a power explanation be equally effective in accounting for the inequality of rewards attached to positions? The difference can perhaps be made clear by appealing to a well-known historical example. The Aryan invasion is said to have been the historical origin of the Hindu caste system. This power event explains why the high-reward positions of priest and warrior were occupied exclusively by members of the conqueror group. It does *not* explain why both the conquerors and the conquered alike (together with many other similar traditional societies) should have regarded the roles of priest and warrior as high-reward positions.

In February, 1963, Wilbert E. Moore's "But Some Are More Equal than Others" answered Tumin and made a re-appraisal of the original Davis-Moore 1945 version.

> My current view is that the Davis-Moore position was incomplete, resulting in some overstatement (as noted by Simpson) and some neglect of dysfunctions. These criticisms have already been noted by Davis. In addition, I should specifically reject any stable equilibrium version of "functionalism" as both incorrect and extrinsic to the position that social inequality is a necessary feature of any social system. . . . The "functional theory of stratification" maintained only that positions of unequal importance would be unequally rewarded, and was silent, regrettably but not criminally, on the subject of systematic changes. . . . Although Davis and Moore were fairly explicit in equating "social stratification" with unequal rewards, that now appears unfortunate. I have some sympathy for Buckley's criticism on this point.[6]

After these modifications Moore turned to re-affirm the original thesis of the 1945 version:

> The single issue to which the present remarks are addressed is whether social inequality is a necessary feature of social systems. . . . The explanation presented here reiterates the thesis that "functional differentiation" of positions will inevitably entail unequal rewards—and adds the thesis that differences in performance must be expected to be and will be differentially valued.[7]

Here Moore reviews the many ways in which "inequality" can arise from the social valuation of "performances, qualities, and achievements," but this misses the point, because neither Tumin nor anyone has argued for the viability of a completely egalitarian order: the issue concerns only the possibility and feasibility of "equivalents" or "alternatives" to "unequal rewards"; namely, whether or not something other than unequal rewards can motivate individuals to occupy the different positions. Moore does not think so.

> Unless intrinsic task equalization is accomplished, it would seem extremely unlikely that equality of rewards—or rather, permitting only

esteem rewards—would be institutionalized by any conceivable system of socialization. This would require a somewhat greater extension of martyrdom than any religious system has yet achieved—and religious martyrs expect future rewards. I believe that Tumin has become entrapped by an ideological position that I see no reason to accept: namely that equality is intrinsically more equitable than inequality.[8]

On the causes of "stratification" (unequal rewards attached to different positions), Moore repeated the 1945 formulation and rejected Tumin's modification:

> The Davis-Moore "functional" interpretation of inequality rested on the unequal functional importance of positions and the unequal supply of talents for filling them. That interpretation, unlike most functional analyses, was explicitly evolutionary, and like many had possible rationalistic overtones. Tumin essentially skirts the issues of importance and talents but rejects the evolutionary explanation, for which he substitutes the view that stratification is an anachronistic survival maintained by self-perpetuating power. (That revolutionary polities establish new modes of social stratification escapes his attention.)[9]

This account of Tumin's views is not quite accurate. Although Tumin did not discuss revolutionary polities, their existence does not constitute a counter-example to his argument. Tumin suggested that the values of relevant power sectors constitute a decisive determinant of "the actual shape of any reward system." And as we saw when we analyzed his argument with the aid of a concrete historical example, power is most certainly a decisive determinant of positional ascription, but it is questionable whether power can explain why within a given socio-historical setting some positions are given high rewards and not others.

Moore argued that the class system of industrial societies exhibits "fragmentation of even nominally singular statuses into comparable analytical subsystems," and that:

> Tumin's position here is compounded of several empirical errors: (1) a class system "really exists"; (2) it is posited upon only one dominant "phase" of social life, the economic, which is associated with (the cause of?) prestige and power; (3) other worthwhile human endeavors are given something less than their "due" because the economy had "invaded" other institutional areas. Not only does this entail an exaggeration of status comparability in industrial societies, but it leads to a perception of status anxieties more pervasive than any evidence indicates.[10]

Moore's formulation, in turn, would seem to rest on an exaggeration. If no class system "really exists" in industrial society because the "analytical subsystems" are really "incomparable," then it would seem to follow that most theories of stratification, including the Davis and Moore theory, are either irrelevant or inapplicable.

In "On Inequality," his reply to Moore, Melvin Tumin argued that the range of social inequality is much greater than that which is institutionalized in unequal rewards.

> Any of the diverse inequalities found in society can become subject to stratification. These inequalities arise from: (1) role specification; (2) ranking according to characteristics intrinsic to the role; (3) ranking according to moral conformity; (4) ranking according to contribution to (a) value and moral ideals and (b) functionally important tasks; (5) diffusion and transfer. Types (1), (2), and (4), have higher likelihood of being taken up into the stratification system, but none *need* so result. Considerable inequality can therefore coexist with little or no stratification.[11]

Here Tumin's main point represents a harmonious addition to the Davis and Moore theory. Tumin's secondary claim that some types of inequality "seem unavoidable as system features for survival of a society over two generations" is more complex and seems to involve disparate elements. First, Tumin is referring to parent-child, man-woman role differentiations (which Davis has explicitly ruled out as possible bases for stratification). Second, Tumin is referring to the universality of invidious valuations: "Everywhere men tend to make comparisons as to who is taller, or prettier, or quicker" (but need he follow the arbitrary functionalist maneuver of translating a cultural universal into an alleged functional necessity?). Third, Tumin is referring to "ranking by functional contribution," which he divides into two major analytical sub-types: (a) "Ranking according to contribution to or exemplification of ideals"; and (b) "Ranking according to functional contribution to desired social goals." In connection with the latter he says:

> Current theory attaches the greatest significance to differential functional importance as a basis of social stratification. It is argued that every society must make judgments about unequal functional importance and must allocate its scarce and desired goods at least partly in line with such judgments.[12]

As an account of what Davis and Moore claim this is surely in error. Once again, it must be emphatically pointed out that differential functional importance is not the same as the judgments or valuations of a given society. Differential functional importance is, presumably, the degree of contribution which each position makes to the preservation or survival of the society.

In his "Rejoinder" to Tumin, Wilbert E. Moore agreed that social inequality and unequal rewards are definitionally different, but he argued that they are empirically closer than Tumin allows. He questioned Tumin's "extremely relativistic view of cultural values and social institutions," and suggested that there is an underlying pattern of necessary functions:

> As I read the evidence, the evaluation of functionally differentiated positions is by no means as randomly variable as his discussion asserts or implies. I suggest that behavior relevant to the maintenance of order, the

provision of economic support, the protection of the society, and the exemplifications of religious and aesthetic values *always* involves differential positional as well as merely personal valuation.[13]

To say that positions in these general areas involve differential valuation is not very enlightening, since presumably all positions in a given society have some degree of positive or negative valuation. Furthermore, and as is the case with all lists of so-called functional prerequisites, the general areas listed by Moore add up to a fairly standard definition of society. It follows from this that the claim that these positions "always" involve valuation is little more than a tautology.

. . .

In October, 1963, Walter Buckley's "On Equitable Inequality" replied to some of the points raised by Wilbert E. Moore's February, 1963, article. Buckley argued that the Davis-Moore theory involves a "competitive fallacy" because it interprets stratification in all societies in terms of an atypical case: "the competitive-achievement syndrome of contemporary industrial societies." He repeated Tumin's point (granted by Moore) that stratification limits or restricts the development of potential talent. He accused Moore of confusing "inequality" with "inequity" (or with using "inequality" in such a way that the meaning of the term shifts from "objective differences" to "inequity"). He argues that the real task of stratification studies should be to determine the minimum range of unequal rewards compatible with an industrial order. Finally, Buckley pointed out that Moore's claim that a class system does not really exist is an artifact created by an artificially restricted definition of "stratum"; and that to adopt Moore's usage would force us to say that "no known society is or has ever been stratified." [14]

In October, 1963, George A. Huaco's "A Logical Analysis of the Davis-Moore Theory of Stratification" attempted a detailed analysis of the notion of differential functional importance.

> The postulate of unequal functional importance means that for any given society, the performance of some roles contributes more to the preservation of survival of that society than the performance of other roles. For this statement we need an independent definition of survival. We also need criteria to measure how much a given role contributes to survival vis-à-vis any other role. Davis mentions the following examples of such criteria.
>
> "Rough measures of functional importance are in fact applied in practice. In wartime, for example, decisions are made as to which industries and occupations will have priority in capital equipment, labor recruitment, raw materials, etc. In totalitarian countries the same is done in peacetime, as also in underdeveloped areas attempting to maximize their social and economic modernization. Individual firms must constantly decide which positions are essential and which are not." [15]
>
> The difficulties with these examples are twofold:
>
> a. Each of them provides a dichotomous (essential/nonessential) criterion which seems to be tautologically derived from an over-all system goal.

But what we need is criteria that permit us to measure the *degree* of contribution to societal survival of any role vis-à-vis any other role; in short, we need ranking criteria.
b. Each of these examples is drawn from a partially or totally planned economic system, and as such, useless for drawing inferences applicable to unplanned systems (and most societies throughout history have been unplanned).[16]

Huaco examined the two "clues" mentioned in the Davis and Moore 1945 version (role uniqueness, and degree to which other positions are dependent on the one in question). He pointed out that there is absolutely no empirical basis for admitting uniqueness and dependency as indicators of anything beyond themselves. Next he examined a claim made by Davis in both the 1945 and 1948 versions. Davis wrote:

Owing to the universal necessity of certain functions in society, which require social organization for their performance, there is an underlying similarity in the kind of positions put at the top, the kind put at the middle, and the kind put at the bottom of the scale. . . . For this purpose we shall select religion, government, economic activity, and technology.[17]

Huaco remarked that this selection of four "necessary" societal "functions" is not only familiar, but it is also in the right order. And that:

As described by Davis, the selected "functions" roughly correspond to the four analytical levels of a well-known model of society:

Davis	*Marx*
Religion	Upper layer of superstructure
Government	Lower layer of superstructure
Economic Activity	Relations of production
Technology	Forces of production

The sole purpose of this comparison is to suggest that Davis and Moore's "universal" and "necessary" societal "functions" are really the various analytical parts of their implicit model of society, or are derived by a series of hidden tautologies from such an implicit model. The "necessity" involved is clearly analytical or logical necessity. It follows from this that Davis' claim that what he has selected are four "universal" and "necessary" societal "functions" is simply a tautology.[18]

Huaco concluded that differential functional importance is "a complete unknown," and that "it cannot serve as a legitimate explanation for unequal rewards."

In Retrospect

Now let us return to our initial analysis of the logical structure of the Davis and Moore theory to try and sort out those portions which have been destroyed by the critics from the more solid and promising fragments. In the first place, it is fairly obvious that the basic concept of the theory, the postulate of differential functional importance, is a fallacy. There is not a shred of evidence that different positions make different degrees of contribution to societal preservation or survival. In the second place, it is also obvious that the assumption to the effect that societies whose stratification systems approach a pure achievement order have greater survival or endurance than more ascriptive societies is not only unwarranted, but probably false. Nevertheless, the remaining fragments of the theory seem to hold considerable promise.

I. *Unequal rewards attached to different positions are a cause of the mobility of individuals into positions.* Despite the technical issue of possible "alternatives," it now seems fairly certain that this is one of the most solid portions of the theory. Evidence for this is indirect, but impressive, and it comes from the area of experimental psychology known as learning theory. Very briefly, Davis and Moore's comprehensive definition of "rewards" corresponds to the psychological notion of "reinforcement." The notion of "high rewards" corresponds to "positive reinforcement" and "low rewards" to negative reinforcement." Learning theorists have considerable experimental evidence that both animals and humans learn and act in response to the manipulation of positive and negative reinforcements.

II. *The existence and operation of the institution of the family is cause of status ascription.* That the particularistic character of kinship bonds tends to generate status ascription is probably self-evident. It is also evident that the existence of the family is an insufficient or incomplete explanation of ascription. We can set up a conceptual model in which the ascriptive propensities of the family are held in abeyance and in which a sizeable amount of status ascription is nevertheless generated. The Norman conquest of England will do as a point of departure: we know that the Norman conquerors reserved for themselves most high reward positions, and limited the conquered Saxons to low reward positions. We know that both societies had extensive family ascription; but the point is that similar ascriptive results would have followed a similar conquest even if both societies had been completely achievement oriented. The explanation of why the conquering Normans reserved for themselves most high reward positions cannot be found in the Norman family, but must be traced to the conquest itself, that is to say to the phenomenon of power.

III. *Differential scarcity of qualified personnel is a cause of "stratification" (unequal rewards attached to different positions).* Let us modify the statement to read: differential scarcity of qualified personnel is a cause of *the range* of unequal rewards attached to different positions. This interesting notion deserves to be developed beyond its brief formulation by Davis and Moore. It seems that we can posit variation along two different dimensions: on the one hand the positional structure of a given society may have high or low requirements for talent and training, on the other hand the population of the same society may have high or low amounts of effective talent and training. A state of relative differential scarcity of personnel can be said to exist whenever there is a sizeable gap between the amount of effective talent and training available in the population and the amount of talent and training required by the positional structure of the society. We can now set up a fourfold table and examine the various possibilities:

Amount of Talent and Training Required by the
Positional Structure of the Society

		High	Low
Amount of Talent and Training Available in the Population	High	Mature Industrial Society	Pre-Revolutionary Society
	Low	Industrializing Society	Traditional Society

1. *Traditional Society:* Here the amount of talent and training required by the positional structure of the society is low and the amount of effective talent and training available in the population is also low. Here it makes little or no sense to speak of a differential scarcity of personnel; and whatever may be the range of unequal rewards, the scope of this range must be explained in terms of other (as yet unidentified) factors.

2. *Industrializing Society:* Here the amount of talent and training required by the positional structure of the society is high but the amount of effective talent and training available in the population remains low. Here there is a differential scarcity of personnel, and the hypothesis would predict that the range of unequal rewards would tend to increase. Historically speaking, this would seem very much to be the case. The period of early West European industrialization, the nineteenth-century American experience, and the period of Soviet industrialization all seem to exhibit an increased range of unequal rewards.

3. *Mature Industrial Society:* Here the amount of talent and training required by positional structure of the society is high, and the amount of effective talent and training available in the population also tends to become high. With a gradual diminution of differential scarcity of personnel, we can predict that mature industrial societies will exhibit a trend toward a gradual shortening of the range of unequal rewards. Again, the historical evidence seems to support this prediction.

4. *Pre-Revolutionary Society:* Here the amount of talent and training required by the positional structure of the society is relatively low but the amount of effective talent and training available in the population becomes relatively high. Instead of a differential scarcity of personnel we have a differential surplus of personnel. This was the situation of Russia in 1917 with its highly educated and underemployed intelligentsia; and it is also the situation of many colonial societies where the colonial administration fosters the simultaneous education and underemployment of a native intelligentsia.

What remains of the Davis and Moore functionalist theory of stratification? Two decades of controversy seem to have effectively sorted out the metaphysical postulate and questionable assumptions from the more valuable ingredients. These ingredients contain considerable insight, but by themselves they do not add up to a fully adequate theory of social inequality, mobility, and ascription, much less of stratification.

NOTES

1. Dennis H. Wrong, "The Functionalist Theory of Stratification: Some Neglected Considerations," *American Sociological Review*, XXIV (December, 1959), 772.
2. Ibid., pp. 774–778.
3. Melvin M. Tumin, "Competing Status Systems," in Arnold S. Feldman and Wilbert E. Moore, eds., *Labor Commitment and Social Change in Developing Areas* (New York: Social Science Research Council, 1960), p. 279.
4. Melvin M. Tumin with Arnold S. Feldman, *Social Class and Social Change in Puerto Rico* (Princeton, N.J.: Princeton University Press, 1961), p. 491.
5. Ibid., p. 508.
6. Wilbert E. Moore, "But Some Are More Equal than Others," *American Sociological Review*, XXVIII (February, 1963), 14–15.
7. Ibid., p. 15.
8. Ibid., p. 16.
9. Moore, loc. cit.
10. Ibid., p. 17.
11. Melvin M. Tumin, "On Inequality," *American Sociological Review*, XXVIII (February, 1963), 18.
12. Ibid., p. 23.
13. Wilbert E. Moore, "Rejoinder," *American Sociological Review*, XXVIII (February, 1963), 27.
14. Walter Buckley, "On Equitable Inequality," *American Sociological Review*, XXVIII (October, 1963), 800.
15. Davis, "Reply," op. cit., p. 395.
16. George A. Huaco, "A Logical Analysis of the Davis-Moore Theory of Stratification," *American Sociological Review*, XXVIII (October, 1963), 803.
17. Davis, *Human Society*, op. cit., p. 371.
18. Huaco, op. cit., p. 804.

Empirical Assessments

After a couple of decades of ideological debate, Stinchcombe proposed that it was time to assess the functional theory empirically. All theories, he noted, have empirical consequences; their truth or falsity is an empirical question —subject to research—and not an ideological issue. Toward this end, Stinchcombe deduced a number of hypotheses from the functional theory. They were presented as untested, but *testable*, hypotheses that could help to clarify the empirical utility of the theory.

He proposed, for example, that in Western European democracies kings have declined in political importance relative to parliaments. Correspondingly, he argued, the rewards of kings have declined; they have less power, less wealth, and the like. Given their reduced importance, the role requirements to be king also have diminished. This is indicated, for Stinchcombe, by more ascriptive successions to the kingships, with fewer palace revolutions to abolish incompetent kings, fewer contested successions to thrones, and so on.

The changes that Stinchcombe hypothesizes have occurred are amenable to historical study. The wealth of kings, the number of contested successions, and the like, all could be examined historically. The trends could be shown to be either consistent or inconsistent with the hypothesis. However, note that the declining functional importance cannot be measured. Without such clues, it remains conjecture whether changes in the rewards or role requirements of kings are due to changes in their functional importance.

Stinchcombe's clearest statement on this issue is that: "Changes in the nature of role-requirements and of the rewards indicate a shift of functions." [19] Unfortunately, this is clearly a tautology. Changes in rewards and requirements are theoretically assumed to be the *consequences* of changes in functional importance. They cannot, therefore, be utilized to indicate that changes in functional importance have occurred.

His other statement on this matter is based on the observation that kings may continue to have important ceremonial roles even though their political roles are more tangential. Their nonpolitical function probably leads them, "to be less important in the eyes of the people." [20] As we have previously noted, however, consensus is a very problematic indicator of functional importance. People's perceptions of importance, in other words, will not necessarily be closely related to the actual contribution of a position to a society. Thus, the same dilemma persists: How is functional importance to be measured?

Given the general inability, as yet, to measure functional importance directly, some critics have argued that the theory is worthless and should be disregarded. This argument is based, however, on a rather limited conception of science; a conception that emphasizes the "products" of any science to the disregard of its "process." In this regard, Abraham Kaplan differentiates between logic in use and reconstructed logic. The former refers to a cognitive style followed, often implicitly, by people within any discipline. The latter involves explicitly formulated logic and need not be identical to the former. For example, Kaplan points out that Newton and his followers made excellent use of calculus in physics, as logic in use. The reconstructed logic of calculus, involving the satisfactory formulation of its foundations, did not occur until about two hundred years after Newton.[21]

The basic question, Kaplan emphasizes, is not whether the facts *can* be reconstructed later, but whether it will prove to be worthwhile to do so. Is there, in other words, "something to be learned" from it? [22] To impose a

---

[19] Stinchcombe, op. cit., p. 806. By the same author, see also *Constructing Social Theories* (New York: Harcourt, 1968), pp. 80–101.

[20] Ibid. On this point, see also Huaco, loc. cit.

[21] Abraham Kaplan, *The Conduct of Inquiry* (San Francisco: Chandler, 1964), p. 9.

[22] Ibid. See, especially, pp. 268–272.

formal deductive scheme prematurely on logic in use may serve only to inhibit scientific progress. With respect to the functional theory, this means that society can be viewed metaphorically as having its own needs if it proves worthwhile to do so—that is, if the assumption leads to the generation of new insights. It means that a theory that cannot now define functional importance according to a reconstructed logic may nevertheless exemplify valuable logic in use. Thus, what can we see, that might otherwise be overlooked or go unexplained, if we assume that the importance of kings has declined?

Raising this question puts the issue into an empirical arena, one place its usefulness should be contested. An example of such an assessment is presented subsequently. It is a test of Stinchcombe's functional deduction that the relative rewards of military positions should exceed the rewards of civilian positions during times of war. The reverse is expected during times of peace. The reasoning behind the hypothesis is clearly the same as in the decline of kingships or the role of the priesthood.

An Assessment of the Functional Theory of Stratification*

Mark Abrahamson

The Effects of War

The basic hypothesis to be tested in this paper, as presented by Stinchcombe (1963), is that during times of war the rewards of positions with direct bearing on the war effort will rise relative to the rewards of positions that are not directly related to the war effort. The assumption, obviously, is that positions which are more directly involved in the war (for example, army captains, diplomats, etc.) attain greater functional importance than their "civilian counterparts." The effects of relative scarcity are not explicitly considered in the formulation by Stinchcombe.

While scarcity is one part of the functional equation, its effects may be ignored in a test of Stinchcombe's hypothesis because of the type of effect attributed to the independent variables. While not explicit on the matter, the Davis-Moore theory implies more an additive than a multiplicative relationship between the two antecedents. Both functional importance and scarcity are viewed as capable of exerting effects upon reward independently of each other (though it is sometimes implied that a value of zero for either variable will nullify the effects of the other, suggesting a multiplicative relationship).

* Abridged from Mark Abrahamson, "Functionalism and the Functional Theory of Stratification," *American Journal of Sociology*, **78**:1239–1246 (1973).

For the most part, however, the implied emphasis upon an additive relationship permits a separation of the antecedents' effects in a preliminary test such as this.[1]

Both operationally and conceptually, two other problems present obstacles to a direct assessment of Stinchcombe's proposition. The first involves the measurement of "civilian counterparts." The second problem entails the designation of peace and war, particularly over the last 25 years. Each will be discussed in turn.

At a conceptual level, the notion of "civilian counterparts" to military positions is rich in imagery. Operationally, however, virtually any criterion on which military and nonmilitary positions could be matched creates problems of contamination because the criterion could also be serving as a reward. This problem was resolved by selecting a very broad, yet relevant, criterion for matching: occupational prestige.

The prestige of an occupation has been shown to be related to job satisfaction, income, community power, and other potential rewards. If, during times of war, a relative increase in a specific type of reward—such as income —could be demonstrated for the military occupation in a comparison of prestige-matched occupations, it would therefore be particularly supportive of the functional expectation.

Specifically, the notion of civilian counterpart was operationalized in this study by the equivalence of occupational prestige scores in the NORC surveys of 1947 and 1963 (Hodge, Siegel, and Rossi 1966, pp. 322–334). Only three specifically war-related positions are included in the NORC survey: corporal in the regular army, captain in the regular army, and diplomat in the foreign service. All three were included in this study. In both 1947 and 1963 there were three civilian occupations whose prestige scores were virtually identical to the military-involved positions and for which comparable data were obtainable; they are: machine operators in a factory, instructors in the public schools, and college professors. The matched occupations and their prestige scores in 1947 and 1963 are listed in Table 1. Further, the high correlation between occupational ranks in 1925 and 1963 ($r = .93$) also suggests these occupations to have been quite comparable prior to 1947 as well (Hodge et al. 1966, pp. 322–334).

In order to test Stinchcombe's (1963) hypothesis, military-related and

TABLE 1
The Matched Occupations

Occupations	Prestige Score in 1947	Prestige Score in 1963
Corporal in the regular army	60	62
Machine operator in a factory	60	63
Captain in the regular army	80	82
Instructor in the public schools	79	82
Diplomat in the foreign service	92	89
College professor	89	90

nonmilitary-related occupations were compared over 4-year intervals between 1939 and 1967. The absence of data in certain years precluded a year-by-year comparison.

The second methodological problem, the unambiguous operationalization of peace- and wartimes, is made difficult because the recent confrontations of the United States (in Korea and Vietnam) have not been formally defined by Congressional declarations of war. Correspondingly, Cold War tensions and actual military conflicts have peaked and ebbed over the last quarter decade resulting in neither peace nor war as absolute conditions. Military expenditures, as a proportion of the GNP, can be used, however, to indicate the society's leanings toward either peace or war.

Data on the cost of war presented by Russett (1969, pp 28–35) show that military expenditures, as a percentage of GNP, increase during times conventionally defined as wartime, then move back toward the prewar level following the confrontation. They do not shrink all the way back, however, as indicated in Figure 1. Instead, there has been a tendency for military expenditures to increase over the last 20 or 25 years. It is reasonable to project from Russett's (1969) data that defense spending in future times of peace will involve a greater share of GNP than times of war did in the immediate past. No arbitrary percentage of military expenses can therefore be utilized to operationalize war or peace. However, the economy's leaning in one or the other direction can be designated by up- or downswings in military expenditures. The substitution of war or peace orientations for the actual conditions does not violate Stinchcombe's reasoning and it more accurately reflects the Cold War situation of the past 25 years.

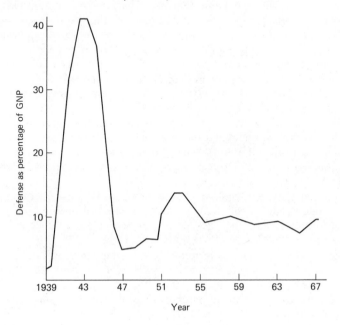

Figure 1

Examination of Figure 1 shows a dramatic increase in the percentage of military spending beginning in 1941 and peaking in 1943 and 1944 (World War II); a less marked increase beginning in 1950 and peaking in 1952 and 1953 (Korea); and a still less marked increase beginning in 1965 and peaking in 1967 and 1968 (Vietnam). By observation it is clear that each succeeding confrontation is more of an orientation toward, than an actual condition of, war.

The three periods of increasing military expenditures define the intervals to be considered wartimes (in orientation). More specifically, as previously discussed, the incomes of occupations are compared over 4-year intervals beginning in 1939 and continuing until 1967. As indicated in Table 2, three of these intervals correspond to periods of increased defense spending and so will be identified as wartime in this analysis.

TABLE 2
**Changes in Proportions of Defense Spending
by Four-Year Intervals, 1939–1967**

Change from 1939–1943	*Change from 1943–1947*	*Change from 1947–1951*	*Change from 1951–1955*	*Change from 1955–1959*	*Change from 1959–1963*	*Change from 1963–1967*
+39%	−37%	+06%	−01%	0%	−01%	+02%

Thus, 1943 (World War II), 1951 (Korea), and 1967 (Vietnam) will designate war intervals. The remaining intervals—characterized by constant or declining percentages of military expenditures—will designate peacetime.

Assessment of the relative gains of occupations began by computing the average (mean) increase in income of each occupation across all time intervals. The average percentage increase of an occupation was then compared to the overall increase of the other occupation in the matched pair. This comparison yielded an expected value; an indication of how the occupations would be expected to do vis-à-vis each other, in general.

In each interval the actual or observed difference between matched occupations was then subtracted from the expected difference. When the resultant value is positive it indicates that the military occupation gained relative to the nonmilitary occupation. Correspondingly, negative values indicate relative gain for the nonmilitary occupation.

In the comparison of diplomats and college professors, for example, the raw salary figures are as follows[2] for diplomats and professors, respectively: 1951, $8,085 and $5,106; 1955, $8,864 and $6,564; 1959, $10,038 and $8,046; 1963, $12,159 and $9,593; 1967, $15,390 and $11,033.

These figures are then converted into percentage increases as follows for diplomats and professors, respectively: 1951–1955, .09 and .22; 1955–1959, .12 and .18; 1959–1963, .17 and .16; 1963–1967, .21 and .13.

Subtracting the percentage increases of professors from diplomats yields the following figures: −.13, −.06, +.01, +.08. The average is −.025 (−.10/4).

The final step is to compare the actual relationship in each interval to the expected (or average). In 1955, for example, professors did .13 better than diplomats. They were expected to do .025 better. Thus, diplomats show a converted percentage value of −10.5 (vis-à-vis professors) in 1955.

It is the direction (positive or negative) of the difference rather than the magnitude that is critical in each comparison. Positive values always indicate relative gain for the military occupation, but to interpret magnitudes would require inferences of variations in relative functional importance and such inferences are beyond the scope of this paper.

The hypothesis is supported if positive values predominate during war intervals (identified as: 1943, World War II; 1951, Korea; and 1967, Vietnam) and negative values predominate during "peace" intervals (1947, 1955, 1959, 1963). The results are presented in Table 3.

In comparing the relative gains and losses of the matched occupations, I found that the data conform to the functional hypothesis that the income of military related positions will rise relative to nonmilitary positions during times of war and decline during times of peace. Differences are in the expected direction in 11 of the 12 compared intervals. (The sole exception is during 1963 when ambassadors rose vis-à-vis college professors. However, while U.S. forces were not yet engaged directly in the Vietnam war they were "on the brink" and there was an increase in diplomatic activity which may account for the relative gain of ambassadors.) Following the binomial distribution, the chance probability of the military gaining during all wartime observations— indicated by a plus in the table—is $P = .031$. Conversely, the chance probability of the nonmilitary gaining in all but one peacetime observation is $P = .054$.

Summary and Conclusions

The discussion of functional theories presented in this paper has viewed a priori assumptions of functional prerequisites as serving to inhibit the generation of empirically testable hypotheses. Treating the Davis-Moore theory as oriented toward variations in reward rather than oriented toward the constancy of need for differential reward clarified the relevance of Stinchcombe's (1963) derivation. The data supported the functional hypothesis that the financial rewards of military-related positions rise relative to those of nonmilitary-related positions during war-oriented times. During peace-oriented times, relative gains are reversed.

Though his discussion of Stinchcombe substantially predates this study, Huaco (1970, pp. 411–428) anticipated the possibility of similar findings with skepticism. The coordination of positions during times of war, he proposes, creates "unusual" (that is, nongeneralizable) social system conditions. Huaco is apparently assuming that: (1) times of war are rare statistically, which they are not (Parsons 1971), and/or (2) relationships which hold during times of war do not hold during times of peace. This latter objection may be true in some cases; however, it is questionable as a general theoretical statement (Coser 1956), and it is not consistent with the findings of this study.

TABLE 3

Relative Income Gains during Peace and War

Occupations	Years							
	1939	1943 (WW II)	1947	1951 (Korea)	1955	1959	1963	1967 (Vietnam)
Corporal* Factory worker†	—	—	—	+ 4	—15	—4	—10	+33
Captain* Public school instructor‡	—	+5	—17	+11	—	—	—	—
Diplomat§ College professor‡	—	—	—	—	—10.5	—3.5	+ 3.5	+10.5

Note: Ratio computed for all intervals in which data for both occupations were available. Thus, data for both corporals and factory workers went back only to 1947; for captains and instructors it began in 1939 but did not continue to 1955; data for diplomats and professors began in 1951.

* Taken each year, as indicated, from World Almanac and Book of Facts.
† Data for production workers (motor vehicles and equipment) from U.S., Department of Labor, Bureau of Labor Statistics (1968).
‡ Data for public school teachers, taken from Statistical History of the U.S.
§ Taken each year, as indicated, from U.S., Bureau of the Budget, data for Foreign Service Officers, Grade 1.

More generally, but tentatively, the findings of this study suggest that the functional theory of stratification, as well as other functional theories, may provide a fruitful source of empirically testable hypotheses. There are a number of additional questions inherent to such theories, however, which deserve high priority in future assessments. Among the foremost of these are questions of: the empirical connotation of inferred differences in functional importance; whether relative scarcity contributes as much explained variance in reward as does functional importance (Lopreato and Lewis 1963, pp. 312–320); and whether psychic rewards operate as "functional equivalents" to material rewards (Wesolowski 1966, pp. 64–69).

NOTES

1. In addition, the field of military eligibles is substantially increased during wartimes by enlarged conscriptions, by relaxing of eligibility requirements, and the like. This may have the effect of lowering the scarcity of persons available for military-related positions in comparison to nonmilitary positions. If so, the effects of relative scarcity would operate against confirmation of the hypothesis.
2. These figures involve direct salaries only. With every increase in the salary of corporals and captains, for example, there was an increase in extra benefits, such as housing allowances. However, these increases are difficult to convert into cash values that are comparable to the fringe benefits in civilian occupations.

REFERENCES

Aberle, D. F. 1950. "Shared Values in Complex Societies." *American Sociological Review* **15** (August): 495–502.

Abrahamson, M. 1972. "On the Structural-Functional Theory of Development." In *Social Development,* edited by M. Stanley. New York: Basic.

Barber, B. 1956. "Structural-Functional Analysis." *American Sociological Review* **21** (April): 131–138.

Buckley, W. 1957. "Structural-Functional Analysis in Modern Society." In *Modern Sociological Theory in Continuity and Change,* edited by H. Becker and A. Boskoff. New York: Holt, Rinehart & Winston.

Coser, L. 1956. *The Functions of Social Conflict.* New York: Free Press.

Dahrendorf, R. 1959. *Class and Class Conflict in Industrial Society.* Stanford, Calif.: Stanford University Press.

Davis, K. 1937. "The Sociology of Prostitution." *American Sociological Review* **2** (December): 744–755.

——. 1953. "Reply to Tumin." *American Sociological Review* **18** (August): 394–397.

——. 1959. "The Myths of Functional Analysis as a Special Method in Sociology and Anthropology." *American Sociological Review* **24** (December): 757–773.

——. 1971. "Sexual Behavior." In *Contemporary Social Problems,* edited by R. K. Merton and R. Nisbet. New York: Harcourt Brace Jovanovich.

Davis, K., and W. Moore. 1945. "Some Principles of Stratification." *American Sociological Review* **10** (April): 242—249.

Gouldner, A. W. 1960. "The Norm of Reciprocity." *American Sociological Review* **25** (April): 161–178.

——. 1970. *The Coming Crises of Western Sociology.* New York: Basic.

Hodge, R. W., P. M. Siegel, and P. H. Rossi. 1966. "Occupational Prestige in the United States: 1925–1963." In *Class, Status and Power,* edited by R. Bendix and S. M. Lipset. New York: Free Press.

Huaco, G. A. 1970. "The Functionalist Theory of Stratification." In *Readings on Social Stratification,* edited by M. Tumin. Englewood Cliffs, N.J.: Prentice-Hall.

Levy, M. J. 1952. *The Structure of Society.* Princeton, N.J.: Princeton University Press.

Lopreato, J., and L. S. Lewis. 1963. "An Analysis of Variables in the Functional Theory of Stratification." *Sociological Quarterly* (1963), pp. 312–320.

Martindale, D. 1960. *The Nature and Types of Sociological Theory.* Boston: Houghton-Mifflin.

————. 1965. "Limits and Alternatives to Functionalism in Sociology." In *Functionalism in the Social Sciences,* edited by D. Martindale. Philadelphia: American Academy of Political and Social Science.

Parsons, T. 1971. *The System of Modern Societies.* Englewood Cliffs, N.J.: Prentice-Hall.

Rex, J. 1961. *Key Problems of Sociological Theory.* London: Routledge & Kegan Paul.

Russett, B. 1969. "The Price of War." *Trans-action* **6** (October): 28–35.

Statistical History of the U.S. 1965. Stamford, Conn.: Fairfield.

Stinchcombe, A. L. 1963. "Some Empirical Consequences of the Davis-Moore Theory of Stratification." *American Sociological Review* **28** (October): 805–880.

Tumin, M. 1953. "Some Principles of Stratification." *American Sociological Review* **18** (August): 387–393.

U.S., Bureau of the Budget. *Budget of the United States.* 1939–1967. Washington, D.C.: Government Printing Office.

U.S., Department of Labor, Bureau of Labor Statistics. 1968. *Employment and Earning Statistics for the U.S., 1909–1968.* Bull. no. 1312–6. Washington, D.C.: Government Printing Office.

Wesolowski, W. 1966. "Some Notes on the Functional Theory of Stratification." In *Class, Status, and Power,* edited by R. Bendix and S. M. Lipset. New York: Free Press.

Whitaker, I. 1965. "The Nature and Value of Functionalism in Sociology." In *Functionalism in the Social Sciences,* edited by D. Martindale, Philadelphia: American Academy of Political and Social Science.

World Almanac and Book of Facts. 1939, 1943, 1947, 1951, 1955, 1959, 1963, 1967. s.v. "Pay Scale of the Armed Services."

It should be apparent that this one assessment cannot provide a definitive test of the functional theory. Indeed, critics have suggested that the assessment indicates the blindness of the functional theory to questions of power, and that the data could be reinterpreted so as to be inconsistent with the theory. The rejoinder, of course, denies the charges and presents further support for the theory.[23]

For the student or scholar who wants definitive answers, this continuing debate can be very frustrating. However, there are some clear signs of progress. At least the functional assumptions are being used to deduce hypotheses that are being examined empirically. In this manner it may be possible yet to answer the question: What is gained, sociologically, by following the functional theory? At this same time, of course, similar questions are being raised about other theoretical perspectives, notably the conflict theory. In the following section we will compare the two directly.

Functional and Conflict Perspectives Compared

Basically, the functional interpretation views stratification as an unconsciously evolved device insuring that the most important positions in society

[23] See Marvin D. Leavy, "Comment on Abrahamson's 'Functionalism and the Functional Theory of Stratification,'" and Beth Vanfossen and Robert Rhodes, "A Critique of Abrahamson's Assessment," in *American Journal of Sociology,* 80:724–732 (1974). In the same issue, see Mark Abrahamson, "In Defense of the Assessment," pp. 732–738.

will be filled by the most capable individuals. The foundation of the functional argument is the premise that the unequal distribution of scarce benefits and rewards serves to motivate individuals to cultivate the talent and obtain the training required by positions that make important contributions to the coordination, integration, and cohesion of society and, further, to motivate individuals to perform the duties and roles encumbent on them by virtue of their position in society. Thus, the amount and composition of rewards attached to a position reflect the importance of the position for the maintenance of society.

In contrast, the conflict interpretation views the structure of social inequality as arising from group competition, conflict, and coercion. According to this perspective, the unequal distribution of rewards and scarce benefits reflect the interests and values of powerful groups rather than fundamental societal needs. These powerful groups utilize their greater access to rewards to justify the status quo and to perpetuate social inequalities across generations through such processes as inheritance. The functional interpretation emphasizes the part played by unequal rewards in motivating individuals to occupy and perform the behaviors attendant to important positions in society, whereas the conflict interpretation emphasizes the way in which differential access to scarce benefits gives rise to distinct social classes that inhibit the discovery of talents and abilities possessed by a large segment of the population. Consequently, social stratification, although recognized to be universal, is seen as detrimental to a society's well-being and especially detrimental to those members whose talents and abilities go unrecognized or are otherwise thwarted by the existing structure of inequality.

The controversy between these two interpretations of stratification has age-old philosophical traditions. Lenski has noted several fundamental disagreements between what he labels conservative (that is, functional) and radical (that is, conflict) perspectives.[24] The first and certainly one of the most basic disagreements is their conception of the *nature of man*. The radical perspective maintains that man is inherently good but is corrupted by social institutions, whereas the conservative perspective maintains that social institutions are necessary to restrain one evil inherent in human nature. This difference leads to a second one concerning the *nature of society*. Conservatives traditionally have maintained that the needs of individuals can be met only if the needs of society are met, whereas radicals have viewed society as the arena of conflict between individuals and groups wherein the structure of social institutions determines the outcome. (This tenet of radical perspective is particularly clear in Marx's work, in which he argues that class

[24] Gerhard E. Lenski, *Power and Privilege: A Theory of Social Stratification* (New York: McGraw-Hill, 1966).

conflicts are determined by relationships to the institutionalized means of production.)

Conservatives and radicals also differ on their explanations of the origins, persistence, and consequences of social inequality. Radicals, particularly those in the egalitarian tradition, have argued that inequality is not inevitable but rather that coercion is the "chief factor undergirding and maintaining private property, slavery, and other institutions which give rise to unequal rights and privileges.[25] The radical perspective also traditionally has argued that the state and the law support the interest of the ruling class and, as such, are instruments for the oppression of the lower classes. Furthermore, according to the radical perspective, inequality and the coercion that it involves are the principal sources of conflict within society.

In contrast, the conservative perspective traditionally has minimized the importance of coercion, maintaining instead that social inequality is inevitable and based on innate differences between individuals. Furthermore, rights and privileges are just and appropriate rewards for hard work and ability, and the role of the state and the legal system has been to promote the common good—not just the interests of the privileged few. Lenski concludes that "The only belief common to all conservatives has been their belief that the existing system of distribution was basically just; the only belief common to all radicals has been their belief that it was basically unjust." [26]

Toward a Synthesis of Functional and Conflict Perspectives

The radical and conservative perspectives generally have been regarded as mutually exclusive and antithetical. However, prompted in large part by the Davis and Moore paper and the debate that followed, several efforts have been made at noting compatibilities and points of convergence between the functional and conflict interpretations of social stratification.

One of the most important of these efforts has been Lenski's study of *Power and Privilege,* in which he extracted basic propositions from each perspective and utilized them to deduce two "laws of distribution." The propositions follow:

1. Survival and the satisfaction of basic needs and human desires require cooperation among individuals and groups.
2. Man is basically selfish; when forced to choose, he will act in accor-

25 Ibid., p. 23.
26 Ibid., p. 29.

dance with his own interests even if his actions are detrimental to the interests and well-being of other individuals.

3. The supply of goods and services is always scarce relative to the demands of human needs and insatiable desires.
4. Conflict will occur between individuals and groups for the control of goods and services beyond those required for subsistence.
5. The outcome of the conflict and, hence, the control of surplus goods and services are determined by the power of the conflicting parties.

Lenski states the two laws of distribution deduced from these propositions:

> *First Law of Distribution*: "Men will share the product of their labors to the extent required to insure the survival and continued productivity of those members whose actions are necessary or beneficial to themselves."
>
> *Second Law of Distribution*: "Power will determine the distribution of nearly all of the surplus possessed by a society." [27]

Lenski goes on to argue that privilege is "possession or control of a portion of the surplus produced by society," [28] which is determined, to a large extent, by power.

The two laws of distribution suggest two testable hypotheses: (1) in societies characterized by a subsistence standard of living, there will be little if any inequality because goods and services will be distributed primarily on the basis of need; and (2) as the size of the surplus of goods and services increases, societies will be characterized by increasing inequality of privilege because an increasing proportion of the surplus will be distributed to groups and individuals on the basis of their power.

Although the productive capacity of a society is a consequence of a number of variables—including environment—clearly the single most important factor is level of technological development. Accordingly, to test his hypotheses, Lenski analyzed the distributive systems and the inequality of societies at different levels of technological development, ranging from simple hunting and gathering societies with a subsistence economy to contemporary industrial societies with their bountiful surplus.

In hunting and gathering societies, technology limits the production of goods and services to that required for survival. In such societies, Lenski noted a virtual absence of inequality. However, beginning with simple horticultural societies, which are characterized by a level of technology sufficient to permit the production of a modest surplus, the size of the surplus increases

---

[27] Ibid., p. 44.
[28] Ibid., p. 45.

at a rapid rate corresponding to the technological advances that characterize advanced horticultural, agrarian, and industrial societies. Lenski provides an impressive array of evidence to support his hypotheses in the case of hunting and gathering, simple and advanced horticultural, and agrarian types of societies. In these societies, as technology advances and yields larger surpluses, the extent of inequality increases and the stratification system becomes increasingly more rigid and increasingly based on power and the second law of distribution. However, the predicted relationship between size of surplus and extent of inequality is not supported in the advanced industrial type of society. As Lenski wrote: "The appearance of mature industrial societies marks the first significant reversal in the age-old trend toward ever increasing inequality." [29]

Lenski offers a number of explanations to account for the greater equality in industrial societies than predicted by the second law of distribution. One explanation stresses knowledge and technical expertise as important sources of power in industrial societies. He wrote:

> Because of the great functional utility of so much of the new knowledge, a host of occupational specialists have appeared who are not interchangeable to any great degree. This introduces into the labor market certain rigidities which favor the sellers of labor, especially in an era in which demand for technical skills is rapidly rising.[30]

It is not surprising that Lenski's efforts at synthesizing the conflict and functional interpretations have been extended by other authors. Nor is it surprising that Lenski's conclusion, that in industrial societies knowledge is power, has been an important point for the continuing comparison and synthesis of functional and conflict perspectives.

[29] Ibid., p. 308.
[30] Ibid., p. 316.

Part Three

Empirical Perspectives

5 The Empirical Origins of Stratification Theory: Studies of the Traditional American Community

In the preceding chapters we reviewed some diverse and competing perspectives on stratification. Characteristic of the development of some of these perspectives was the tendency to rely on intuition rather than systematically obtained empirical data. Thus, we often describe these perspectives as armchair theories. The image conveyed by this label is that of a social scientist perched in a comfortable chair beside a fireplace, surrounded by dusty books and papers thinking profound thoughts about the nature of social reality. The stereotype suggests a non empirical approach, leading to generalizations based on speculation rather than observation.

In reality, however, some kinds of data were probably always used as a basis for generalization. These included the theorist's own experiences as an actor in various environments, his responses to these experiences, and reflection about why they occurred. In addition, almost all of these men were perceptive observers of what was occurring in their social contexts. Furthermore, they relied on observations made by others before them.

These perspectives, then, had some empirical basis. The earlier theories could not, and our contemporary theories cannot, therefore, be differentially assessed simply because there are or are not data to support the underlying assumptions. The question is rather: How *systematically* were the data obtained? The nineteenth-century varieties of social science may be seen from this perspective as contributing theories whose content and emphasis were highly influenced by the unique life-experiences of the individual theorists. Even though more contemporary theories continue to be influenced by the same kinds of personal experiences, a greater reliance on systematically obtained data helps to reduce the influence of personal biases and to make assessments more empirical, more impersonal and, as a result, more objective.

Even when data are systematically obtained, however, there is a basic difference in the degree to which these data are explicitly used to test formal hypotheses. During the early part of the twentieth century, sociologists systematically collected a voluminous amount of data. These observations were typically used to describe, in a very deliberate way, some specific segment of the activities in a given society. Sometimes they were used also to defend a particular point of view. Only infrequently were data utilized to enable the explicit testing of a hypothesis. As a prevalent practice, the formalization of procedures involving an intense and reciprocal relation between theory and systematic data is a much more recent phenomenon.

In this chapter we briefly trace the development of systematic studies of stratification in the United States. This entails an initial focus on the ecological approach primarily associated with sociologists at the University of Chicago. Although these studies were not concerned primarily with stratification, they provided the backdrop from which later studies of stratification emerged. To present this historical perspective accurately also necessitates an initial concern with largely descriptive studies to be followed by an examination of explicit assumptions and the critical testing of hypotheses.

The Chicago School of Ecology

The classical pioneers of American sociology were active during the latter part of the nineteenth and the first two decades of the twentieth centuries. Although the greatest impact of their ideas was felt later, they did influence the work of sociologists at the University of Chicago who came to dominate American sociology particularly during the 1920s and 1930s. Chicago's reign over American sociology was expressed in several ways: by establishing and publishing the most prominent sociology journal of that period; by training more sociologists and awarding more graduate degrees in sociology than all other departments combined, thereby providing Chicago-trained faculty for other emerging departments; and by fostering empirical approaches, including the ecological approach, which influenced the direction of sociological research regardless of the original training of sociologists elsewhere.

The early school of human ecology, as one of a number of contributions, grew out of the work of Robert Park, Ernest Burgess, Roderick D. McKenzie, and their students.[1] A basic assumption of this ecological view was that within a society men are highly interdependent. The key variable differentiating groups of men from one another is their accessibility to various human and material resources. And variations in accessibility are conceptualized in terms of space and distance.

Much of the analysis was analogous to the studies of lower plant and animal life conducted by biological ecologists. Thus, areas of a city were viewed as subject to the same processess of invasion and succession as a natural ecological community. The turbulence of life in developing cities, like Chicago in the 1920s, made notions analogous to an evolutionary struggle for survival seem meaningful.[2] Much of early human ecology was in fact considered biosocial, as opposed to purely sociological.

Substantively, a major thrust of this early school involved a description and analysis of spatial relations in American cities. The concentric zone theory of urban growth and development offered by Park and Burgess is probably the best known of these works, and it provides a good illustration of the application of this perspective.[3] Park and Burgess viewed the downtown business district as the center of any city, the *nucleus*. Unless the topography of the city prevented it, urban growth was viewed as the adding of successive circles moving out of the central business district, which was called zone 1. Zone 2 was called transitional, involving both businesses and private dwellings. In succeeding zones land use became increasingly specialized and, because it was more desirable, competition became intensified. Within each of the zones, the inhabitants were exposed to similar social circumstances and were relatively alike in many respects. The transitional zone, for example, had the "down-and-outers." The next zone contained recent European immigrants. In the series of rings moving out toward the suburbs, the number of recent immigrants declined while the quality of homes and the relative affluence of the inhabitants increased. Although there was some variation within each zone, there appeared to be greater similarity within than between zones in the residents' social characteristics and life-styles.

Deviance, social disorganization, and crime were also prominent

[1] See Robert E. L. Faris, *Chicago Sociology 1920–1932* (San Francisco: Chandler, 1967).

[2] See the Introduction by Amos Hawley in *Roderick D. McKenzie on Human Ecology* (Chicago: U. of Chicago, 1968).

[3] Ernest W. Burgess, "Introduction to a Research Project," *Proceedings of the American Sociological Society,* **18**:85–89 (1923).

focuses of the early Chicago school.[4] There were probably several reasons for this interest. To begin with there was widespread antiurban sentiment throughout the United States, especially in the Middle West. Suicide, mental illness, crime, and the like were all viewed as distinctly urban phenomena that could not be ignored by these early students of cities.[5] In fact, they were particularly sensitive to them after finding variations in rates associated with various zones. Finally, there was a general *action orientation* associated with the perspectives of these sociologists that made deviance and disorganization likely interests. Park and Burgess, for example, were consultants to various city agencies, and McKenzie prepared numerous reports for governmental commissions. Thus, they stimulated a multitude of studies ranging from concern with juvenile delinquency and prostitution to mental illness and racial discrimination; and they chronicled the activities of drug peddlers and confidence men and such now rarely heard of "operators" as jack rollers and taxidancers. All of these were studied in the context of their distributions in space throughout the various areas of cities.

In sum, the focus of the Chicago school was primarily on spatial or ecological relations and secondarily on substantive concerns including social disorganization and deviant behavior. Although social stratification per se was not a major interest, at least an implicit view of stratification as an ecological phenomenon did grow out of analyses of the characteristics of residents in various zones. A particularly interesting example was E. Franklin Frazier's analysis of the distribution of black families in the city of Chicago.[6]

Frazier's original assumption was that the process of selection and segregation characterizing the spatial distribution of the black community as urban areas expanded were a microcosm of processes in the community at large. He began by describing the spatial distribution of blacks, which in Chicago involved a point of origin just south of the Loop (12th Street) and which continued south (to 71st Street); an area approximately six miles long and one mile wide.

In zone 1, Frazier found the highest percentage of Southern-born family heads, the highest rate of illiteracy, and the lowest per cent of the population in professional or white-collar occupations. These characteristics of residents

---

[4] See for example, Frederick M. Thrasher, *The Gang* (Chicago: U. of Chicago, 1927); Harvey W. Zorbaugh, *The Gold Coast* (Chicago: U. of Chicago, 1929); Clifford R. Shaw et al., *Delinquency Areas* (Chicago: U. of Chicago Press, 1929); and Robert E. L. Faris and H. Warren Dunham, *Mental Disorders in Urban Areas* (Chicago: U. of Chicago, 1929).

[5] Morton White and Lucia White, *The Intellectual Verses the City* (New York: Mentor, 1964).

[6] E. Franklin Frazier, "*The Negro Family in Chicago,*" (Ph.D. diss., University of Chicago, 1931). It was published under the same title by U. of Chicago, 1932. A revised paper, with the same title, appears in Ernest W. Burgess and Donald J. Bogue, eds., *Urban Sociology* (Chicago: U. of Chicago, 1964).

varied rather consistently by zone, and in zone 7 there is the lowest rate of Southern-born family heads, the lowest rate of illiteracy, and the highest percentage of blacks in professional and white-collar occupations. Generally speaking, therefore, the poorer newcomers to the city were concentrated in zones adjacent to the center, and increasing assimilation to the city and increasing wealth and prestige were associated with a movement outward.

In order to assess the generality of his findings, Frazier subsequently analyzed the population distribution in Negro Harlem during the early 1930s. One obvious difference was initially observed in the form of the expansion process. In Chicago, the black population had expanded initially out from the center along major thoroughfares that cut across a number of concentric zones. In Harlem, by contrast, the population expanded from the center of the black community in all directions. It resulted in a distribution resembling a *self-contained city* with five concentric zones emanating from a center to the periphery. Historically, as business and manufacturing structures declined in each zone, there was a succession of black families into the zone. Despite differences in the nature of the zones, however, Frazier was able to show changes in population characteristics in each zone that were consistent with Chicago's pattern.

Studies such as Frazier's necessarily involved the very considerations that would be crucial to the study of stratification; but they were treated in a very different manner. There was typically little concern with the importance of social position per se, for example, or with how social positions were related to other aspects of social organization. In looking back at his research thirty years later, Frazier viewed it as a contribution to the study or urban growth. However, he realized very well the limitations of an ecological approach. Such studies fail, he contends, "to show the social stratification of the community which would provide the most important frame of reference for studying . . . social changes. . . ." [7]

The Social Anthropologists

Beginning during the 1920s, simultaneously with the ecological analyses, were a number of social anthropological studies of American communities. Like the ecological studies they involved highly detailed empirical investigations, but unlike the ecological, they were primarily concerned with questions of social organization. Also unlike the ecological studies, they focused extensively on stratification as an aspect of social organization.

One of the pioneering studies of American communities was the study of a small city in Indiana, given the pseudonym Middletown, by Robert and

[7] Frazier, in Burgess and Bogue, ibid., p. 238.

Helen Lynd.[8] In their attempt to study a typical small American city, the Lynds and their associates did examine the spatial distribution of the town's social classes, and they did note examples of succession in the expansion of Middletown. More important, however, their analysis helped to set a precedent for ensuing studies by focusing on stratification apart from ecological relationships.

Because they sensed fairly soon that the nature of work had great implications on all spheres of life, the initial focus of the Lynd's study was on work in Middletown. Workaday life in Middletown, at first appearance, included an apparently haphazard assortment of specific activities. A second, and closer look, however, suggested to the Lynds that there were two basic types of activities associated with what appeared to be two categories, or classes, of people based on their connection with work: a working class and a business class. They categorized about 30 per cent of Middletown's work force as business class and the remaining 70 per cent as working class. What characterized the business class in their daily routine was their intense involvement with people. In their occupational roles they sold, promoted, and managed. Those in the working class, by contrast, were primarily oriented to things, such as machines and tools, rather than people. In making this same distinction in more recent studies, sociologists have used other labels, such as manual and nonmanual, blue collar and white collar. However, the essential distinction remains the same.

In addition to their broad observations the Lynds proceeded to examine a number of specific *correlates* of class. They observed that members of the working class, in contrast to the business class, were less educated, were more likely to have been raised on farms, had less money, and had a higher percentage of working wives. The Lynds painted a picture of a more generally difficult day-to-day struggle for existence in the working class.

Interestingly, they suggested that innate capacities were, in part, responsible for some of these class differences, primary evidence for this assertion being based on a comparison of intelligence-test scores for working- and business-class children. About one-fourth of the children of business-class parents were described as having "superior" intelligence (that is an IQ of more than 110) in comparison to only 6 per cent of the working class children. At the other extreme, they found that more than 40 per cent of the working-class children were "below normal" as compared to 13 per cent of the business-class children.

These basic differences in capacity, they concluded, are related to differences in all other aspects of life, such as the quality of child rearing,

[8] Robert S. Lynd and Helen M. Lynd, *Middletown* (New York: Harcourt, 1929). See, also, Robert S. Lynd and Helen M. Lynd, *Middletown in Transition: A Study in Cultural Conflicts* (New York: Harcourt, 1937).

home making, and community participation. The Lynds did recognize that intelligence, as measured, was a product of the interplay between both genetics and environment but they emphasized the genetic component more than would more contemporary sociologists.[9]

In analyzing the correlates and consequences of work, the Lynds emphasized what they termed, "the long arm of the job." In family life, leisure activities, community affairs, and politics, various features of a person's job exerted important constraints on the roles played in these other contexts. "As one prowls Middletown streets about six o'clock on a winter morning," they observed, "one notes two kinds of homes: the dark ones where people still sleep, and the ones with a light in the kitchen where the adults of the household may be seen moving about, starting the business of the day." [10] It is almost exclusively the working class who are awake, and the business class who are still sleeping.

In a variety of both obvious and subtle ways, these differences in the rhythm of daily routine created class differences. For example, one prominent citizen proposed that the solution to the generation-gap problems of their time was to make breakfast "a time of leisurely family reunion." He just did not realize, the Lynds point out, that this solution could not work in as many as two-thirds of Middletown's families where fathers were at work an hour or two before the children were awake. There were also direct conflicts that emerged from similar class-linked phenomena. In the spring of 1925, for example, there were heated debates about changing the clocks to daylight saving time (DST). The business class urged moving clocks back to provide an additional daylight hour for golf and to make Middletown's time more congruent with that of eastern enterprises, for business reasons. The working class, by contrast, supported DST because of the summer heat. By moving the clocks up, they would get an extra hour of cooler early morning sleep before going to work. "Each group," the Lynds report, "thought the other unreasonable." [11]

PLAINVILLE, USA. Beginning shortly after 1850 and continuing most dramatically until about 1950, there was a very rapid increase in urbanization in the United States, if urbanization is viewed as the per cent of a country's population living in urban areas.[12] As might be expected, there was a great

---

[9] For a review of studies on genetics and social class, see I. I. Gottesman, "Biogenetics of Race and Class," in *Social Class, Race and Psychological Development*, Martin Deutsch, et al., eds. (New York: Holt, 1968).

[10] Lynd and Lynd, *Middletown*, op. cit., p. 53.

[11] Ibid., p. 71.

[12] Until 1850, only 15 per cent of the population of the United States lived in urban areas. This figure reached 40 per cent by 1900 and 64 per cent by 1950. The *rate* of increase has declined since. See Murray Gendell and Hans Zetterberg, *A Statistical Almanac of the United States* (New York: Scribners, 1964), Table 9.12.

public interest in this process, and as a corollary this general interest was reflected in numerous sociological studies of urbanization and its conse- quences. The ecological investigations of urban growth previously described here are a clear example of this increased interest. The study of Middletown also reflected increased concern with the change from rural to urban living, as did the Yankee City studies with which we will deal subsequently. Socio- logical research was focused less often on stratification in rural areas. One of the most notable exceptions to this general trend was a study in rural Missouri conducted between 1939 and 1941 by a social anthropologist who used the pseudonym of James West.[13] West called this community Plainville.

West observed that a sizeable number of the citizens of Plainville denied the existence of social classes in their community. They often claimed, "This is *one* place where everybody is equal. You don't find no classes here." [14] However, West's observations led him to believe that Plainville's classes created a "superorganization" or *masterpattern* that, in reality, accorded a relative social ranking to every person, every family, and every association in the community. He offered two kinds of support for his inference: (1) in daily life people seemed to behave as though they knew the "rules" of Plainville's stratification system, and (2) the "thinking" persons in the middle class described a class system that (apparently) coincided with West's own observations.

West proposed a basic division of Plainville society into two social classes. In this respect, it was similar to the Lynds', even though the social correlates of the classes were different, reflecting Plainville's rural nature. However, West—more than the Lynds—further subdivided the two classes into subclasses.

The basic division was into an "average, self-respecting, and refined" class and a "lower" class. This higher group included one special subcat- egory, the "upper crust," whereas the lower ranked class had two additional subcategories, a "lower" element and "people who lived like animals." The five groupings of persons that resulted were briefly characterized by West as follows: (1) the upper crust, small in number, they "set the tone for the society" (most persons in this category would actually deny membership in it, but they are seen by others as "people who stand out"); (2) The average, self-respecting people, the greatest in number, who provide the "backbone" of the community; (3) the good lower class, the next largest in size, which includes those who most closely resemble the class above in am- bition and morals; (4) the lower element, a smaller group with still fewer of the preceding qualities; and (5) the people who live like animals, a still

13 James West, *Plainville, U.S.A.* (New York: Columbia U.P., 1945).
14 Ibid., p. 25.

smaller group who, as the label implies, cannot be judged by the "conventional standards of responsible people."

The people in West's upper class (1 and 2 here) tended to be "prairie" people, whereas those in the lower class tended to be "hill" people, and many of the class distinctions followed from this difference. Most of the prairie land was better suited to farming, especially with modern technology. As a result, the prairie farmers used more modern machinery, which was related to higher status. They also tended to be wealthier, which reinforced their higher standing. Thus, according to West, the "most visible and obvious criterion of class status happens to be geographical." [15] A more recently developed criterion was family lineage, which divided Plainville into "good families" and "trashy families." Prairie families were disproportionately in the first category, whereas hill families were in the second, although some kinship ties did cut across the geographical barrier. Of all the criteria, however, lineage was perhaps the most inflexible. It provided, West states, rigid restrictions on patterns of courtship, visiting, and worship.

Another criterion involved morality and religion, but it tended to be used only in evaluating people in the lower class. This specifically entailed honesty, ambition, temperance, gambling, and church membership. Related to morality and religion were what West called manners or life-styles. This criterion involved all of the others, and in some ways superseded them. "People on the prairie," West states, "have better and more modern cars, improvements, farming implements, livestock, furniture, clothing, etc. These things," he continues, "represent not only the greater productivity, or wealth, of the prairie; they represent also the habits and tastes of prairie people, and their 'feelings' of what it is appropriate for their class to possess, use and display. . . ." [16] In short, it is possible to differentiate two distinct styles of life in Plainville: one associated with prairie people, the other with hill people.

W. Lloyd Warner and Yankee City

The 1930s were characterized by a proliferation of studies of community stratification that—like the studies by the Lynds, West, and others—attempted to describe stratification and social organization in great depth and detail. However, unlike the Middletown and Plainville studies, researchers associated with the Warner school went on to develop formalized

---

[15] Ibid., p. 120.
[16] Ibid., p. 124.

methods and techniques of social-class analysis. The two names most identified with this approach are W. Lloyd Warner and A. B. Hollingshead.

Perhaps the best known of all the American community studies are Warner's studies of a small New England community called Yankee City.[17] The initial research orientation to stratification in Yankee City was economic; that is, Warner expected the town's residents would rank one another in class positions according to their wealth. Warner's rationale for this expectation was that "the fundamental structure of our society, that which ultimately controls and dominates the thinking and actions of our people, is economic. . . ." [18] Once Warner and his associates began talking to residents of Yankee City, however, they began to take noneconomic factors into account. In this regard they soon recognized that where people lived—their ecological location—seemed to make a difference in their relative rank in the community. So, too, did the kinds and numbers of associations a family member joined, or was asked to join. In fact, members of the highest-status families in Yankee City belonged to organizations that were so exclusive many middle-class respondents did not even know of their existence.[19]

What emerged finally were various indications of differential lifestyles. Just as in Plainville, where a person lived, the kinds of organizations he belonged to, his recreational interests, and the like all combined to provide a picture of his manner of living. Because of its New England location and its industrial and urban nature, however, the differentiating characteristics of life-styles in Yankee City were different from those in Plainville.

---

[17] See, for example, W. Lloyd Warner and Paul S. Lunt, *The Social Life of a Modern Community* (New Haven: Yale, 1941). Our selection of studies to be reviewed should not be regarded by the reader as a simple ranking, based on the authors' values, of what are the best studies of community stratification in America. Our choice reflects an interest in describing some of the variety of studies undertaken and, more important from our perspective, their connection with more recent, formal studies of social stratification. Some of the acknowledged classics that are omitted at this point are John Dollard, *Caste and Class in a Southern Town* (New York: Harper, 1937); Allison Davis and G. M. Gardner, *Deep South* (Chicago: U. of Chicago, 1941); and St. Clair Drake and Horace Cayton, *Black Metropolis* (New York: Harper, 1945). In addition, see Robert S. Lynd and Helen M. Lynd, *Middletown in Transition* (New York: Harcourt, 1937). The critical appraisal of James West's class analysis in the restudy of Plainville is similarly excluded here, although it does deal with methodological matters. Cf., Art Gallaher, Jr., *Plainville Fifteen Years Later* (New York: Columbia U.P., 1961). For a complete review of the work of Warner and his associates, see H. W. Pfautz and Otis Dudley Duncan, "A Critical review of Warner's work in Community Stratification," *American Sociological Review*, **15**:205–215 (April, 1950); and H. W. Pfautz, "The Current Literature on Social Stratification: Critique and Bibliography," *American Journal of Sociology*, **58**:398–418 (Jan. 1950).

[18] Warner and Lunt, op. cit., p. 81.

[19] Warner was able to differentiate most of Yankee City's organizations by the social-class positions of members and then relate these differences back to the organizations. Those with upper-class members, for example, tended to have charitable goals; organizations with middle-class members were usually occupationally organized; and those with relatively lower-class members tended to be fraternal orders.

Warner also found, as did West, that the preferences reflected in different alternatives often involved comparable economic costs.[20] On the other hand, one could not ignore the observation that stylistic preferences generally are not completely divorced from purely economic considerations.

Warner held, based upon his observations, that the evaluations and ratings of local residents reflected six social classes (or strata) in Yankee City. They were described as follows:

CLASS 1, UPPER UPPER.   Class 1 is very elite and small (only about 1 per cent of Yankee City families were placed here). The most distinguishing characteristic of class 1 was the presence of traditional family wealth; that is, money had been in those families for several generations. Thus, because people were born into those families, the rank was more of an *ascribed* than an *achieved* status position. Because economic solvency was taken for granted in the upper-upper class, a strong orientation to leisure rather than work also characterized the group. Leisure rather than labor was dignified, and the capacity to afford help made extensive amounts of leisure possible.

CLASS 2, LOWER UPPER.   Class 2 was also a small and elite class, but the absence of a prominent family name differentiated these persons from those in class 1. They often possessed wealth that was comparable to that of class 1 families, but it was "new money." In other words, they either earned it themselves or, if inherited, it was too recent for its origins to have been forgotten.

A good deal of time and effort was expended by class 2 families in trying to emulate the behavior they associated with class 1. There was a life-style difference, however, revolving primarily about an "involved-detached" dimension. For example, there was active involvement by class 2 members in professional activities (many of the men were doctors and lawyers) and in civic affairs. Interest in class 1, by contrast, was directed toward activities associated with hunting clubs, summer homes, and winter vacations.

CLASS 3, UPPER MIDDLE.   Class 3 was larger and less exclusive than those above it, but it was still ranked well above the "common man." (Warner estimated about 10 per cent of Yankee City to be in this category.) Many of the class 3 men were also professional, but they tended to have less money and different life-styles generally. Included in this category was also a large number of the community's more successful wholesale and retail businessmen.

---

[20] For example, the cost of a better home in a working-class neighborhood of a city is often about the same as a less-expensive home in a middle-class suburb. Which of them a person chooses is indicative of this type of noneconomic life-style preference.

CLASS 4, LOWER MIDDLE.   The persons in class 4 closely resembled those in class 3, but they tended to have fewer high-status occupations—many of them were clerks and skilled workers—and there were differences in the quality and condition of their homes. Characteristic of class 4 (also of class 3, but less so) was an orientation that involved hard work, striving for prestige, attending church, and extolling morality. From Warner's perspective they were solid and respectable, if perhaps a bit dull.

CLASS 5, UPPER LOWER.   Class 5 was the largest in Yankee City, containing about one third of the classified residents. Ethnicity was a conspicuous factor in class 5 categorization: 30 per cent of its members were foreign born, and the majority of the community's Irish, Armenian, Jewish, French-Canadian, and Italian populations were in this class.

The men typically had little occupational skill and they worked in large factories, on construction projects, and in similar occupations. They tended to view themselves as the backbone of the community, but as viewed from above (with a degree of disdain), they were the poor but honest folk who seemed to be on a treadmill.

CLASS 6.   Class 6 was the bottom; they were West's "people who live like animals." They were poor, but unlike the class 5 families, they were the "disreputable poor." Many were unemployed and they lived in small run-down houses. Viewed from above, this group was held in contempt for their apparent lack of ambition and morality.

A. B. Hollingshead: Elmtown and New Haven

ELMTOWN.   Hollingshead's classic study of a midwestern communty, called Elmtown, began with assumptions similar to Warner's.[21] However, from the outset, Hollingshead, presumably benefiting from Warner's earlier work, seemed to be more aware of the importance of noneconomic criteria in rank-linked behavior: religion, family background, life-style, and the like. Warner, in contrast, had to hear comments from residents such as: "You have to have a little money but it is the way one uses it which counts," before he became sensitive to these factors.

Elmtown represented an extension of Warner's work in New England, and what had been learned earlier became the base for an expanded understanding of the relationship between given factors, including economic ones,

[21] A. B. Hollingshead, *Elmtown's Youth* (New York: Wiley, 1949). The report on the same community by Warner and his associates, including Hollingshead, is W. L. Warner et al., *Democracy in Jonesville* (New York: Harper, 1949).

and stratification-linked behavior patterns. Thus, Warner's work in Jonesville, with which Hollingshead was associated prior to his independent work, built on what had gone before.

One of the main thrusts of Hollingshead's study was toward behavior patterns among adolescents in the community. He found that the same stratification distinctions made in the adult community were almost perfectly reflected in the status evaluations of the adolescent community. Activities in the high school, membership in friendship cliques, and the like tended to be class-based, and the youths from relatively lower-class backgrounds were the objects of class discrimination. In addition, Hollingshead noted, similar class-based processes of discrimination were inherent in the school system. Teachers and administrators, following the morality and ambition codes associated with the middle class, generally closed off opportunities to lower-class adolescents because of differences in motivations, values, and life-styles.

Using a variety of criteria for class placement in Elmtown, Hollingshead constructed a stratification system for the community much like Warner's. It was also based on similar considerations. However, Hollingshead did not differentiate between Warner's classes 3 and 4. Rather, both were combined into a single "middle-class" category. In general, the two sets of descriptions are too alike to bear repeating. Therefore, a summary of the characteristics of the social classes, combining both Warner's and Hollingshead's observations, is presented in Table 5.

Warner and Hollingshead emerged as the most influential students of community stratification in the United States prior to and following World War II, a period characterized by more and more refined research methods and increasing clarification of stratification concepts. But there was to be a reassessment, if only short lived, including an effort to appraise the usefulness of combining the ecological approach of the early 1920s and 1930s with the stratification perspectives we have just described.

NEW HAVEN. Following his research on Elmtown in the Midwest, Hollingshead shifted his attention and residence eastward, to southern New England, where he continued his studies of social stratification in America. In New Haven, Connecticut, he found a unique combination of elements representing the vestiges of a class structure not unlike Yankee City's on the one hand, and a rapidly emerging fluid system of stratification characterizing the proliferation of a mass society on the other. Furthermore, the fact that New Haven was a sizeable city, whose population was 240,000 at the time of Hollingshead's first studies (1950), enhanced the value of the research because the earlier studies had been done in smaller, less urbanized, and, perhaps, less typical cities.

Building on Maurice R. Davie's earlier ecological research in New

TABLE 5
Composite Class Differences*

	Median Age of Marriage	Dominant Occupations	Residence	Associations	Religion	Children's High School	Magazines Preferred
Class 1	28	Professional, proprietary	Private homes; large and in good condition	Social and charitable	Unitarian, Episcopal	Private, preparatory	National Geographic, Saturday Evening Post, Sports Afield
Class 2	27	Professional, proprietary	Private homes; large and in good condition	Social, charitable and economic, professional	Unitarian, Episcopal	Private, preparatory	National Geographic, Saturday Evening Post, Time
Class 3	26	Retail dealers, professional, proprietary	Private homes; medium sized, in good condition	Social, charitable and economic	Unitarian, Baptist, Christian-Science	Public (college-preparatory program)	National Geographic, Better Homes & Gardens Ladies Home Journal
Class 4	25	Clerks, skilled and semiskilled	Rented; small and medium homes, in fair condition	Men's fraternal	Congregational, Episcopal	Public (vocational)	Needlecraft, Pictorial Review, Better Homes & Gardens
Class 5	24	Unskilled and semiskilled	Rented; small, poor, and fair condition	Men's and women's fraternal	Catholic	Public (vocational)	Needlecraft, Pictorial Review, Cosmopolitan
Class 6	23	Unskilled, semiskilled, and unemployed	Rented; small, poor condition (often in business buildings)	Men's and women's fraternal	Presbyterian, Methodist, Baptist, Congregational, Catholic	Public (vocational)	Needlecraft, Cosmopolitan, Pictorial Review

* Based on Warner et al., loc. cit., and Hollingshead, loc. cit., to describe and combine Yankee City and Jonesville-Elmtown data.

Haven,[22] Hollingshead developed an index, the Index of Social Position, to classify respondents in the city, with the objective of testing hypotheses relating social-class position to a variety of behavior patterns, one of which was mental illness and its corollaries.[23] Unlike the earlier studies in which ordinary members of the community were selected to rank families by reputation and thus provide the criteria for placement of the remaining population of families into categories, Hollingshead and his associate, Jerome K. Myers, both residents of the community, independently ranked a sample of families and selected salient criteria from the groups ranked. Three factors appeared to be influencing the placement process: (1) where a family lived, (2) the way a family made its living, and (3) its tastes, cultural orientation, and ways of using leisure time.[24] Thus, the ecological factor was used explicitly as an indicator of social-class position, along with occupation and education.

Five classes were described in the Hollingshead and F. C. Redlich study, *Social Class and Mental Illness,* and associated with differential diagnosis and classification of illness, differential assignment to treatment, and differential consequences of treatment, to name but a few of the many important corollaries of class position that were discovered in the study.

For the study of social stratification in America, however, Hollingshead was able to demonstrate that the types of approaches developed by both the ecologists and the students of community class structure could be fused into a useful research tool. But this fusion was short lived and the three-factor Index of Social Position was soon to be superseded by a two-factor index that deleted the ecological variable.[25] The march toward simpler, more useful indicators of social stratification continued.

Thus far in this chapter we have traced the development of systematic studies of social stratification and their emergence out of the concern of early American sociologists with the spatial and temporal distribution of activities. These studies, which have their roots in biosocial analysis of human ecology, were seen as becoming increasingly more "sociological" and focusing more and more on social stratification and the unequal distribution

[22] Maurice R. Davie, "The Pattern of Urban Growth," in *Studies in the Science of Society,* ed. G. P. Murdock (New Haven: Yale, 1937, pp. 133–161; and J. K. Myers, "Note on the Homogeneity of Census Tracts," *Social Forces,* **32**:364–366 (May 1954).

[23] A. B. Hollingshead and F. C. Redlich, *Social Class and Mental Illness* (New York: Wiley, 1958).

[24] op. cit., p. 390.

[25] Earlier ecological studies of Chicago described patterns of distribution of mental disorders that anticipated, two decades earlier, some of Hollingshead and Redlich's findings. Cf., R. Faris, L. Faris, and H. Warren Dunham, *Mental Disorders in Urban Areas* (Chicago: U. of Chicago, 1939). On greater refinement of the social class variables influencing behavior patterns associated with mental disorders a recent work by one of Warner's students (in collaboration with others) is Leo Srole et al., *Mental Health in the Metropolis* (New York: McGraw-Hill, 1962).

of scarce benefits as an aspect of social organization. This development was marked by the sociological and social anthropological investigations of stratification and social organization in presumably "typical" American communities.

Two aspects of this development that have not been fully treated in this chapter are the continual refinement of research methods and some very basic assumptions and ideologies about the nature of social organization, particularly in the United States. We will take up issues relating to research methodology in the final section of this chapter. First, however, the following paper will present a review of American stratification research that locates that research within competing ideological frameworks.

Ideological Currents in American Stratification Literature*†

John Pease, William H. Form, and Joan Huber [Rytina]

In his preface to the English edition of Karl Mannheim's *Ideology and Utopia*, Louis Wirth (1936, pp. xxii–xxiii) wrote that "the most important thing . . . that we can know about a man is what he takes for granted, and the most elemental and important facts about a society are those that are seldom debated and generally regarded as settled." Nowhere is Wirth's instruction more pertinent that in the American study of stratification; for although individual sociologists sometimes make early and penetrating analyses of the social scene, the profession usually ignores these findings until times of social crises. Thus the disclosure that one-fourth of the nation lives in poverty was as surprising to the average sociologist as it was to the average congressman. The Negro movement was as unexpected by most sociologists as it was by most other middle-class people who thought that things were getting better. The warning by a conservative president that a military-industrial complex threatens pluralistic politics is haltingly being accepted by many sociologists ten years later. Such observations underscore the salience of another of Wirth's instructions, namely, that the American study of social stratification "should be viewed in the light of the fact that American society and American scholarship largely take the democratic value of equality of opportunity for granted" (1953–1954, p. 280).[1]

The dominant American ideology has generally permeated most sociological thinking about social stratification, and advances in stratification theory

*   Reprinted with permission from *The American Sociologist*, 5:127–137 (May 1970).
†   This article was prepared with financial support of the Office of Manpower Policy, Evaluation, and Research, United States Department of Labor through grant #91–24–66–44, pursuant to provisions of the Manpower Development and Training Act of 1962. We are grateful for the Department's support.

have tended to be systematically ignored in research. The purpose of this paper is to critically review the impress of this ideology in the American sociological literature on social stratification.

We define social stratification as the institutionalization of power arrangements that perpetuate intergenerational economic, political, and social inequality among collectivities. Although this definition is found in both American and European literature, the Europeans have generally clung more closely to it.

The two major intellectual currents underlying most American stratification literature are "evolutionary liberalism" and "structural realism." Evolutionary liberalism holds that amorphous classes emerge as a consequence of individual mobility which represents the process of natural selection of those who are socially and biologically most "fit." Structural realism holds that distinct classes emerge as a consequence of socially created arrangements that maintain economic, political, and social inequality. American sociologists have responded primarily to the former and have made only formal obeisance to the latter. Even in American studies of the distribution of power, research findings say more about personal influence than about the differential allocation of resources.

This tendency to adhere to a perspective that exaggerates individual opportunity for mobility and justifies the consequences of a "free" economic order has not been uniquely American. European scholars have expressed similar ideas. But the distinction of American sociologists is that they have persistently embraced and supported this view while they adopted new vocabularies that masked their basic ideological position.

Early American Sociology

Evolutionary liberalism clearly pervades the work of three early American sociologists—William Graham Sumner, Charles Horton Cooley, and E. A. Ross —who specifically addressed themselves to the subject of social stratification. As early as 1883 Sumner asked *What Social Classes Owe to Each Other*, and his answer was "nothing." In Sumner's view, class stratification was

> the outcome of natural social-evolutionary processes, with the members of the various strata arranged in accordance with their individually unequal physical, moral, and intellectual endowments for progress. Social superiority and contribution to progress were identical (Hinkle and Boskoff 1957, p. 377).

Ross viewed social stratification largely as a mechanism of social control, and he angrily denounced social arrangements that perpetuated economic, political, and social inequality. "In a society cleft by parasitism the poor are poor," he wrote, "because they are held under the harrow and not because they are less capable and energetic than the classes that prey upon them" (Ross 1924, p. 394). In Ross's view, however, America was not such a society.

> In a really competitive society [U.S.A.] the hopelessly poor and wretched are, to a large extent, the weak and incompetent who have accumulated

at the lower end of the social scale because they or their parents have failed the tests of the competitive system (Ross 1924, p. 394).

This evolutionary and optimistic view about American stratification was also embraced by Cooley. Although he recognized the unequal distribution of wealth, he was optimistic that "under conditions which a country of opportunity, like the United States, affords, great masses of people rise from poverty to comfort, and many of them to opulence" (Cooley 1909, p. 295).

In short, although Ross and Cooley as well as Lester Ward and, most of all, Albion Small viewed class stratification as more of an arbitrary and artificial arrangement than did Sumner, they too thought that the stratification system of the United States was "open" and that the natural evolutionary forces of a "private" economy and a "democratic" polity would continue to limit the pith and permanence of stratification in America. The analysis of class phenomena occupied a decidedly secondary place in their work, and, as their historian Charles Page has argued, they "gave voice to class theories which were, in the final analysis, highly colored by the 'classlessness' of the American scene" (1969, p. 250). In one way or another, said Page, they were "impressed by the anti-class elements of the American democracy and by the social virtues of that 'classless' segment of society—the middle class" (1969, p. 250).

Although the thesis is extravagant that "the poor quality and (comparatively) limited quantity of American studies of class before the nineteen-twenties are to be explained by the high social mobility and low degree of stratification in American society" (MacRae 1953–1954, p. 11),[2] it seems clear that the "ideology of the American dream was a major deterrent to the study of class" (MacRae 1953–1954, p. 16). As American sociology entered its second generation, it did so with "little class research in progress, a minimum of theoretical consideration of the precise meaning of the term, and practically no recognition of the class framework as a major area of investigation (Gordon 1958, p. 8).

Apart from the contributions of the "founding fathers," the study of stratification was largely ignored during the half-century following Sumner's (1883) essay,[3] despite the important exceptions of Thorstein Veblen and Pitirim Sorokin. Veblen's 1899 classic, *The Theory of the Leisure Class*, was the first serious analysis of stratification in the annals of American sociology although, as Wirth (1953–1954, p. 280) pointed out, this study was largely neglected in its own time. Three decades later Sorokin (1927) published his classic *Social Mobility*, which was a comprehensive summary and a detailed commentary on most of the previous research relevant to stratification—but it did not stimulate any major research. Stratification did not appear to be worth studying.

The Nineteen-Thirties

"It was not until the great depression of the 1930's that any appreciable amount of intellectual effort was devoted by social scientists in America to careful scientific analyses of social stratification and social mobility" (Wirth 1953–1954, p. 280). As the depression deepened, sociologists began to recognize widespread poverty and immobility, and they began to question the ability of private enterprise and political democracy to maintain prosperity and to minimize economic and social inequality.[4]

In *The Modern Corporation and Private Property*, Adolph Berle and Gardiner Means (1933) documented in sterile tones what Veblen (1923) had written years earlier in *Absentee Ownership*. The massive TNEC reports[5] requested by the federal government and the rural monographs[6] sponsored by the Works Progress Administration demonstrated the American failure to provide an open class system. In *Middletown in Transition* Robert and Helen Lynd (1937) recorded the reality of the bifurcation of class in a "typical" American community. Frank Taussig and Carl Joslyn (1932), while asserting that social mobility was an individual responsibility, nonetheless found in a nationwide study of *American Business Leaders* that it was more difficult to become a leader in the 1930's than it had been earlier. Percy Davidson and Dewey Anderson (1937) found a high degree of inheritance for all major occupational categories in their study of *Occupational Mobility in An American Community*; and in *Ballots and the Democratic Class Struggle*, they (Anderson and Davidson, 1943) demonstrated the political consequences of differential mobility.

Alfred Winslow Jones's *Life, Liberty, and Property* (1941), a study of ideology in an American industrial city, documented the differential perception, by occupation, of the ability of the private property system to provide social justice. Lewis Corey (1934) showed a structural orientation in *The Decline of American Capitalism*, and he attributed the changing distribution of income to the changing structure of American capitalism. In *The Crisis of the Middle Class*, Corey (1935) along with Alfred M. Bingham in *Insurgent America* (1935) showed how economic forces were shattering the economic, political, and social solidity of the American middle class. Shortly thereafter, Goetz Briefs (1937) published *The Proletariat*, a study of the proletarianization of American labor during the depression and an analysis of the probable impact of the social security program on this process. For the first time, American sociologists appeared to be disposed to abandon adherence to the liberal *laissez-faire* ideology and to be willing to examine the economic and political underpinnings of institutionalized stratification. But the inclination to look hard at the structural sources of institutionalized inequality didn't last long.

The Nineteen-Forties

As the country recovered from the depression of the 1930's, the momentum for the empirical study of stratification continued in spite of a change in focus which T. B. Bottomore (1966, p. 105) characterized as one where

> the manifestations of social prestige in the local community, evaluated in terms of consumption patterns and styles of life, or occupational prestige and individual mobility through the educational system . . . absorbed the attention of sociologists. The underlying conception was that of America as a middle-class society in which some people were simply more middle class than others.

W. Lloyd Warner and Paul Lunt's (1941) research on *The Social Life of a Modern Community* provided the model. Stratification research took on a distinctly middle-class quality that was especially well expressed in the work of Warner, his associates, and adherents.[7] Stratification was viewed not so much as a matter of economic and political inequality as a matter of difference in values and style of life. The emphasis was on status, prestige, and esteem.[8] The study of stratification became especially suited for "American consumption . . . essentially middle class, status-involved, and ethnocentric" (Reissman 1959, p. 44). The critics charged that Warner had ignored the historical context, neglected power, generalized beyond the data, muddled the conceptualization, committed assorted methodological errors, and espoused support of the status quo (see, for example, Mills 1942; Miller 1950; Pfautz and Duncan 1950; Goldschmidt 1950; Lipset and Bendix 1951a; Lipset and Bendix 1951b; Mayer 1953; Kornhauser 1953; Gordon 1958; and Thernstrom 1964, pp. 225–239). But Warner endured.

Although some of the criticism of the Warner school was derived from a close reading of Max Weber (Mills 1942), and although some of Weber's writing on stratification was translated at about this time (Weber 1944, 1947), his ideas had little effect on empirical research.[9] Subsequent community studies politely acknowledged Weber's concepts of class status, and party, but thereafter concentrated only on status, either not knowing or neglecting the fact that Weber had analyzed status largely as a mode of the distribution of power. Indeed, while Weber is often praised in American sociology for his adroit handling of the conceptual distinctions in stratification—such as, "Weber's analytical distinctions offer the most meaningful framework for interpreting and understanding stratification in a modern industrial society" (Reissman 1959, p. 69)—the praise is deceptive. He is footnoted more than he is used.

Nearly two decades ago, for example, Oliver Cox noted that while "no writer on the general subject of 'class,' social status, and caste has been cited by American students with such finality as Max Weber . . . Weber's conclusions have seldom been quoted directly as illuminants in theoretical studies or as hypotheses in empirical research" (1950, p. 223). More recently, W. G. Runciman reported that "surprising as it seems, there is as far as I know no major writer on social inequality who has explicitly formulated and consistently retained the tripartite distinction" (1966, p. 37).

Most American students of stratification simply use Weber's authority to assert that stratification is not simple and unidimensional (implying, incorrectly, that Karl Marx said it was) and that class and status are analytically distinct (implying, as Weber did not, that the two are therefore equally consequential in social life). Most researchers eagerly welcomed Weber's addition of status to the stew of stratification concepts as a corrective to the one-eyed Marx who (they alleged) had myopically dealt only with class and power. Thus was Weber speedily de-Marxed and effectively Warnerized.

But even Warner was Warnerized. Many of the important contributions of the Warner school were never fully exploited, even by Warner himself. No other major stratification theorist advanced Warner's analysis of the place of

Negroes in the community stratification systems of the North and South (Davis et al. 1941); none advanced the seminal theory of the social allocation of various ethnic groups in the local labor market (Warner and Lunt 1941). The concept of the job ceiling for Negroes (Drake and Cayton 1945) and the specification of how the educational institution perpetuated the class system (Warner et al. 1944, 1949; Hollingshead 1949)[10] lay fallow for fifteen years. Generally American sociologists seized two things from the Warner school: a recipe for measuring social class (that is, socio-economic status) and a rationale for the empirical study of social status in the small community. The study of community status that Warner pioneered has been continuous, and most of it has merely aped him.

In 1945 Kingsley Davis and Wilbert Moore presented "Some Principles of Stratification." In what is now called the "functional theory of stratification," the authors asserted that stratification is functionally necessary because every society must have some mechanism for inducing its members to occupy positions that are socially important and require training. The differential distribution of class and status rewards ensures that "the most important positions are conscientiously filled by the most qualified persons" (Davis and Moore 1945, p. 243). Social stratification is therefore functional, necessary, and inevitable. In their view, stratification "becomes essentially an integrating structural attribute of social systems, and interclass relations are typically viewed as accommodative" (Pfautz 1953, p. 392).[11] The thesis was not new. Indeed, it was yet another declaration of evolutionary liberalism—that the economic order selects the most able for the highest positions and the least able for the lowest, assuring not only an open class system but one that is "best" for the economy and society.

Postwar Studies

Since the end of the Second World War, American research and writing on stratification has steadily increased.[12] "The work in the field has been extremely scattered in character and reflects a wide range of interests and concerns" (Lenski 1958, p. 521), from the meticulous North–Hatt scale of occupational prestige (North and Hatt 1947), that leaves unattended the question of relevance to the central issues of stratification, to C. Wright Mills's (1951) *White Collar*, that combines economic, historical, and institutional data on a scale reminiscent of Veblen. Despite this range of interests, some significant trends are discernible.[13] For example, doubts about generalizing from community data led to an increased use of national survey research studies (for example, North and Hatt 1947; and Centers 1949).

One of the most significant postwar trends was the critique of functionalism.[14] "Owing to its blatant inconsistency with many sociological facts" (Wesolowski 1962, p. 28), several clarifications and modifications of the functional theory appeared after Melvin Tumin's influential criticism. As a "continuing debate," these are centrally located in: Davis and Moore (1945), Tumin (1953a), Davis (1953), Moore (1953), Tumin (1953b), Buckley (1958), Davis (1959), Levy (1959), Buckley (1959), Moore (1963a), Tumin (1963), Moore (1963b), and Buckley (1963). Other, but not all, contributions important to the evaluation of this position are, chronologically: Parsons (1940), Davis (1942), Davis (1949, pp. 366–378), Parsons (1953), Anderson (1954), Tumin (1954), Schwartz (1955), Tumin (1955), Sieradzki (1956), Simpson (1956), Tumin (1956), Dahrendorf (1959), Reissman (1959, pp. 69–94), Wrong (1959), Cohn (1960), Tumin (1960), Cohn (1961), Sgan (1961), Tumin (1961, pp. 467–511), Queen (1962), Wesolowski (1962), Huaco (1963), Lewis and Lopreato (1963), Lopreato and Lewis (1963), Montague (1963, pp. 30–38), Miller and Hamblin (1963), Ossowski (1963), Stinchcombe (1963), Harris (1964), Wrong (1964), Tausky (1965), Lenski (1966), Harris (1967a, pp. 15–24, 79–81), and Harris (1967b).

The most important consequence of the debate was the withdrawal from the ranks of sociological "principles" of the assertion that stratification ensures that the ablest and best-trained persons conscientiously fill the most important positions in the society. As the critics pointed out, such an assertion assumes that all have equal opportunity to acquire training and that all those who are equal in training have equal opportunity to occupy positions that yield the highest reward. Moreover, as John Porter observed, "The functional view of social class cannot escape the charge of being a product of a conservative ideology and a theory to support the *status quo*. It does not sound unlike the view of society put forward by associations of manufacturers" (1965, p. 17).

A temporary shift of emphasis in stratification research from prestige to power was contemporaneous with the critique of functionalism. Since 1942, Mills had argued that while the study of community prestige structures was relevant, prestige was neither the sole nor the central concern of stratification analysis. Especially noteworthy departures in the American style of stratification research were two studies of power: Floyd Hunter's *Community Power Structure* (1953) and C. Wright Mills's *The Power Elite* (1956); both of these studies viewed stratification primarily as an unequal distribution of economic power, and they owed more to Marx and Weber than to Parsons and Warner. They did not hold sway for very long.

Sociologists quickly seized Hunter's recipe for identifying community influentials, just as they had earlier seized Warner's recipe for identifying social classes, and a spate of community power studies followed.[15] These studies, however, were not generally thought of as part of the stratification literature. Rather, they were thought either to represent a new area or to be part of political sociology, which, contrary to Weber, was not considered a part of the study of social stratification. These community studies were notably less concerned with the study of power structure than with the identification of individual community influentials, thus personalizing both power and social structure. Moreover, in conjunction with political scientists, sociologists examined many low-level, middle-class community issues, erroneously assuming that they were studying community power structure. Since they failed to investigate the economic and political bases of local and national institutionalized power, they confirmed the traditional liberal ideology that several occupational groups share in decision-making and that power is distributed pluralistically. Their findings constitute a fairly accurate description of middle-class views of middle-class politics.

Just two years after Mills (1956) wrote *The Power Elite*, Gerhard Lenski warned that "an undue emphasis is coming to be placed on economic power to the neglect of other forms of power" (1958, p. 530). "If the trend to phrase questions pertaining to stratification in terms of power becomes a trend to phrase questions solely in terms of economic power," Lenski admonished, "the gains which will accrue will very largely be offset by corresponding losses both in theoretical insight and in predictive value" (1958, p. 531). The caveat was needless. In 1960, for example, Robert E. L. Faris wrote, "Nor is power a class matter. . . . Power in reality comes from the millions of voters and purchasers, organized and unorganized, in a complex flow of forces" (Faris 1960, p. 1). And so the study of power quickly settled into a study of middle-class issues at the community level.[16]

Another postwar trend was a renewed concern for vertical mobility because, to quote William Kenkel, "it became apparent that our society was 'on the go' again" (1965, p. 569). The findings of mobility research in this period "coincided with a rejection of the doctrine of the nineteen-thirties that the rate of mobility in American society [was] declining" (Lenski 1958, p. 523).[17] Stuart Adams (1950; 1951; 1953; and 1954), Seymour Lipset and Reinhard Bendix (1952a and 1952b), William Peterson (1953), Natalie Rogoff (1953), Gideon Sjoberg (1951), W. Lloyd Warner and James Abegglen (1955), and others[18] presented studies suggesting that "the rate of mobility in American society is at least as high today as it has been at any time in the last fifty to one hundred years, if not higher" (Lenski 1958, p. 524). Not only were data unavailable to justify this conclusion, but the conclusion itself could, with equal justification, be put in negative terms—the rate of mobility today is at least as low on the average as it has been during the past century.

At the same time that studies were documenting high occupational mobility, some sociologists were testifying to the unreality of stratification in postwar America. According to mass society theory, affluent America was classless because nearly everybody was in the middle class. Peter Drucker (1953) contended that America was an "employee society," and in a society where everyone was an employee, the study of stratification was no longer relevant.[19] Meanwhile, Talcott Parsons recorded the disappearance of "the traditional 'bottom' of the occupational pyramid" and argued that "if anything this will tend to make our class structure even more predominantly 'middle-class' than it already is" (1953, pp. 124–125). Daniel Bell (1949) applauded "America's Un-Marxist Revolution" and heralded *The End of Ideology* (1960). John Kenneth Galbraith (1958) signalized the achievement of *The Affluent Society* and Robert Nisbet (1959, p. 16) maintained that "so far as the bulk of Western society is concerned, and especially in the United States, the concept of class is largely obsolete." The outstanding feature of American social structure was said to be the absence of any significant class stratification. According to Faris (1960, p. 1), who was then president of the American Sociological Association.

the sociological meaning of the evolution of our nation toward a general middle-class condition is simply that the complex organization which civilized man lives by continues to grow and to embrace more fully the hitherto less organized strata at the lower income and educational levels. It is essentially a trend toward a more complete participation of these people in modern civilization.

Ironically, the same year that Faris celebrated the extension of middle-class civilization to the lower class American sociologists learned that millions of other Americans lived in poverty (see, for example, Brand, 1960). Sociologists seemed prepared to accept equally the judgments that the United States of America was a middle-class society and a stratified society (Mayer, 1963, for example). Much of the research on poverty that has been undertaken since poverty was "rediscovered" has assumed that

> in a really competitive society [U.S.A.] the hopelessly poor and wretched are, to a large extent, the weak and incompetent who have accumulated at the lower end of the social scale because they or their parents have failed to meet the tests of the competitive system (Ross 1924, p. 394).

Stratification Studies Today

How could American sociologists, after eighty years of varying concerns with problems of social stratification, so persistently neglect the economic and political aspects of institutionalized social inequality?

One reason is that the dominant American ideology has always stressed individualism: the idea that a man's position in the social order is the direct consequence of his personal attributes. The sociological approach, on the contrary, assumes that a man's position is the consequence of the kind of social order in which he lives. But sociologists, as all other men, are exposed to the dominant ideology and the social set of givens that most people in a society take for granted.

A second reason is that the structural explanation not only runs contrary to public ideology, but it is also conceived by the public (and many sociologists) as a Marxist position. Thus, the acknowledgement of even a modest intellectual debt to Marx is usually accompanied by an elaborate statement of Marx's errors. As Leonard Reissman (1959, pp. 6–7) has remarked, "The evasions from what are relevant Marxian observations are noticeable in much of the sociological literature; are evident in the back-handed way that many have adopted of explicitly rejecting those observations of Marx that clearly are not applicable or of interpreting narrowly and then rejecting ideas that Marx did not seem to intend." Apparently, most American sociologists cannot fully appreciate the structural orientation to stratification of sociologists such as Weber, Toennies, Mosca, Michels, and many others. The climate of American opinion makes a theoretical focus on the relationship of political and economic institutions to the stratification system somewhat hazardous. As Page (1969, p. xviii) recently concluded,

> the "middle-class" coloration of research and writing on social stratification ... is consistent with and partly a reflection of long-standing themes in American culture: an individualism that resists structural interpretations

of social arrangements and processes, a voluntarism that rejects deterministic explanations of social action, a pragmatism that suspects abstract theories. These are prominent themes in folk thought and folk sentiment, in popular culture, and in intellectual and artistic endeavor. These themes, clearly, significantly influenced the discursive theories of the pioneers of American sociology; and they have intruded, I believe, into the more objective and rigorous social science of recent years.

A third reason is that sociology has been struggling for scientific status, and part of this struggle involves the improvement of quantification procedures, a concern that has come into focus especially since World War II. The discipline has overresponded to the opportunity for quantification which at this time is more difficult in the study of institutional sources of economic and political inequality than in the study of individual behavior. Sociologists therefore tend to design research that is suited to available machinery, and survey research is especially well suited.[20] Status is more easily studied with survey techniques than is power and wealth. Power is difficult to operationalize, especially when the individual is not the unit of analysis; and respondents are assumed to be unwilling or unable to give the detailed information necessary for a study of income and wealth. Unfortunately, the emphasis on status does not automatically lead to questions of politics or social change.

Summary

The ideology of students of American stratification has remained optimistic, individualistic, and evolutionary. Belief that the stratification system selects for mobility those who are biologically and socially most fit has generally prevailed since the inception of the discipline. Sociologists have also believed that rates of occupational mobility have tended to verify the dominant ideology because the "relatively high" rates have reduced extremes of economic, social, and political inequality and have created a middle-class society. A corollary of this basic functional argument suggests that status differences become increasingly important as economic equality and political enfranchisement become more widespread (see, for example, Mayer 1959).

A recent argument is that the society is evolving from a middle-class to a middle-mass society, as Bernard Barber (1968) has told. This argument holds that such processes as urbanization, industrialization, professionalization, and bureaucratification have made American society so homogeneous that the conception of a stratified political and economic order is no longer applicable. (This is a persistent theme, for instance, in Hodges 1964.) What matters now is not how much money a man has, but the taste and style he can display in spending it. According to Nisbet (1959, p. 16), for example,

> about the most that research comes up with is that wealthy persons spend their money more freely, choose, when possible, better schools for their children, buy clothes at Brooks or Magnin's rather than at Penney's, avail themselves of better medical attention, and belong to more clubs. But while all of this is interesting, it says little about anything as substantive as a social class is supposed to be.

In their identification of the many unresolved questions regarding stratification in the United States, the authors of a recent report about *Social Class and the Urban School* list as the first question: "Is social stratification a reality in America?" (Herriott and St. John 1966, p. 16). Sociologists who view stratification as a matter of individual occurrences rather than social structure, who study consumption to the neglect of distribution and production, who study the labor market but not the credit and commodity markets, who emphasize status, oversimplify class, neglect wealth, define power as being outside stratification, and who fail to see "race relations," minority status, and poverty in the context of stratification[21] confirm Robert Lynd's observation that when it comes to matters of class stratification, "the social sciences tiptoe evasively around the problem" (1949, p. 17).

The contributions of Marx and Weber still wait beyond the American ken.

NOTES

1. Parenthetically, at the time of Wirth's commentary, Faris, in his presidential address to the Pacific Sociological Association, denied the reality of stratification in America: "In the light of modern research knowledge . . . is there any justification for employing such an expression as 'the class system' of this country? To such questions we should at least be ready to answer a flat 'no' " (1954, p. 83).

2. "Undoubtedly in certain regions mobility was high, and strata were ill-defined, but in the East and South this was not the case. Nor was class-consciousness lacking; the end of the nineteenth and the early twentieth century were periods of acute class-conflict and class-feeling among the industrial workers. . . . On the whole the failure of the 'fathers' —Ross and Cooley are partial exceptions—is probably largely to be explained in terms of reaction from what must, falsely, have appeared to be a sharpening class-conflict" (MacRae 1953–1954, p. 11). Also, Nisbet has reported: "Recently I treated myself to a re-reading of some of the first-water novels of the turn of the century. . . . It is an instructive sociological experience, if only to be reminded that the idea of social class was then as vivid and widely accepted as is today the idea of status mobility" (1959, p. 11).

3. "Only two of the 125 papers presented at the annual meetings of the American Sociological Society before 1917 treated subjects having to do predominantly and obviously with some aspect of rank" (Hinkle and Boskoff 1957, p. 376). It should be added that there was discussion and writing about child labor, unemployment, etc., during this period, but these topics were not generally considered in a stratification context.

4. The renewed interest in Marxism during the 1930's was also related to the political events in Germany. "The rise of Nazism focussed attention on the class-structure of Germany and turned inquiry to the understanding of the social roots of the new regime. . . . In addition the Nazis' social policy sent a flood of scholars into exile through the world, above all to France, Britain and America. . . . There was inevitably a new sympathy for Marxism which then appeared both the major opponent of Nazism and its major interpreter" (MacRae 1953–1954, p. 15).

5. There were more than two dozen reports in this series. Two of the most cited are *Economic Power and Political Pressures* (Temporary National Economic Committee, 1941) and *Competition and Monopoly in American Industry* (Temporary National Economic Committee, 1940).

6. About two dozen research monographs and nearly the same number of "special reports" were published in this series during the 1930's. One of the best of the research monographs is *Landlord and Tenant on the Cotton Plantation* (Woofter et al. 1936).

7. For an extensive bibliography of the "Warner school," see Gordon (1958).

8. This is not to suggest that the interest in status was original with Warner, but in his work it was the *dominant* interest, just as it has been in the American study of stratification

ever since. In a recent general review of American stratification research, there is no mention of class as a political or economic phenomenon. The entire discussion is centered on the concept of social status. For example, there is no mention of income, inequality, money, power or wealth (Kenkel 1965).

9. The first empirical research in the annals of American sociology that explicitly used Weber's conceptual scheme was that of Form (1945).

10. These studies gave educators a methodology and a perspective that have affected their policies toward working-class students from the date of their publication to the present.

11. Four years after Pfautz's observation, Warner lamented that "the literature on class conflict is far greater than that on the common tasks of society, or than on organized apportion (in Simmel's sense) among those who collaborate" (1957, p. 233).

12. This is reflected in the proliferation of instructional volumes in social stratification. Prior to 1953 there were only two volumes that, viewed broadly, were considered stratification textbooks: North (1926) and Sorokin (1927). Since 1953 eight general social stratification texts have been published: Cuber and Kenkel (1954), Barber (1957), Kahl (1957), Reissman (1959), Bergel (1962), Hodges (1964), Lasswell (1965), and Lenski (1966). Also available are five "primers" of social stratification: Svalastoga (1965), Bottomore (1966), Tumin (1967), Owen (1968), and Mayer and Buckley (1969)—a revision of Mayer (1955). In addition, eight edited collections in social stratification have been published since the early 1950's, and two of these are in their second edition: Bendix and Lipset (1953; 1966), Mack 1963; 1968), Smelser and Lipset (1966), Kahl (1968), Lane (1968), Heller (1969), Roach, Gross, and Gursslin (1969), and Tumin (1969).

13. Other trend assessments of the study of stratification in American sociology vary in quality and scope of coverage; in chronological order they are: Shils (1948, pp. 10—15), Goldschmidt (1950), Bendix and Lipset (1953, pp. 7–16), Pfautz (1953), MacRae (1953–1954), Wirth (1953–1954), Anderson (1955), Keller (1956), Hinkle and Boskoff (1967), Warner (1957), Gordon (1958), Lenski (1958), Murphy (1964), Svalastoga (1964), Kenkel (1965), Bendix and Lipset (1966, pp. xiii–xviii), Boskoff (1969, pp. 249–277), Jackson (1969), Page (1969; originally published in 1940) and Reissman and Halstead (1969).

14. The Davis and Moore (1945) statement was slightly modified prior to any critical analysis of it. See Davis (1949, pp. 364–389). The first major critique was that of Tumin (1953a).

15. For a recent listing of much of this literature, see Pellegrin (1967).

16. See, for example, Polsby (1963). According to Anton (1963a, p. 454), the pluralists deny that power is permanently structured. If they find no evidence of community power, they tend to conclude that further investigation is a waste of time. And, says Anton, the pluralists claim to have no ideology "other than commitment to empirical science—a commitment which emphasizes that which is rather than that which ought to be." For a critical commentary of Anton's essay, see Dahl (1963). Then see Anton's (1963b) rejoinder.

17. The only notable exception to these data and interpretations was the report by Hertzler (1952) that points to a declining rate of mobility. For a comprehensive review of the mobility literature see Miller (1960).

18. For example, Kahl has stated that "American society is not becoming markedly more rigid" (1957, p. 268). Barber (1957, p. 468) has reported that "there has not been a trend toward less mobility, as has frequently been asserted recently. There may even have been slightly more mobility in the present than in the past." Kenkel's summary of post-depression mobility trends in the U.S. was that "most, but not all, subsequent research indicates that at least from generation to generation there is a great deal of vertical mobility, probably as much as there ever has been" (1965, p. 569). Blau and Duncan, who reported that "men who start careers in manual work are less likely than others to achieve an occupational status that differs from that of their fathers" (1967, p. 424), also reported that "the rates of upward mobility in the United States today are still high" (1967, p. 426).

19. For a critical commentary of Drucker's thesis, see McKee (1953).

20. Reissman and Halstead (1969) arrived at a similar conclusion.

21. Although this is characteristic of the American study of stratification, there are notable exceptions. Lenski (1966), for example, has focused upon power, wealth (privilege), and the distributive process. Wiley (1967) has made imaginative use of Weber's ideas. Heberle (1959) has rightly asseverated the usefulness of class theory. Leggett (1968) has inspirited the area of class-consciousness. Perhaps the most notable exception to the mode of American stratification study today is the work of S. M. Miller and his associates (see, for example, Miller et al. 1967).

REFERENCES

Adams, S.
1950 "Regional differences in vertical mobility in a high-status occupation." *American Sociological Review* **15** (April): 228–235.
1951 "Fact and myth in social class theory." *Ohio Journal of Science* **51** (November): 313–319.
1953 "Trends in occupational origins of physicians." *American Sociological Review* **18** (August):404–409.
1954 "Trends in occupational origins of business leaders." *American Sociological Review* **19** (October):541–548.

Anderson, C. A.
1954 "The need for a functional theory of social class." *Rural Sociology* **19** (June): 152–160.
1955 "Recent American research in social stratification." *Mens en Maatschappii* **30**: 321–327.

Anderson, Dewey, and Percy Davidson
1943 Ballots and the Democratic Class Struggle: A Study in the Background of Political Education. Stanford: Stanford University Press.

Anton, T. J.
1963a "Power, pluralism, and local politics." *Administrative Science Quarterly* **7** (March): 425–457.
1963b "Rejoinder." *Administrative Science Quarterly* **8** (September):257–268.

Barber, Bernard
1957 Social Stratification: A Comparative Analysis of Structure and Process. New York: Harcourt, Brace and World.
1968 "Social stratification structure and trends of social mobility in western society." Pp. 184–195 in Talcott Parsons (ed.), American Sociology: Perspectives, Problems, Methods. New York: Basic Books.

Bell, D.
1949 "America's un-Marxist revolution." *Commentary* **12** (March):207–215.
1960 The End of Ideology: On the Exhaustion of Political Ideas in the Fifties. Glencoe, Ill.: Free Press.

Bendix, Reinhard, and Seymour Lipset (eds.)
1953 Class, Status, and Power: A Reader in Social Stratification. Glencoe, Ill.: Free Press.
1966 Class, Status, and Power: Social Stratification in Comparative Perspective. 2nd ed. New York: Free Press.

Bergel, Egon
1962 Social Stratification. New York: McGraw-Hill.

Berle, Adolph, Jr., and Gardiner Means.
1933 The Modern Corporation and Private Property. New York: Macmillan.

Bingham, Alfred M.
1935 Insurgent America: The Revolt of the Middle-Classes. New York: Harper.

Blau, Peter, and Otis Duncan
1967 The American Occupational Structure. New York: Wiley.

Boskoff, Alvin
1969 Theory in American Sociology: Major Sources and Applications. New York: Thomas Y. Crowell.

Bottomore, T. B.
1966 Classes in Modern Society. New York: Pantheon.

Brand, H.
1960 "Poverty in the United States." *Dissent* **7** (Winter):334–354.

Briefs, Goetz
1937 The Proletariat: A Challenge to Western Civilization. New York: McGraw-Hill.

Buckley, W.
1958 "Social stratification and the functional theory of social differentiation." *American Sociological Review* **23** (August):369–375.
1959 "A rejoinder to functionalists Dr. Davis and Dr. Levy." *American Sociological Review* **24** (February):84–86.
1963 "On equitable inequality." *American Sociological Review* **28** (October):799–801.

Centers, Richard
1949 The Psychology of Social Classes: A Study of Class Consciousness. Princeton: Princeton University Press.

Cohn, W.
1960 "Social status and the ambivalence hypothesis: some critical notes and a suggestion." *American Sociological Review* **25** (August):508–513.
1961 "Reply to Sgan." *American Sociological Review* **26** (February):104–105.

Cooley, Charles H.
1909 Social Organization: A Study of the Larger Mind. New York: Charles Scribner's Sons.

Corey, Lewis
1934 The Decline of American Capitalism. New York: Covici, Friede.
1935 The Crisis of the Middle Class. New York: Covici, Friede.

Cox, O. C.
1950 "Max Weber on social stratification: a critique." *American Sociological Review* **15** (April): 223–227.

Cuber, John, and William Kenkel
1954 Social Stratification in the United States. New York: Appleton-Century-Crofts.

Dahl, R. A.
1963 "Letter to the editor." *Administrative Science Quarterly* **8** (September):250–256.

Dahrendorf, Ralf
1959 Class and Class Conflict in Industrial Society. Stanford: Stanford University Press.

Davidson, Percy, and H. Dewey Anderson
1937 Occupational Mobility in an American Community. Stanford: Stanford University Press.

Davis, Allison, Burleigh B. Gardner, and Mary R. Gardner
1941 Deep South. Chicago: University of Chicago Press.

Davis, K.
1942 "A conceptual analysis of stratification." *American Sociological Review* **7** (June): 309–321.
1949 Human Society. New York: Macmillan.
1953 "Reply." *American Sociological Review* **18** (August):394–397.
1959 "The abominable heresy: a reply to Dr. Buckley." *American Sociological Review* **24** (February):82–83.

Davis, K., and W. E. Moore
1945 "Some principles of stratification." *American Sociological Review* **10** (April): 242–249.

Drake, St. Clair, and Horace R. Cayton
1945 Black Metropolis. New York: Harcourt, Brace.

Drucker, P. F.
1953 "The employee society." *American Journal of Sociology* **58** (January):358–363.

Faris, R. E. L.
1954 "The alleged class system in the United States." *Research Studies of the State College of Washington* **22** (June):77–83.
1960 "The middle class from a sociological viewpoint." *Social Forces* **39** (October):1–5.

Form, W. H.
1945 "Status stratification in a planned community." *American Sociological Review* **10** (October):605–613.

Galbraith, John K.
1958 The Affluent Society. Boston: Houghton Mifflin.

Goldschmidt, W. R.
1950 "Social class in America: a critical review." *American Anthropologist* **52** (October-December):483–498.

Gordon, Milton
1958 Social Class in American Sociology. Durham: Duke University Press.

Harris, E.
1964 "Prestige, reward, skill, and functional importance: a reconsideration." *Sociological Quarterly* **5** (Summer):261–264.

1967a Essays in General Sociology. New York: American Press.
1967b "Research methods, functional importance, and occupational roles." *Sociological Quarterly* **8** (Spring):255–259.

Heberle, R.
1959 "Recovery of class theory." *Pacific Sociological Review* **2** (Spring):18–24.

Heller, Celia (ed.)
1969 Structured Social Inequality: A Reader in Comparative Social Stratification. New York: Macmillan.

Herriott, Robert, and Nancy St. John
1966 Social Class and the Urban School: The Impact of Pupil Background on Teachers and Principals. New York: Wiley.

Hertzler, J. O.
1952 "Some tendencies toward a closed class system in the United States." *Social Forces* **30** (March):313–323.

Hinkle, R. C., Jr., and A. Boskoff
1957 "Social stratification in perspective." Pp. 368–395 in Howard Becker and Alvin Boskoff (eds.), Modern Sociological Theory in Continuity and Change. New York: Dryden.

Hodges, Harold, Jr.
1964 Social Stratification: Class in America. Cambridge, Mass.: Schenkman.

Hollingshead, August
1949 Elmtown's Youth: The Impact of Social Classes on Adolescents. New York: Wiley.

Huaco, G. A.
1963 "A logical analysis of the Davis-Moore theory of stratification." *American Sociological Review* **28** (October):801–804.

Hunter, Floyd
1953 Community Power Structure. Chapel Hill: University of North Carolina Press.

Jackson, J. A.
1969 "Editorial introduction–social stratification." Pp. 1–13 in J. A. Jackson (ed.), Social Stratification. Sociological Studies No. 1. Cambridge: Cambridge University Press.

Jones, Alfred W.
1941 Life, Liberty, and Property: A Story of Conflict and a Measurement of Conflicting Rights. Philadelphia: J. B. Lippincott.

Kahl, Joseph
1957 The American Class Structure. New York: Holt, Rinehart and Winston.

Kahl, Joseph (ed.)
1968 Comparative Perspectives on Stratification: Mexico, Great Britain, Japan. Boston: Little, Brown.

Keller, S.
1956 "Sociology of social stratification, 1945–1955." Pp. 114–119 in Hans L. Zetterberg (ed.), Sociology in the United States of America. Paris: UNESCO.

Kenkel, W. F.
1965 "Recent Research." Pp. 567–572 in Thomas E. Lasswell, John H. Burma, and Sidney H. Aronson (eds.), Life in Society: Introductory Readings in Sociology. Chicago: Scott and Foresman.

Kornhauser, R. R.
1953 "The Warner approach to social stratification." Pp. 224–255 and 675–678 in Bendix and Lipset (eds.), Class, Status, and Power: A Reader in Social Stratification. Glencoe, Ill.: Free Press.

Lane, W. (ed.)
1968 Permanence and Change in Social Class: Readings in Stratification. Cambridge, Mass.: Schenkman.

Lasswell, Thomas
1965 Class and Stratum: An Introduction to Concepts and Research. Boston: Houghton Mifflin.

Leggett, John
1968 Class, Race, and Labor: Working-Class Consciousness in Detroit. New York: Oxford.

Lenski, G. E.
1958 "Social stratification." Pp. 521–538 in Joseph S. Roucek (ed.), Contemporary Sociology. New York: Philosophical Library.
1966 Power and Privilege: A Theory of Social Stratification. New York. McGraw-Hill.

Levy, M., Jr.
1959 "Functionalism: a reply to Dr. Buckley." American *Sociological Review* **24** (February):83–84.

Lewis, L. S., and J. Lopreato
1963 "Functional importance and prestige of occupation." *Pacific Sociological Review* **6** (Fall):55–59.

Lipset, S. M., and R. Bendix
1951a "Social status and social structure: a re-examination of data and interpretations, I." *British Journal of Sociology* **2** (June):150–168.
1951b "Social status and social structure: a re-examination of data and interpretations, II." *British Journal of Sociology* **2** (September):230–254.
1952a "Social mobility and occupational career patterns, I: stability of job holding." *American Journal of Sociology* **57** (January):366–374.
1952b "Social mobility and occupational career patterns, II: social mobility." *American Journal of Sociology* **57** (March):494–504.

Lopreato, J., and L. S. Lewis
1963 "An analysis of variables in the functional theory of stratification. *Sociological Quarterly* **4** (Autumn):301–310.

Lynd, R. S.
1949 "Tiptoeing around class." *Review of the Psychology of Social Classes* by Richard Centers. *New Republic* **121** (July 25):17–18.

Lynd, Robert, and Helen Lynd
1937 Middletown in Transition: A Study in Cultural Conflicts. New York: Harcourt, Brace and World.

Mack, Raymond (ed.)
1963 Race, Class, and Power. New York: American Book Co.
1968 Race, Class, and Power. 2nd ed. New York: American Book Co.

McKee, J. B.
1953 "Status and power in the industrial community: a comment on Drucker's thesis." *American Journal of Sociology* **58** (January):364–370.

MacRae, D. G.
1953– "Social stratification: a trend report." *Current Sociology* **2** (No. 4):7–73.
1954

Mayer, Kurt
1953 "The theory of social classes." *Harvard Educational Review* **23** (Fall):149–167.
1955 Class and Society. Studies in Sociology. Rev. ed. New York: Random House.
1959 "Diminishing class differentials in the United States." *Kyklos* **12** (Fasc. 4):605–628.
1963 "The changing shape of the American class structure." *Social Research* **30** (Winter): 458–468.

Mayer, Kurt, and Walter Buckley
1969 Class and Society. Studies in Sociology. 3rd ed. New York: Random House.

Miller, L. K., and R. L. Hamblin
1963 "Interdependence, differential rewarding, and productivity." *American Sociological Review* **28** (October):768–778.

Miller, S. M.
1950 "Social class and the 'typical' American community." *American Sociological Review* **15** (April):294–295.
1960 "Comparative social mobility: a trend report and bibliography." *Current Sociology* **9** (No. 1):1–89.

Miller, S. M., M. Rein, P. Roby, and B. M. Gross
1967 "Poverty, inequality, and conflict." *Annals of the American Academy of Political and Social Science* **373** (September):16–52.

Mills, C. Wright
1942 Review of "The Social Life of a Modern Community," by W. Lloyd Warner and Paul S. Lunt. *American Sociological Review* **7** (April):263–271.

1951 White Collar: The American Middle Classes. New York: Oxford.

1956 The Power Elite. New York: Oxford.

Montague, Joel, Jr.

1963 Class and Nationality: English and American Studies. New Haven: College and University Press.

Moore, W. E.

1953 "Comment." *American Sociological Review* **18** (August):397.

1963a "But some are more equal than others." *American Sociological Review* **28** (February):13–18.

1963b "Rejoinder." *American Sociological Review* **28** (February):26–28.

Murphy, R. J.

1964 "Some recent trends in stratification: stratification theory and research." *Annals of the American Academy of Political and Social Science* **356** (November):142–167.

Nisbet, R. A.

1959 "The decline and fall of social class." *Pacific Sociological Review* **2** (Spring):11–17.

North, Cecil

1926 Social Differentiation. Chapel Hill: University of North Carolina Press.

North, C. C., and P. K. Hatt

1947 "Jobs and occupations: a popular evaluation." *Opinion News* **9** (September):3–13.

Ossowski, Stanislaw

1963 Class Structure in the Social Consciousness. Translated by Sheila Patterson. New York: Free Press of Glencoe.

Owen, Carol

1968 Social Stratification. The Students Library of Sociology. New York: Humanities Press.

Page, Charles

1969 Class and American Sociology: From Ward to Ross. New York: Schocken Books.

Parsons, T.

1940 "An analytical approach to the theory of social stratification." *American Journal of Sociology* **45** (May):841–862.

1953 "A revised analytical approach to the theory of social stratification." Pp. 92–128 and 665–667 in Bendix and Lipset (eds.), Class, Status, and Power: A Reader in Social Stratification. Glencoe, Ill.: Free Press.

Pellegrin, R. J.

1967 "Selected bibliography on community power structure." *Southwestern Social Science Quarterly* **48** (December):451–465.

Peterson, W.

1953 "Is America still the land of opportunity? what recent studies show about social mobility." *Commentary* **16** (November):477–486.

Pfautz, H. W.

1953 "The current literature on social stratification: critique and bibliography." *American Journal of Sociology* **58** (January):391–418.

Pfautz, H. W., and O. D. Duncan

1950 "A critical evaluation of Warner's work in community stratification." *American Sociological Review* **15** (April):205–215.

Polsby, Nelson

1963 Community Power and Political Theory. New Haven: Yale University Press.

Porter, John

1965 The Vertical Mosaic: An Analysis of Social Class and Power in Canada. Canadian University Paperbacks. Toronto: University of Toronto Press.

Queen, S. A.

1962 "The function of social stratification: a critique." *Sociology and Social Research* **46** (July):412–415.

Reissman, Leonard

1959 Class in American Society. New York: Free Press of Glencoe.

Reissman, L., and M. N. Halstead

1969 "The subject is class." Paper delivered at the annual meeting of the American Sociological Association, San Francisco.

Roach, Jack, Llewellyn Gross, and Orville Gursslin (eds.)
1969   Social Stratification in the United States. Englewood Cliffs, N.J.: Prentice-Hall.

Rogoff, Natalie
1953   Recent Trends in Occupational Mobility. Glencoe, Ill.: Free Press.

Ross, Edward A.
1924   Social Control: A Survey of the Foundations of Social Order. New York: Macmillan.

Runciman, W. G.
1966   Relative Deprivation and Social Justice: A Study of Attitudes to Social Inequality in Twentieth-century England. Berkeley: University of California Press.

Schwartz, R. D.
1955   "Functional alternatives to inequality." *American Sociological Review* **20** (August): 424–430.

Sgan, M.
1961   "On social status and ambivalence." *American Sociological Review* **26** (February): 104.

Shils, Edward
1948   The Present State of American Sociology. Glencoe, Ill.: Free Press.

Sieradzki, G. F.
1956   "The structural-functional theory of social stratification: a critical analysis and suggested revision." *Berkeley Publications in Society and Institutions* **2** (Spring): 1–14.

Simpson, R. L.
1956   "A modification of the functional theory of social stratification." *Social Forces* **35** (December):132–137.

Sjoberg, G.
1951   "Are social classes in America becoming more rigid?" *American Sociological Review* **16** (December):775–783.

Smelser, Neil, and Seymour Lipset, eds.
1966   Social Structure and Mobility in Economic Development. Chicago: Aldine.

Sorokin, Pitirim
1927   Social Mobility. New York: Harper.

Stinchcombe, A.
1963   "Some empirical consequences of the Davis-Moore theory of stratification." *American Sociological Review* **28** (October):805–808.

Sumner, William G.
1883   What Social Classes Owe to Each Other. New York: Harper.

Svalastoga, Kaare
1964   "Social differentiation." Pp. 530–575 in Robert E. L. Faris (ed.), Handbook of Modern Sociology. Chicago: Rand McNally.
1965   Social Differentiation. McKay Social Science Series. New York: David McKay.

Tausky, C.
1965   "Parsons on stratification: an analysis and critique." *Sociological Quarterly* **6** (Spring):128–138.

Taussig, F., and C. Joslyn
1932   American Business Leaders: A Study in Social Origins and Social Stratification. New York: Macmillan.

Temporary National Economic Committee
1940   Competition and Monopoly in American Industry. Monograph No. 21. Washington, D.C.: U.S. Government Printing Office.
1941   Economic Power and Political Pressures. Monograph No. 26. Washington, D.C.: U.S. Government Printing Office.

Thernstrom, Stephen
1964   Poverty and Progress: Social Mobility in a Nineteenth Century City. Cambridge: Harvard University Press.

Tumin, M. M.
1953a   "Some principles of stratification: a critical analysis." *American Sociological Review* **18** (August):387–393.

1953b "Reply to Kingsley Davis." *American Sociological Review* **18** (December):672–673.

1954 "Obstacles to creativity." *Etc.: A Review of General Semantics* **11** (Summer): 261–271.

1955 "Rewards and task-orientations." *American Sociological Review* **20** (August): 419–423.

1956 "Some disfunctions of institutional imbalance." *Behavioral Science* **1** (July): 218–223.

1960 "Competing status systems." Pp. 277–290 in Wilbert E. Moore and Arnold S. Feldman (eds.), Labor Commitment and Social Change in Developing Areas. New York: Social Science Research Council.

1961 Social Class and Social Change in Puerto Rico. Princeton: Princeton University Press.

1963 "On inequality." *American Sociological Review* **28** (February):19–26.

1967 Social Stratification: The Forms and Functions of Inequality. Foundations of Modern Sociology Series. Englewood Cliffs, N.J.: Prentice-Hall.

1969 Readings on Social Stratification. Englewood Cliffs, N.J.: Prentice-Hall.

Veblen, Thorstein

1899 The Theory of the Leisure Class: An Economic Study in the Evolution of Institutions. New York: Macmillan.

1923 Absentee Ownership and Business Enterprise in Recent Times: The Case of America. New York: B. W. Huebsch.

Warner, W. L.

1957 "The study of social stratification." Pp. 221–258 in Joseph B. Gittler (ed.), Review of Sociology. New York: Wiley.

Warner, W., and James Abegglen

1955 Occupational Mobility in American Business and Industry, 1928–1952. Minneapolis: University of Minnesota Press.

Warner, W., and Associates

1949 Democracy in Jonesville. New York: Harper.

Warner, W., Robert Havighurst, and Martin Loeb

1944 Who Shall be Educated? The Challenge of Unequal Opportunities. New York: Harper.

Warner, W., and Paul Lunt

1941 The Social Life of a Modern Community. New Haven: Yale University Press.

Weber, Max

1944 "Class, status, party." Translated and edited by H. H. Gerth and C. Wright Mills. *Politics* **1** (October):271–278.

1947 "Social stratification and class structure." Translated by Talcott Parsons. Pp. 424–429 in The Theory of Social and Economic Organization. Translated by A. M. Henderson and Talcott Parsons. Edited by Talcott Parsons. Glencoe, Ill.: Free Press.

Wesolowski, W.

1962 "Some notes on the functional theory of stratification." *Polish Sociological Bulletin*, Nos. 3–4 (5–6):28–38.

Wiley, N.

1967 "America's unique class politics: the interplay of the labor, credit, and commodity markets." *American Sociological Review* **32** (August):529–541.

Wirth, L.

1936 Preface (pp. x–xxx) to "Ideology and Utopia: An Introduction to the Sociology of Knowledge," by Karl Mannheim. Translated by Louis Wirth and Edward Shils. Harvest Books. New York: Harcourt, Brace and World.

1953– "Social stratification and social mobility in the United States." *Current Sociology*
1954 **2** (No. 4):279–303.

Woofter, T., Jr., with the collaboration of Gordon Blackwell, Harold Hoffsommer, James G. Maddox, Jean M. Massell, B. O. Williams, and Waller Wynne, Jr.

1936 Landlord and Tenant on the Cotton Plantation. Research Monograph V. Washington, D.C.: Works Progress Administration.

Wrong, D. H.

1959 "The functional theory of stratification: some neglected considerations." *American Sociological Review* **24** (December):772–782.

1964 "Social inequality without social stratification." *Canadian Review of Sociology and Anthropology* **1** (February):5–16.

Conceptual and Methodological Issues

Although the Lynds' study of Middletown was probably the pioneering study of stratification and social organization in American communities, it is probably the research of W. Lloyd Warner that has had the most lasting influence on stratification research in the United States. Warner's influence was twofold: through the direct impact of his own writings and through his influence over other community analysts who were trained (and sometimes supervised) by him. Therefore, the theoretical assumptions that guided Warner are of great initial importance.

A convenient place to begin discussing the pattern of the Warner school is with Warner's field research in Australia (1926–1929). His analysis focused on eight Murngin tribes that were viewed rather easily as sharing a common culture. They were physically removed from each other, but each had established almost identical groupings, based on the same kinship-oriented structure. These tribes, Warner later wrote:

> have the same kinship system, the same form of local organization, largely the same myths and ceremonies, and, in general, the same culture, with only those minor variations found in any homogeneous civilization.[26]

Warner's experience in studying aboriginal Australian tribes, and those of other social anthropologists in New Guinea, Central America, and elsewhere, provided the background for his American community studies. More specifically, they led to the conceptual and methodological skills that were applied. In a later introduction to Yankee City, Warner (with the assistance of Paul S. Lunt) wrote:

> The more simple types of communities—with their smaller populations, less numerous social institutions, less complex ideational and technical systems— provide the social anthropologist with the equivalent of a laboratory wherein to test his ideas and research techniques. By investigation of these simple societies, he is able to equip himself better for the analysis of more complex forms of human society.[27]

The clarification of three concepts recurrently used by these social anthropologists[28] is essential to understanding their approach. The three concepts are culture, society, and community.

1. Culture is "a synonym for society."
2. Society is "a group of mutually interacting individuals."

[26] W. Lloyd Warner, *A Black Civilization* (New York: Harper, 1937), p. 108.
[27] Warner and Lunt, op cit., p. 3.
[28] As used by Warner, this denoted "comparative sociologists."

3. Community is "a body of people having common interests and living in the same place under the same laws and regulations and all the individual members have social relations directly or indirectly with each other." [29]

Thus, culture, society, and community are concretely and essentially one and the same, although a given society or culture could be represented in more than one community. By viewing these concepts as having virtually identical referents, it was then possible to link the simple primitive tribes and bands to contemporary American communities in a theoretically meaningful way. To Warner, primitive *or* modern communities:

> are essentially the same in kind. All are located in a given territory which they partly transform for the purpose of maintaining the physical and social life of the group, and all the individual members of these groups have social relations directly or indirectly with each other.[30]

Robert and Helen Lynd, in their classic study of Middletown, offered a legitimation for this comparison a decade earlier. In examining diverse communities, they concluded that there are "not so many major kinds of things that people do." [31] In effect, although the overt trappings may vary, all people make a home, train their young, engage in religious practices, and so on. It was in Warner's writing, however, that the notion of cross-cultural uniformities in the nature of communities was most fully developed:

> Culture . . . has often been called . . . "a chaotic jumble." . . . Obviously, if the facts to be studied exist in "chaos," it is impossible to apply scientific methods to them. . . . This viewpoint . . . represents only . . . one school of anthropological thought. . . . The exact opposite of this position is held by another group.
>   To Durkheim and others . . . "the essential and permanent aspects of humanity" are those generalizations which can be made by the inductive method after an examination of various kinds of social phenomena. . . .[32]

Given this conception of communities, the type of analysis that closely fit, and was in fact generally used, was *functionalism*. This perspective has its origins in many disciplines, and its use by American social scientists was strongly influenced by Emile Durkheim and by the essays of A. R. Radcliffe-Brown who, incidentally, directed Warner's research in Australia.

A functional approach begins with a "system." Briefly defined, a system

29 Warner and Lunt, op. cit., p. 15.
30 Ibid., pp. 16–17.
31 Lynd and Lynd, *Middletown*, op. cit., p. 4.
32 Warner and Lunt, op. cit., pp. 9–10.

is a conceptualized whole whose composition is a product of the interrelations among its components. Thus, it is the interrelations among enzymes, stomach, intestines, and so on that constitute a digestive system in biology. The continued operation of any system is generally assumed to require that the components continue to make the same contribution to its maintenance. A change in the relationship among any components forces the entire system to undergo changes and disruption, unless other components can take over and provide the missing contribution.

One of the distinct advantages of a functional analysis is that it facilitates the identification of similarities in different contexts. For example, the rituals and norms associated with gift giving vary greatly from society to society; so, too, do the objects exchanged. By approaching gift giving from a functional perspective, however, it has been possible for social scientists to view diverse forms as functional equivalents; that is, as making similar contributions to the maintenance of the social systems in which they occur. Specifically, the offering and acceptance of a gift may be viewed as serving to reinforce social relationships.[33] Coming as they do at intervals—such as birthdays and special holidays—gift-giving occasions are opportunities to prevent kinship and friendship ties from dissolving. In a society such as our own, gift giving may also serve relatively unique functions, such as offering a discreet apology or conspicuously demonstrating wealth. However, by focusing on the cross-societal similarities, a functional approach permits an observer to classify similarly such seemingly different events as the Trobriand Islanders' ceremonial exchange of necklaces and armshells and the Americans' exchange of ties and gloves at Christmas.

The functional approach that guided Warner and his students in community studies is clearly expressed in the following quotation from the introduction to Yankee City:

> the investigator viewed the total community as a complex configuration of relations, each relation being a part of the total community and mutually dependent upon all other parts. Yankee City, we assumed, was a "working whole" in which each part had definite functions which had to be performed, or substitutes acquired, if the whole society was to maintain itself.[34]

The application of functional analysis to a modern social system required a community small enough to be conceptualized as a funtionally integrated whole. A large city, such as New York or Chicago, would be too large. In addition, their segregated ethnic groups represent different subcultures that would have destroyed the isomorphism of society, culture, and

---

[33] This view is presented by Marcel Mauss, *The Gift* (New York: Free Press, 1954).

[34] Warner and Lunt, op. cit., p. 14.

community. Therefore, as noted earlier by the Lynds, the kind of site selected had to be, "compact and homogeneous enough to be manageable."[35]

To examine these "typical" communities, the investigators selected a participant-observer methodology; that is, they (along with their families and assistants) typically moved into the community, often for a period of years. Their general goal was to observe, without personally influencing what they observed. They wanted to know who interacted with whom, how people thought, and what they felt, particularly with respect to local stratification patterns. As expressed by Hollingshead:

> No aspect of the field work was experimental, since we were interested in observing and gathering information about what the study group did under the conditions then prevailing in the community and under the conditions they themselves created by their activities, rather than in seeing how they would react to controlled situations presented to them, perforce, in an artificial manner.[36]

PARTICIPANTS OR OBSERVERS?   One of the most consistently raised methodological questions about the community stratification studies, in general, concerns whose perception of social classes was being presented: a compendium of all the residents; the views of only the more articulate residents; or those of the outside investigator? Certainly the answer makes a difference in the interpretation of these studies but, unfortunately, the community analyst themselves often appeared unable to answer the question.

The complexity of this issue was clearly pointed up by Allison Davis and Burleigh and Mary Gardner in their study of a "traditional" Southern community.[37] Their data indicated that there were patterned variations in the perceptions of stratification according to the class position of the respondents. Specifically, persons in the upper strata (that is, Warner's classes 1 and 2) made few distinctions in describing people at the bottom. Both the lower-lower ("disreputable poor") and the upper-lower ("poor but honest folk") were lumped together in their perceptions and categorized solely as "poor whites." Correspondingly, the people at the bottom did not differentiate between the upper middle and the two upper classes. All three categories were combined into what was considered, "Society." Thus, the amount of perceived differentiation varied inversely with social distance; that is, the greater the social distance between rater and subjects, the fewer were the perceived distinctions.

Davis and the Gardners also reported a tendency for invidious comparisons to increase as social distance decreases. In other words, people eval-

35 Lynd and Lynd, *Middletown,* op. cit., p. 7.
36 Hollingshead, op. cit., p. 10.
37 Allison Davis, Burleigh Gardner, and Mary Gardner, *Deep South* (Chicago: U. of Chicago, 1941).

uated those just above or below them with disdain and resentment, whereas more socially distant categories were more impersonally described. People in the lower middle class, for example, saw the upper middle as "People who think they are somebody." Similarly, the lower lower class saw people in the upper lower class as, "Snobs trying to push up." By contrast, people tended to evaluate their own class in quite favorable ways. Thus, in terms of self-conceptions the upper middle class saw themselves as "People who should be upper class." The lower lower class described members of their class as, "People just as good as anybody."

In reporting that there are six classes in this Southern community, it is apparent that Davis and the Gardners put together the perceptions of some highly diverse respondents; that is, they compiled the views of persons at various rank levels. Therefore, the resultant description is "real" only to the investigators. Perhaps no single individual in the community would see the town's social classes in the same way as the researchers.

In his analysis of Plainville, West resolved inconsistent perceptions in the same way. Placements were difficult to make, he reported, because the idea of social classes in Plainville was normatively disapproved. Thus, class placements were "more frequently made by inference and innuendo than by outright statement." Furthermore, "no two people [know] exactly the same facts about an individual, nor do they weigh the facts equally." [38]

Warner, and several other community analysts, were less consistent in how they handled this issue. At one point, for example, Warner insisted that he was only summarizing the distinctions made by the people themselves. At other times, however, he claimed that people were often insensitive to stratification, or that their perceptions were severely limited by their own positions. Presumably, then, Warner also was forced to construct a personally meaningful view of Yankee City's classes.[39]

Perhaps the overriding issue raised in this discussion concerns what social stratification meant to the community analysts. Were social classes those configurations that were subjectively real to the residents? Or were they the placements that seemed to make sense to the observer? The answer appears to be that the community analysts typically compromised; that is, their descriptions of stratification were partly real to the respondents, but partly real only to themselves. Whose reality *should* matter—that of the participant or that of the observer—is a very sensitive issue in sociology, and it is not confined to the study of social stratification.[40] The issue becomes highly salient in the study of stratification, however, because of the abstractness of the concepts involved—that is, social class, life-styles, and the like.

[38] West, loc. cit., p. 118.
[39] Warner and Lunt, loc. cit.
[40] This issue underlays the debates surrounding ethnomethodology as a contemporary sociological approach. In stratification, the issue is discussed in Milton Gordon, *Social Class in American Sociology* (Durham: Duke University, 1958).

These conceptions have no immediate or direct empirical referrant. Rather, they are generalizations and abstractions that have been developed in order to explain and summarize a great number of discrete empirical observations. Seen in this way, the issue then becomes not which view is "real," but which provides a more useful perspective for understanding and analyzing social stratification. At this point in our discussion it is sufficient to raise this issue; in ensuing chapters it will be assessed more fully.

SIZE AND GENERALIZATION.   Following any investigation, one must wonder about the degree to which the results may be generalized. The conclusions reached may apply only to the specific case studied, or they may be applicable to a wide variety of situations. In the last analysis, this question is empirically answered by the results of replicating studies. By examining the design of a study, however, it is initially possible to reflect on the likelihood of replication in different situations.

A question that, in this context, comes immediately to the fore concerns the size of most of the communities analyzed. The communities selected, such as Elmtown and Yankee City, were generally small. Their populations were typically less than ten thousand in size. In addition, they were often relatively isolated communities. To what extent, we must ask, are they representative of other American communities both now and at the time they were conducted?

During the 1930s approximately one half of the United States lived in metropolitan areas with populations of fifty thousand and more. In 1975, it is estimated, about 70 per cent of the total population lived in such metropolitan areas.[41] Sociologically, size is primarily important as an independent variable because of its effects on the form of interaction and the nature of social organization. As a community increases in size, there is a tendency for subgroup norms to become more highly differentiated and for intergroup conflicts to intensify; for coordinative problems to become magnified and for the overriding authority structure to become more formalized.[42] As these and other changes occur, they will necessarily affect the nature of social stratification and alter its relationship to the social organization.

In a large urban community, status assessments, for example, often must be made in a more fleeting and anonymous manner. "The urbanite may frequently rely upon appearance rather than reputation."[43] Thus, as we noted earlier, symbols—such as modes of dress, manners, cars, and conversational styles—replace family background and reputation as evaluations become less intimate and less enduring.

---

[41] See Gendell and Zetterberg, op. cit.
[42] See Paul E. Mott, *The Organization of Society* (Englewood Cliffs, N.J.: Prentice-Hall, 1965).
[43] William Form and Gregory P. Stone, "Urbanism, Anonymity, and Status Symbolism," *American Journal of Sociology,* 3:227–241 (1957).

Perhaps the greatest representativeness of the communities studied lies in their "typical-sounding" pseudonames. Consider how different an image would be conjured up if investigators called their communities by their true names, which included Muncie, Indiana; Newburyport, Massachusetts; and Morris, Illinois.

In the chapters immediately following we will consider the consequences, with respect to generalization, of studying selected communities. We may ask now, however, why communities of this type were selected? Part of the answer has been suggested already. The methodological framework of social anthropological studies initially required application in a community sufficiently small to permit examination of the whole. In addition, the previously discussed similarities of referent assumed among the conceptions of culture, society, and community required not only a small, but a homogeneous, study site. This point is clearly illustrated in Warner's explanation of his preference for either New England or Southern towns.

> It seemed wise to choose a community with a social organization which had developed over a long period of time under the domination of a single group with a coherent tradition. In the United States, only . . . New England and the Deep South, we believed, were likely to possess such a community. New England still contains many towns and cities where Puritan tradition remains unshattered. . . . The Deep South, too, changes in terms of an old and well-defined tradition.[44]

It was important to select communities of this type because, within them, there was likely to be the greatest congruence between culture and society, and it was likely that these would be distinctive communities.

As previously discussed, Warner and other researchers did not differentiate between culture and society. However, sociologists have typically done so, especially because in an urban society (such as our own) the distinction is useful. Specifically, a culture is typically defined as involving two components, material and social. The former consists of the technology and artifacts by which people meet their material needs. The second component entails shared traditions, values, and beliefs. A society, by contrast, involves a common culture and a distinctive geographical location; but, it also involves a social organization and patterns of social relations.

In a densely populated urban area—such as Detroit or Philadelphia—there are likely to be cultural and societal incongruities at the same time that there are shared patterns. Furthermore, and importantly, different ethnic or religious groups may not subscribe to a single set of values or traditions. The conceptualizations and methodology of the community studies initially could not accommodate to these kinds of discrepancies, derived as they were from highly integrated and homogeneous primitive

---

[44] Warner and Lunt, op. cit., p. 5.

societies. Thus, only one aspect of community life was studied, that which reflected the homogeneity of its groups.

Finally, there is the matter of community. In a large city without a single set of traditions and values, it is even more difficult to apply the concept of community. There may actually be many communities—that is, many areas with distinct geographical or social boundaries. However, our most recent experience in several cities has indicated that many of the ethnic-religious communities, formed during the latter part of the last and the first third of this century, have lost their distinctive identities as a result of assimilation.

Although it may appear initially that this process has simply eroded any kind of connection between individuals and whole or subcommunities, it is well to keep in mind that this may *not* be the case. The dissolution of ethnic communities has freed third- and fourth-generation Americans for absorption into the larger urbanized communities, allowing for different kinds of identification. Indeed the local-cosmopolitan distinction, which, on the basis of recent research, appears to be associated with different behavior patterns, suggests that some kinds of new identities have been formed that are relevant to life in mass, urbanized societies. The idea of community is somewhat elusive in complex societies, but it may still be meaningful to view most urban areas as communities.[45]

Thus, as noted earlier, Hollingshead, in his study of New Haven, provided a link between the Warner studies of small towns and cities and the urban research that began in the 1920s and continues to this day. That one can view this large eastern city as a community is clearly illustrated by the existence of a community-based social structure both distinctive of New Haven and similar to other cities and by attitudes and values reflecting orientation to and identification with the city as a whole.[46] If New Haven, clearly a part of the new megalopolis stretching across the eastern seaboard, still enjoys some identity as a community, then it is likely that this is an aspect of many large urban areas in the United States.[47]

Whatever the case, it appears that the controversy surrounding the significance of the idea of community in general and the sociological value of the various studies by the Lynds and Warner—to select the most prominent —will not be resolved in this volume. However, more recent research and developments in conceptual and methodological spheres do provide bases for drawing judgments about these issues. It is to these that we now turn.

[45] In this context see M. Stein, *The Eclipse of Community* (Princeton: Princeton University Press, 1960).

[46] Hollingshead and Redlich, op. cit.

[47] On the relationship between urbanism and community, see selected items in P. Meadows and E. H. Mizruchi, eds., *Urbanism, Urbanization and Change* (Reading, Mass.: Addison-Wesley, 1969).

6   Classes and Strata: Concepts and Measurement

The Debate Over Class in America

The research conducted during the first half of the twentieth century by American sociologists raised more questions about social stratification in the United States than it answered. Part of the reason for this, no doubt, is that for the most part the research was atheoretical—its focus was not the development of sociological theory by the systematic testing of research hypotheses. Rather, its principal focus was descriptive. Thus, research accomplished during the 1920s and 1930s by the "ecological school" inadvertently described some features of social organization and stratification, and the community studies executed by Warner, Hollingshead, and their disciples during the 1940s added considerable depth to our understanding of the nature of social stratification and its consequences in the United States.

However, one of the central, and indeed elementary, questions left unanswered by this research was whether the stratification system in American society was a hierarchy of finely graded strata or a hierarchy of clearly differentiated social classes. On one side are those who interpret the research findings as indicating that the stratification hierarchy is characterized by a number of discrete social classes. On the other side are those who argue that the research suggests that the stratification hierarchy is a continuous distribution of social strata without meaningful divisions along it.

Those who argue that American society is stratified into social classes have some basis for arguing that social classes are "real"; they are real in terms of their consequences, or real in terms of how they are subjectively perceived. The Lynds, Hollingshead, and others, have argued that social classes are objectively real as indicated by a variety of consequences. Within each class people share common life-chances, for example, and the most meaningful associations occur within each class.[1] By contrast, social psychologist Richard Centers and others have maintained that social classes are subjectively real. Individuals have a feeling of belonging to social classes, Centers argues, and this differentiates a class from a *stratum*.[2] The latter involves a category of persons placed together in some category (for example, an income group); but a stratum does not involve the psychic sense of identification associated with a class. The underlying premise of this subjective-reality argument is that members of American society believe that social classes exist; and they employ class labels (for example, middle class or working class) in order to categorize and rank themselves and others. Therefore, it is argued, these perceived class divisions are real; at least in the minds of individuals and, in that context, they are real in their consequences for behavior.

What we have termed the objective- and subjective-reality arguments are not contradictory; nor are they necessarily mutually exclusive. The writings of Marx, for instance, reflect both the objective and subjective positions. In Chapter 3 we noted that Marx implied that social classes are composed of individuals who share a common relationship to the land, labor, and capital of a society. These means of production provide the basis for a class division between the bourgeoisie, who own and control them, and the proletariat, who are employed by the bourgeoisie as "a class of labourers, who live only as they find work, and find work only so long as their labour increases capital." [3] In this passage Marx clearly implies that social classes are objectively real; that an individual's class position can be determined simply in terms of his relationship to the means of production. However, Marx also indicates that a subjective reality in the form of "class consciousness" will inevitably arise in response to the conflict and oppression that is inherent in the class system. Thus, Marxian theory predicts that the bourgeoisie will unite in common defense against the proletariat, which, in turn, unites in order to rid itself of the oppressive yoke of the ruling bourgeoisie.

---

[1] For a discussion of class, and classless, stratification, see Joseph A. Kahl, *The American Class Structure* (New York: Holt, 1957).

[2] Richard Centers, *The Psychology of Social Classes* (Princeton: Princeton University Press, 1949).

[3] Karl Marx, *The Communist Manifesto,* in *Selected Works* (New York: International Publishers, n.d.), p. 7.

The Continuum Theorists

John F. Cuber and William F. Kenkel[4] were the first to give systematic
expression to the position that the stratification hierarchy in the United
States consisted of a finely graded continuum and that conceptions of social
classes as discrete and identifiable groups in American society were both
unwarranted and incorrect. In support of this contention, continuum
theorists have pointed out certain inadequacies and inconsistencies in research based on the idea that classes are real. To begin with, they note the
widespread disagreement among theorists and researchers holding to the
classes-are-real argument concerning the exact number of social classes
in American society or in a given community. Marx's analysis of capitalist
societies, for instance, notes the existence of divisions between two basic
social classes, with the upper class subdivided into the aristocracy, the
bourgeoisie, and the petty bourgeoisie and the lower class subdivided into
the proletariat and the *lumpenproletariat*. James West's study of Plainville
also reflected the existence of two principal social classes, with the lower
class subdivided into three categories respectively defined by the residents
as "good lower-class people," "the lower element" and "people who live
like animals."[5] John Useem and his associates, however, in focusing
their analysis on what they termed the polar extremes of the "Tops" and
the "Bottoms" implied the existence of at least three distinct social classes.[6]
Centers, a leading proponent of the subjective-reality position, notes the
existence of four social classes: upper, middle, working, and lower. Hollingshead, on the other hand, points to five social classes in his study of Elms-
town's Youth, and Warner and his associates define five and sometimes
six. The point is that there appear to be as many social classes as there are
theorists or researchers. This leads to the interpretation that the reality
of social classes may be more a consequence of a priori decisions or
research methodologies than an accurate reflection of social organization
or stratification.

In addition, continuum theorists point to a lack of empirical evidence
to support the claim that individuals think of themselves and of others as
members of distinct social classes. At the same time they supply evidence
to the contrary. Lenski, for example, observed that when residents were
asked to rank a sample of families from their community, they did not agree
on either the number of social classes or the location of the boundaries

[4] John F. Cuber and William F. Kenkel, *Social Stratification in the United States*
(New York: Appleton, 1954).

[5] James West, *Plainville, USA* (New York: Columbia U.P., 1945).

[6] John P. Useem et al., "Stratification in a Prairie Town," *American Sociological
Review*, 7:47–59 (1942).

between them.[7] Thus, the placement of a segment of the population into social classes appears to be ambiguous, which may require the researcher to make somewhat arbitrary decisions. For example, according to Warner's rules for class placement, which we will take up later in this chapter, nearly one third of the workers he studied obtained scores intermediate between social classes. In order to resolve this dilemma, Warner arbitrarily assigned one half of the workers to each of the adjacent classes. Lenski interpreted his results as evidence that even the well-informed members of the community "were not accustomed to thinking of the community as divided into discrete social strata." [8]

Focusing specifically on the arguments that social classes are subjectively real, continuum theorists have noted that the individual's self-placement in a social class is dependent to a large extent on the structure of the question to which he or she is responding. Centers, for example, found that given the alternative of upper, middle, working, and lower class, 51 per cent of the respondents said that they belonged to the working class, 40 per cent said the middle class, and only 3 per cent located themselves in each of the lower and upper classes, respectively, whereas another 3 per cent either did not know to what class they belonged or denied the existence of social classes in American society. Kahl and Davis replicated Centers's study and found a similar distribution of responses when the same fixed alternative social classes were provided. However, in the same study they found that when the alternatives were not provided (that is, when the question was open-ended), the results were appreciably different. The open-ended question yielded a distribution of 1 per cent who said they were upper class; 51 per cent who claimed membership in the middle class; 2 per cent who thought of themselves as members of the lower class; and an important 32 per cent who either did not know to what class they belonged or denied the existence of social classes.[9] The Kahl and Davis findings imply that classes are real in the minds of individuals to the extent that reality is suggested by the researcher.

Research reported by Harold A. Mulford and Winfield W. Salisbury raises still another critical argument against Centers's position that social classes are part of an individual's ego and personality. They investigated the salient characteristics of the individual's self-concepts utilizing a modified version of the Twenty Statements test. In this test subjects were asked to respond to the question: "Who am I?" Mulford and Salisbury found that only one of the 1,213 respondents gave a self-definition in terms of social-

[7] Gerhard E. Lenski, "American Social Classes," *American Journal of Sociology,* **58**:139–144 (1952).

[8] Ibid., p. 143.

[9] Joseph A. Kahl and James Davis, "A Comparison of Indices of Socio-Economic Status," *American Sociological Review,* **20**:317–325 (1955).

class membership.[10] This finding suggests that social-class position is not a salient characteristic of an individual's self-concept as argued by Centers.

Continuum theorists also support their interpretation of the stratification system in the United States by citing data on the distribution of critical stratification variables such as income, education, and occupational prestige within American society. One of the best-known and most-cited examples is the National Opinion Research Center's (NORC) study of occupational prestige.[11] This data does not provide evidence of any discernable cleavage effect occurring along the occupational prestige hierarchy. Robert A. Ellis[12] has responded to this finding by noting that NORC's work

> only confirms what Warner has already reported and documented: namely, the single factor of occupation does not provide a satisfactory means for accurately assigning individuals to their appropriate social class.[12]

Nevertheless, additional studies by Stanley A. Hetzler[13] and Kenkel,[14] which involve stratification variables in addition to occupational prestige, similarly bolster the continuum interpretation of the American stratification system.

The controversy between the discrete and continuum interpretations of the stratification system has been eased by the recognition that the concepts of social class and social strata and the placement of individuals into one class or strata as opposed to another can be of hueristic benefit to the researcher without necessarily implying a reification of the concept.[15] Furthermore, sociologists have largely come to agree with Werner S. Landecker's conclusion, which appears in the following article.

[10] Harold A. Mulford and Winfield W. Salisbury, "Self Conceptions in a General Population," *Sociological Quarterly,* **5**:305–316 (1964).

[11] Cecil C. North and Paul K. Hatt, "Jobs and Occupations," *Public Opinion News,* **9** (1947).

[12] Robert A. Ellis, "Social Stratification and Social Relations," *American Sociological Review,* **22**:118 (1957).

[13] Stanley A. Hetzler, "An Investigation of the Distinctiveness of Social Classes," *American Sociological Review,* **19**:96–105 (1953).

[14] Kenkel, as reported in Cuber and Kenkel, op. cit.

[15] Robert W. Hodge, "Social Integration, Psychological Well-Being and Their Socioeconomic Correlates," in *Social Stratification,* Edward O. Laumann (ed.) (Indianapolis: Bobbs-Merrill, 1970).

Class Boundaries*

Werner S. Landecker

Students of stratification disagree about the presence or absence of structural divisions in social status systems. This issue has been raised primarily, although not exclusively,[1] with respect to stratification in the United States. It involves two contrasting views, which may be considered as alternative hypotheses of a sociographic or descriptive character. One of these is designated here as the "class structure" hypothesis, the other as the "status continuum" hypothesis.

Status Continuum Versus Class Structure

The *class structure* hypothesis is represented by the familiar assumption that the status systems of American communities are composed of distinct structural units, described in terms of a limited number of "classes."[2] In part, the widespread acceptance of this hypothesis may have resulted from the fact that the analysis of stratification had its origin in societies with highly visible class lines. Moreover, to researchers engaged in a variety of stratification studies the "class structure" assumption has offered a particular advantage: it has provided them with a meaningful criterion for the construction of their statistical tables. Without this assumption, the categories into which a status range is divided must be treated as purely arbitrary "intervals"; with it, they can be conceptualized as "social classes."

Advocates of the *status continuum* hypothesis do not deny the presence of social stratification in the United States. They doubt, however, that it can be described by means of a few structural categories. Status differences in American society are thought to be of a merely gradual character and to lack in "natural breaks." Thus it is claimed that status differences in American society form continuous rather than structured hierarchies.[3] This hypothesis originated in response to research findings which seemed not to be readily compatible with the conventional image of discrete social classes. An analysis of variations in socio-economic attitudes by social status revealed a prevalence of merely minor differences in such attitudes between contiguous status levels.[4] Further doubt regarding the existence of discrete social classes was provoked by the observation that a panel of well-informed local citizens showed no substantial agreement as to the number of social classes in their community.[5]

While it is true that such findings lend plausibility to the status continuum

* Reprinted with permission from *American Sociological Review*, **25**:868–877 (Dec. 1960).
    This study is part of a larger project conducted jointly with Gerhard E. Lenski within the framework of the Detroit Area Study at the University of Michigan. Grants from the Social Science Research Council and from the Faculty Research Fund of the University of Michigan are gratefully acknowledged. Helpful suggestions were made by Robert C. Angell, Gerhard E. Lenski, and Alberta Z. Potter.

hypothesis, their relevance to the hypothesis is indirect, and they support it only by way of inference.[6] In order to probe the issue with more conclusive evidence it seems advisable to employ a direct method of detecting the presence or absence of structural divisions in a stratification system, based on an examination of its internal properties.

The Concept of Class Boundaries

Like any other methodological objective, the problem of how to deter-mine the existence of structural divisions in a status distribution can be pur-sued in various ways. The present approach reflects a basic interest in a particular aspect of a stratification system, namely, the interrelationship among its constituent rank systems.[7] The entire system of stratification in a given population can be viewed as a composite of several rank systems. In any one of these, the entire population is ranked on the basis of a single status factor, such as occupation or ethnic-racial ancestry. Thus, within a given system of stratification, all rank systems are distributions of the same population, but each is based on a different criterion of status.

A total system of stratification can be divided into different layers, each of which cuts across all rank systems. Every layer is a horizontal constellation of ranks located at mutually equivalent levels in different rank systems. Such ranks can be compared with regard to similarity or difference in their composi-tion. If they are very similar in composition, that is, if they have nearly the same incumbents, they form jointly a distinct structural unit of stratification.

In populations characterized by rapid change, however, it is more com-mon that equivalent ranks of different rank systems are at least moderately *dissimilar* in their composition. Under these conditions, there is a large pro-portion of persons each of whom holds discrepant statuses in the several rank systems. Figuratively speaking, these rank systems are linked in a network of crisscross connections. Such a network, however, is not necessarily unstruc-tured. Disparate but interrelated ranks of different rank systems can form a cluster, demarcated from other ranks by observable boundaries. One may think of a boundary as being located between two consecutive ranks insofar as their respective interrelations with other rank systems gravitate in opposite direc-tions. In other words, two consecutive ranks are separated by a boundary to the extent that the upper rank is linked to levels above it, and the lower rank to those below it.

In its simplest form, a boundary may be described by means of a model consisting of two rank systems (A and B), both containing four ranks (1–4). This model is shown in Figure 1. The model assumes a population of four persons (a–d), each of whom holds disparate statuses in the two rank systems. The particular status combinations for each person are designed in such a manner that a boundary occurs between rank levels 2 and 3. Rank 2 gravitates upward in the sense that each person who occupies rank 2 in one rank system combines it with rank 1 in the other rank system. Rank 3 is combined with rank 4 in every instance and thus gravitates downward. This model serves as a rudimentary and "ideal-typical" sketch of the more complex constellations of status which are the actual subject-matter of boundary analysis. The model

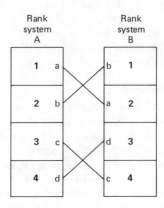

Figure 1

provides guidelines for the elaboration of a method by means of which that kind of analysis can be undertaken.

Once such a method has been worked out, the issue posed by the class structure and status continuum hypotheses can be translated into empirical problems of boundary analysis. Insofar as the analysis would fail to reveal the existence of boundaries, the findings would conform to the status continuum hypothesis; insofar as the presence of boundaries is ascertained, such evidence would support the class structure hypothesis. In order to make explicit the fact that boundaries have this heuristic significance, they are designated as *class boundaries*.[8]

This translation of the controversy into problems of class boundary analysis constitutes more than a change in terminology. In their initial formulation, the two hypotheses seemed to assert mutually exclusive situations: no compromise between these alternatives was readily apparent.[9] This aspect of the issue is modified when the concept of class boundary is introduced.

In the first place, whereas such terms as "social classes" or "class structure" are descriptive of a total system of stratification, this is not true of the concept of class boundary. The latter refers to a particular location within the larger system and claims no additional characteristics of the system as a whole. Therefore, this concept directs the investigator's attention to the possibility that he may find class boundaries within a limited range of a status system but not elsewhere in its remaining range. In this event, one segment of the observed system would conform to the class structure hypothesis, another to the status continuum hypothesis.

A second feature of the class boundary concept is its essentially quantitative character, which becomes more apparent below in its operational treatment. A class boundary is a matter of degree. The manner in which a class boundary is ascertained is a procedure of measuring its relative magnitude. Therefore, the concept brings into focus a wide span of measures, ranging from the strongest to the weakest boundaries. In this respect, the concept permits a greater variety of observations than is anticipated in either hypothesis.

A Method of Ascertaining Class Boundaries

The problem of how the presence of class boundaries can be determined empirically arose within the context of a more comprehensive study of social stratification in the metropolitan area of Detroit. The data for this study were obtained through interviews with 749 subjects, selected by means of an area sampling technique.[10] The stratification system of Detroit was treated as a composite of four rank systems, namely, the occupational, income, educational, and ethnic-racial.[11] Each rank system can be envisaged as a separate table showing the distribution of subjects in ranked categories. For example, one table might show a percentage distribution by year of school completed.[12] another by annual income in intervals of 1,000 dollars.

The choice of the four rank systems reflects an attempt to select as broad a variety of systems as permitted by the available data. Thus, while the occupational, educational, and income rank systems constitute different varieties of achieved status, the ethnic-racial rank system was included to represent ascribed status. For the same basic reason, it seemed desirable to avoid qualitative similarities among rank systems; this explains why only one rank system was chosen from several possible indicators of financial status.

These four rank systems were used as the raw material for boundary analysis. The various steps of that analysis are described in the remainder of this section.

1. A Uniform Measure of Rank.　In Figure 1 two hypothetical systems were drawn, each consisting of four ranks. The assumption that rank levels 2 and 3 are divided by a boundary rested on the implicit premise that status in both rank systems is measured in identical units. It was assumed, in other words, that ranks 2 in rank systems A and B are mutually equivalent in status, that rank 1 in rank system A is superior in status to rank 2 in rank system B, and so on.

Empirical rank systems, however, do not permit this assumption; they present the investigator with such questions as: How much income is the status equivalent of how much education? It becomes necessary, therefore, to reduce the initial diversity in units of measurement to a common denominator. For this reason, the various ranks of any rank system were treated uniformly as a population distribution, described in terms of cumulative percentages which were counted up from the lowest rank. The midpoint of the cumulative percentage range occupied by a given rank was used as its status score.

2. The Basic Criterion for Boundary Analysis.　The model shown in Figure 1 illustrates a major criterion for the determination of class boundaries. This criterion can be observed in the manner in which the population stratified in one rank system is distributed in the other rank system, and *vice versa*. The presence of a boundary is indicated by the fact that incumbents of contiguous ranks in one rank system occupy noncontiguous ranks in the other rank system. A crucial methodological task is to replicate this criterion under actual conditions. Toward this end, one rank system was selected initially, and for all persons in a given rank the arithmetic mean of their status scores in another rank system was computed. The occupational rank system may serve as an example. For each occupational rank, the mean income status associated with it was ascertained. Correspondingly, for each occupational rank its respective means of ethnic-racial and educational status were obtained. This treatment of the occupational rank system is illustrative of a procedure which was applied to the other three rank systems as well.

3. Standardizing the Unit of Measurement.   It might seem that the preceding step yields a sufficient criterion for judging the size of a break or the "distance" which separates consecutive ranks within a rank system. The difference between the mean status scores carried by their respective incumbents in other rank systems may appear to be such a criterion. For instance, if a greater difference in mean income status were found between the incumbents of certain occupational ranks than between those of other occupational ranks, this might suggest that the first set of occupational ranks is divided by a greater distance than is the second set.

This conclusion, however, is weakened by the fact that even *within* a rank system there may be greater or smaller status differences between any two consecutive ranks, irrespective of the way their incumbents are distributed in *other* rank systems. Two such ranks may differ widely in the status scores assigned to them in their own rank system, while two other ranks in the same system may differ much less. Variations in this respect are apt to distort the results of the investigation, since the amount of status difference between two ranks within their own rank system will affect the difference between their means in other rank systems. For example, if the difference in means of income status is greater between occupational ranks 1 and 2 than between ranks 2 and 3, the greater magnitude of that difference may be an insignificant artifact, created by a larger discrepancy in occupational status between 1 and 2 than between 2 and 3. Conversely, a given income difference between two occupational ranks is all the more significant, the less these ranks differ in their occupational status. It is necessary, therefore, to cancel out the effect of this variable before any conclusions with respect to class boundaries are drawn.

For this reason, mean income differences between occupational ranks were weighted by a factor inversely proportionate to the difference in occupational status between the same ranks.[13] In accordance with their weighted differences from one another, the original means of income status were converted into "adjusted means." [14] The same procedure of standardization was extended to all means of status which had been computed previously (step 2). This resulted in three series of adjusted means for each of the four rank systems, every series representing one particular rank system in relation to one other rank system.

4. "Distances" within a Rank System.   The extent to which contiguous ranks differ in their adjusted means constitutes a multiplicity of criteria for ascertaining the existence of breaks between such ranks. Not only do these criteria vary from one rank system to another, but even for any one of them there are different sets of adjusted means which compete as indicators of breaks *within* the rank system. Thus, for purposes of judging the extent to which there are breaks in the income rank system, alternative and not entirely uniform criteria are provided by its adjusted means of occupational, educational, and ethnic-racial status, as may be seen in Table 1. For example, the two highest income ranks differ from each other most sharply in their adjusted means of educational status, less so in their corresponding means of occupational status, and not at all in their means of ethnic-racial status. Generally speaking, for each of the four rank systems in question, its respective distribution in each of the three other systems would yield diverse criteria of distance between its ranks.

TABLE 1
Distances among Income Ranks, As Measured by Differences
among Their Adjusted Means in Three Other Rank Systems

Income Ranks		Adjusted Means in the			Means of	
Ranges (A)	Status Scores (B)	Occupational Rank System (C)	Educational Rank System (D)	Ethnic-Racial Rank System (E)	Adjusted Means (F)	Inter-rank Distances (G)
(1) 93.4–100.0	97	80.4	78.9	57.5	72.3	15.5
(2) 90.5– 93.3	92	69.4	43.5	57.5	56.8	0.9
(3) 81.2– 90.4	86	71.6	36.8	59.4	55.9	6.4
(4) 68.2– 81.1	75	61.0	34.0	53.6	49.5	1.8
(5) 46.8– 68.1	57	56.7	33.2	53.2	47.7	4.1
(6) 18.1– 46.7	32	49.8	29.2	50.4	43.1	−0.4
(7) 10.1– 18.0	14	50.2	30.0	50.7	43.6	5.2
(8) 4.9– 10.0	7	48.4	21.8	40.6	36.9	−0.4
(9) 0.0– 4.8	2	47.8	15.4	50.5	37.9	

But the methodological goal of the analysis was to produce a single measure of boundaries for the stratification system as a whole rather than for one rank system at a time, let alone three different criteria for each rank system. It was necessary, therefore, to combine all of these limited measures into a single index of class boundaries. This procedure was carried out in two stages. In the first, the three criteria for the gauging of breaks in a given rank system were combined into a single measure of the "distance" between any two of its ranks. In the second stage, these measures of distance, each specific to a different rank system, were used as components of an over-all index of class boundaries.

The manner in which distances within a rank system were computed is illustrated in Table 1 with reference to the income rank system.[15] In the first place, the table shows each of the adjusted means of status held by the incumbents of a given income rank in each of the three other rank systems. These three means of status were combined into their over-all mean (column F). The difference between the over-all means for a given income rank and the *next lower* over-all mean of a lower income rank was used to measure an inter-rank distance. Depending on the location of the next lower over-all mean, distances were calculated sometimes between contiguous ranks[16] and sometimes between non-contiguous ranks.[17] For each income rank, its distance from a lower income rank is shown in the last column.[18]

The same procedure which has been described with reference to the income rank system was used in each of the three other rank systems. Thus, distances in the occupational rank system were calculated by combining the mean educational status, income status, and ethnic-racial status, which are associated with a given occupational rank, into an over-all mean, and by determining the difference between the over-all means for one occupational rank and another. In basically the same way, inter-rank distances were obtained for the educational and the ethnic-racial rank systems.

5. The Class Boundary Index.   While, then, a variety of limited indicators were merged into fewer and more comprehensive measures of distance, any set of such measures is restricted to a single rank system. The remaining task, therefore, was to combine the four sets of distance measures into an over-all index of class boundaries. The desired function of such an index is to summarize in each of its values a cross-section of inter-rank distances which are found in different rank systems at similar locations.

As indicated above, any "rank" represents a range of percentage scores within the cumulative percentage distribution of a rank system. The lowest score of the range covered by a given rank is designated as its "lower rank-limit" in Table 2. It is the point at which a rank is separated from lower ranks and, therefore, is the potential location of class boundary. The table shows the amount of distance by which the ranks of each rank system are divided at each lower rank-limit,[19] thereby providing a basis for assessing the magnitude of a class boundary formed by a horizontal series of lower rank-limits.

Several lower rank-limits were combined into a horizontal series in accordance with the following rule: No rank system may be represented more than once in a single series, and different lower rank-limits must be similarly located in their respective rank systems. They were treated as being "similarly located" if they fell into the same interval of status percentiles. Each such interval consisted of five consecutive percentiles. It was found that such breaks in this particular set of data can be represented most adequately by selecting status percentiles 2–6 as the base line for the entire array of equal intervals.[20] The class boundary index is the arithmetic means of inter-rank distances at those lower rank-limits which fall within a single interval. The last column of Table 2 presents the values of this index. Since some intervals do not contain any lower rank-limits, there are corresponding gaps in the array of index scores. The use of parentheses signifies that the score shown is a single inter-rank distance rather than an average of several.

Findings and Their Implications

Location and Magnitude of Class Boundaries.   When the various scores of the class boundary index are compared, one fact stands out clearly: a single class boundary by far surpasses all others in magnitude. This boundary is found in the interval of status percentiles 92–96 and separates a small "elite" range from the remainder of the stratification system. The elite range is characterized by a completed college education, occupations on a high professional or

TABLE 2

Class Boundaries, as Measured by the Means of Inter-Rank Distances

Intervals of Status Percentiles	Occupational Rank System		Income Rank System		Educational Rank System		Ethnic-Racial Rank System	
	Lower Rank-Limits	Inter-rank Distances	Lower Rank-Limits	Inter-rank Distances	Lower Rank-Limits	Inter-rank Distances	Inter-rank Distances	Class Boundary Index
92–96	94	9.8	93	15.5	—	14.1	—	13.1
87–91	—	—	90	0.9	89	9.0	3.5	4.5
82–86	—	—	—	—	—	—	—	—
77–81	72	4.7	81	6.4	78	1.9	3.1	3.8
72–76	—	—	68	1.8	72	0.4	-1.6	1.5
67–71	—	—	67	—	—	—	—	1.1
62–66	—	—	—	—	—	—	—	—
57–61	—	—	61	—	59	-1.3	0.6	-0.4
52–56	—	—	51	—	—	—	-1.2	2.7
47–51	43	3.2	43	4.1	50	5.1	0.1	0.8
42–46	—	—	—	—	42	-0.8	—	—
37–41	—	—	32	—	—	3.2	—	(3.2)
32–36	—	—	—	—	—	—	—	—
27–31	—	—	—	—	—	—	—	—
22–26	—	—	18	-0.4	25	—	-3.7	(-3.7)
17–21	—	—	—	—	16	—	4.9	(4.9)
12–16	8	1.8	10	5.2	20	3.3	-6.0	-1.0
7–11	—	—	8	—	6	6.1	—	4.4
2–6	—	—	5	-0.4	—	—	-12.5	-6.5

executive level, and incomes whose recipients constitute approximately the highest seven percent of all income-earners.

The class boundary index yields other positive, but much smaller, scores in several locations. The highest of such scores, those exceeding four points each, are—at best—suggestive of two further segments of the status system. One of these represents a barely distinguishable "lower" stratum; the other is placed in an "upper-middle" area, immediately below the elite range. Between them lies a very large range whose internal boundaries are so feeble that it can be considered as almost undifferentiated.

The upper-middle sector is demarcated from this range by a minor boundary (interval 87–91) which derives its limited support primarily from a break in the educational rank system. This break separates persons who have completed a substantial amount of college study[21] from those on lower educational levels. An additional basis for this minor boundary is provided by a division between the highest ethnic rank, composed of persons of English ancestry, and the next-lower level of the ethnic-racial rank system. On the other hand, the segment which lies below the minor boundary in the interval 7–11 is characterized by unskilled service occupations, relatively little formal education,[22] and by the lowest nine percent of all personal incomes.

While it is possible, then, to delineate a few relatively small structural units—designated in the above as "elite," "upper-middle," and "lower"—this merely structural description requires quantitative modification. The three structural units differ greatly in the magnitude of the class boundaries by which they are set off, and therefore also in the degree of their structural distinctness. The elite sector is demarcated by a class boundary which is almost three times stronger than any other, as measured by their index scores. Only the elite boundary is of significant magnitude to indicate a tendency of adjacent strata to "gravitate" in opposite directions. To detect such a tendency is the purpose for which the class boundary index has been designed. The inverse of that tendency is signified by negative index scores. They show the extent to which there is overlap, rather than separation, between the strata concerned. It is only because negative and extremely low positive scores are so prevalent in the total array of index values that the few indications of minor boundaries seemed to merit recognition at all.

Related Research Problems.   The preceding findings rest upon one among several available criteria for the determination of class boundaries. Whether or not the use of other criteria would produce similar results is an open question. An alternative to the approach taken here might be to infer the existence of class boundaries from other phenomena in which they may be manifested, such as low rates of vertical mobility between contiguous strata,[23] low frequencies of person-to-person contacts across contiguous strata, or sharp differences between them with regard to attitudes and behavior. It is likely indeed that such variables are fairly sensitive to the prevailing system of stratification; they are acceptable as indices of its structural properties if there is no better alternative.

Instead of taking recourse to indirectly relevant observations of this kind, it seemed preferable to determine the location and magnitude of class boundaries by means of direct evidence, that is, through an examination of the relationships among the various rank systems of which the total system of stratification is constituted. This procedure has the major advantage of permitting the investigation of research problems which otherwise would be obscured. Since class boundaries were not measured in terms of attitudinal and behavioral variables, the relationship of these variables to class boundaries can be studied as an empirical question.

This type of research problem can be exemplified as follows. Some years ago, a comprehensive review of public-opinion data revealed that the sharpest break in attitudes on socio-economic issues occurred between a small, upper set of well-to-do persons and the remaining 80 to 90 percent of the population.[24] This break in the distribution of attitudes is near the point where the only major class boundary was found in the present study. While these findings may be unrelated, their similarity suggests a general problem: Are differences in socio-economic attitudes held by consecutive strata proportionate to the magnitude of class boundaries between them? Similar questions for research concern the relationship between class boundaries, as measured here, and several other variables noted above as alternative indicators.

Furthermore, the findings have implications for a methodological problem in stratification research. When seeking to ascertain behavioral or attitudinal concomitants of stratification, the investigator sometimes is faced with the task of deciding which of several possible cutting-points in a status distribution is likely to reveal the most significant status differences among his subjects. Theoretical considerations which can be traced to Thorstein Veblen have given support to the view that it is advantageous to split a population into "white collar" and "blue collar," or "middle class" and "working class." [25] In urban samples, each category created by this split constitutes a major portion of the entire status range.[26]

The adequacy of this approach, however, is not beyond question. Especially among thinkers who treat American society largely as a power structure, it has been claimed that the chief structural components of the population are a small "elite" and a much larger "mass." [27] While the present study has no bearing on the political and socio-psychological aspects of "elitist" theory, it does strengthen the view that the main break in the stratification system occurs very near the top. It seems probable, therefore, that a status dichotomy which overlaps this break, as does the cut between white collar and blue collar, will be impaired in its discriminatory power as an instrument of research.

The "Structure"-"Continuum" Controversy. The analysis of class boundaries was occasioned by two alternative conceptions of social stratification in the United States, called here the class structure and the status continuum hypotheses. Being merely descriptive statements, these hypotheses would not clash if each were applied to a different population. Thus, the class structure hypothesis may fit the situation in one community, while the status continuum hypothesis may be closer to the facts in another. In order to establish the relevance of the present findings for *both* hypotheses it is necessary to assume, therefore, that *each* would have given rise to a different prediction for the particular community treated in this study. This seems to be a reasonable assumption and is taken as a premise for the following conclusions.

It is readily apparent that neither hypothesis is wholly corroborated or contradicted by the data examined here. The *class structure hypothesis* derives its strongest support from the existence of a major class boundary. However, in line with the hypothesis itself, one would have expected to find structural divisions throughout the entire system of stratification. Accordingly, one would have predicted that as wide a range as lies below the "elite" level is subdivided by at least one class boundary of major proportions. While minor boundaries within that range were tentatively identified, they provide only the most limited support for the hypothesis; their very weakness signifies the extent to which the observed facts fall short of the anticipated pattern.

The *status continuum hypothesis*, on the other hand, denies the existence of *any* major structural break in a given system of stratification. It is clear that the evidence does not substantiate this hypothesis in its radical sense. But the hypothesis implies also the more limited assumption that a stratification system will show at least a greater *degree* of coherence, covering a wider *range* of its levels, than would be compatible with the traditional notion of "class structure." This assumption is supported by the fact that the condition of an unbroken status sequence is closely approximated throughout a large segment of the observed system.

In summary, the measurement of class boundaries attempted in this investigation reveals the presence of one major class boundary, by which the topmost strata are divided from the bulk of the population. Below this elite boundary, the dominant feature is a status gradation of considerable continuity, aside from a few minor indentations. The view suggested by these findings is that neither the class structure nor the status continuum hypothesis takes precedence over the other, but rather that each is appropriate to a different portion of the total system of stratification.

NOTES

1. See Robert A. Ellis, "Social Stratification and Social Relations: An Empirical Test of the Disjunctiveness of Social Classes," *American Sociological Review*, 22 (October, 1957), pp. 570–578; Renate Mayntz, "Gedanken und Ergebnisse Zur Empirischen Feststellung Sozialer Schichten." *Kölner Zeitschrift für Soziologie und Sozialpsychologie*, Sonderheft 1 (1957), pp. 79–104.

2. This view has been taken in many community studies listed in Harold W. Pfautz, "The Current Literature on Social Stratification: Critique and Bibliography," *American Journal of Sociology*, 58 (January, 1953), pp. 391–418, esp. pp. 400 ff. The opposite view is explicitly rejected in favor of the class structure hypothesis by Ellis, *op. cit.;* and by Joseph A. Kahl, *The American Class Structure*, New York: Rinehart, 1957, pp. 12 ff.

3. This hypothesis is favored by Arthur W. Kornhauser, "Analysis of 'Class' Structure of Contemporary American Society—Psychological Bases of Class Divisions," in G. W. Hartmann and T. Newcomb, editors, *Industrial Conflict*, New York: Cordon, 1939, Chapter 11, esp. pp. 250, 261: Gunnar Myrdal, *An American Dilemma*, New York: Harper, 1944, p. 675; Oliver C. Cox, *Caste, Class and Race*, Garden City, N.Y.: Doubleday, 1948, pp. 301—310; Gerhard E. Lenski, "American Social Classes: Statistical Strata or Social Groups?" *American Journal of Sociology*, 58 (September, 1952), pp. 139–144; Stanley A.

Hetzler, "An Investigation of the Distinctiveness of Social Classes," *American Sociological Review*, 18 (October, 1953), pp. 493–497; John F. Cuber and William F. Kenkel, *Social Stratification in the United States*, New York: Appleton-Century-Crofts, 1954, pp. 12, 23–29, 150 ff., 303–309; Bernard Barber, *Social Stratification*, New York: Harcourt, Brace, 1957, p. 77; and John L. Hear, "Predictive Utility of Five Indices of Social Stratification," *American Sociological Review*, 22 (October, 1957), pp. 541–545.

4. Kornhauser, op. cit.
5. Lenski, op. cit.
6. Unless one employs a more nearly psychological than sociological framework and conceives of stratification in terms of attitudinal and perceptual variables.
7. Ronald Freedman et al., *Principles of Sociology*, New York: Holt, 1952. Chapter 7; Gerhard E. Lenski, "Status Crystallization: A Non-Vertical Dimension of Social Status," *American Sociological Review*, 19 (August, 1954), pp. 405–413; Werner S. Landecker, "Class Crystallization and its Urban Pattern," *Social Research*, 27 (Autumn, 1960).
8. The use of class boundaries as criteria of class structure has a logical implication for the corollary concept of "class." Aside from other specifications which one may wish to include in a definition of this concept, the present approach leads one to stipulate as a basic property of a class its separation from the remainder of the stratification system by a class boundary.
9. An exception is the discussion by Milton M. Gordon in *Social Class in American Sociology*, Durham: Duke University Press, 1958, pp. 183–189.
10. Leslie Kish, "A Two-Stage Sample of a City." *American Sociological Review*, 17 (December, 1952), pp. 761–769.
11. For details, see Lenski, "Status Crystallization . . . ," op. cit., pp. 406 ff.
12. This measure of educational status is admittedly crude insofar as it fails to take account of informal status differences among schools represented on the same formal level of education.
13. Whenever the higher of two adjoining occupational ranks had also the higher mean of income status, the difference between the two means of income status, multiplied by 10, was divided by the difference in occupational status between the same ranks. Any mean of income status which exceeded that of a higher occupational rank was kept in its proportionate relation to the next higher and lower means.
14. The weighted differences were subtracted cumulatively from the highest mean. The result of each single subtraction was an "adjusted mean."
15. Corresponding tables were constructed for each of the three other rank systems but are omitted because of space limitation.
16. Thus, referring to specific cells of Table 1, $G1 = F1 - F2$; $G2 = F2 - F3$; $G3 = F3 - F4$; and $G4 = F4 - F5$.
17. Thus, $G5 = F5 - F7$; and $G7 = F6 - F9$.
18. Reversals between the over-all means of contiguous ranks resulted in negative values of distance. The structural significance of a reversal for the rank system as a whole seemed to depend partly on the relative size of the smaller of those ranks between which the reversal occurred; negative distance values were weighted accordingly. Thus

$$G6 = \frac{A7\,(F6 - F7)}{X_\Delta} \; ; \text{ and } G8 = \frac{A9\,(F8 - F9)}{X_\Delta} \,.$$

19. Inter-rank distances for the income rank system are taken from Table 1. Inter-rank distances for each of the other rank systems were calculated in the same manner, as shown above in step 4.
20. The methodological principle involved here is not that a class boundary index always requires the particular intervals used in this instance, but rather that they should be chosen so as to provide the best possible fit for the actual distribution of lower rank-limits. Some flexibility in this respect will enhance rather than reduce the comparability of indices for different sets of data.
21. For persons under 40 years of age, three years of college; for persons 40 or more years of age, two or three years of college.
22. For persons under 40 years of age, less than an 8th grade education; for persons 40 or more years of age, less than a 4th grade education.
23. This criterion has been proposed by Andreas Miller in "The Problem of Class Boundaries and its Significance for Research into Class Structure." *Transactions of the Second Congress of Sociology*, Paris, 1954, Vol. 2, pp. 343–352.
24. Kornhauser, op. cit., pp. 253, 261.

25. Seymour M. Lipset and Reinhard Bendix, *Social Mobility in Industrial Society,* Berkeley: University of California Press, 1959, pp. 14–17, and passim.
26. See, e.g., C. Wright Mills, *White Collar,* New York: Oxford, 1953, p. 63; and Morris Janowitz, "Social Stratification and Mobility in West Germany," *American Journal of Sociology,* 64 (July, 1958), Tables 1 and 2.
27. C. Wright Mills, *The Power Elite,* New York: Oxford, 1956, pp. 321–324; see also Harold D. Lasswell and Abraham Kaplan, *Power and Society,* New Haven: Yale University Press, 1950, p. 202.

Measurement of Social Position

There are three principle methods for determining the rank of an individual or family in the stratification hierarchy.[16] The first, or objective, method determines class or strata rank in terms of criteria such as: educational attainment; amount of income (that is, either total family income or income of the head of the household); source of income (that is, whether the income is earned in the form of salaries and wages or as profits from self-employment, sale of stocks, interest on savings, or land holdings); occupation; racial or ethnic background; life-style; and so on. The investigator may utilize any one of these or other indicators or may combine several of them to form an "index" of position in the class or strata hierarchy. The objective method assumes that social classes or strata are objectively real and can be differentiated by such factors or indicators. The choice of indicators, however, is largely dependent on the theoretical persuasion of the investigator and the research question of interest. For example, research guided by the writings of Marx and concerning itself with the question of class conflict would most appropriately use "source" of income as an indicator of class membership; the same research guided by the writings of Weber would most appropriately use "amount" of income as an indicator of position in the class (for example, economic) hierarchy. The validity of the objective method, therefore, depends on the researcher having a clear conceptual definition of precisely what is meant by social class or social strata and choosing indicators accordingly.

The second method of ranking individuals in the stratification hierarchy is self-placement, in which individuals are simply asked to which social class or strata they belong. This method clearly assumes that social classes or strata have a subjective reality and that individuals share perceptions and definitions of the class hierarchy. As we have noted already, however, the individual's self-placement is greatly affected by the manner in which the question of class membership is presented.

The third principal method of placement is according to reputation. In general, the reputational procedure involves asking knowledgeable mem-

---

[16] Typically, all persons in a family are given the score assigned to the head of the household.

bers of the community to describe the stratification system and rank several families in their respective social classes. The investigator can then place the remaining members of the community in the social class described by the judges. This method of class placement assumes that social classes are real in the minds of (at least) "informed" community members. However, one of the principal shortcomings of this method is that it is appropriate only for relatively small communities in which the knowledgeable judges know virtually everyone in the community.[17]

In the early community studies, investigators typically reported that the placement of individuals into specific strata or social classes was accomplished by utilizing a number of criteria such as income, occupational standing, area of residence, family lineage, memberships in particular formal associations, and so on. The relative importance of each of these criterion was moot. Equally moot were questions of the validity and reliability of placement.

One of the first techniques offered as a systematic procedure for plac-ing an individual in the stratification hierarchy was Warner's reputational method. He called it Evaluated Participation (EP).[18] The first task in utilizing the EP method is for the investigator to locate and interview a number of informants of different social backgrounds. These informants are assumed to be knowledgeable about the stratification hierarchy in the community and it is from their judgments that the investigator is able to describe the social-class hierarchy. Only if the informants agree on their judgments can the investigator assume that there are clear and pervasive class divisions in the community. Having determined these divisions, the investigator can place remaining members of the community into social classes according to where others say they belong; according to the types of organizations to which they belong; by comparison to others who have already been placed; or by the types of status symbols they possess.

It is clear that EP is a vague procedure in which an investigator retains a great deal of freedom. However, Warner's efforts—to be properly understood—must be viewed also within a historical context because many sociologists at that time were critical of efforts to develop techniques. Many of Warner's contemporaries agreed that he had "oversystematized what is essentially an intuitive procedure based on trained, clinical judgment." [19]

Despite the ambiguities of the EP technique, it represented a clear advancement in systematic methodology. In addition, it appeared able to yield fairly reliable ratings. In this context, reliability refers to the ability of any measuring instrument to produce consistent results. It is obviously

---

[17] W. Lloyd Warner et al., *Democracy in Jonesville* (New York: Harper, 1949).
[18] Ibid.
[19] See Kahl, op. cit., p. 39.

very difficult for anyone to replicate the intuitive judgments of another. Therefore, because of the scientific importance of replication, systematic procedures are highly valued.

In order to demonstrate the empirical reliability of EP, Warner compared some of his results to those of Hollingshead. Working independently of each other, both investigators had analyzed the stratification patterns of the same midwestern community. (Hollingshead called it Elmtown, Warner called it Jonesville.) Hollingshead's method involved the construction of a control list. This list consisted of twenty families who were well known and consistently placed in the community. Respondents then were asked to locate other families by comparing them to those on the control list. (For example, a respondent could indicate that "The Browns are higher than the Smiths, but lower than the Gordons.")

Warner rated 134 families with EP that Hollingshead had rated with the control list. Their agreement in placements ranged from a low of 72 per cent in the upper lower class, to a high of 100 per cent in the upper class. (However, the latter contained only two families.) The over-all mean (or average) degree of agreement was 80 per cent. Thus, despite problems of methodological vagueness, there was a substantial degree of agreement between the EP and the control-list techniques. In a small town, however, where perceptions are relatively salient and widely shared, a reliability of 80 per cent is not very high. It implies that in a larger, more heterogeneous sample the reliability might be quite low. (Confirming evidence will be introduced later.)

Warner felt that in using EP he was able to describe stratification in a valid way. Given the problem of replication, however, his subsequent step was to look for a more systematic measure whose results would be consistent with EP. In order to develop such a measure, he correlated a number of specific indices with EP.

Warner found that there were four characteristics that, in combination, provided the best prediction of EP placement. This combined measure is labeled the Index of Status Characteristics (ISC):

1. Occupation: Categories are scored according to prestige from 1 (professional) to 7 (unskilled manual).
2. Source of income: Types are scored according to their prestige value from 1 (inherited) to 7 (public relief).
3. House type: A 7-point scale is used following local prestige values.
4. Dwelling area: Same as for characteristic 3.

Each of these four measures yields a placement of individuals that is highly related to EP placement. The ranking of the magnitude of the correlations follows the preceding listing—that is, occupation first ($r = .91$)

and dwelling area last ($r = .82$). The measures also can be combined and their predictive value assessed with a multiple correlation.

In this case, the multiple correlation coefficient of .97 is near perfect.[20] Thus, the difficult-to-replicate EP can be duplicated almost perfectly by the more systematic Index of Status Characteristics. In fact, based on the obtained coefficient of .91, even occupation by itself could be used as a placement index.

It is important to point out that certain prominent indexes—such as (absolute) income and organizational membership—are not included in the ISC, but not because they are unrelated to EP placement. We already know that they are related. Rather, they are excluded because they are redundant; that is, the variation in placement they explain is already explained by the included indices. Income, for example, is related to strata placement; but, it is also related strongly to occupation and to source of income. Because of the latter relationships, over-all prediction of EP placements is not enhanced by including income in addition. Thus, the four included characteristics present the optimum balance between parsimony and predictability.

Several other measures of class or strata position have been developed. F. Stuart Chapin has developed a measure that utilizes home furnishings and other status symbols (for example, the presence of books in the living room of a home) as indicators of social position,[21] whereas William H. Sewell has developed an index particularly suited to the measurement of the social position of farm families.[22] Hollingshead combined occupational standing and education into a two-factor Index of Social Position.[23] Similarly, Robert Ellis, W. Clayton Lane, and Virginia Olesen have offered the Index of Class Position, which combines occupational standing with a fixed-alternative self-placement question.[24]

Subsequent methodological developments involved an increasing concern with representativeness as well as reliability. Studies increasingly focused on a single component of status, such as occupational prestige, and examined its distribution in broader, less restrictive samples. These developments were largely associated with an increasing focus specifically on occupational prestige as *the* stratification index, and it is to this topic that we now turn our attention.

[20] Warner, op. cit.

[21] F. Stuart Chapin, *Measurement of Social Status* (Minneapolis: University of Minnesota, 1935).

[22] William H. Sewell, *The Construction and Standardization of a Scale for Oklahoma Farms,* Technical Bulletin no. 9 (Stillwater: University of Oklahoma, 1940).

[23] A. B. Hollingshead et al., "Community Research," *American Sociological Review,* 13:161–169 (1949).

[24] Robert A. Ellis, W. Clayton Lane, and Virginia Olesen, "The Index of Class Position," *American Sociological Review,* 28:205–215 (1963).

Focus on Occupations

There are a number of reasons to suggest that occupational criteria should be singled out the most in studies of contemporary stratification. There is the empirical evidence of their importance, as previously indicated, stemming from Warner and others. In the following pages, we will encounter a great deal of additional collaborative evidence; however, there are also some compelling conceptual arguments.

The consequences of the nature of work are multiple, not only for the employed individual, but for the employee's family. Consider the obvious aspect of hours of employment: recreational, social, and other family activities are influenced profoundly by whether an individual works a night shift or is on a nine-to-five routine; and on whether he or she is generally home, or on the road traveling, and so on. The income associated with a job also has obvious effects on the kind of community in which the family lives, the kinds of aspirations to which children will be exposed, and so on. Thus, both socially and economically, occupational characteristics profoundly influence family standing. Edward Gross provides a dramatic description of the historical significance of work:

> Work provides us with one of the major bonds through which we are united with our fellows. A few people work alone—the lonely artist struggling in a rat-infested garret for contact with the infinite comes to mind. But most persons work in association with others on some common endeavor. Sometimes the resulting organizations may be very complex. In medicine, the doctor finds himself caught up in a vast network of organizations which includes medical schools, medical societies, health insurance societies, state licensing bodies, hospitals, X-ray laboratories, and so on. Or the organization may be of the sort found in modern, large-scale industry, or government, or commercialized recreation, or education. And, it is through our membership in such work organizations that we are provided with a fundamental index of status and self-respect. A hundred years ago, in rural America, when two strangers met, the first question was likely to be: "Where are you from?" And the answer meant something. When the newcomer mentioned a given town, or said "From the hill country," the other was then able to place him in his scale of values. He could make a shrewd estimation of the man's probable wealth and previous work experience. If it happened that they were both from the same area, then the next question was sure to be about each other's names. Again, in a period of stable residence, where one family lived on the same farm for generations, a name meant something. The family had a reputation—good or bad—and to be known as one of the Hatfields was very different from being known as one of the McCoys.[25]

[25] Edward Gross, *Work and Society* (New York: Crowell, 1958), p. 4.

Shortly after Warner's development of the ISC, further empirical support for the importance of occupation as a stratification index came from an analysis by Kahl and Davis. They interviewed and rated a sample of men on a wide variety of stratification measures: how they saw themselves, their sources of income, their occupational standing, formal education, residential area, and so on. The various measures were then subjected to a factor analysis.[26] The primary factor obtained by Kahl and Davis analysis dealt with occupation. The items that clustered together focused on occupational prestige and income; in turn, this occupational factor was strongly related to other stratification variables such as formal education, self-conception, and so on. The investigators concluded, in accord with theoretical expectations, that an occupational measure is the single best indicator of an individual's over-all location in a stratification system.

Simultaneously with the community studies, sociologists were attempting to develop specialized measures of occupational standing, although these efforts have been more prevalent recently. One of the first such scales was developed by Alba Edwards in conjunction with his work at the United States Bureau of the Census. This lent an "official aura" to Edwards's scale, which involved six basic categories: (1) professionals, (2) proprietors, managers, and officials, (3) clerks and kindred workers, (4) skilled workers and foremen, (5) semiskilled workers, and (6) unskilled workers. Each of the six categories, according to Edwards, combines important economic aspects, such as income and its source, with related attitudes and special interests. "Each of them is thus a really distinct and highly significant social-economic group." [27]

For the most part, the Edwards index makes distinctions that are congruent with the stratification distinctions previously made by Warner and others. Like Warner, Hollingshead, and the others, Edwards used the scale to divide American society into social stratas that were congruent with other empirical findings regarding stratification, and it was relatively easy to place most of the population into one of the six categories. However, it did not differentiate the population on stratification dimensions to a finer degree than nonoccupational indexes. Greater differentiation really occurred in 1947 with the publication of the first NORC, or North-Hatt, Occupational Prestige Scale.

The scale offered two rather important advantages over most of the scales that had been developed previously:

1. It presented a prestige ranking of ninety major occupations. Thus, it permitted stratification differentiation (based on occupation) to a very

[26] Kahl and Davis, op. cit.

[27] *Occupational Statistics for the U.S., 1870–1940* (Washington, D.C.: Govt. Printing Office, 1943), p. 179.

extensive degree. Furthermore, it could not be translated directly
into social classes, thereby forcing sociologists to reconsider the relationship between stratification and strata.

2. It was an empirically developed scale, based on an analysis of a representative cross-sectional sample of adults. Thus, it permitted evaluation
   of occupational standing according to representative judgments, rather
   than those of specific (and perhaps atypical) communities.

Specifically, North and Hatt asked almost three thousand respondents,
from all sections of the United States, to give their "own personal opinion
of the general standing" of each of the ninety occupations. Each respondent
was presented with five response alternatives: excellent, above average,
average, below average, or poor. Each of those responses was then given a
mathematical value, as follows: 100 for excellent, 80 for above average,
60 for average, 40 for below average, and 20 for poor. Each occupation
was then given an average score. A select sample of resultant occupational
ratings is presented in the following table.

NORC Rating*

Occupation	Score	Rank	Occupation	Score	Rank
Physician	93	2	Author of novels	80	31
Mayor of a large city	90	6	Public school teacher	76	36
College professor	89	7	Radio announcer	75	40
Banker	88	10	Insurance agent	68	40
County judge	87	12	Policeman	67	53
Dentist	86	15	Barber	59	65
Lawyer	86	15	Taxi driver	49	78
Civil engineer	84	23	Garbage collector	35	88

* North and Hatt, loc cit.

One of the noteworthy findings of the North-Hatt survey was the very
high prestige the public accorded to government officials. Only mayors of
large cities are included in the table, but the survey also included state
governors (score 93), representatives in Congress (score 89), and others.
The average score of all such officials was 90.8. In other words, they were
rated typically about halfway between excellent (100) and above average
(80). The next highest category contained thirty professional and semi-
professional occupations (for example, physicians and public school
teachers), whose average score was 80.6. Proprietors, managers, and (nonfarm) officials constituted the next category, with an average score of 74.9.
Thus, when occupations are placed into these categories, government officials are seen to be the prestige leaders, by a substantial margin. Remember,

too, that this survey was conducted in the mid-1940s; therefore, the assertion that President Kennedy made public service desirable probably shows a callous disregard for the traditionally high prestige of government offices in the United States.

Occupational Prestige: Some Cross-National Evidence

Before attempting to explain the obtained ratings, it will be useful to broaden our perspective and analyze the results in comparison to those obtained in other societies. Fortunately, numerous comparative studies are available and enough comparable occupations are involved generally to make comparison meaningful.

In Japan, for example, a 1952 survey of the urban Japanese population followed a procedure similar to that of the 1947 NORC survey.[28] The scoring technique was different, however, so we will focus on the comparability of ranks.[29] To begin, we can compare the adjusted ranks of the five occupations listed in the preceding table that also were included in the Japanese study.

U.S.–Japanese Comparison

Occupation	Adjusted Rank in U.S.	Adjusted Rank in Japan
College professor	8	7
Public school teacher	40	37
Insurance agent	54	67
Policeman	59	57
Banker	72	73

It is obvious that the two rankings are not identical, but they are in substantial agreement. This agreement is clearly reflected in correlational analyses.

The first extensive intersociety comparison of occupational prestige was reported by Alex Inkeles and Peter H. Rossi.[30] They took a basic sample of fifteen occupations and compared their ranking in six of the most

[28] Kunio Odaka and Shigeki Nigihera, *Social Stratification and Mobility in the Six Large Cities of Japan*, Transactions of the Second World Congress of Sociology (London, 9, 1954).

[29] The Japanese survey included only thirty occupations. To compare it to the United States, adjusted scores are created by dividing an occupation's rank in each country by the size of the total list.

[30] Alex Inkeles and Peter H. Rossi, "National Comparisons of Occupational Prestige," *American Journal of Sociology*, **61**:329–339 (1956).

industrialized societies. In addition to the United States and Japan, they included the USSR, Great Britain, New Zealand, and West Germany.

The results show a very extensive degree of intersocietal congruence. Specifically, the correlations among occupational rankings are typically in excess of .91. The investigators explain the observed similiarities by viewing any industrialized system as generating a consistent set of occupational values. Given an industrial-occupational structure, they propose, "there is a relatively invariable hierarchy of prestige—even—in the conext of larger social systems which are otherwise differentiated. . . ." [31] In addition, they viewed certain other values as generated by an industrial nation state which, in turn, reinforce the prestige hierarchy. For example, there is a consistent emphasis on health, which partly accounts for the high standing of physicians; on education, which results in the high status of professors, and so on.[32]

More recently, Hodge, Treiman, and Rossi have attempted to expand this focus by examining the similarity of occupational rankings in a sample that included the same six industrial nations as well as twenty-two other nations, many of which were much less industrialized (for example, Chile, India, Turkey).[33] In addition to correlating the ratings of specific occupations in these varied nations, the researchers also examined the comparisons among blue-collar, white-collar, and all nonfarm occupations. This latter analysis followed from their assumption that cultural differences might account for specific variations in occupational ratings that might be obscured unless one focused on specific categories:

> Cultural variation may act to produce inversions among occupations within a narrow range of prestige positions. Thus, disagreement in the relative ratings accorded to such functionaries as priests, high government officials, scientists and businessmen . . . may be the major consequence of cultural differences. . . . But we can hardly expect that cultural traditions will produce inversions of dominant functionaries and blue collar workers. . . .[34]

In addition, when the similarities among all occupations are examined, the resultant correlations probably will be influenced by the extreme occupations; that is, some occupations are always very high, whereas others are always very low. Therefore, when a strong correlation coefficient results, it may obscure inconsistencies among middle scoring occupations.

The findings, even with specific categories, however, continue to in-

[31] Ibid., p. 337.

[32] Ibid., p. 338.

[33] Robert W Hodge, Donald Treiman, and Peter H. Rossi, "A Comparative Study of Occupational Prestige," in *Class, Status and Power*, Rinehard Bendix and Seymour Martin Lipset (ed.) (New York: Free Press, 1966).

[34] Ibid., pp. 311–318.

dicate very strong intersocietal similarities. Between all nonfarm occupations in twenty-three varied countries for which they had data, the average correlation is still slightly greater than .90. Even within the white-collar category, it is nearly .90, although the average over-all blue-collar occupations is a somewhat lower, .83. They conclude:

> Major institutional complexes serving central societal needs which exist in all societies, and the common bureaucratic hierarchy imposed by the nation-state, act to insure . . . similarity between nations in the white-collar prestige hierarchy . . . but these factors cannot be expected to induce a corresponding degree of prestige similarity at the blue-collar level. However, the fundamental conclusion that wide differences in cultural traditions . . . are insufficient to produce major inversions in the occupational-prestige hierarchy is not altered by these findings, since even the lower average within blue-collar titles is still sizeable.[35]

Perhaps, surprisingly, the investigators have seen that these strong similarities are noted even when societies vastly differing in industrialization are compared. This suggests modification of the earlier Inkeles-Rossi conclusion, which emphasized industrialization as generating consistent occupational values. Rather, these similarities are produced, they now conclude, by similarities in more fundamental structural organization. Essentially, they conceptually differentiate between societies according to degree of complexity. This pushes us toward a dichotomous view of primitive societies, on the one hand, and modern ones on the other. The former are characterized by a general lack of social differentiation. The specialization common to modern societies, regardless (within limits) of their degree of industrialization, produces needs for control and coordination, as well as values that uniformly emphasize health, education, and so on. These needs and values, in turn, result in uniform occupational prestige hierarchies.

Implicit in this formulation is the functional theory of stratification. We may now apply it in a more explicit way and at least offer some tentative conclusions. With increasing differentiation within a society, it may be assumed, there is an increasing need for coordination and regulation of specialized activities. Typically, this will involve political roles, and it might account for the relatively high prestige of governmental positions not only in the United States, but in all differentiated (or complex) societies. It is interesting to note that even though he did not pursue the point in his community studies, Warner initially began to study stratification from a very similar perspective. In large, heterogeneous, and differentiated societies, he proposed, there is a great need for coordination. The occupants of positions that are expected to provide coordination receive high prestige. In

[35] Ibid., p. 318.

other cases, the prestige of a position becomes sufficient—for the position—to be allocated a coordinating role. In either event though, Warner expected the prestige of positions to be intimately related to vital coordinating activities.[36]

In addition, the existence of certain uniform values, which transcend the stratification system, also may be inferred in most highly differentiated societies. These values emphasize the importance of health, education, and other related activities. As a result of these values, physicians, professors, scientists, and others are uniformly accorded high prestige because of the congruence between their functions and salient cultural values. In sum, the relative prestige ranking of occupations is seen to be quite consistent in most highly differentiated societies. This consistency is, in turn, viewed as the result of the importance of coordination in differentiated societies. Specifically, those positions—notably governmental—whose function is to provide coordination are typically the highest in prestige. Cultural values that stress health and education, themselves the apparent consequences of differentiation, also are seen to explain the uniformly high prestige of related positions. To this point, however, insufficient attention has been given to the measurement of occupational prestige.

The Measurement of Occupational Prestige Assessed

The 1947 NORC study, it will be recalled, scaled occupational prestige according to the average score given to a position by the sampled raters. The ninety occupations were in this way hierarchically arranged by average scores ranging from 96 to 33. This procedure has been widely criticized, with most of the criticism directed at two points: (1) the overlapping of response distributions and (2) the ambiguity of responses.[37]

The first point involves the information that may be ignored when an occupation's average score is computed. Assume, for example, that we are going to examine two occupations, X and Y, in detail. For the sake of simplicity, further assume that only one hundred individual ratings are involved. Now, let us say seventy of them rank occupation X as "above average," mathematically valued as 80; and one half of the remaining thirty say "excellent" (that is, 100) and the other one half say "average," or 60. The mathematical average of the ratings will be 80. In the case of occupation Y, let us assume that fifteen people say "excellent," seventy say "above average," five say "average," and ten say "below average." The mathematical

[36] W. Lloyd Warner, *Social Classes in America* (Chicago: Science Research Associates, 1949).

[37] Albert J. Reiss, Jr., *Occupations and Social Status* (New York: Free Press, 1961).

average of Y is then 78. In the actual scale, an occupation with a score of 80 is ranked 31st, whereas an occupation with a score of 78 is ranked 36th. The rank of difference is 5; but note that an identical number of respondents rated the two occupations as both above average and excellent. Should their ranks then be differentiated? And, of greater importance, if the study were done again, would the same differences between X and Y be obtained?

The second point, the ambiguity of responses, refers to the knowledge or information of the raters. What percentage of the respondents in a representative sample of the United States can really be expected to know what a nuclear physicist, for example, does? Those who do not—and this probably includes most people—are rating on the basis of stereotype, or a vague image. To support this contention, it can be pointed out that chemists, psychologists, sociologists, and biologists all are scored substantially lower than college professors; but, many of the persons in these fields are college professors! Thus, to the extent that people are ignorant with respect to the definition of an occupation, their ratings may be inconsistent.[38]

Albert J. Reiss and O. D. Duncan have developed an alternative procedure, based on the preceding considerations, that is labeled the Duncan index. What they have tried to predict is the percentage of above-average and excellent responses given to an occupation. Their results have indicated that the education and income typically associated with a position are the best predictors. In combination, their correlation with prestige is .91. In other words, education and income (combined) account for 83 per cent of the variation in the percentage of above-average and excellent ratings given to an occupation.[39]

There are two advantages in using the Duncan scale. First, it decreases the variability about an occupation's score, thereby reducing scale error. Secondly, education and income are more easily quantified than prestige, and occupations not included in the original survey can be scored without a new survey. However, the basic assumption behind the rejection of the NORC survey is the presumed difficulties in replication. The overlapping and the ambiguity of responses both imply this difficulty. Now, the matter of replication is an empirical question and, fortunately, there have been replication attempts, so we can reflect on the question in the appropriate empirical manner.

Sixteen years after the first survey, in 1963, Hodge, Trieman, and Rossi again questioned a national sample. They utilized both the same ninety occupations and the same method of scoring. Thus, their results are directly comparable. The correlation they obtained between 1947 and 1963

---

[38] Respondents could always say, "Don't know." However, for eighty-three of the ninety occupations, fewer than 10 per cent chose this response.

[39] Reiss, op. cit.

ratings was .99. Thus, during the sixteen-year interim occupational prestige ratings remained almost identical.[40]

To further check on the stability of occupational prestige, the investigators also correlated their results with those obtained by George S. Counts in 1925. Counts had questioned a sample of midwestern high school students and was interested in using the results to counsel students in their vocational choices. However, his results are comparable due to the similarity of the question he asked: arrange these occupations "in order of social standing." [41]

Between 1925 and 1963, there were some changes in occupational standing. The relative standing of lawyers and barbers increased slightly, for example, whereas that of clerks and store managers declined. However, there was an overwhelming similarity between the rankings of 1925 and 1963, as indicated by an obtained correlation of .93. Thus, during this period of nearly forty years, the prestige of occupations remained relatively constant. In other words, even if people are unsure of what the practitioner of a specific occupation does, there is a collective judgment of how much prestige to accord that remains largely unchanged over long periods of time.

Correlates of Occupation

The discussion and evidence cited here suggest that occupation is a central factor according to which individuals are ranked in the stratification hierarchy. It is not surprising, therefore, to find that occupational standing is frequently used in sociological research to explain differences in rates and types of mental illness; fertility and mortality; political as well as religious attitudes and behaviors; family structure and child-rearing practices; ability, personality, and achievement; tolerance of minority groups, discrimination, and prejudice; participation in formal and informal associations; leisure activities and consumption patterns; and values, attitudes, and ideology.

A concrete example of the connection between occupational position and general life-situation is found in this passage from a study of social class, social values, and anomie in American society.*

Another factor in middle-class anomie involves the more general significance of work in the middle-class *milieu*. One's total way of life is circum-

---

[40] Harold W. Hodge, Donald Trieman, and Peter H. Rossi, "Occupational Prestige in the U.S.," *American Journal of Sociology*, **70** (1964).

[41] George S. Counts, "The Social Status of Occupations," *School Review*, **33** (1925).

* Ephraim H. Mizruchi, *Success and Opportunity* (New York: Free Press, 1964), pp. 110–113. The stratification scale used was the Hollingshead Index of Social Position and the anomie index used was the Srole Anomia scale.

scribed by the specific occupational role to which one is committed. It is thus the middle-class respondents who experience the greatest amount of stress based on failure to achieve occupational aspirations.

For the lower classes, however, goals are more limited. We have already underlined Durkheim's suggestion that poverty is a force that limits both aspiration and expectation. Our data confirm this suggestion . . . . In addition to finding their aspirations more circumscribed, the lower classes are exposed to other factors conducive to greater demoralization. Their status in the community is very similar to that of a minority group. In the event of failure in the occupational sphere, middle-class Americans have been trained to utilize an alternative response to anomie, a response that is not readily available to lower-class Americans: Achieving recognition in other than the economic sphere. Everett C. Hughes, discussing the nature of careers, has enumerated other sources of attainment outside the occupational sphere:

> But the career is by no means exhausted in a series of business and professional achievements. There are other points at which one's life touches the social order, other lines of social accomplishment—influence, responsibility, and recognition. A woman may have a career in holding together a family or raising it to a new position. Some people of quite modest occupational achievements have careers in patriotic, religious, and civic organizations. (1958, p. 64.)

We agree with Hughes that participation in highly valued activities of the community provides an alternative channel for the attainment of *achievement* goals. Middle-class Americans are involved to a much greater extent in the various formal associations in the community, which serve as established avenues to attainment of prestige and recognition. These activities may traverse the distance between their own and higher class levels. By active community works, a class 3 person may find himself in close contact with a class 1 person. To be sure, their relative class positions are not equalized as a result of such contact. However, by increasing one's association with segments of the community enjoying higher position and status honor one's own relative prestige in the community increases. One often notices that many of the most dedicated workers in formal associations are people with modest achievement as a result of occupational attainment. A case, selected from unpublished data gathered by this writer, illustrates this point.

> Mrs. L is the wife of the owner of a very small appliance store which both she and her husband operate. Mrs. L cares for the store when Mr. L goes out on maintenance calls. The L's have limited educational backgrounds, neither one having gone beyond high school, and although they own the business, their income is modest. Although the L's are in social class 3, Mrs. L plays a very active role in the community. She organized the plan and program to distribute Salk polio vaccine to the children in her school district and has been very active as a leader in other community projects. It was she whom the County Commissioner of Health suggested as *the* person in the town who could be most helpful in organizing support for

our research in the health sphere. In spite of their modest backgrounds, the L's enjoy relatively high prestige in the community and in some of the semi-selective clubs in the area, including the country club.

This case illustrates, not only how a person of relatively modest occupational achievement can utilize an alternative avenue to a middle-class goal, but also how middle-class patterns themselves can provide a springboard to catapult the motivated individual into a *milieu* that provides acceptance and recognition. In sharp contrast to the case of Mrs. L, is Mrs. C's subjective reaction to a similar process, community involvement.

> Mrs. C is the wife of a tannery laborer. The C's live in the center of a small village, and Mrs. C does not participate in the organized activities of the town. She attributes her isolation at least partially to the recency of her arrival in the community. In her own words, "We're new people in town. Those who've lived here all their life are in these associations. As one of my neighbors put it, 'If you're born here you're welcome, if you're not you're going to have a tough time!' " When asked what the neighbor meant, Mrs. C replied, "She meant you wouldn't fit in, you wouldn't get invited into the organizations in town. Some people get in if they have relatives who are well-to-do. That kind gets in easy." When prodded into further description of what types of people are invited to join associations, she replied, "Just about anyone who is well-to-do gets in. If you are in that class that can throw money around that's fine. Lots of money, that is what they like around here."

Conspicuous in the reaction of Mrs. C, an "isolate," is her concern with socio-economic factors and the problems of "fitting-in" with others in the community. These factors, rather than her recent arrival, dominate her response. It is particularly clear that, for Mrs. C, voluntary associations are not likely to provide an avenue either to attainment of recognition in the community or to a sense of belonging to the community and its activities.

Mrs. L's opportunities for attaining recognition, as well as for a sense of involvement are much greater. Indeed, they are characteristic of the middle-class way of life. Regardless of the personal motives that direct one's social participation, middle-class patterns themselves provide channels through which attainment of recognition in the community is possible.

It seems from our analysis that the lower classes are more prone to despair, as a result of both limited opportunities to attain their limited goals and of limited opportunities to pursue alternative goals—a combination we shall call "double circumscription." It is clear that Mrs. C is a lower-class woman who aspires to a degree of acceptance into the formal associations of her community, and it is equally clear that she has found her opportunities for acceptance limited. The reaction of Mrs. C reflects a certain amount of malaise, one of several possible personal reactions to social structural anomie.

Part Four

Social Mobility

7 Social Mobility: Concepts and Measurement

Social Stratification and Social Mobility

When the term *mobility* is used in everyday conversation, people generally have either of two referents in mind: geographic mobility or social mobility. The former refers to changes in physical space, or what the biological scientists call motility. The latter referent, or social mobility, means a change in "social space"—that is, a change in the way people are evaluated and where they are located or ranked in a social hierarchy, such as the stratification system. Any ambiguity between geographic and social mobility stems from the fact that the population of the United States is probably the most mobile in the world, with approximately one out of five families changing its residence each year and the fact that social mobility often accompanies geographic mobility. Nonetheless, it is social mobility independent of geographic mobility that we are particularly interested in here.

We have defined social mobility as a change in social space and the evaluation of individuals' or groups' ranking in the stratification hierarchy. In Chapter 4 we reviewed the work of Max Weber and took particular note of his suggestion that power, wealth, and honor are the important dimensions, or hierarchies, of social stratification. Accordingly, amount of wealth, leisure, power, and life-style come to mind as the continuums, or

203

dimensions, along which individuals or groups can be socially mobile. However, these continuums, or hierarchies, are not necessarily of equal importance; nor do they serve our purpose equally well. Rather, we will focus the study of social mobility on changes in occupational prestige in view of the fact that occupational prestige is the single best indicator of the individual's location in the stratification hierarchy. To further substantiate the selection of occupational prestige as the most important dimension for assessing social mobility, consider the following: Would an individual who earned $20,000 per year as bodyguard to a kingpin of organized crime be considered "upwardly mobile" relative to his father if his father earned $15,000 per year as manager of a small drugstore? The answer to this is probably not—despite the fact that the son earns more money, probably has more leisure time, and undoubtedly leads a more glamorous and exciting life. In fact, the son is likely to be evaluated as having taken a step *down* in the stratification hierarchy. In contrast, if the father made $20,000 per year managing the drugstore and his son or daughter earned $15,000 per year as a college professor of nuclear biology, the son or daughter would, in all probability, be considered upwardly mobile, despite the fact that he or she makes less money. As we learned from Warner's extensive research, it is not how much money an individual makes, but how it is earned that, among other things, determines location in the stratification hierarchy. In brief, it is the factors associated with or implied by occupation prestige that weigh most heavily in our evaluation and ranking of positions individuals occupy in the stratification hierarchy.

Thus far we have implied that social mobility is the vertical—that is, upward or downward—movement of individuals or groups within the hierarchy of occupation prestige. However, social mobility can also occur in a nonvertical, or horizontal, direction. Consider the son or daughter of a laborer in a coal mine who moves to the city and takes a job as a taxi driver; or the individual who quits a job as a carpenter to become a mail carrier. In either case, the social mobility that occurs is horizontal in that neither individual has been mobile across strata of the occupational prestige hierarchy. The taxi driver has the same occupational prestige as his or her father in the coal mine, and the carpenter gained or lost no prestige in giving up the job to become a mail carrier. Of course, becoming a taxi driver may facilitate upward social mobility in the long run by providing access to opportunities that are not as readily available to an individual working in the coal mines, such as the range of college and technical education programs available in urban areas.[1] Similarly, the carpenter who becomes a mail carrier may be motivated to make such a job change by anticipations of a

---

[1] Seymour Martin Lipset, "Social Mobility and Urbanization," *Rural Sociology,* **20**:220–228 (Sept. 1955).

downturn in construction activity and the threat of unemployment, as compared to anticipations of job security and potential advancement (that is, upward social mobility) through the ranks of civil employment with the federal government.

Types of Social Mobility Compared

There are at least two reasons that underlie why we study social mobility. The first is concerned with the extent to which social inequalities and differential access to advantages, opportunities, and scarce benefits are perpetuated across generations. At one extreme is the rigidly closed caste system in which position in the stratification hierarchy is inherited and fixed, with a virtual absence of social mobility. At the other extreme is the egalitarian system of stratification in which an individual's location in the social hierarchy is independent of his parents' location. We are, thus, concerned with social mobility in terms of the correlation or the degree to which parent's position in the social hierarchy determines the position of their offspring. A high correlation between parental and offspring position defines an impermeable stratification system, whereas a low correlation defines a system in which social classes or social strata are permeable. Thus by definition, permeable stratification systems involve high rates of social mobility; however, a high rate of social mobility by itself does not necessarily mean that the stratification system is highly permeable. We study the rate of social mobility in a society, therefore—or, more to the point, the correlation between parental and offspring status—to assess the degree of permeability of the stratification system.

Beyond our concern with the degree of permeability of the system and the rate of social mobility in the population, we are concerned with the magnitude, or *range,* of vertical movement. In particular, we are concerned with whether social mobility is restricted to movement between adjacent classes or strata or whether mobility occurs across a broader range of the stratification hierarchy. In Figure 7-1 two alternative situations appear. In

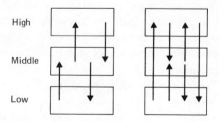

Figure 7–1

the situation depicted by the figure on the left, vertical movement occurs between adjacent strata only, whereas in the situation on the right, movement occurs between nonadjacent classes, or strata. In this latter situation, it is possible for the offspring of high-class parents to be downwardly mobile into the low class, and vice versa. Accordingly, the latter situation exhibits a greater range of social mobility.

These characteristics, permeability, rate of social mobility in the population, and range of social mobility are important for describing the structure of social inequality manifest in a given society and for comparing the structures of social inequality of several societies.

A second purpose for studying social mobility is to locate the social structural and psychological factors that play a role in the status attainment. (that is, social mobility) of individuals. By and large, most of the empirical studies in American sociology that fall under the label of social-mobility research have focused on the question of individual status attainment, rather than on the persistence of structured social inequality per se. This research has attempted to measure the relative importance of such background, or structural, characteristics as parental socioeconomic status, race, and years of education completed, as well as such social psychological attributes as achievement motivation and aspirations for the status attainment of individuals. Needless to say, the results of this approach and research implicity tells us something about the structure of opportunities and, therefore, the structure of social inequality in a society.

Measuring Social Mobility

In discussing the distinctions between vertical and horizontal social mobility, comparisons have been made between the occupational prestige of parents and their children and between the occupation prestige of an individual at two different points in time. These comparisons measure aspects of *inter-generational* and *intragenerational* mobility, respectively. To be more precise, the extent of social mobility, either across or within generations, can be measured in the differences in *status of origin,* which refers to the status of the parents during the time the individual was growing up; *status of entry,* which refers to the prestige of the first full-time occupation engaged in upon entrance into the labor force; and, *status of destination,* which is the individual's principal occupation.

Although it is relatively easy to distinguish between inter- and intragenerational mobility at the conceptual or theoretical level, it is a considerably more difficult matter to differentiate them methodologically or operationally.[2] Consider the following alternative comparisons for assessing inter- and intragenerational mobility:

1. Compare the entry status of consecutive generations. In other words, compare the entry status of offspring with the entry status of their parents. We may ask: What are the probabilities of the offspring of a blue-collar worker entering the labor force in a blue collar occupation and in a white-collar occupation; and, what are the probabilities of the offspring of a white-collar worker entering the labor force in a blue-collar occupation and in a white-collar occupation? High probability values indicate that the system is (relatively) impermeable, meaning again that the status of offspring is highly dependent on parental status.

The advantage of this alternative is that it reveals the mobility that occurs across a generation of career starting points in the occupational hierarchy. However, this measure of vertical movement across generations obscures processes, particularly the magnitude of intragenerational mobility experienced by the parent, which may be important for the status attainment of the offspring. The parent's mobility experiences are important because vertical movement in the occupational hierarchy carries with it certain increases or decreases in advantages and opportunities for children that ultimately may translate into higher- or lower-prestige occupations as initial jobs. To illustrate this point consider the case of a child born to a parent employed in his first occupation at an assembly-line job in an automobile plant. Suppose that the parent completes a college education, goes to graduate school to earn a Ph.D. degree, and becomes a college professor—

[2] W. Z. Billewicz, "Some Remarks on the Measurement of Social Mobility," *Population Studies*, **9**:96–100 (July 1955). S. M. Miller, "The Concept of Mobility," *Social Problems*, **3**:65–73 (Oct. 1955), and *The Concept and Measurement of Mobility. Transactions of the Third World Congress of Sociology*, **3**:144–154 (London: International Sociological Association, 1956); Melvin M. Tumin and Arnold S. Feldman, "Theory and Measurement of Occupational Mobility, *American Sociological Review*, **22**:281–288 (June 1957); Charles F. Westoff, Marvin Bressler, and Phillip C. Sagi, "The Concept of Social Mobility: An Emperical Inquiry," *American Sociological Review*, **25**:375–385 (June 1960); James A. Geschwender, "Theory and Measurement of Occupational Mobility: A Re-examination," *American Sociological Review*, **26**:451–452 (June 1961); Richard T. Curtis, "Conceptual Problems in Social Mobility Research," *Sociology and Sociological Research*, **45**:387–395 (July 1961); Peter M. Blau, "Inferring Mobility Trends from a Single Study," *Population Studies*, **16**:79–85 (July 1962). Otis Dudley Duncan, "Methodological Issues in the Analysis of Social Mobility," in *Social Structure and Mobility in Economic Development*, ed. Neil J. Smelser and Seymour Martin Lipset (Chicago: Aldine, 1966), pp. 51–97, and "Social Stratification and Mobility: Problems in the Measurement of Trend," in *Indicators of Social Change*, ed. Eleanor B. Sheldon and Wilbert E. Moore (New York: Russell Sage Foundation, 1968); Leo A. Goodman, "On the Measurement of Social Mobility: An Index of Status Peristence," *American Sociological Review*, **34** 831–850 (Dec. 1969); and Roland Hawkes, "Some Methodological Problems in Explaining Social Mobility," *American Sociological Review*, **37** 294–300 (June 1972).

all before the child is ten years of age. Furthermore, suppose that the child goes to college and then directly on to graduate school and enters the labor force in a first job as college professor. A comparison of the child's entry status with the entry status of the parent indicates that there has been considerable upward social mobility across a single generation. However, for a substantial part of his or her life the child benefits from whatever advantages and opportunities accrue from a parent engaged in a high-prestige occupation. The child actually enters the labor force at a level of occupational prestige equal to that held by the parent during the child's early (that is, formative) years. Thus, what appears to be a "pure" measure of intergenerational mobility may actually turn out to be "contaminated" by the intragenerational experiences of the parent. Our illustration suggests a second alternative.

2. Compare destination statuses for two generations; that is, assess the differences in occupational prestige between the parent's principal occupation and the principal occupation engaged in by the offspring. In a sense this comparison matches the intragenerational mobility of the two generations such that differences in occupational prestige may, at least in part, be attributed to intergenerational mobility. The principal inadequacy of this alternative is that it does not shed any light on the process of occupational mobility or on the relationship between the status of parents when their children are growing up and their offspring's subsequent status attainment in the occupation hierarchy. This inadequacy suggests a third alternative.

3. Compare status of origin with destination status for a single generation; that is, compare the prestige of the parent's occupation with the prestige of the individual's occupation. This comparison implicitly takes into account the benefits parents provide their children in the form of status of origin and assesses the magnitude of mobility occurring across generations as the difference between status of origin and destination status. However, this comparison provides only an over-all measure of mobility occuring across generations; it does not differentiate between intergenerational and intragenerational components. In other words, this comparison does not isolate the magnitude of mobility that results from differential access to the opportunities and advantages parents provide (that is, status of origin) their children that can be translated into first jobs (that is, status of entry). Nor does this comparison indicate the magnitude of intragenerational mobility or status attainment that can occur between status of entry and destination status.

4. The deficiency of the third alternative suggests a pair of comparisons that will yield a more complete and accurate picture of structured social inequality and social mobility. Specifically, first, compare status of origin with status of entry for a single generation. That is, compare the prestige of an individuals' first full-time occupation with the prestige of the occupation

his or her parent was engaged in when he or she was growing up. This comparison focuses specifically on the relative advantages and opportunities parents make available to their children and the extent to which offspring are able to translate these advantages into career starting points (for example, entry statuses) in the occupational hierarchy. In this respect, this comparison takes into account the persistence of differential or preferrential access to scarce benefits and the extent to which this differential access is transmitted across generations. It is interesting to note, however, that, for reasons we will see later, the offspring of parents with high-prestige occupations tend to enter the labor force in first jobs that have less prestige than their status of origin. Therefore, for offspring of parents with high-prestige occupations, the comparison tends to indicate downward social mobility across a generation even though, in the long run, such individuals often experience considerable upward intragenerational mobility and attain a position in the occupational prestige hierarchy that equals or surpasses that attained by the parent. Accordingly, the comparison of status of origin with status of entry ignores the intragenerational mobility experienced by an individual and, for this reason, this comparison by itself yields an incomplete picture of structured social inequality.

The second comparison between status of entry and destination status completes the picture of social mobility occuring across generations. Differences between the prestige of the first full-time occupation and the prestige of principal occupation indicates the magnitude of intragenerational mobility in the occupation hierarchy. We, thus, have a model of social mobility that is represented in Figure 7-2. It allows for the assessment of the relative importance of social origins (for example, status of origin) and occupational career beginnings (for example, status of entry) for prestige of principal occupation (for example, destination status).

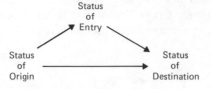

Figure 7–2

Each of the alternative comparisons presented here offers certain advantages as well as certain disadvantages. Which alternative is appropriate depends on the investigator's paramount research question. However, regardless of which question is central to the research and which alternative methodology is utilized, certain conceptual and methodological problems remain that warrant discussion.

The first of these problems is the inherent relationship between occupational prestige and magnitude of social mobility, which is depicted in Figure 7-3. The hatched portion of the graph indicates upward and downward social mobility that cannot occur. We see that as occupational prestige increases (along the *x* axis), the potential magnitude of upward social mobility decreases and the potential magnitude of downward social mobility increases. The floor and ceiling effects can be explained as follows: if the parent is employed in the lowest prestige occupation, then the prestige of the offspring's occupation can be equal to or greater than, but not less than, that of the parent, and the maximum range of upward social mobility is possible across generations. If, however, the parent is employed in the highest-prestige occupation, then the prestige of his or her offspring's occupation must be less than or equal to, but not greater than, that of the parent. Then there is no possibility for upward social mobility, but there is the potential for maximum range of downward social mobility across generations. We also see that the offspring of parents engaged in occupations constituting the middle of the occupation hierarchy can experience either upward or downward social mobility across generations. These floor and ceiling effects are, in part, the reason why the first occupation of offspring of high-prestige parents tends to indicate downward social mobility, whereas the first job of offspring of parents engaged in low-prestige occupations tends to indicate upward social mobility. An example may serve to clarify the relationship between vertical status and social mobility: if the offspring of a shoeshiner enters the same occupation there is no social mobility; however, if he or she is engaged in any other occupation he or she is, by definition, upwardly mobile because all other occupations are higher in prestige than shoeshiner. In contrast, the offspring of a United States Supreme Court Justice must also be a Justice of the Supreme Court or be downwardly mobile because all other occupations are lower in prestige than Supreme Court Justice. Of course, the maximum possible downward mobility is experienced by the offspring of the Supreme Court Justice who becomes a shoeshiner, whereas the maximum possible upward social mobility is experienced by the offspring

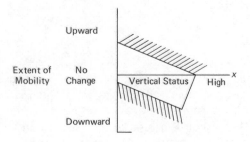

Figure 7–3

of the shoeshiner who becomes a Supreme Court Justice. Needless to say, and in spite of Horatio Alger, neither of these two alternatives is very likely to occur!

Some Additional Methodological Problems

Additional problems are encountered when we try to asses the social mobility of women. It is particularly difficult to measure the intergenerational mobility of females in terms of occupational prestige because of the role women have historically played in the labor force and in the hierarchy of occupations. In 1900, for example, only about 20 per cent of women aged eighteen to sixty-four were in the labor force. By 1940 this percentage had increased to 30 per cent and by 1970 approximately 50 per cent of women between the ages of eighteen and sixty-four were in the labor force.[3] Furthermore, in recent history, many of these women have been engaged in part-time employment. Those who have been employed full-time have been limited to factory work, although this is true to a lesser extent today, and more recently they have been employed at lower-prestige white-collar (for example, clerical and secretarial) occupations. Accordingly, as Joan Acker has so aptly put it, "if women are to be seen as persons rather than as appendages to males, how do we define their social status, particularly if they are not working for pay and cannot be categorized on the basis of their own occupation and income?" [4]

Partly as a result of their traditional role in the labor force (and partly as a result of male bias) female mobility generally has been measured by comparing the status of a woman's husband with the status of her father. This measurement procedure clearly assumes that married women gain their position in the stratification hierarchy by virtue of a marriage contract and that this position is indicated by the prestige of their husband's occupation. Moreover, the assumption commonly has been made that female mobility is tied to male mobility either through marriage (for example, the daughter of a plumber who marries a physician) or through the vertical mobility or status attainment of their husbands after marriage (for example, the daughter of a plumber who marries the son of a plumber who subsequently becomes a physician) rather than through their own personal status attainment in the occupational hierarchy. Along this line Norville D. Glenn, Andreain A.

[3] Valerie Kincade Oppenheimer, "Demographic Influence on Female Employment and the Status of Women," *American Journal of Sociology*, **78**:947 (Jan. 1973); see, also, *The Female Labor Force in the United States: Demographic and Economic Factors Governing Its Growth and Changing Composition.* Population Monograph Series, no. 5 (Berkeley: University of California, 1970).

[4] Joan Acker, "Women and Social Stratification: A Case of Intellectual Sexism," *American Journal of Sociology*, **78**:941 (Jan. 1973).

Rose, and Judy Corder Tully have recently written that "Although personal attainment may be more important in the future than mobility through marriage, most female mobility apparently has been (and perhaps still is) through marriage." [5] However, as more and more single and married women enter the labor force and embark upon occupational careers of their own, the soundness of these assumptions becomes increasingly more problematic and a greater emphasis on female status attainment in the occupation hierarchy becomes necessary.

Furthermore, as more women engage in full-time employment and gain access to higher-prestige occupations, certain additional problems develop with respect to measuring the inter- and intragenerational mobility of both males and females. The difficulty arises because working mothers contribute to the advantages, aspirations, and opportunities available to their children just as do working fathers. Consequently, the mobility indicated when a father in a low-prestige occupation has a son or daughter attaining a high-prestige occupation cannot unequivocally be assumed to be the consequence of the advantages afforded the child by virtue of the father's occupational prestige. It may very well be the case that it was the income earned by the working mother that paid the tuition that enabled her child to attend college and enter a higher-prestige occupation than he or she would ordinarily have been able to. Accordingly, to estimate the extent of social mobility across generations, one is confronted with the dilemma of selecting a comparison between the father's occupational prestige and that of the son or daughter; the mother's occupational prestige and that of the son or daughter; whichever is higher, the prestige of the mother's or father's occupation and that of the son or daughter; or some combination of the prestige of the father's and mother's occupations and that of the son or daughter.

It should be readily apparent that evaluating the relative openness of the stratification system in terms of the vertical mobility of either males or females can lead to very misleading results and inaccurate conclusions. The mobility careers of males and females may not be identical or even parallel. If, for example, the openness of the system is assessed in terms of male status attainment, the results are likely to "overstate" the openness of the system to the extent that males have differential or preferential access to those advantages that translate into occupational opportunities and mobility. As late as 1969, for instance, males accounted for 58.5 per cent of those receiving the B.A. and first professional degree, whereas approximately seven males received the doctorate degree to every one awarded to a female.[6]

[5] Norval D. Glenn, Adreain A. Ross, and Judy Corder Tully, "Patterns of Intergenerational Mobility of Females Through Marriage," *American Sociological Review,* **39**:684 (Oct. 1974).

[6] Derived from the *1969 Handbook on Women Workers,* Woman's Bureau Bulletin no. 294 (Washington, D.C.: Department of Labor, 1969), and from *Statistical Abstracts of United States, 1970* (Washington, D.C.: Bureau of the Census, 1970).

Thus, if years of education completed and academic degree earned open up occupational opportunities, males have been in an advantaged position in the labor force, whereas females, for this and other reasons that we will discuss in Chapter 9, are, or at least have been, in a disadvantaged position. It would seem to follow, therefore, that evaluating the openness of the system in terms of female status attainment would tend to understate the permeability of the system. However, an examination of the correlation between parental status and offspring status indicates that males are thwarted by less permeability in the stratification system than females. In other words, a recent analysis reveals "origin to be more highly correlated with destination for males than for females." [7] Part of this disparity seems to be a consequence of the female's mobility via marriage and the proclivity of females to marry up in the stratification hierarchy—or so the argument goes.

Treating males and females separately in studying the permeability of the stratification system may lead to contradictory or erroneous conclusions; the same is true with respect to treating majority and minority groups. That is, members of minority groups may experience obstacles to social mobility that are not experienced by the majority of Americans, and any measure of the "openness-closure" of the stratification system ought to reflect these differences.

The importance of the methodological problems inherent in studying social mobility cannot be overstated because inappropriate or erroneous methods can yield grossly inaccurate and biased results. In Tokyo, for example, a comparison of father and son statuses, when both were of the same age, shows particularly higher statuses for the younger sons, indicating recently increasing rates of upward mobility in Japan. However, if a son's current status is compared to his father's main job status, the reverse is indicated; that is, upward mobility appears to be declining. This spurious effect occurs because fathers of older sons have had longer occupational careers in which to experience intragenerational mobility.[8]

Social Mobility As a Consequence of Social Change

In the preceeding sections we have described some of the complex problems inherent in the conceptualization and measurement of inter- and intragenerational social mobility. We will now turn to the problem of differentiat-

[7] Glenn, et al., op. cit., p. 694. The hypothesis that females marry up the stratification hierarchy is referred to as the hypergamy hypothesis; see, for example, R. M. Pavalko and N. Nager, "Contingencies of Marriage to High-Status Men," *Social Forces*, **46**:523–531 (June 1968); and Z. Rubin, "Do American Women Marry Up? *American Sociological Review*, **30**:514–527 (Aug. 1970).

[8] Saburo Yasudo, "A Methodological Inquiry into Social Mobility," *American Sociological Review*, **1**:16–23 (Feb. 1964).

ing between social mobility as a voluntary movement of individuals and groups within the stratification hierarchy, or to what Natalie Rogoff has termed "social distance mobility," and "demand mobility"—which is mobility instigated by structural changes within society.[9]

It is common for every generation of parents to tell their children how much opportunities have changed; how when they were young they did not have the rich range of alternatives and advantages that their children have. For their part, the children often do not take this argument seriously. However, as our data on the occupational structure will indicate, perhaps they should. There are at least two basic and closely interrelated processes that affect the range of advantages and opportunities, the permeability of the stratification system, and the magnitude and rate of social mobility existing in a society. The first of these processes is changes in the demands for skill, training, and a wide range of other attributes that may be required of individuals in the performance of social roles. Lipset and Bendix note in this context that "Complex societies change, and whether social change is slow or rapid it leads sooner or later to a change in the demands which different positions make on those who occupy them." [10] These changes result from the increasing division and specialization of labor that accompany the techno-logical innovations of industrialization and urbanization.

As a society undergoes the transition from a rural-agrarian economy to an urban-industrial complex, large segments of the population must be recruited to fill a wide range of newly emerging occupations.

A study by Robert M. Marsh provides some insight into demand mobility as a consequence of industrialization. Marsh examined the inter-relationships between degree of industrialization, measured as the per cent of males in the labor force engaged in nonagricultural occupations; *elite demand,* measured as the per cent of the labor force in the two highest occupational strata (which include professionals, higher administrators, managers and officials, and owners of large enterprises); and (3) *elite mobility,* measured as the per cent of sons of rural or urban manual workers who enter the two highest occupational strata. According to Marsh:

> The theory states three propositions: (1) elite demand is positively cor-
> related with degree of industrialization; (2) elite mobility is positively co-
> related with elite demand; and (3) elite mobility is positively correlated with
> degree of industrialization.[11]

[9] Natalie Rogoff, *Recent Trends in Occupational Mobility* (New York: Free Press, 1953).

[10] Seymour Martin Lipset and Reinhard Bendix, *Social Mobility in Industrial Society* (Berkeley: University of California Press, 1967), p. 2.

[11] Robert M. Marsh, "Values, Demand and Social Mobility," *American Sociologi-cal Review,* 28:575 (Aug. 1963).

In a sample of ten societies, which ranged in degree of industrialization from Puerto Rico, with 53 per cent of its male labor force engaged in non-agricultural occupations, to Great Britain, with 94 per cent of its male labor force engaged in nonagricultural occupations, Marsh found correlations of .214 between degree of industrialization and elite demand; .945 between elite demand and elite mobility; and, .380 between degree of industrialization and elite mobility. Furthermore, the correlation between degree of industrialization and mobility into elite occupations in "high-demand" societies was found to be only .339 whereas for "low-demand" societies the original correlation of .380 was reduced to .129. This indicates that mobility into elite occupations is more highly correlated with elite demand than with degree of industrialization. However, in a sample of thirty-two nations that was more representative of the range of industrialized societies, the correlation between degree of industrialization and elite demand was found to be .874, as compared with the .380 found in the subsample of ten nations. This suggests that the proportion of elite and middle class in a society increases with industrialization. Thus, Marsh concluded that the process of industrialization increases social mobility *"provided that increasing industrialization is accompanied by increases in elite demand."* [12]

The combined social processes of urbanization and industrialization are accompanied by a proliferation of occupations and occupational specialties and by a corresponding change in demand for various occupational skills and training. As a consequence of industrialization, there is an increase in the per cent of the labor force engaged in white-collar occupations and a decrease in the per cent in agricultural occupations. Table 7.1 traces these changes in terms of the percentage distribution of the labor force in the United States in 1900 and for the last three decennial censuses.

At the turn of the century, the United States was primarily a rural-agrarian society with just under 40 per cent of the population residing in urban areas and about an equal percentage of the labor force engaged in agriculture. Workers in white-collar occupations constituted only 17.6 per cent of the labor force, whereas 35.8 per cent were engaged in blue-collar jobs. By midcentury, however, dramatic changes had occurred in the rural-urban distribution of the population and in the occupational distribution of the labor force. In 1950, more than 60 per cent of the United States population resided in urban areas[13] and by 1970 this figure had risen to 72 per cent.

---

[12] Ibid, p. 576.

[13] The large increase in per cent urban is partly a consequence of the use of a new definition of urban by the United States census. In 1950, the census began to define as urban places any area having 2,500 residents regardless of whether the area was incorporated or unincorporated. The old definition used by the census prior to 1950 defined urban places as incorporated areas with populations of 2,500 or more. According to the "new" definition, 64 per cent of the United States population resided in urban places in 1950, whereas according to the "old" definition, 59 per cent of the population was urban in 1950.

TABLE 7.1
Percentage Distribution of Labor Force by Occupation of 1900, 1950, 1960, and 1970

	1900*	1950†	1960†	1970†
Total labor force		59,648	66,681	78,627
White-collar per cent of total	17.6	37.5	43.1	48.3
Professional, technical, and kindred	4.2	7.5	11.2	14.2
Managers, officials, proprietors (except farm)	5.9	10.8	10.6	10.5
Sales	4.5	6.4	6.6	6.2
Clerical and kindred	3.0	12.8	14.7	17.4
Blue-collar per cent of total	35.8	39.1	36.3	35.3
Craftsmen, foremen, and kindred	10.6	12.9	12.8	12.9
Operatives and kindred	12.8	20.4	18.0	17.7
Laborers (except farm)	12.4	5.9	5.5	4.7
Service workers	9.0	11.0	12.5	12.4
Farm workers	37.6	12.4	8.1	4.0

* From United States census, reported in Murray Gendell and Hans T. Zetterbert, *A Sociological Almanac for the United States* (New York: Scribners, 1964).
† *Statistical Abstract of the United States,* 1972 (Washington, D.C.: Bureau of the Census, 1972). Adapted from Table 336, p. 230.

This increase in per cent urban was accompanied by a dramatic decrease in the per cent of the labor force engaged in agricultural occupations. The decrease in the percentage of the labor force engaged in agricultural occupations during the first half or the twentieth century was from 37.6 per cent in 1900 to 12.4 per cent in 1950. During this same fifty-year period, there was only a slight increase in the per cent of the work force in blue-collar occupations with, as expected, most of the increase occuring in industry and factory occupations (that is, for operatives and kindred jobs). However, the greatest and most significant change in the distribution of the labor force during this period was the large increase in white-collar workers from 17.6 to 37.5 per cent. Particularly important is the quadrupling of the per cent in clerical and kindred white-collar occupations.

Between 1950 and 1960, and again between 1960 and 1970, the per cent of the labor force in farm occupations further declined to where in 1970 it was only 4.0 per cent. Also, during the last two decades, and in contrast to the changes that occurred between 1900 and 1950, the percentages in blue-collar occupations have declined. The only category of blue-collar occupations that has remained stable over the last twenty years in terms of the percentage of the labor force has been craftsmen and foremen. In contrast, the per cent of the labor force in white-collar occupations has consistently risen, although the percentages in the sales and in the managers, officials, and proprietors categories have remained relatively stable since 1950. However, what is striking to note is the consistent and large increase in the per cent engaged in lower white-collar clerical and kindred occupations. Even more striking is that, in 1970, 14.2 per cent of the labor force was engaged in professional and technical occupations, which is nearly double the per cent in this occupational category just two decades ago.

The second social process that creates demand mobility in any society is changes in the size of the population resulting from the basic demographic factors of immigration, fertility, and mortality. These demographic processes are important in that they in a large part determine the size of the labor pool. They determine one supply of personnel from which individuals are recruited to fill positions in the occupational hierarchy that are vacated by mortality, retirement, or emigration, as well as positions that are created by technology in newly emerging and expanding occupations. The distribution of the population throughout the stratification system, and more directly the distribution of the labor force throughout the occupational hierarchy, is thus subject to change entirely as a consequence of natural demographic factors. For instance, if the offspring's occupational status is perfectly determined by parental occupational status, the structure of occupational inequality is impermeable and the distribution of the labor force at any point in time reflects historical differences in fertility and mortality in the various occupational strata. In contrast, if the occupational hierarchy is perfectly permeable and there is a zero correlation between parental and offspring occupational status, then the occupational distribution of the labor force is unaffected by any historical differences in the reproductivity of occupational strata.[14]

There are two forms of differential fertility that must be distinguished since they are consequential to the structure of social inequality and to social mobility in different ways. The first form of differential fertility is that which occurs between strata of the social hierarchy. Table 7.2 provides some indication of the magnitude of fertility differences between occupational groups for the last three decennial censuses. Strata in which there are more children born than required to fill positions vacated by mortality (and retirement) as well as new positions created by industrialization and technological innovations become suppliers of labor and thereby foster social mobility. In contrast, strata in which there are fewer children born than

---

[14] Judah Matras, "Differential Fertility, Intergenerational Occupational Mobility and Change in the Occupational Distribution," *Population Studies*, **15**:187–197 (Nov. 1961).

TABLE 7.2
Average number of children ever born to wives aged 35–44 by Spouse's Occupation

	1950[a]	1960	1970
Professional, technical, and kindred	1.825	2.417	2.941
Managers, officials, proprietors (except farm)	1.949	2.431	2.941
Sales	1.827	2.656	2.891
Clerical and kindred	1.827	2.302	2.841
Craftsmen, foremen, and kindred	2.313	2.607	3.119
Operatives and kindred	2.523	2.730	3.179
Service workers[b]	2.103	2.484	3.018
Laborers (except farm and mine)	3.004	3.008	3.367
Farmers and farm managers	3.204	3.170	3.578
Farm laborers and foremen	3.796	3.988	4.296
Total	2.343	2.596	4.296

[a] The 1950 census combines sales with clerical and kindred workers.
[b] Includes private household.

required to fill vacated and newly created positions foster social mobility in that they become consumers of labor. For the past three decennial censuses, it has consistently been the case that professional and other white collar workers have had fewer children than farm and blue collar workers.

Samuel H. Preston has analyzed the effects of differential fertility across occupational groups on the structure of inequality and social mobility in the United States. His analysis reveals that if there had been no fertility differences, 41 per cent of the professional and technical workers (in 1962) would have been born to parents in professional or technical occupations. However, only 38.7 per cent of the white professional and 31.8 per cent of the nonwhite professionals were actually born to parents in professional and technical occupations. Furthemore, if there were no differences in fertility, we would expect to find 22.6 per cent of the white-collar workers to have been recruited from the offspring of blue-collar and farm workers. This compares with an actual recruitment of 32.3 per cent and 25.9 per cent for whites and nonwhites, respectively. This difference between the expected and observed recruitment percentages suggests that the upper strata of the occupational hierarchy are more open and permeable as a consequence of differential fertility than would be the case if no fertility differences existed across occupational strata. However, even though the upper strata appear to be more fluid as a consequence of differential fertility, the lower strata appear to be more closed.[15] Preston comments on the importance of the mobility effects of differential fertility:

> This greater fluidity [of the upper strata] could have a number of consequences, of course: a continued revitalization of the upper classes from greater exposure to the fresh perspectives of ambitious recruits; and an increase in the tensions and anxieties resulting from incongruities between status of origin and destination. . . . A smaller proportion of the lower classes at any point in time has descended from the upper. These classes are thus relatively deprived of whatever benefits accrue from fresh outlooks and diversified recruits and are, one could speculate, possibly encouraged to view the world in conspiratorial terms. The mobility effect of differential fertility is clearly a double-edged sword.[16]

The second form of differential fertility that is important to the study of social mobility—particularly the status attainment of individuals—is the unequal distribution of children across families. Differences in family size and average number of siblings are each directly related to the concentration of childbearing. If childbearing were evenly distributed across families and each family were to have exactly two children, then there would be no differences in family size (assuming all families to be complete—that is, mother, father, and children) and each child would have only one sibling. However, if childbearing were concentrated among half of the families and these families had four children and the other half of the families had no children, then half of the families would be three times larger than the other half and each child would have three siblings, even though the total number of children born would be the same in both instances.

The significance of family size and number of siblings to the study of social mobility lies in the ability of a family to provide the range of opportunities and advantages to their children that the offspring can translate ultimately into status attainment and social mobility. Families with few children are in a position to concentrate their resources to maximize the achievement potentials of their offspring. Families with a large number of children must spread their resources thinly and, thus, possibly directly or indirectly thwart the status attainment of their offspring.

In their comprehensive analysis of the occupational achievement of a generation of American men Peter M. Blau and Otis D. Duncan found that men from small families—those with fewer than four siblings—attain higher educational levels and achieve considerably higher occupational status than men from families with five or more children. In fact, men from small families

---

[15] Samuel H. Preston, "Differential Fertility, Unwanted Fertility, and Racial Trends in Occupational Achievement," *American Sociological Review,* **39**:492–506 (Aug. 1974).

[16] Ibid., p. 502.

generally complete at least a high school education, whereas those from larger families often drop out of school at the legal age.[17] This difference of nearly two years in average educational attainment translates into higher career starting points in the occupational hierarchy and higher status of destination. One might suspect that these differences in years of education completed and achievements in the occupational realm are a consequence of differences in socioeconomic status of origin in that larger families generally are concentrated in the lower occupational strata and upper-strata families tend to have fewer children (see Table 7.2).

Blau and Duncan write:

> Sons in large families are doubly disadvantaged. They not only tend to have low-status parents, who usually have no tradition of going to college or even graduating from high school, and who have meager total financial resources, but they also must share the total parental resources with more siblings than children from small families on the same socioeconomic level.[18]

However, their analysis revealed that even after differences in socioeconomic status of origin are taken into account, men from small families continue to attain higher educational levels and achieve greater occupational status than men from large families. But, if controls are introduced simultaneously for socioeconomic status of origin and for educational attainment, the differences in occupational achievements between men from small and large families virtually disappear. These findings clearly suggest that the advantage of coming from a small family, with respect to occupational achievement, lies in the superior educational opportunities and attainment that a small family fosters.

Consequences of Social Mobility

To this point we have demarcated the study of social mobility. We may now ask: "What are the consequences of social mobility for the structure of society and for the lives of the individuals who experience it?[19] In response to this question we reprint a paper written by Melvin M. Tumin. Although this paper appeared about two decades ago, the rapid changes occurring in

---

[17] Peter M. Blau and Otis Dudley Duncan, *The American Occupational Structure* (New York: Wiley, 1967).

[18] Ibid., pp. 304 and 306.

[19] Harold T. Wilensky, "Measures and Effects of Mobility," in Smelser and Lipset, op. cit., pp. 98–140; Miles E. Simpson, "Social Mobility, Normlessness and Powerlessness Two Cultural Contexts," *American Sociological Review,* **35**:1002–1013 (Dec. 1970); and Ralph H. Turner, "Upward Mobility and Class Values," *Social Problems,* **11**:359–371 (Spring 1964).

the United States during the late 1960s and early 1970s coupled with the economic dilemmas faced by the industrial nations of the world during the middle of the 1970s may indeed show Professor Tumin's comments to have been very prophetic.

Some Unapplauded Consequences of Social Mobility in a Mass Society*

Melvin M. Tumin

The process of getting to be better-off than one used to be does not ordinarily make one sit and reflectively balance what he may have lost against the advantages gained. For, if being reasonably well-off is a novel experience— as is implied when we talk of mobility—it may take a long time for the novelty to wear off. One begins to spend time and energy in cultivating the new habits of consumption and the new modes of living appropriate to his new position. And, perhaps one's most ardent wish is that no one should rock the boat, or raise questions about other dimensions of life on which this experience of mobility may be having an impact.

But this is what I propose to do here, briefly, and, in large part, impressionistically, since while much attention has been given to measuring mobility and to comparing the mobility rates of various groups in various societies,[1] relatively little attention has been paid to the range of consequences generated.

I

In the broadest sense, any economic improvement of heretofore disadvantaged persons strikes us as valuable.[2] This is true whether we start with a Marxist orientation toward the factors which determine man's fate, or a twentieth century liberal's version of what constitutes the good life; or the most conservative of political orientations, which ultimately joins with a version of Marxism in insisting that the economic welfare of the society is the basis of the total welfare of that society.

Even a smattering of sociological sophistication, however, informs us that economic changes do not occur in a vacuum;[3] that other conditions precede, accompany and follow; that a range of values is affected; and that general social change, and not simply economic change, is necessarily implied. Surely, then, the consequences of any phenomenon as broadsweeping as socio-economic mobility are likely to be diverse and mixed—diverse in their institutional ramifications and mixed in their implications for other values.

* Reprinted with permission from *Social Forces*, **36**:32–37 (Oct. 1957).

The same bit of sociological sophistication will also inform us that mobility is too broad a term to allow for more than vague generalizations, unless we further specify the kinds of mobility, the rates of occurrence, the conditions under which it transpires, and the segments of the population affected.[4]

With these requirements in mind I wish now to specify more closely the mobility about which I am here talking. I refer first to the current American scene, and, within that, to the improvement in the standard of living, both relative and absolute, of large numbers of members of various ethnic minority groups. The improvement is preceded and accompanied by a reallocation of persons to higher-rated occupational groups, in which these higher incomes are earned.[5] I refer secondly to the fact that much of this has occurred within the last fifty years, or less than two demographic generations; and that a very substantial portion of the change is attributable to the opportunities presented by the second World War and the Korean incident. I cite these specific events only as convenient indicators of the time periods involved.

These transformations have occurred in a contest of what we are now wont to call a "mass society." The referents of that term are numerous and mixed.[6] For our purposes here, as a minimum, when we speak of a "mass society" we shall have reference to the following things:

1. There are media for rapid interchange and transfer of ideas, persons, incentives and styles.
2. Economic motives include specific intents to produce for and distribute to all available segments of the population.
3. Inexpensive duplication of elite items of consumption is a dominant theme in production and consumption.
4. Traditional criteria of prestige, such as membership in exclusive kinship groups are rapidly vanishing. First appraisals and appraisals of status-rank are made increasingly on the basis of apparent income, as manifested in items openly consumed.
5. The "ideal" values insist that existing lines of social differentiation, including class and caste barriers, are temporary, and in the long run, insignificant; that all men are ultimately equal, some temporarily more equal than others; but that in some way we take turns at being more equal, since this is a condition which is theoretically available to everyone under the right happenstances.
6. It is theoretically permissible and even well-mannered to compete with everyone, no matter what his rank.

Running through this type of social order is a major theme of status striving which, for our present purposes, we need not try to explain, but rather will take as given. Sometimes and some places this motif is at bottom a search for some token by which to assure oneself of the rightness of self-esteem. Other times and other places it is egregiously insistent upon formal and overt recognition by others of one's right to an elevated place and a differentiated set of powers. Whatever the motive to which status-rivalry can be reduced, and whatever the forms it may assume, it is an intense focus of social activity and interpersonal relations, especially among mobile-minded Americans.[7]

These features then roughly and approximately describe the types, conditions, rates, and participants in social mobility to which we have reference.

A further word of caution needs to be inserted before we proceed to the main analysis in hand. Some of the consequences to be cited will refer only to some of the most mobile segments of the population; some of them and those with whom they come in contact during their movement or at their temporary resting places; some to the relations between them and their kin; some have to do with phenomena which emerge in the interplay between strains toward mobility and those toward stability; some are only dimly visible while others are already well-developed. In short, the sweep, coverage, intensity, and importance of the consequences we are about to specify are as mixed as the conditions which give rise to them.

II

1. The Fragmentation of the Social Order

I have reference here in general to the numerous ways in which rapid social mobility, in a mass society in which status rivalry is a dominant theme, leads to the proliferations of interest groups, associations and temporary social congeries, all oriented toward the accumulation and symbolization of prestige.

This proliferation is set in motion when status-mobiles, with full credentials in hand, knock upon the doors of elite membership groups, demanding acceptance and recognition, and are then denied the final bestowals of grace on grounds quite irrelevant to those which presumably determine one's right to such recognition. Even though sufficient income, education, occupational rank, commodiousness of residence, and auxiliary criteria have been met, the occupants of the top statuses invoke other criteria, such as kinship, ethnic origin, table and bar manners, and coldness of emotional toning, in order to justify the denial to the status-mobiles of access to intimacy with them in their own highly-ranked associations.

These criteria—precious and refined—are not only irrelevant to the major themes in the culture, but essentially hostile to democratic values. Their invocation, in denying admission to aspirants, leads to actions on the part of the mobiles which intensify certain anti-democratic and anti-open-society tendencies.

Thus, for instance, one finds the rejected aspirants creating dual and triple sets of elite facilities such as social clubs, country clubs, recreational facilities, residential sites, and even colleges and universities. These tend to be justified on the grounds that where opportunity has been illegitimately cut off; it is proper to create such facilities. Whatever pleasures and proprieties these dual facilities may insure for the participants and whatever pleasure of restricted intimacy this may residually grant to the older elite, the creation of such facilities, along lines of ethnic, racial, and religious distinctions, gives further strength to these anti-democratic distinctions. Moreover, because the *elites* of various ethnic and religious persuasions engage in such distinctions, these styles of social intercourse are likely to be emulated at other class levels.

Within these separate hierarchies status-rivalry becomes heightened and intensified, and there is sharper insistence on class-oriented behavior. This intensification of class distinctions within ethnico-religious status-hierarchies is not unmixed in its implications for a democratic, open society.

Under these circumstances, one may expect some loss of faith in the fairness of the social process and in the democratic quality of the culture. For if the major criteria of equal status have been satisfied, but personal recognition is nevertheless withheld, there is good ground to disbelieve the value-themes which emphasize the equality of all men and the worthwhileness of supporting the society in general, without reference to ethnic or religious origin.

Still another consequence may be cited. Highly mobile members of ethnic and religious groups tend to impose upon their mobile co-ethnics the same criteria of disability with which they were earlier afflicted. Thus, Negroes use color as bases of distinction within their group; Jews use Jewish folk-characteristics of language, gesture, and food. In short, denigrated minority groups absorb, accept, and apply to themselves the very anti-democratic criteria which their status-superiors earlier imposed upon them. In the extreme cases, the ethnics tend to blame their own rejection upon the persistence of these identifying traits of origin among their less mobile co-ethnics. The phenomenon of Negro and Jewish self-hatred has often been partially and correctly explained on these grounds.

The implication for self-esteem and mental health of such self-depreciation are obvious. What may not be quite so obvious is the way in which this shift of focus misplaces the responsibility for the existing barriers to social mobility, redirecting it mistakenly from the institutional restraints and anti-democratic tendencies in the older elites where it properly belongs.

2. The Denial of Work

A good deal of the social energy and drive which have made mobility possible for many of the heretofore underprivileged groups in America derived from the belief that hard work pays off. This belief was tied in and compatible with prior value commitments to the inherent virtue of work.

But now the emphasis has shifted from the importance of work and striving to the urgency of appearing to be successful. In at least some important elite circles, the social productivity of one's occupation, the social value of products which one distributes, and the skill required to produce these items are systematically ignored. Instead, almost exclusive preference is given to the open portrayal of *being* successful, as measured by the power and property which one openly consumes.

No one in any society has more quickly oriented himself to what is the right way to succeed in our status-conscious society than the new-mobile. Being a mobile and seeking further mobility makes it imperative that one adopt the standards which rule the market. In adopting those standards, and playing the game by them, he helps institutionalize them and make them the themes into which the next generations are socialized and indoctrinated. In this manner, the fact of rapid social mobility contributes importantly to the loss of a theme of the instrumental importance and the inherent dignity of work. In their place has been substituted the cult of the quick buck, with its theme that nothing succeeds like success.

Most of the major consequences of the triumph of the cult of the quick buck are well known. Some of the less obvious but equally important consequences bear scrutiny for a moment.

We may note, in the first place, the development of a Cult of Opportunity, Unlimited. That is, there has spread through the younger members of the more mobile groups in our population a sense that only success is in store for them; that the paths to this success are pretty clearly indicated; that no downward turns of the economy are possible; and that the insistence upon a horizon of despair is simply a neurotic hankering for the past on the part of those who have not quite made the grade.

This set of attitudes leads to an uncritical acceptance of the strength and durability of those economic and social arrangements which have recently yielded such high standards of living. In turn, this makes any ideas regarding the need for checks, controls, and contingency mechanisms, designed to cushion cyclical downturns, seem like morbid, gloomy, and radical prophecies of doom. Such policies and legislation as may be required to provide just these contingency cushions and provisions for possible economic disaster, fail to receive at least the kind of attention which our past history has indicated they merit. It would be one thing to reject them after scrutiny, on the grounds that the fears for the possible future are pointless. It is quite another to dismiss them out of hand as undeserving of consideration. Nothing is likely to contribute so much to the possibility of a bust as the denial, during the boom, of that possibility.

The denial of work also has consequences for social integration. For the only system of social recognition which makes it possible for all men in a society to achieve a sense of their worthiness to that social order, and thus to be integrated within it, must contain important reference to the dignity of work, *at any level*, and to the worthiness of conscientiousness regardless of the level of skill or income associated with the work. Any tendency which denies the dignity of work and which, in turn, insists upon consumption of high income as a criterion of social worth, undermines the possibility of widespread social integration. For, thereby, large numbers of men are deprived of the only basis on which they can achieve a sense of their equality. It is extremely difficult for a democratic ideology to have vital meaning at all levels of skill and income when we denigrate work and applaud income.

3. The Loss of Social Criticism

I have reference here at the outset of the numerous ways in which the ranks of social critics and the ideas of social criticism are being depleted under the impact of the illusions and fantasies which social mobility for large numbers has generated.

There are evident signs of the emergence of "a cult of gratitude" among significant sections of the mobile population. Members of this cult tend to lose sight of the history of effort and struggle which have been required for past mobility. They engage in a type of euphoric wallowing in present comforts. They organize their perspectives around a sense of gratitude to the social order for making the present pleasures possible.

A prime case in point concerns some intellectuals. Perhaps never before has there been so much room in the well-paying portions of the occupational ladder for the skills and talents of intellectuals. Again it may be inconsequential that ideas now become commodities, or gain much of their value from their marketability. It is consequential, however, for the total society, that many of the ablest critics of the social order, whose criticism and ideas were important in making past mobility and present comfort possible, have been in a sense, bought off by the social order. This reference is not alone to political critics operating directly in the field of political ideology, but also to men of creative imagination and ideas operating in the fields of literature, mass entertainment and the media of mass-know-how-enlightenment.

Any social order stands in danger when it becomes smug regarding its past and even smugger about its future. The presence of an alert, critical-minded and creatively-oriented group of men of ideas is an indisposable antidote to such smugness. The mobility of the society in general has made creative criticism highly undesired and unpopular. And the mobility of prior critics has made significant numbers of them deny their histories and the value of their prior criticism. Those denials have helped them move quickly and surely into the ranks of those who feel it important to applaud. The active pursuit of open and sharp debate—an indispensable condition for the maintenance of an open society—is thus seriously endangered.

4. The Diffusion of Insecurity

Anomie spreads through any social order when its personnel moves rapidly through a series of statuses and roles, whose definitions or rights and responsibilities are constantly shifting. This is generally what occurs in any society when much of the population experiences rapid social mobility, and when styles of behavior are oriented primarily toward status-acceptance and prestige-ranking, rather than some persistent and assured sense of what the social welfare requires.

In its simplest terms one sees this process occurring when the primary orientation is upon moving out of given levels into others as rapidly as possible; and when each of the major roles at any of these levels—whether parental, occupational, or community-members role—is defined in accordance with the class level. There is neither time nor inclination to become absorbed in a set of traditional responsibilities and to cultivate the expectations of traditional rights. The stability of bearing and the security deriving from adequate role-playing are thereby surrendered in preference for the constant readaptation of onself and his role performances to the requirements of the next income level.[8]

Insecurity is also spread under such conditions, when, in addition, one takes his bearings on his worth to himself and his social order by his position on the prestige-ladder, and when that position is primarily defined by income and its correlates. For in a society with differentiated income-classes, almost everyone is outranked by someone else who, by his own criteria, is more worthy.

Moreover, no source or criterion of prestige is quite so shaky and unstable as wealth, especially when that wealth flows from commerce rather than from proprietary estates based on land. Many of the very same persons who today are wealthy and therefore prestigeful have known in their own life-times what it has meant to be poor, therefore low-ranking, to become wealthy and improve their ranking, to become impoverished once again and lose their ranking, and finally, now once again, to be wealthy and be back in the high ranks. It is difficult to see how there could be any deeply built-in sense of security under such circumstances. It is easy to see how a gnawing, though perforce, concealed, sense of the ephemerality and impermanence of their present conditions might permeate such a population.

Rapid social mobility of the type we have experienced, and under the circumstances which have prevailed, has led to an extreme emphasis upon income-accumulation and consumption as the basis of ranking. Thus, there has tended to diffuse throughout significant portions of the population at all levels an insecurity regarding place and position. An illustration in point is the intense demand for reassurance that we are loved. This is exemplified in its most unself-conscious form in the cult of "palship" among cafe society habitués. To insist that a true friend is one who sticks by one through all varying economic fortunes, and, in turn, to place the value of that kind of friend above all other values except money, is to testify to the instability of money as a measure of worth in general, and the uncertainty regarding one's personal worth, so measured, in particular.

III

Time forbids the detailed analysis of any other set of consequences of social mobility. Yet a number of these may be mentioned in passing, to indicate how truly mixed are those consequences, in contrast to the general bland assumption that social mobility is eminently and predominantly benign process.

5. We must recognize, therefore, that rapid social mobility, under the conditions stated, leads to a severe imbalance of institutions, insofar as it encourages the invasion of such institutions as family, religion, and education by criteria derived from the market place. The success of role-performances in these institutions tends to be measured by some income yardstick, thus endangering seriously the major functions they have traditionally performed.[9]

6. Comparably, the possibilities of genuine cultural pluralism in our society are seriously diminished by some results of the process of rapid social mobility. For in leading to the criterion of dual and triple hierarchies on new class levels, ethnic groups have become converted into status-competing hierarchies rather than the culture-contributing peer groups which a theory of a pluralist society envisions.

7. Along with the loss of social critics and criticism goes the depreciation of taste and culture which occurs in a highly mobile society when marketability becomes the criterion of aesthetic worth and when one consumes such products as the taste merchants assure us that the elite are presently enjoying.

8. Finally, it may be observed that rapid social mobility generates in the older

portions of the population a cranky and bitter conservatism and worship of the past; and in the new-mobile segments a vituperative contempt for traditions. If it is true that the age of a custom is no guarantee of its contemporary fitness, it is equally true that the age of a custom is no guarantee of its inadequacy. Any society will be the loser which either wallows in its past indiscriminately or, equally indiscriminately, rejects it.

IV

Marx somewhere says that the philosopher with his eyes upon the stars is betrayed by his lower parts into a ditch. Without being silly enough to try to improve upon that formulation, I would try to adapt it to the present situation, by noting that the mobiles, with their eyes upon the higher reaches of the social ladder, are betrayed into their ditches by their overly careful devotion to how and where they might next move.

NOTES

1. See, for instance, three book length studies: N. Rogoff, *Recent Trends in Occupational Mobility* (Glencoe, Illinois: The Free Press, 1954); W. L. Warner and J. C. Abegglen, *Occupational Mobility in American Business and Industry, 1928–1952* (Minneapolis: University of Minnesota Press, 1955); D. V. Glass (ed.), *Social Mobility in Britain* (Glencoe, Illinois: The Free Press, 1954); also, an earlier review of the literature in P. Sorokin, *Social Mobility* (New York: Harper & Bros., 1927).
2. Robin Williams, Jr., *American Society: A Sociological Interpretation* (New York: A. Knopf, 1951) on the dominant values of American society.
3. See Wilbert Moore, *Economy and Society* (Garden City: Doubleday & Co., 1955), especially chap. 2.
4. Melvin Tumin and Arnold Feldman, "Theory and Measurement of Occupational Mobility in Puerto Rico," *American Sociological Review*, XXII, 3, (June 1957).
5. See H. P. Miller, *Income of the American People* (New York: John Wiley & Sons, 1955).
6. Daniel Bell, "The Theory of the Mass Society," *Commentary*, 22, No. 1 (July 1956), pp. 75–83, presents an historical survey of the meanings ascribed to the term "mass society."
7. In Melvin M. Tumin, "Some Disfunctions of Institutional Imbalance," *Behavioral Science*, I, No. 2 (July 1956), the consequences of heavy emphasis upon status as measured by economic achievement are argued in some detail.
8. See Melvin Tumin, "Rewards and Task Orientations," *American Sociological Review*, XX (August 1955).
9. Melvin Tumin, "Some Disfunctions of Institutional Imbalance," loc. cit.

Before proceeding with an analysis of social mobility in the United States and then on to a cross-national comparison of mobility, let us review briefly the points made in the preceding discussion concerning the conceptual and measurement problems that are inherent in social-mobility research. We have pointed out that social mobility is analytically distinct from, although often occurring in conjunction with, geographic mobility. Furthermore, we noted that social mobility can occur in either a horizontal or vertical direction. We have further differentiated between the mobility experienced by an individual during the course of his or her lifetime (for example, intragenerational mobility) and the social mobility that occurs between parents and their offspring (for example, intergenerational mobility) across a generation. In the process of making these distinctions we noted the difficulty of holding constant the effects of either intra- or intergenerational mobility in order to evaluate the effects of the other. However, we suggested that the extent of social mobility between generations or within a single generation can be assessed by comparing an individual's status at three points during his or her life: status of origin; status of entry; and, status of destination. We also have distinguished between (1) social mobility as voluntary movement, or as the circulation of individuals throughout the social hierarchy, and (2) social mobility that is demanded by structural changes such as industrialization and differential fertility. Finally, we have seen what Tumin termed some of the "unapplauded consequences" of social mobility.

8 Social Mobility in the United States

The American Dream

One of the most pervasive themes characterizing American society is that of "rags to riches." The subject of countless novels, short stories, speeches, movies, and folk tales, the theme lauds the presumably greater opportunity for Americans to improve their social position than their European counterparts. The American Dream is the manifestation of the all-pervasive expectation that social mobility is a right and a reality for all Americans to enjoy. More dramatically, it is more than a right, it is a mandate. Making an effort to improve one's economic and social position is obligatory, and those who remain satisfied with their achievements are perceived by others as deviant.[1]

Given such a profound and pervasive emphasis on social mobility in the United States, it is not surprising that American society has been popularly characterized by its *presumed* high rate of social mobility. In the mind of the

[1] For analysis of this theme cf. Ephraim H. Mizruchi, *Success and Opportunity* (New York: Free Press, 1964); Robert K. Merton, "Social Structure and Anomie," *Social Theory and Social Structure* (New York: Free Press, 1957); and Irvin Wyllie, *The Self Made Man in America* (New Brunswick, N.J.: Rutgers University Press, 1954).

typical American, including social scientists, there is probably no other society that provides comparable opportunity.

In the previous chapter we commented on some of the conceptual and methodological problems involved in the study of social mobility. We also reiterated the relationship between the extent of social mobility and the permeability of the stratification system and noted some of the unapplauded consequences of social mobility in mass society. In this chapter we review and assess the extent of social mobility in the United States, which, in the next chapter, we will analyze from a comparative (that is, cross-national) perspective. In the following excerpt the author discusses and reports research on the relationship between social stratification, social mobility, and the American Dream.

Social Class and Social Values*

Ephraim H. Mizruchi

Success Values

Our major concern in this work is to test hypotheses systematically by utilizing empirical data gathered for that specific purpose. Our definitions and methods must not only be sociologically meaningful, but they must also be adequate for empirical analysis. Questions "concerning the objectivity of values [or] . . . their quality of absoluteness or lack of it,"[1] as Williams points out need not concern us here. For our purposes, we can accept Kluckhohn's definition of value: "A value is a conception, explicit or implicit, distinctive of an individual or characteristic of a group, of the desirable which influences the selection from available modes, means, and ends of action."[2]

From our point of view, then, a value is a group's conception of the desirable. The specific nature of the value-referent, although we will make extensive references to it, is not crucial to the test of our hypotheses. In our analysis, we use care in distinguishing between what are often referred to as values—the reified referents of the process of valuation—and the underlying conceptions that influence our judgments of these values. It is only in the latter case that we are truly dealing with values, while in the former we are focusing on what may, for purposes of convenience, be called value-referents.

The specific values, indices of which we are attempting to analyze, are those associated with the American notion of "success." Lyman Abbott, a late

---

* Reprinted, with permission of the publisher, from *Success and Opportunity*, New York: The Free Press, 1964.

nineteenth-century clergyman, "a true prophet of the success cult," describes this American concept with a great deal of clarity and succinctness:

> The ambition to succeed may be and always ought to be a laudable one. It is the ambition of every parent for his child. It is emphatically an American ambition; at once the national vice and the national virtue. It is the mainspring of activity; the driving wheel of industry; the spur to intellectual and moral progress. It gives the individual energy; the nation push. It makes the difference between a people that are a stream and a people that are a pool; between America and China. It makes us at once active and restless; industrious and overworked; generous and greedy. When it is great, it is a virtue; when it is petty, it is a vice[3] (Wyllie 1950, p. iii).

Wyllie, a historian, traces the idea back to sixteenth-century England and describes its growth as a source of motivation in America for more than three hundred years. He asks:

> But what is success? Americans have defined it in various ways. Politicians equate it with power, publicists with fame. Teachers and moralists rate themselves successful when they have influenced the minds and characters of others. Men of creative instinct strive for self-realization. Humanitarians identify success with service, reformers with the alteration of the social order. To the devout, success is salvation, and to thousands of plain people it is nothing more than contentment and a sense of happiness. Each of these definitions embodies worthy ideals, and all have their champions. But no one of these concepts enjoys such universal flavor in America as that which equates success with making money. "Everyone knows that success with the great masses spells money," said John C. VanDyke in 1908 in his book *The Money God*. "It is money that the new generation expects to win, and it is money that the parents want them to win. The boy will make it, and the girl, if she is not a goose, will marry it. They will get it in one way or another" (Ibid, pp. 3–4).

Although Wyllie has placed a great deal of emphasis on money as a concrete goal, we should violate his meaning if we failed to note what he points out in a later passage on European stereotypes of Americans:

> It is a mistake, however, to deduce the motives of an entire people from the careers of a few representatives, for though some Americans look upon wealth as an end in itself, and sacrifice everything to its acquisition, many more view it only as an instrumentality[4] (Ibid. p. 5).

Sociologists have also treated the striving toward success. The Lynds in their study of Middletown during the 1920s, for example, noted that "in season and out, regardless of such vicissitudes as unemployment, everybody who gets a living in Middletown is theoretically in process of 'getting there'; the traditional social philosophy assumes that each person has a large degree of freedom to climb the ladder to ever wider responsibility, independence, and money income" (1929, p. 65). We have already remarked that Merton has provided us with an elaborate description of the cultural mandate to achieve success in his essay, "Social Structure and Anomie."

Williams has also described factors associated with success in American society and has made some important comments on the relationship between money and success, taking into account some complexities of empirical analysis:

> Santayana's insight has more accurately indicated the central function of money in the American value system: "It is the symbol and measure he [the American] has at hand for success, intelligence, and power; but as to money itself, he makes, loses, spends and gives it away with a very light heart." In a society of relatively high social mobility, in which position in the scale of social statification basically depends upon occupational achievement, wealth is one of the few obvious signs of one's place in the hierarchy. Achievement is difficult to index, in a highly complex society of diverse occupations, because of the great differences in abilities and effort required for success in various fields. At the same time, the central type of achievement is in business, manufacturing, commerce, finance; and since traditionalized social hierarchies, fixed estates, and established symbols of hereditary rank have had only a rudimentary development, there is a strong tendency to use money as a symbol of success. Money comes to be valued not only for itself and for the goods it will buy, but as symbolic evidence of success and, thereby, of personal worth[5] (1960, pp. 420–421).

It seems clear, from these observations, that, as far as a good many historians, philosophers, and sociologists are concerned, success is a pervasive motivating force for the American people. Our job is to provide empirical evidence that will help confirm or reject this expectation.

Although there are several possible ways of approaching the study of values empirically, we use only one, an indirect approach to verbal value responses. We have asked a series of questions designed to elicit descriptions of behavior and possessions that reflect basic value systems. Although we are attempting to tap as broad a range of values as possible, we do not attempt to describe a total value system or even a sub-system. Let us now turn to the data for a more concrete description of the value ascribed to success.

We begin our empirical analysis by examining the distribution among the several social classes of selected values pertinent to our problem. An attempt will be made here to answer the following questions: What is the distribution of success values among the classes? To what extent do members hold values that aid or hinder them in their efforts to achieve success? To what extent do members believe that opportunities of getting ahead are available to them.[6]

Social Class

In addition to our brief comments about the empirical assessments of success values, it is advisable to comment on social class and the use of indices in this sphere.

Without making too pretentious an attempt to define class, we would suggest that classes are broad social categories that, at least in part, reflect similarities in styles of life.

The life styles associated with people in the same class categories include, among other things, particular orientations to manners, speech, clothing styles, education and, especially, "success." All these elements involve both reactions to and manipulation of symbols. These symbols serve as guides for the classification of individuals in class categories and, consequently, for description of differential group associations.

There is a tendency for people with similar styles of life to participate together in both formal and informal groups, to marry one another, and to choose activities that reflect their similar value orientations. In American society, in particular, although there are clear-cut patterns of discrimination along social class lines, it is difficult to demonstrate that *class consciousness* is a significant phenomenon. The norms associated with equality of opportunity are so strong that class awareness among Americans is quite nebulous.

Discrimination along class lines in the form of acceptance or rejection of those adopting certain symbols usually involves little cognitive perception of class differences. As our own data indicate—and those of other students of class—subjective perception of class differences lacks the articulation associated with conscious awareness of class. Indeed, were Americans clearly aware of class differences, it seems unlikely that Vance Packard's *The Status Seekers* would have been so widely read.

What is of great interest to us at this juncture, however, is the use of social-class indices in research. An index is a rough measure that is associated with but does not explain a given phenomenon. For social class, for example, we might use monetary income as an index to the patterns of consumption among different segments of the population. The actual amount of monetary income at any one time in an individual's career would be a relatively poor index to his style of life, however, because *how* he uses his money is more closely related to style of life than how much he has to spend.

Monetary income can be an *index* to class, but it does not determine class. On the other hand, an index based on occupation and education may reflect different styles of life and value orientations with more clarity than does income. Indeed, more recent developments in the methodology of social-class-analysis support this view.

Our analysis utilizes an *index* to social class based upon occupational rank and educational attainment . . . . This index focuses on *objective* class position, in which the observer assigns a class category to the respondent.

We have also used several *subjective* indices, in which the respondent ranks himself in relation to his parents, in one case, and in relation to others. Other subjective indices are also used.

Our data should therefore allow us to make generalizations about our respondents as we see them and as they see themselves, as far as social class is concerned.

Social Class and "Getting Ahead"

In Merton's essay, "Continuities in Social Structure and Anomie," he attempts to evaluate several studies designed to test his hypothesis. In commenting on Hyman's findings that differences *do* exist among classes, in terms of values related to success in American society, he makes the following statement:

> The survey data available to Hyman do not discriminate between the *degrees* of commitment to the goal but indicate only the relative *frequency* with which individuals in the samples drawn from the several social strata express some unknown degree of acceptance of the success goal and of related values . . . it appears that subsequent inquiry might be usefully directed toward studying the intensity as well as the extent to which these values are held in diverse groups, social strata, and communities (1957, p. 171).

In order to test the Merton hypothesis, we selected what seemed a well designed question to elicit the kind of response necessary for adequate assessment of the distribution of success values in American society. Morris Rosenberg has used a measure of the degree of importance placed upon striving for success in American society.[7] This measure has been pretested and used in other studies as well. Rosenberg has formulated his question in terms of "getting ahead,"—"How important is it to you, personally, to get ahead in life?"—which may appear initially to be an indefinite rephrasing of "striving for success." We believe, however, that this goal is by its very nature nebulous and that an indirect question phrased in layman's language does provide an adequate index to his aspirations. Merton lacks precision on the specific nature of his goal, although he focuses on pecuniary success in his analysis. Note the following quotation:

> It would of course be fanciful to assert that accumulated wealth stands alone as a symbol of success just as it would be fanciful to deny that Americans assign it a place high in their scale of values. In some large measure, money has been consecrated as a value in itself, over and above its expenditure for articles of consumption or its use for the enhancement of power. "Money" is peculiarly well adapted to become a *symbol of prestige*. As Simmel emphasized, money is highly abstract and impersonal. However acquired, fraudulently or institutionally, it can be used to purchase the same goals and services. The anonymity of an urban society, in conjunction with these peculiarities of money, permits wealth, the sources of which may be unknown to the community in which the plutocrat lives or, if known, to become purified in the course of time, to serve as a *symbol of high status*. Moreover, in the American dream there is no final stopping point. The measure of "monetary success" is *conveniently indefinite and relative* (1957, p. 136. Italics added).

A close examination of this statement offers a clue to Merton's fundamental notion of success. "Success" is reflected in prestige and high status, which is a result of a particular relationship to certain symbols.[8] Wealth, in these terms, is simply one symbol of relative success, as is a particular occupational achievement. Emphasis upon "pecuniary success" may prove useful in an analysis of *deviant* reactions to discrepancies between aspirations and achievements, but it is not so useful in gaining insights into *normative* reactions or even to reactions in general. In sum, what is significant in assessing Merton's theory is the subjective and indefinite nature of success goals as he conceives of them. Whatever the precise nature of the goals, for our purposes—the assessment of Durkheim's theory as formulated by Merton—it is not so important as the degree of their accessibility. If a goal is culturally prescribed and if, for those who aspire to it, it is structurally unattainable, it meets the requirements for assessment of the theory. We shall not ignore the specific nature of success goals as our respondents perceive them, however. We are merely attempting here to clarify one problem associated with empirical assessment of the theory.

Rosenberg's question is phrased, "How important to you, personally, is it to get ahead in life?" Of the 226 respondents to Rosenberg's question in our survey, 174 (77 per cent) answered that "getting ahead" is important, while only fifty-two replied that "getting ahead" is unimportant to them. Rosenberg found that 88 per cent of his respondents thought "getting ahead" was important (1957, p. 159). His subjects were, however, college students, whom we should expect to be more involved in striving for success than our respondents, many of whom have already achieved some of their life goals.

Not only do *most* of our respondents feel that getting ahead is important, but our data indicates that it is slightly more important to the lower-class segments of the population.[9] The lower-class respondents show a greater "degree of commitment," in Merton's terminology, as well as greater frequency of acceptance of success goals.

These data, if taken alone, might provide additional support for the findings of Srole and others that anomie is greater in the relatively low classes. It could then be argued that, since success is apparently more important to lower-class respondents and since anomie is already known to be higher among the lower classes, the greater degree of importance placed on success is a cause of anomie. In order to make a more complete assessment of the theory, however, it is necessary to relate anomie to class when acceptance of success goals is constant among all classes.

Social Class, Success, and Related Values

Our second question about the relationship between social class and values is, To what extent do members of the different classes have values that aid or inhibit them in their efforts to achieve success? What is success from the point of view of the respondent, how is it attained, and what part does his conception of success and its corollary values play in his opportunities for achievement?

Hyman (1953, p. 430) has focused on the importance attributed to college education and particular types of occupation. We shall describe the class distribution of perceived symbols of success, the kinds of success goals associated with the several classes, and the class differential perceptions of means for achieving success.

Social Class and Success Symbols.   One method of exploring Americans' conception of the nature of success is to analyze the importance attributed to the symbols they associate with it. In an effort to uncover these symbols, we asked, "Could you list, in order of importance, those things which you believe to be signs of success in our society?" Six possible responses were read by the interviewer, and the respondent stated an order of preference. The six elements were based on a code taken from open-ended replies to the same question in an earlier study. It is sufficient for our purposes to present only the first choices. The class categories, from the highest (I) to the lowest (V), are taken from Hollinghead's Two-Factor Index of Social Position . . . . The basis for our classification is occupational and educational attainment of the male head of the household in which the respondent resides.

As Table I indicates, there are several tendencies associated with the selection of success symbols among our respondents. The symbol rated first in importance by the greatest proportion of our sample (31 per cent), was home ownership. "Having a good education" was ranked most important by 29 per cent and "having a good, steady job" by 23 per cent. When we review the distribution by class, we notice certain trends. Home ownership tends to be selected more frequently as class declines. There is also a slight similar tendency in selection of job security. Education, however, tends to be selected more frequently as we ascend the class structure.

TABLE 1
Class and Most Important Symbol of Success as Selected by Respondent
(in Percentages)

	Class					Totals Per Cent	N
	I	*II*	*III*	*IV*	*V*		
Education	61	37	30	26	21	29	63
Many friends	0	10	17	5	3	7	16
Prestige	8	10	4	6	5	6	13
Job security	15	21	17	27	24	23	51
Home ownership	8	16	32	31	41	31	70
Money	8	6	0	5	6	4	10
Totals	100	100	100	100	100	100	223
N	(13)	(19)	(47)	(81)	(63)		

Chi-square $= 12.6$, 3 d.f., $P = .01$.

A closer examination of the data suggests that these relationships are not simply the result of chance. By grouping job security, home ownership, and money into a category designated "material-economic symbols," as contrasted with "non-material-economic symbols," we find that class and category of success symbol are associated. A chi-square analysis yields a probability of .01, a much greater concentration of "material-economic" responses in the lower classes than we would expect by chance alone. It is clear, then, that symbols of the attainment of success are different for respondents in the several classes.

There are at least three possible interpretations of this finding that are worthy of consideration. First, the data may reflect the degree of awareness, that is, the limited range of experience, among the lower classes, of certain symbols and their referents. This reflection is analogous to the oft-noted suggestion that those at the bottom of the class structure know very little about those at the top. This observation is particularly true of life styles, tastes, and other class-related symbolic behavior. The symbols of success in the lower classes are limited, then, to the attainments they have had opportunities to see, particularly the most conspicuous. These goals are concrete and easily identified.[10]

A second possible interpretation is that people value most what they have least. On the lower levels, therefore, people still strive for the basic necessities, and only after attaining them do they seek other goals (cf. Inkeles, 1960). The process of attainment in a society in which products are constantly being introduced and improved and goals are frequently reformulated—a society that tends toward a great deal of anomie in its subsystems—involves reaching goals and then seeking still other goals, endlessly. This process has been called the "escalator process." The mass media of communication, children and neighbors, and a host of other influentials encourage people to continue accumulating and trading in the old model for the new. In the middle classes, goals have shifted beyond the material, which presumably anyone can attain, to more intangible goals.

Finally, and this explanation provides a broad enough framework for incorporation of our first two, there are elements—reflected in these choices of symbols—of Williams's distinction between "achievement" and "success." He has written:

> Whereas achievement refers to valued accomplishments, success lays the emphasis upon rewards. Amoral success-striving may not have gone to the lengths suggested by some observers, but the important point is that once success goals are divorced from the ultimate values of society, the way is opened for a corrosion of regulative norms. In the United States, the available evidence suggests that, even though success is often regarded as an end in itself and sometimes there is almost no positive linked to achievement, achievement is still associated with work, and relation between success and moral virtue, yet the success pattern is still work is still invested with an almost organic complex of ethical values. Thus, success is still not a primary criterion of value in its own right, but rather a derivative reward *for* active, instrumental performance (1960, p. 419).

Setting aside, for the present, the possible implications of this statement for Merton's theory of social structure and anomie, let us attempt to view our data in terms of the distinction between achievement and success.

The lower-class symbols are clearly *success* symbols as contrasted with the middle-class *achievement* symbols.[11] Occupational pursuits in the lower-class groups, for example, are much less likely to lead to achievement. Even the skilled technician has difficulty thinking of his work in such terms, as does the clerk in the same class category (Class IV). In contrast, the engineer, the scientist or the small business owner who constantly speaks of "building" his business demonstrates a broader dimension of aspiration. It is not until the minimal *success* symbols have been attained that *achievement* becomes a goal in contemporary American society. In this respect, the lower classes do not suffer from structured strain so much as those in the higher classes. There is comparatively little struggle for abstract goals, which are difficult to attain, among those in the lower classes. Their problem is the attainment of goals that are inherently more limited. The middle-class American, however, does seek goals that are more difficult to attain—though he often does manage to attain them —and struggles also with questions about the relative legitimacy of his *success* or lack of *success*, as contrasted with *achievement*. It is on the higher-class levels that we observe the consequences of structured strain of a particular type. For certain occupational groups, particularly the intellectuals, the gap between success and achievement is wide. While many have achieved some degree of prominence in their occupational spheres, they have often not been rewarded with adequate symbols of success. From this group come many of the intellectual-political critics of industrial societies.[12] Furthermore, there is a tendency toward the converse as well. The groups that have attained *success* without having *achieved* tend to look upon themselves and be looked upon by others as not quite legitimate. Americans are reluctant to give power to those who have not earned their wealth—a prototype is the speculator who seeks control of a long established business enterprise—and they accord less status honor to the attainers of success alone than to those whose success is the result of their own achievements. This point is suggestive for Max Weber's theory of social stratification (1946, pp. 180–195; cf. Lenski, 1954). In a well integrated social system, wealth, prestige, and power would be held in relatively the same measure by the participants. In societies undergoing transition, we find discrepancies among the three. The distinction between success and achievement, reflecting the distribution of wealth and accomplishment respectively, has implications that go beyond our data to broader questions of social structure. Such questions are beyond the scope of our study. We shall, however, make some brief comments on them in our concluding chapter.

Characteristics Associated with Success.   In addition to asking more abstract questions about "getting ahead" and "signs of success," we attempted to reach much more concrete levels of perceived success. One type of question was designed to project the respondent momentarily into his community setting, in order to describe a particular phenomenon (an element of this approach was embodied in our question on signs of success). One concrete example is the question, "If you were asked to describe a successful person in your community how would you do it?" Response categories to this question were precoded in order to classify the characteristics stressed. The question was, however, open-ended, and the coding was done after the interview was completed.

Our data were grouped to combine cells in which there were very few cases into broader, yet meaningful categories. Most of our respondents stressed characteristics of success that fell into the prestige-recognition category. Of the 179 respondents, eighty-eight (49 per cent) stressed factors associated with "good" reputation in the community. Sixty-two (35 per cent) emphasized those associated with the accumulation of material goods and security. Only 16 per cent described success in terms of factors associated with family welfare or personal happiness. A chi-square analysis of these results yields a value significant at the .05 level of probability. There is a marked difference in perceptions of success among the several classes, the lower classes stressing material symbols.

These data are consistent with those presented earlier and suggest that both sets reflect underlying value systems that influence the choice of value-referents. The data, as a result, support our distinction between success and achievement, as a reflection of different value configurations among the classes.

The Differential Significance of Money and Security. Since the foregoing analyses have suggested that money and security are preferences that characterized the responses of the lower-class subjects and since the several studies of social class and anomie have shown that anomie has a greater impact on these classes, we shall investigate the relationship between money and security, on one hand, and social class, on the the other. In analyzing two types of response, we may be able to assess the relative valuation associated with each among the several social classes.

Hyman reports some findings of a 1942 Roper survey based on a national sample of high school students, who were asked "to express their preference for one of three types of job: a low-income but secure job, a job with good pay but with an even risk of losing it, or a job with extremely high income and great risk" (1953, p. 433). According to Hyman, "The poor youth cannot accept the risk involved in becoming less poor" (ibid.). Another sample taken by Roper in 1947 is reported by Hyman and provides data on adult responses to this question, reflecting a similar class pattern. "Thus, for example, a low income but secure job is chosen by 60 per cent of factory workers but only by 26 per cent of professional and executive persons. In 1949, a question presenting a similar choice situation between a secure job and a risky but promising career in one's own business yielded parallel results" (ibid., p. 434). Although Hyman's purposes in reporting these specific data were different from ours— he was concerned with types of occupational aspiration—Roper's findings do suggest that security is of more concern to lower-class respondents than is money.

Our own interest is in the relative significance of money as a goal, compared to security, since our over-all findings suggest that both are more highly valued in the lower classes than they are in the middle class. The same question Hyman asked was used in our study.

Of the 222 respondents to this question, 145 (63 per cent) indicated that their choice of occupation would be one that pays only a low income but is secure. Only thirty-three (16 per cent) would choose jobs that pay extremely high salaries to the successful, with a high risk of dismissal for the unsuccessful. A chi-square analysis of the association between social class and occupational choice yields a value with a probability of .001. Our data clearly indicate that the segments of the population for whom security is more important are the Class IV and V respondents, which is consistent with our other findings. These data also clarify the *specific* values that seem most important to lower-class respondents and help to support our explanation for the absence of emphasis upon *achievement* in the lower classes. *Security* has been isolated as a major concern of lower-class respondents. Hyman's data also support our explanation. The significance of money for those in the lower classes is, however, open to questions that go beyond our specific interests in this study (cf. Inkeles, 1960).

Education as a Value.   Because education has been found to be a relatively important symbol of underlying values and because it plays a major role in opportunity for advancement, we attempted to take a closer look at the part education plays in the evaluative perceptions of our respondents. Hyman has devoted a large part of his analysis to the value placed on formal education. As he points out, the degree to which education is valued is a significant factor in differential opportunities to achieve success. He suggests that:

> Part of the ideology of American life is that important positions are not
> simply inherited by virtue of the wealth of one's parents, but can be
> achieved. Such achievement, however, requires for many types of im-
> portant positions considerable formal education. One cannot, for
> example, become a physician or a lawyer or an engineer without advanced
> education. Consequently, insofar as the lower classes placed less value
> on higher education, this would constitute an aspect of a larger value
> system which would work detrimental to their advancement (1953, p. 429).

Hyman proceeds to show that there is differential preference among the classes for college education, increasing with higher class position. Even though our own data support Hyman's findings and generalizations, we should approach his interpretation with some caution. The use of indices of "preference for college education" as a means of assessing educational values seems to this writer to involve a middle-class bias on the part of the investigator. We believe that success in a lower-class position can be achieved with high-school education alone. The skilled technician and the shop foreman, for example, have certainly attained modest degrees of success in an objective sense, and college education for them seems superfluous if not completely meaningless. For those of the middle classes whose aspirations include professional achievement, however, college education may be much more meaningful.

We are dealing here with *means-values* rather than with *ends-values.* College education is being viewed as a means toward other ends, one of several alternative means for achieving "success." Our earlier findings, however, suggest that education is more highly valued by the middle classes as an *end-value* than it is by the lower classes. We hypothesize that the greater importance of education as an *end-value* for the middle classes provides them with greater opportunities for advancement *because* they view it as an *end-*

value. As Hyman suggested, the nature of the value systems themselves limits or expands opportunities for success.

Values can have consequences that are either compatible or incompatible with the objectives of the actors in a social system, and these consequences may or may not be known to actors or to group members generally. There may, in fact, be latent, that is, unrecognized consequences for values for particular groups. Education's role as an *end-value* for the middle classes for example has the latent consequence of providing relatively greater chances of attaining both success and achievement goals, while for the lower classes the *lack* of education as an important *end-value* has the latent consequence of limiting chances for reaching goals in skilled, commercial, or professional occupations.

We should, then, expect to find that education itself is evaluated differently among the several classes. In order to test this hypothesis, our respondents were asked the following question taken from Williams (1956). "Here are some reasons different people have given for wanting to have their children finish a certain amount of education. Which *one* of these would you say is most important?" The responses were grouped into two categories: instrumental perception of education and noninstrumental perception of education.

Our findings are reported in Table 2. The 205 respondents were almost evenly divided between the instrumental and noninstrumental categories. Fifty-two per cent perceived education as a *means-value*, while 48 per cent perceived it as an *ends-value*. There is a marked tendency for instrumental perception of education to increase inversely to social class. A chi-square analysis indicates that lower social class and perception of education as instrumental are associated at the .01 level of probability. Our middle class respondents, then, tend to see education, not only as a means of achieving a better job or income, but also as a source of personal satisfaction. We should guess that our lower-class respondents tend to view education as something that would have helped them in adulthood had they pursued it in childhood and adolescence. While they see it as a means to success, they do not evaluate it so highly as other symbols (see Table I). Floud and his colleagues, in a study

TABLE 2
Class and Instrumental and Noninstrumental Perception of Education
(in Percentages)

	Class					Totals	
	I	*II*	*III*	*IV*	*V*	*Per Cent*	*N*
Noninstrumental	91	72	55	46	44	52	107
Instrumental	9	28	45	54	56	48	98
Totals	100	100	100	100	100	100	205
N	(11)	(18)	(47)	(68)	(61)		

Chi-square = 11.5, 3 d.f., P = .01.

entitled *Social Class and Educational Opportunity*, also noted the lower evaluation of education among working-class parents in England (1957, p. 81).

Our lower-class respondents are caught in a situation analogous to Merton's conception of anomie on the social structural level. In the rational or *cognitive* sphere, education is viewed realistically by the lower classes as a means for the attainment of success. In the nonrational, *evaluative* sphere, education is not highly valued. There is thus a disparity between the cognitive and evaluative dimensions that fosters a greater tendency to limited achievement in the lower classes. This disparity reflects strain between the subcultural system and the requirements of the lower-class social structure, an additional source of structured strain.

Bronfenbrenner has made a similar observation:

> Perhaps this very desperation, enhanced by early exposure to impulse and aggression, leads working-class parents to pursue new goals with old techniques of discipline. While accepting middle-class levels of aspiration he has not yet internalized sufficiently the modes of response which makes these standards readily available for himself or his children. He has still to learn to wait, to explain, and to give and withhold his affection as the reward and price of performance (1958, p. 423).

It should be noted, however, that our data do not totally support Bronfenbrenner's assumption that the "levels of aspiration" are identical with those of the middle class.

In answer to our second question—To what extent do members of the several classes hold values that aid or hinder them in their efforts to attain success in American society?—we must conclude that, although our lower-class respondents are aware of the utility of education as a means for getting ahead, that they do not view it as a high *end-value* does limit their chances for even modest advancement. We must agree with Hyman that the lower-class population does thus share a self-imposed tendency to nonachievement of success goals.[13]

Social Class and Perceived Opportunity

We have so far attempted to answer the first two of our three questions about class distribution of success values and the relationship between certain values and their roles in the process of striving for success. The third question is, To what extent do members of the various classes believe that opportunities for getting ahead are available to them? We turn again to Hyman for suggestions on what we may expect to learn from our data. In interpreting Roper's data, Hyman indicates that the lower classes believe that economic opportunities are limited for them in comparison to opportunities for higher classes (1953, p. 437). He also suggests that there are class differences in perceptions of the most important factors in job advancement. We should expect that such perceptions are an important factor in the study of effects of social structural anomie on group participants.

We asked three questions about perception of opportunities for success, which will be explored further. Now, however, we shall limit our discussion here to the relationship between responses to these questions and social class. Specifically, the questions deal with perceptions of universalistic or particularistic criteria for advancement; implicit acceptance of the success ideology and the opportunities of the striver; perception of the respondent's own chances of getting ahead as indicator of a class determined reaction; and the discrepancy between sought and achieved occupational rank.

Ability as a Factor in Success.   In order to gauge perception of the degree to which legitimate striving will be rewarded, we asked, "Do you feel that a person with ability has a good chance of achieving success in our society, or do you feel that ability has little to do with it?" Of the 224 subjects who responded, only fourteen replied that ability had little to do with it. Of the fourteen, however, it is interesting to note that none was a member of Class I or Class II; only two members of Class III; and six members each of Classes IV and V. A chi-square analysis of these data, however, indicates that there are no class differences in response to this item.[14] It appears, then, that the American dream of equal opportunity for all who have ability remains a potent ideological force in American society.

We use the term "ideological" with a clear understanding of its implications. We believe that, since objective conditions demonstrate that success is limited for those born into lower-class families and since the vast majority of lower-class respondents in our study still believe that ability is a major factor in advancement toward success, there is a disparity between the cognitive and evaluative dimensions of class perception. It should be clear from their perspective that ability *is not* a major factor in achieving success in our society unless they are willing to admit that they, as members of the lower classes, are people of low abilities. One way to close the gap between objective social circumstances and the group's limited capacity to deal with them is through ideology, that is, a set of beliefs and sentiments that will provide the group with goals, realistic or not, to give life meaning. In the American ideology of success, if one remains faithful to his task, continues to strive and to hope, he too will be rewarded by advancement.[15] We hold that the ideology provides support only as long as objective conditions do not cause too great a gap between aspirations and opportunities for achievement. As the gap widens, the supportive potential of the ideology lessens. This factor is one of several that may explain our observation that average anomia decreases with age, climbing sharply upward only after age 55.[16]

Perceived Chances of Getting Ahead.   Our second finding supports this interpretation. As our data show, there is a class differential in the respondents' perceptions of their own chances of getting ahead. As class declines, we note an increase in responses that reflect awareness and expectations of limited success even though the over-all distribution of responses is relatively even. Fifty-three per cent saw their chances as excellent or fair, compared to 47 per cent who saw them as limited or almost nonexistent. The data provide a sharper picture when we combine Classes I and II, our smallest groups. Then we find 83 per cent giving responses of "excellent" or "fair" and 17 per cent giving less hopeful replies. A chi-square analysis yields a probability of less than .01.

It can be concluded, from this finding, that the lower classes in our sample tend to see their objective chances of success as limited. How does this result fit with our finding that most respondents in the same class had, only moments before in the interview, replied that a person with ability has a good chance of achieving success? We should expect from these two replies that those on the lowest rungs of the social-class ladder believe themselves lacking the *ability* to get ahead. Yet these data may also be interpreted as providing support for our suggestion that the disparity between *cognitive* perception and *evaluative* perception—another instance of socially structured strain—creates a vacuum that is filled by the ideology of success.

Merton is correct in pointing out that the system is not threatened by the failure of particular individuals to achieve their aspirations. The system, as our data show, is not put to the test. Instead, the individual continues to hope for eventual reaping of rewards, or he turns the blame for failure upon himself. If we compare those in the lower classes who feel their chances are fair or excellent to those in the lower classes who feel their chances are limited, anomia scores reflecting structured strain will be higher for the latter. On one hand, using perception of limited opportunities as an index to the malfunctioning of the success ideology, we should expect anomia to increase with the decrease in expectation of success. On the other, we should expect this relationship to be stronger in the lower classes because they are more likely to see their chances as limited. A controlled analysis suggests that this expectation is not borne out. Anomia is associated with perception of limited expectations for the *middle* classes only! How do we explain this unexpected finding?

We begin by noting that the middle-class respondents are more involved in the competitive struggle for success. They affirm the American dream, and, while their chances of attaining success or achievement, are greater, their chances of failure are greater too. Those in the lower classes do not have far to fall if they fail. The lower-class respondent, furthermore, sees about him others whose opportunities are circumscribed, and rationalization comes more easily under these circumstances. By contrast, the middle-class *milieu* is one of success and continuous striving. Among those who have had access to education and job opportunities, what excuses can be offered for failure? Our preliminary results, which indicate that income and anomia are significantly associated only for those respondents who have gone to high school and college provide further support for this hypothesis. The college educated respondents who earned less than $5000 a year were more likely to become anomic than were members of any other educational group.

Social Class and Aspiration for Achievement.   The third general question we set out to answer in this chapter was, what is the relationship of disparity between aspiration and achievement to social class? Although this question is, in reality, a test of the Durkheim-Merton hypothesis, since such a disparity may be viewed as an index to anomie, we are treating it here in the limited context of the relationship between social class and social values.

In an effort to develop a measure of structured strain independent of Srole's anomia scale, we decided to combine two separate items into what is, for the time being, a crude index to the disparity between the respondent's past occupational preference and his current occupational rank. Both elements were ranked according to the Hollingshead scale of occupations, a part of his index of social position. We asked, "Do you wish you had gotten into another line of work when you were younger?" The respondents who replied "yes" were then asked to describe the occupation to which they had formerly aspired. Since some of the respondents selected occupations different from their own on a horizontal plane—occupations with the same rank—we excluded them from our analysis. It is on the vertical plane that we should expect the effects of anomie to manifest themselves, since disparity in occupational level is our major concern.

TABLE 3
Class and Disparity between Earlier Occupational Aspiration and Achievement (in Percentages)

Disparity	Class			Totals	
	I, II, III	IV	V	Per Cent	N
Low	44	35	18	31	26
Moderate	25	32	15	26	21
High	31	33	67	43	36
Totals	100	100	100	100	83
N	(16)	(40)	(27)		

Chi-square = 9.3, 4 d.f., P = 0.06.

Our findings are reported in Table 3. Thirty-six of the eighty-three respondents (43 per cent) fell into the high disparity group, and twenty-six (31 per cent) into the low disparity group.[17] The distribution of low disparity declines from Classes I, II, and III to Class V, and that for high disparity ascends comparably. The few cases in the analysis also suggest marked differences in responses among class groupings. A chi-square analysis indicates that class and degree of discrepancy are significantly associated at the .06 level of probability. Our findings, then, indicate specifically that there is a greater gap between earlier occupational aspiration and occupational achievement in the lowest class (V) and, more generally, that the Durkheim-Merton hypothesis is supported.

Summary

Our problem in this chapter has been to explore the distribution of success values among the several social classes as reflected in responses to questions dealing with the importance of getting ahead; symbols of success; perceived characteristics of successful people; the selection of occupations in terms of security and monetary compensation; and the quality of educational preferences. In addition, related questions were asked on the role that ability plays in achieving success and on differential perceptions of opportunities for advancement.

Several sociologically interesting themes are evident. The importance of getting ahead is stressed, not only by most of our respondents throughout the class structure, but most heavily by the lower classes. This finding is true for both the extent and intensity of belief in getting ahead and therefore satisfies Merton's criterion for an "adequate" test of his theory. This index to the importance of success clearly lends support to Merton, Srole, Bell, and others who have assumed that Americans share similar life goals. We can report, then, at this stage of our analysis, that there is evidence to support the Durkheim-Merton hypothesis.

We have also found that, by using Williams's distinction between "success" and "achievement," we obtain a clearer understanding of the nature of values and greater insights into the differential aspects of striving for success in the several classes. The distinction leads us, for example, to explore and to explain middle-class anomie.

Our data, at the same time, indicate that the idea of limited opportunity for the attainment of life goals is more complicated than Merton recognized. The tendency for the lower classes to select material symbols and preferences supports Hyman's suggestion that those objects and activities they rank highest are those that contribute least to the attainment of success. There is, as Hyman has noted, a self-imposed tendency to anomie in the lower classes thanks to low evaluation of the cultural mechanisms—objects and activities—instrumental in the attainment of success. This low evaluation is particularly true of education. In the middle classes, where education is valued more highly, the pursuit of learning, no matter how minimal or superficial, furnishes by-products that become assets in later life. We have suggested that when the question of future achievement is assessed cognitively, the middle-class adolescent, for example, has already developed many of the social and intellectual skills necessary to movement up the ladder of success. For the lower-class respondent, it is often too late. Although he can recognize education and its concomitants as instruments for the climb, there is little he can do to recapture his formative years. The lower classes, as a result, are "boxed in" by the consequences of a kind of structured strain, the discrepancy between their evaluative and cognitive perceptions of education.

This process, combined with the limitations imposed by the social structure and, more specifically, by the objective requirements for occupational advancement, leads to a cyclical phenomenon analogous to a self-fulfilling prophecy (Merton 1957, pp. 421–438). Lack of education blocks advancement and opportunities to move out of the lower-class *milieu*. Furthermore, lack of opportunity to incorporate middle-class values reinforces the tendency to seek more available means for getting ahead. "To him that hath shall be given."

We have implied that the lower-class situation is very much like that of the minority group. The nature of the values that characterize the lower classes by themselves explain much of the failure to advance from those classes.

We generalize that the belief that a man with ability can get ahead in

American society is uniformly held throughout the class structure. The American dream remains intact, in spite of the objective social conditions of the lower-class milieu. Nevertheless, a number of respondents see their own chances of getting ahead as limited. Purely rational self-analysis might be expected to lead to a corresponding belief that such limited chances are owing to low ability. The success ideology, which effectively fills the gap between the cognitive and evaluative spheres, however, provides solace and hope that sooner or later success will be won as a just reward for legitimate striving. That this ideology protects the social order from disruptive criticism has been demonstrated by Merton. We add that this particular ideology fills the gap between the objective conditions of the "working class," as Marx described them, and their lack of revolutionary orientation. Marx assumed that the working class would eventually become aware of its condition and would overthrow the "capitalist" classes.

We have already noted that Marx failed to take account of alternative ideologies in his analysis. The success theme is such an alternative. Our view is that lack of class identification is not in itself what is responsible for so-called "working-class apathy" but the specific quality of the American dream itself. As Merton has noted, the American who believes he has equal opportunity for advancement has only himself to blame if he fails to succeed. Our findings support this suggestion.

Finally, we assessed the disparity between earlier occupational aspiration and current achievement and found it greatest among the lower classes. This finding provides a test of the Durkheim-Merton theory and lends it at least initial support.

In sum, we have managed to isolate four sources of structured strain in the social-class system of the small city from which our data are taken.[18] One was suggested by Merton and may be designated "external" to particular classes. He focused on the limits imposed upon the lower classes by the middle classes, which place obstacles in the path of those attempting to attain culturally prescribed goals. Three sources that are reflected in our data arise from class value systems themselves and may be described as "internal." Our choice of these terms is based on the extent to which groups other than those acting to achieve a particular goal are a primary source of strain (external) and on factors within the group that are primary sources of strain (internal).

Of the internal sources, there is first the disparity between the success ideology, particularly the belief that all can achieve success, and the objective conditions of American life, which limit achievement and success to relatively few at each level of the class structure. For example, only a few singers can join the Metropolitan Opera Company, even though there may be many who are capable. Second, there is a disparity between the lower-class value system and the requirements for attainment of success in American society. The values themselves tend to circumscribe opportunities among the lower classes. Finally, there is the distinction between achievement and success.

Whether or not these observations clarify processes at work in other communities can be determined only by systematic observation. It is our view that they represent significant focal points for the study of social structure and anomie in American society.[19]

NOTES

1. Robin M. Williams, Jr., American Society (New York: Knopf, 1960), p. 402.
2. Talcott Parsons and Edward Shils, Toward A General Theory of Action (Cambridge: Harvard University, 1951), p. 395.
3. Irvin G. Wyllie, The Self Made Man in America (New Brunswick, N.J.: Rutgers University 1954).
4. Note that Wyllie makes a distinction between money as a goal and money as a means. We will also use this distinction later, referring to *ends-values* and *means-values*.
5. The quotation from George Santayana is from *Character and Opinion in the United States* (New York: Charles Scribner's Sons, 1920), p. 185. Note that there is an implied difference between achievement and success in Williams's comments. We shall deal with this distinction later.
6. The data we use for this analysis of values are limited to those gathered in our second sample (N = 227), since questions on values were not asked of our larger sample.
7. Morris Rosenberg, *Occupations and Values* (New York: The Free Press of Glencoe, 1957; Robin M. Williams, Jr., ed. *Friendship and Social Values in a Suburban Community* (Eugene: Dept of Sociology, University of Oregon, 1956, Mimeographed); and Rose K. Goldsen, Morris Rosenberg, Robin M. Williams, Jr., and Edward Suchman, *What College Students Think* (New York: Van Nostrand, 1959). I should like to thank Professor Robin M. Williams Jr., for permission to use questions that he has developed in connection with his research on values and for a number of important suggestions about the kinds of problem associated with research on the relationship between aspiration for success and anomie.
8. Note that Merton does not distinguish, in the above quotation between "achievement" and "success" as does Williams, although their points of view are very similar.
9. Chi-square = 4.7, 2 degrees of freedom, P = .10. Although we are suggesting an arbitrary limit to acceptance or rejection of a probability statement as support for a particular finding, we want to avoid holding ourselves to any limit. We shall be content if the reader interprets the findings as they are presented, using his own judgment of whether or not they appear *theoretically* significant.
10. James Beshers has suggested that secrecy about symbols is a means of maintaining a status group intact and keeping lower status groups in subordinate positions. See *Urban Social Structure* (New York: The Free Press of Glencoe, 1961). Note also that this suggestion explains why socially mobile groups grasp the symbols that are most concrete and conspicuous, those that they recognize as associated with higher status, only to find that they are not the symbols that count
11. Robert and Helen Lynd have made a similar observation, pointing out that the lower classes are concerned in their jobs with *things* while the middle classes are concerned with *people* (1929, p. 22).
12. That this criticism represents structured strain is supported by our findings, reported later, that only the college- and high school-educated tend to be anomic when their incomes are below $5000 a year (P = .001 and P .03, respectively). It has often been suggested that the late President Franklin D. Roosevelt organized groups of artists, writers, and scholars into workshops during the depression of the 1930s to avert organized criticism of the system by this influential and potentially radical segment of the population. This insight was suggested to the writer some years ago by Professor St. Clair Drake.
13. Additional support is provided by our finding that class and the selection of specific means for the achievement of success are not associated—that there is no difference in the degree to which one means is selected over others, by class. It is clearly not in the *cognitive* sphere but in the *evaluative* sphere that obstacles to "getting ahead" are found in the lower classes. We hazard the hypothesis that cognitive perception is capable only of providing motivation for short periods of time. In order for motivation to be patterned and persistent, it must be "built into" the group's participants. Only then is it effective in the long run. This observation is apparently a tacit assumption in the theory of institutions.
14. The greatest number of such responses came from those classes with the greatest number of respondents. We do not know what the results would have been with a larger sample of middle-class respondents. There is a relationship, however, between *anomia* and perception of the role of ability as a factor. The greater the anomie, the more frequent the rejection of ability as an important factor in success (chi-square = 8.6, 2 d.f., P = .02, N = 224). This datum, it should be noted, is clearly consistent with Merton's notion that anomie results in utilization of illegitimate means.

15. It is clearly relevant to note here the weakness of Marx's assumption of rationality in the working-class's perception of its social-situation and his failure to take alternatives to revolutionary ideologies into account. See Leonard Broom and Philip Selznick, *Sociology* (2nd ed.; New York: Harper & Row, 1958), pp. 578–579; Richard Centers, *The Psychology of Social Classes* (Princeton, Princeton University Press, 1949), pp. 28–29.
16. A class-controlled analysis indicates that, for lower-class groups, the curve rises after age 60, while, for the middle classes, the rise begins after age 55.
17. "High disparity" means that three or more rank levels separated the aspired and achieved; "moderate," two levels; and "low," one level.
18. See Leon Festinger, *A Theory of Cognitive Dissonance* (New York: Harper & Row, Publishers, 1957) for a discussion that offers a possible method of integrating the social psychological and sociological approaches to structured strain.
19. These analyses suggest that now is the time for intensive exploration of the qualitative nature of values. We should expect that the kinds of value held by a particular group play a role in its group functions. Money as a value provides interesting analytical possibilities for the study of aspiration and anomie. Because, as Simmel has shown, money is easily transferred, easily accumulated, and so forth, money as an *end-value* may be more predisposing to anomie than goals more difficult to measure quantitatively. The thirst for money cannot be so easily quenched as that for formal education. By its very nature, it would therefore seem to have a greater potential for anomie. A similar analysis of norms is presented in Mizruchi and Perrucci (1962), Ephraim H. Mizruchi and Robert Perrucci, "Norm Qualities and Reactions to Deviant Behavior," *American Sociological Review, 27* (June), 1962.

The Nineteenth Century

The nineteenth century was an era of large-scale immigration into the United States. During the first three to four decades large numbers of families arrived from the United Kingdom; during the 1830s, 1840s and 1850s, immigrants arrived from Ireland, the Scandanavian countries, and from the Rhine River Valley in Central Europe. During the next few decades the immigrants to this country came from Eastern Europe, whereas the last quarter of the century and the period until the eve of World War I saw the arrival of a large number of individuals from Italy and other Southern European and Mediterranean countries. There are more differences between these waves of immigrants than simply their date of arrival in the United States. In fact, it is useful to distinguish between those immigrants who came from the United Kingdom, Central and Eastern Europe, and the Scandanavian countries from those who journeyed from Southern Europe and the Mediterranean region. The former are often called the "old immigrants" and the latter are collectively referred to as the "new immigrants."

The old immigrants, particularly those who left Central Europe and the Rhine River Valley around the time of the Civil War in the United States were primarily farmers or semiskilled laborers. They came to America to make a new life. Entire families arrived in the ports of the eastern seaboard; many of them settled in Baltimore, Philadelphia, and New York City; many others migrated westward to the cities of Buffalo, Chicago, and Milwaukee; and still others settled the land in the Midwest that had been made available by the Homestead Act of 1864.

TABLE 8.1
Immigration into the United States

Decade	Approximate Total	Source		
1821–1830	150,000			
1831–1840	600,000	British Isles		
1841–1850	1,710,000			Old immigrants
1851–1860	2,600,000			
1861–1870	2,310,000	Central and Eastern Europe		
1871–1880	2,810,000			
1881–1890	5,250,000			
1891–1900	3,690,000	Southern Europe and Mediterranean region	New Immigrants	
1901–1910	7,800,000			
1911–1920	6,740,000			

The new immigrants, particularly the nearly two million who emigrated from Southern Italy, were from rural areas. They settled in the growing cities of the eastern United States and established the ethnic enclaves, or ghettoes, that persist in many Northern American cities. What is important to note is that unlike the old immigrants, many of the new immigrants arrived in a land where the free acreage provided by the Homestead Act was no longer available and where urbanization and its corollary industrialization were beginning to gather momentum. Most important, a disproportional number of the new immigrants were males who had left their families in the "old" country in order to make their fortune in the United States and return to their homeland as rich men. Many, if not most, of these immigrants were unskilled and depended on word of mouth for day-to-day jobs as laborers in the large cities. For example, at the turn of the century it is estimated that 90 per cent of the laborers engaged in constructing the subway system in New York City were Italian immigrants.

Our knowledge of social mobility during the nineteenth century in the United States is sketchy, owing to a lack of data in which the occupational careers of a cohort of individuals can be traced. Much of the work done by sociologists on the social organization and stratification of nineteenth-century America has focused on the history and assimilation of the various ethnic groups that immigrated to the United States during the century.[2] A pervasive and characteristic theme of much of this work is that America is "God's crucible," a giant melting pot in which cultural differences blend

[2] See for example, Milton M. Gordon, *Assimilation in American Life: The Role of Race, Religion, and National Origins* (New York: Oxford U.P., 1964); Israel Zangwill, *The Melting Pot* (New York: Macmillan, 1909); Will Herberg, *Protestant-Catholic-Jew* (New York: Doubleday, 1955); and Nathan Glazer, "A New Look at the Melting Pot," *The Public Interest,* **16**:180–187 (Summer 1969).

together to provide equal opportunity for all regardless of race, creed, or ethnic background.

Nevertheless, the rags-to-riches ideology has not gone untested. Several social scientists have explored the "social origins" of the nineteenth-century business elite. C. Wright Mills, for example, found that only 9.8 per cent of the business leaders listed in the *Dictionary of American Biography* who were born before 1907 were the sons of skilled craftsmen, semiskilled, or unskilled workers, whereas 13.2 per cent born between 1820 and 1849 had similar blue-collar origins.[3] Mills concluded that even though the business elite of the nineteenth century was drawn primarily from among the sons of high-status fathers, it contained more sons of blue-collar origin than at any other time in the history of the United States. In similar studies Susanne Keller found that of 254 business leaders born in about 1820, only 3 per cent were the sons of fathers in low white- and blue-collar jobs.[4] Similarly, Reinhard Bendix and Frank W. Howton found the percentage of industrialists coming from working-class origins to be about 2 per cent, 1 per cent, and 2 per cent for those born during the periods 1801 to 1830; 1831 to 1860; and 1861 to 1890, respectively.[5] Although each of these studies is based on small (and not necessarily representative) samples, in combination they suggest that about 95 per cent of the nineteenth-century business elite were drawn from the ranks of sons of business leaders and that only about 3 per cent had fathers in lower-status blue-collar occupations. As Herbert G. Gutman notes: "Andrew Carnegie was an important American in 1900, but hardly any men of his economic class or social position shared with him a common career pattern." [6]

Recently, urban historians have begun to rummage through the dusty manuscripts of the census of the United States for the decades 1790 through 1890, as well as through several other sources of information such as directories, tax records, and marriage licences in an effort to piece together a picture of social mobility and the structure of inequality in nineteenth-century America.[7]

[3] C. Wright Mills, "The American Business Elite: A Collective Portrait," in *Power, Politics and People: The Collected Essays of C. Wright Mills,* ed. Irving Horowitz (New York: Oxford U.P., 1962), pp. 110–139.

[4] Susanne Keller, "The Social Origins and Career Lines of Three Generations of American Business Leaders," (Ph.D. diss., Columbia, 1953).

[5] Reinhard Bendix and Frank W. Howton, "Social Mobility and the American Business Elite," in *Social Mobility in Industrial Society,* ed. Reinhard Bendix and Seymour Martin Lipset (Berkeley: University of California Press, 1959), pp. 114–143.

[6] Herbert G. Gutman, "The Reality of the Rags-to-Riches 'Myth': The Case of Paterson, New Jersey, Locomotive, Iron, and Machinery Manufacturers, 1830–1880," in *Nineteenth Century Cities,* ed. Stephan Thernstrom and Richard Sennett (New Haven: Yale, 1969), p. 98.

[7] For a review of some of this literature and a comparison of the results of several studies, see Lawrence E. Hazelrigg, "Occupational Mobility in Nineteenth Century U.S. Cities: A Review of Some Evidence," *Social Forces,* 53:21–32 (Sept. 1974).

One of the larger problems encountered in this type of research is the difficulty of obtaining a random sample of families or individuals for whom occupational data are available at several points in time. Nineteenth-century cities in the United States witnessed large-scale movements of population. Many of the urban dwellers were perpetual migrants moving from city to city in search of opportunity. Stephan Thernstrom has estimated that in the years between 1837 and 1920, the population migration into and out of Boston was so great that 25 per cent of the population residing in the city at any one point in time had lived elsewhere only a year earlier.[8] In fact, the migration into and out of the nineteenth-century cities was so extensive that it may have involved more people than were enumerated in the city's decennial census. For example, in 1880 Boston had a population of less than one-half million but gained nearly sixty-five thousand during the decade as a result of migration. However, "more than a million people moved through the city in those years to produce that net gain." [9]

The migration into and out of nineteenth-century cities was a highly selective process. Single males were more likely to leave a city than were married males or males with families. The poor, the unemployed, and those engaged in unskilled occupations were more likely to migrate than skilled workers or the wealthy—probably because they anticipated improved employment opportunities elsewhere.

The problem of tracking such a migrant population throughout its occupational career is exacerbated by incomplete data for any one point in time. Census data are estimated to underenumerate the population by 8 or 9 per cent each decade, whereas other sources of data such as city directories may have twice the number of errors. As a result, the populations studied are highly selective and are, therefore, not necessarily representative of the urban populations of nineteenth-century America.

Nevertheless, Thernstrom has analyzed mobility in nineteenth-century Boston by constructing a sample of white males from census records, marriage license and tax records, and the city directory. He has organized the sample into four birth cohorts: 1850–1859; 1860–1879; 1880–1889; and 1900–1909. These data span the years of massive immigration beginning with the Irish, who arrived in the 1850s through the arrival of the Italians during the 1890s and early years of the twentieth century. Of greatest interest to us are the 1850–1859 and 1860–1879 cohorts.[10]

[8] Stephan Thernstrom, "Working Class Social Mobility in Industrial America," in *Essays in Theory and History*, ed. Melvin Richter (Cambridge: Harvard U.P., 1970).

[9] Stephan Thernstrom, "Reflections on the New Urban History," *Daedalus*, **100**:366 (Spring 1971).

[10] Stephan Thernstrom, "Immigrants and Wasps: Ethnic Differences in Occupational Mobility in Boston, 1890–1940," in Thernstrom and Sennett, op. cit., pp. 125–164.

Those born in the decade preceeding our Civil War were entering the labor force in around 1880, whereas those born between 1860 and 1879 were new entrants to the labor force at around the turn of the century. The measures of mobility used by Thernstrom were comparisons of father's job, which approximates what we have termed *status of origin;* son's first job, defined as "the first job to be held by a sample member, so long as it was held prior to age thirty," which approximates *status of entry* into the labor market; and son's last job, defined as "the last job held in Boston as revealed by the tracing method, so long as it was held at the age of thirty or older." [11] "Last job," as defined by Thernstrom, is a reasonable estimate of destination status in view of the "marked slowing of occupational mobility for men thirty and above" [12] observed by Thernstrom.

Some of the data from Thernstrom's study are presented in Table 8.2. The data reveal a substantial increase in the proportion engaged in white-collar occupations. Whereas 36 per cent of the fathers were in white-collar jobs, 56 per cent of the sons in the sample ended their work careers in non-manual occupations. However, not all sons born between 1850 and 1879 had an equal opportunity to start or end their work careers in upper-status occupations. As expected, Thernstrom's data show that sons of white-collar fathers and white-Ango-Saxon Protestants (WASPs) were in advantageous positions relative to sons of blue-collar workers and second-generation ethnics with respect to attaining higher-status occupations.

The importance of parental status for the occupational careers of sons is clear. Sons of white-collar workers were more than twice as likely to enter the labor force in white-collar jobs than sons of blue-collar parents. Further-more, the advantage of having white-collar parents persisted throughout the work career. Of the 19 per cent of white-collar sons who experienced down-ward mobility to blue-collar first jobs, more than one third experienced up-ward mobility to white-collar last jobs. In contrast, of the three in five blue-collar sons who entered blue-collar first jobs, only 19 per cent were to later experience a similar intragenerational mobility into a white-collar occupation. Sons of higher-status parents were also in an advantageous position with respect to retaining their white-collar entry status. Only 8 per cent of the white-collar sons who entered the labor force in white-collar jobs skidded into the blue-collar ranks, whereas 22 per cent of the blue-collar sons who managed to begin their careers in white-collar occupations experienced downward mobility to blue-collar status.

Important differences between the work careers of WASP and second-generation ethnics also were found. Sixty-one per cent of the WASP fathers occupied white-collar jobs, whereas 80 per cent of the fathers of second-

11 Ibid., p. 162.
12 Ibid.

TABLE 8.2
Comparisons of Son's First and Last Occupation, by Father's Occupation and Ethnic Generation, for an 1850–1879 Birth Cohort of Boston Sons*

Father's Occupation	Son's First Occupation	Ethnic Generation								
		All Sons			WASP			2nd Generation		
		Son's Last Occupation			Son's Last Occupation			Son's Last Occupation		
		White Collar	Blue Collar	n	White Collar	Blue Collar	n	White Collar	Blue Collar	n
All Sons N = 756	White Collar	85	15	415	93	7	220	77	23	195
	Blue Collar	21	79	341	21	79	66	21	79	275
	n	427	329		218	68		208	262	
White Collar N = 269	White Collar	92	8	219	95	5	155	84	16	64
	Blue Collar	36	64	50	50	50	19	26	74	31
	n	219	50		157	17		62	33	
Blue Collar N = 487	White Collar	78	22	196	88	12	65	73	27	131
	Blue Collar	19	81	291	9	91	47	21	79	244
	n	208	279		61	51		147	228	
		N = 756			N = 286			N = 470		

* Adapted from ibid., Table 4, p. 143.

generation sons were engaged in blue-collar occupations. However, 76 per cent of the WASP sons ended their work careers in white-collar jobs, whereas only 56 per cent of the second-generation sons ended in blue-collar occupations. This indicates a slight decline in the WASP's advantaged position in white-collar jobs and suggests that the rapidly expanding white-collar work force was recruited from the sons of immigrants.

Even though considerable upward mobility occurred among second-generation ethnics, ethnic generation continued to have an important impact on the occupational careers of Boston sons. Among the sons of white-collar workers, nine out of ten WASPs, compared to 67 per cent of second-generation sons, entered white-collar jobs. Nearly all (that is, 95 per cent) of the WASPs continued to hold white-collar jobs, whereas second-generation sons were more than three times as likely to be downwardly mobile from their white-collar origins and entry occupations. Furthermore, WASP sons who began in blue-collar jobs were about twice as likely to be upwardly mobile to white-collar destinations than second-generation ethnics. As a result, the advantage of being a WASP *increased* for white-collar sons over the generation.[13] Whereas 89 per cent of the WASP sons began in white-collar jobs, compared to 67 per cent of second-generations sons (a difference of 22 per cent), 90 per cent of the WASPs, but only 65 per cent of the second-generations sons (a difference of 25 per cent), ended their careers in white-collar occupations.

The mobility patterns of blue-collar sons were somewhat different. Three out of five WASP sons, compared to one out of ten of the second-generation sons entered the labor force in white-collar occupations. WASP sons were more likely to retain their higher status, whereas second-generation sons entering white-collar jobs were twice as likely to be downwardly mobile during their work career. However, a contrary pattern occurred among blue-collar sons who entered blue-collar jobs. In this case, 21 per cent of the second-generation sons attained white-collar status, whereas only 9 per cent of the WASP sons with similar origins and career starting points experienced upward mobility to white-collar destinations. This suggests that WASP sons of blue-collar workers lost whatever advantage their ethnic background gave them for attaining white-collar status when they began their occupational careers in blue-collar jobs.

A more concise picture of the relative importance of ethnic generation, parental status, and career starting point is presented in Figure 8–1. The (phi) coefficients are measures of the strength of association between variables in the "causal model." The values in parentheses are partial coeffi-

---

[13] Thernstrom notes that the advantage of being WASP declined over the generation. However, this conclusion is based on an erroneous calculation in his Table 4, ibid., pp. 143 ff.

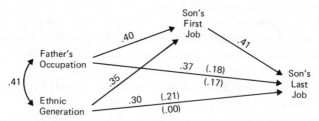

Figure 8–1

cients: those above the arrows are the strength of associations for sons entering the labor force in white-collar jobs; those below the arrows are for blue-collar starters.

All of the correlations in the model are moderately strong, indicating that the social-origin variables of ethnic generation and father's occupation had a moderately strong effect on a son's career starting point and that social origins and first job each had a moderately strong effect on a son's occupational destinations. However, the partial coefficients indicate that the effects of a father's job on a son's destination were mediated largely by the type of occupation in which the son began his career. Furthermore, the son's ethnic generation continued to have an impact on his destination status when he began his work career in a white-collar occupation. But for sons beginning their work careers in blue-collar occupations, the effects of ethnic generation on career destinations vanished altogether. In other words, WASP sons who began work in white-collar jobs had an advantage over second-generation sons in terms of remaining in higher-status occupations. In contrast, ethnic background was neither an advantage nor a liability for sons who started in blue-collar jobs; their intragenerational mobility experiences were determined more by the type of occupation in which their fathers had engaged than by their ethnic background.

The findings we have presented here are consistent with at least a dozen studies of social mobility from 1850 to the earliest part of the twentieth century. These studies report about one third of the working-class families to have been upwardly mobile into white-collar occupations and middle-class status, whereas only about one in five families experienced downward mobility from the middle class to blue-collar occupations and working-class status. These findings contradict any notion that the rapid industrialization of the United States during the nineteenth century led to a permanent and rapidly growing class of the poor. At the same time, however, these findings do not constitute overwhelming support for the opposite contention that the United States was the land of equal opportunity. Clearly, then as now, some were more equal than others.

The Early Twentieth Century

One of the most extensive studies of occupational mobility during the earlier part of the twentieth century was reported by Rogoff. The study focused on rates of intergenerational mobility in 1910 and 1940 in the metropolitan area of Indianapolis, Indiana.

Rogoff's basic data were taken from marriage licence applications, which, in Indiana, require the applicant to list both his own occupation and that of his father. A comparison of father-to-son rates of occupational inheritance in 1910 and 1940 showed highly similar patterns, especially when structural changes in the occupational system were taken into account. Rogoff's findings, for a selected list of major occupational categories, are presented in Table 8.3.[14]

TABLE 8.3
Percentage of all sons in an occupation whose fathers were in the same occupational category, and relative size of that category, in 1910 and 1940.

Occupation	1910	Relative Size	1940	Relative Size
Per cent professional and semiprofessional	20	4	24	6
Per cent proprietors, managers, and officials	36	12	32	12
Per cent clerical and sales	16	6	21	11
Per cent skilled	30	26	46	28
Per cent unskilled	35	12	30	7
Per cent farming	83	26	65	16

Examination of the table shows that rates of inheritance in 1940 were substantially like those observed for 1910. The notion of demand mobility in this context can be grasped by viewing changes in amount of inheritance in light of changes in the relative size of an occupational category. This indicates that when the rate of inheritance declined from 1910 to 1940 there was typically a decline in the relative size of the occupational category as well. (The unskilled and farming categories are clear examples.) This association between declining size and declining inheritance indicates that all of the lower percentage of sons not following in their father's footsteps were not in "voluntary circulation." In other words, as the number of jobs within an occupation declines, some sons who might otherwise have "inherited" their fathers' occupational type are forced out of the category.

[14] Natalie Rogoff, *Recent Trends in Occupational Mobility* (New York: Free Press, 1953).

The opposite trend is also indicated in Table 8.3 namely, that when the percentage of inheritance increases, the relative size of the occupational category tends to increase also. (The clerical and sales occupational category is a clear example.) In these cases, just the reverse process is in effect. The increased number of jobs within the category makes it possible for a larger proportion of sons to follow in their fathers' occupational footsteps.

Blau proposes that when there is an increase in the demand for practitioners of a given kind, leading to expansion, the occupation (or occupational category) is reorganized to attract outsiders.[15] This tends to increase the attractiveness of the occupation in the eyes of the sons of the current practioners as well. Expansion then occurs by retaining a high percentage of sons within the occupation and recruiting others from fathers of highly diverse backgrounds. Occupations of this type are labeled *consumers*. In 1940, the clerical and sales fields were good examples; salaried professionals and managers are contemporary examples. Prestige also is involved, as the consumers tend to be concentrated in high-status occupations, which contributes to their ability to retain sons.

When the demand for an occupation's contribution declines, by contrast, the constriction that follows has the opposite effect. Sons follow their fathers to a lesser degree, outsiders are not widely attracted, and the occupation becomes a "producer"; that is, there is a flow of sons out of the category. Farmers and unskilled laborers illustrate producer categories both for 1940 and today. The alert reader will notice that prestige is again involved, as the producers tend to be concentrated in relatively low-status occupations (especially by comparison to the consumers).

Occurring within the context of these macroscopic changes, Rogoff noticed that between fathers and sons there was a tendency for mobility patterns to exhibit a regression toward the mean; that is, the sons of fathers with above-average standing tended to attain above-average standing themselves, but to a less marked degree than their fathers. Correspondingly, sons of lower-than-average-standing fathers tended to move up toward the mean. As a result of these two lines of regression toward the mean, Rogoff was able to identify cutoff points. Slightly above the mean was one cutoff point; if the father was located above this point, intergenerational mobility was disproportionately downward. The second cutoff was just below the mean; a preponderance of upward mobility was experienced by sons whose fathers were below this point.

When an occupational hierarchy is being modified—either through structurally forced mobility or voluntary circulation—these cutoff points will vary. For example, if there is an excess of upward to downward mobility

[15] Peter M. Blau, "The Flow of Occupational Supply and Recruitment," *American Sociological Review,* **30**:475–490 (Aug. 1965).

during a thirty-year interim, it will result in raising of the cutoff point located above the mean.

Rogoff's findings were that from 1910 to 1940 the rate of occupational inheritance, when structural changes were taken into account, remained largely the same. Furthermore, the ratio of upward to downward mobility—when inheritance did not occur—remained substantially the same.[16] Particularly indicative of the absence of change were Rogoff's cutoff points, which virtually were unchanged between 1910 and 1940.

Even though Rogoff's data are drawn entirely from an Indianapolis (and surrounding Marion County) sample, the extensiveness of that sample, and the apparent representativeness of that metropolitan area, help to make hers the most reliable study of the period in question. In addition, Rogoff inferred mobility by comparing two different groups at two different times. By contrast, most other studies of the period attempted to infer trends from a single group, studied at one time only. Specifically, men of varying ages would be interviewed, all at the same time. However, rates of intergenerational mobility are difficult to control with this alternative procedure, and there are serious questions concerning how the representativeness of such a sample can be assessed.

Of the studies conducted at a single point in time, we need only note that their results, although imprecise, tend to be in agreement with the conclusions of Rogoff. During the early 1930s, for example, Percey E. Davidson and H. Dewey Anderson analyzed the mobility experienced by a sample of men in San Jose, California. For the most part, the occupational status of the men in the sample was the same as that of their fathers. When changes did occur they were very small in magnitude, leading the investigators to conclude that substantial intergenerational movement—either upward or downward in direction—occurs for only a "minor fraction" of men.[17]

One final, but very noteworthy, study of this period was part of the Yankee City series of studies, reported by Warner and his associates. The actual town was Newburyport, Massachusetts, a small New England town with a large shoe manufacturing industry. Based on their observations, Warner and his colleagues felt that the nostalgic view of American mobility opportunities would not be present in the future; opportunities for the modern urban laborer and his children, they argued, were declining.[18]

This conclusion followed from Warner and J. O. Low's acceptance of a nostalgic view of the past. It was a romantic view in light of Thernstrom's

---

[16] In fact, there was a very slight excess of downward to upward mobility in 1940, compared to 1910.

[17] Percey E. Davidson and H. Dewey Anderson, *Occupational Mobility in an American Community* (Stanford: Stanford University Press, 1937).

[18] W. Lloyd Warner and J. O. Low, *The Social System of the Modern Factory* (New Haven: Yale, 1947).

findings. In fact, according to Thernstrom, Warner and Low conjured up a "never-never land." [19] Their reasoning, however, was congruent with widespread beliefs throughout the society. Therefore, it is of interest despite its factual inaccuracies.

Traditionally, Warner and Low proposed, work and production were harmoniously interwoven into the fabric of the community. Implicitly, a guild system served as their historical point of reference. In this type of system, every youngster presumably became an apprentice, then a journeyman, and then a master. As the youngster learned the skills, moving up in the hierarchy was a virtual certainty. In other words, intragenerational mobility was assured.

The complex technology associated with the mechanization of production was assumed to have several effects that ultimately destroyed the earlier system. Most important, perhaps, complex technology required a large capital investment that could not be met within the local community. As outside money came in, the community lost its economic self-sufficiency. The absentee owners—outsiders—were viewed as creating an unbridgeable social gulf between themselves, the management, and the workers. This terminated, they concluded, the previous feelings of community solidarity and ended opportunities for mobility that had been assured in the past.

The changes they described were viewed by Warner and Low as inhibiting both inter- and intragenerational mobility. The new urban laborer, "created" by the technological transformation, was expected by them to have little chance to move up during his own lifetime. The distinction between laborer and manager was too great, based on too many qualitative differences, and there was no longer the solidifying influence of the community. The sons of laborers also were forced to enter the occupational hierarchy at a low position, and for the same reasons, had little chance to be upwardly mobile.

In 1933 a strike closed all of Newburyport's shoe factories, and changed the impression of tranquility that had previously characterized the town. The demands of workers were typically expressed in terms of better working conditions, higher salaries, and the like. The basic underlying reason, however, according to Warner and Low, was the change in industrial organization. The workers were perceived as clinging to traditional values that could not be actualized within the new technological context. Thus, the strike was viewed as representing a symbolic mourning for an open system that had been killed by industrial changes.

However, Thernstrom points out that strikes had occurred regularly in Newburyport from about 1850 on, and had their origin in 1800. Further-

[19] Stephan Thernstrom, "Yankee City Revisited: The Perils of Historical Naiveté" *American Sociological Review,* **30**:234–242 (April 1965).

more, the guild system, which had been viewed as open, actually always had been a rigid hierarchy that was quite closed. To support his contention that the pre-1900 organization did not offer mobility opportunities, Thernstrom analyzed a large sample of workers and their sons between 1850 and 1880. He could not find within his sample a single case of upward mobility into the managerial category, or even into the ranks of foreman.

What Warner did not anticipate was that industrialization would create more than offsetting demands for professional and technical personnel; that, in fact, industrialization would correlate with higher rates of mobility by leading to an expansion of higher-status positions and a contraction of lower-status (unskilled) positions.

From World War II to the Present

One of the most complete estimates of mobility trends during the years following World War II is provided by Elton F. Jackson and Harry J. Crockett, Jr.[20] Their data were taken from two sources: from Centers's national sample, conducted during 1945[21], and from a Survey Research Center sample taken in 1957.[22] The earlier study unfortunately did not include farmers, unemployed persons, or nonwhites. In order to make the two groups comparable, such persons had to be excluded from the latter sample. Thus, the analysis applies only to urban, white employed males (both samples included about six hundred persons with these characteristics). As we suggested earlier, inconsistencies in the status question that allow for different amounts of intragenerational mobility would invalidate direct comparisons. However, virtually identical questions were asked at both points in time.

Of initial interest are the findings concerning gross rates of mobility in the two periods. The findings, which are summarized in Table 8.4, indicate an increase in the over-all amount of intergenerational mobility. Viewed conversely, sons were less likely to inherit their fathers' occupational position in 1957 than in 1945. It is interesting to note that almost the entire increase in movement resulted in upward mobility. Approximately one fourth of both samples continued to experience downward movement, although there was a substantial increase in upward mobility. Jackson and Crockett's

[20] Elton F. Jackson and Harry J. Crockett, Jr., "Occupational Mobility in the United States: A Point Estimate and Trend Comparison," *American Sociological Review,* 29:5–15 (Feb. 1964).

[21] Richard Centers, "Occupational Mobility of Urban Occupational Strata," *American Sociological Review,* 13:197–203 (April 1948).

[22] Reported in Gerald Gurin et al., *Americans View Their Mental Health* (New York: Basic Books, 1960).

TABLE 8.4
Gross rates of mobility for two periods

	1945	1957
Per cent mobile	61.5	67.7
Upward	29.7	39.8
Downward	27.0	25.7
Per cent structural	16.8	14.5
Per cent circulation	44.7	53.2

findings further suggest that this upward movement was increasingly due to voluntary circulation. Specifically, it accounted for a larger percentage of the mobility in 1957, whereas the contribution of structural factors slightly declined after 1945. Finally, the investigators computed Cramer's V, a measure of association reflecting the relationship between the positions of fathers and sons. It takes both demand and circulation mobility into account, and indicates the degree to which the mobility experiences of a sample are congruent with a "full-equality" model: in other words, a completely open system in which status of origin has no influence on one's occupational attainments (for example, status of destination). When this is the case, V will attain a value of O. However, there probably is no such society in reality, so interpretation in fact involves assessing how close societies come to the full-equality model.

In 1945 they obtained a V value of .297. It was lower in 1957, $V =$ .233. Thus, in 1957 there was greater congruence with a full-equality model than in 1945. Taking into account, also, the increase in upward mobility, it seems fair to conclude that in the decade or so after the war, the actual mobility patterns in the United States moved closer to congruence with the traditional ideals of the American Dream. The only discordant note stems from the constancy of downward mobility for slightly over one fourth of those studied; a rate that probably seems surprisingly high to most people and makes all the more unfortunate the almost total lack of sociological study of downward mobility.

The trend toward greater actualization of ideals described between 1945 and 1957 also was observed to have been carried into the 1960s by Blau and Duncan.[23] From their data it appears that about three fourths of

[23] Peter M. Blau, "The Flow of Occupational Supply and Recruitment," *American Sociological Review*, **30** (1965); Otis Dudley Duncan, "The Trend of Occupational Mobility in the United States," *American Sociological Review*, **30**:491–498 (Aug. 1965); Peter M. Blau and Otis Dudley Duncan, *The American Occupational Structure* (New York: Wiley, 1967).

the sons were mobile in 1962, as compared with about two thirds in 1957, and that the previously seen trend toward increasing rates of upward mobility continued into the 1960s too. These trends are indicated in Figure 8-2.

The single most comprehensive and authoritative study of occupational mobility in the United States was conducted by Blau and Duncan and reported in their classic volume *The American Occupational Structure*. In 1962, with the cooperation of the Bureau of the Census, Blau and Duncan gathered data on 20,700 American males between the ages of twenty and sixty-five. This sample was highly representative of approximately forty-five million American men in the civilian noninstitutionalized population.

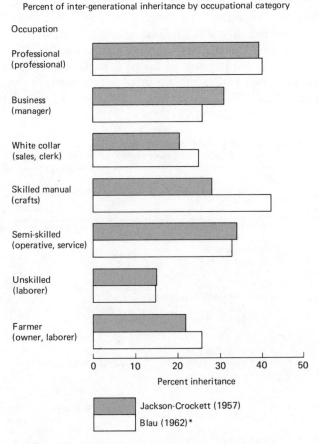

Percent of inter-generational inheritance by occupational category

*The fathers who were not in the labor force and their sons, were excluded from these calculations in order to make Blau's figures comparable to those of Jackson and Crockett, loc cit.

Figure 8–2

Their analysis of mobility patterns utilized seventeen categories of occupation, which were ranked in terms of socioeconomic status as determined by members' median income earned and median years of schooling completed (see Table 8.5).

Blau and Duncan began by analyzing the flow of manpower between the seventeen categories of occupation. Each occupational group can be considered a "consumer" of manpower in the sense that it recruits members from other occupations; it is a "supplier" of manpower in the sense that its members and their offspring are destined for employment in other occupations. The extent to which an occupation is a consumer and a supplier of manpower is a function of at least three factors: (1) changes in the occupational structure over time, particularly over a generation; (2) differential fertility and mortality among members of an occupation; and (3) the permeability of the occupational hierarchy. (The first two factors constitute aspects of demand mobility, which we discussed in Chapter 7.)

By far the occupational strata with the highest rate of self-recruitment was farmers. Eighty-two per cent of the men engaged in farming in 1962 were sons of farmers, whereas only about 18 per cent were the sons of men in other occupations. The self-employed professionals', proprietors', and

TABLE 8.5
Socioeconomic rank of seventeen occupation categories for males fourteen and over employed in 1962*

Professionals:	
1. Self-employed	Upper white collar
2. Salaried	
3. Managers	
4. Salesmen, other	Middle white collar
5. Proprietors	
6. Clerical	Lower white collar
7. Salesmen, retail	
Craftsmen:	
8. Manufacturing	
9. Other	Upper blue collar
10. Construction	
Operatives:	
11. Manufacturing	
12. Other	Middle blue collar
13. Service	
Laborers:	
14. Manufacturing	Lower blue collar
15. Other	
Farm:	
16. Farmers	
17. Farm laborers	

* Adapted from Blau and Duncan, op. cit., p. 27.

farm laborers' strata also exhibited *relatively* high rates of occupational inheritance. About 16 per cent of the proprietors and 14.5 per cent of the independent professionals and farm laborers were in occupations their fathers had been in. Three of the high-inheritance occupations (self-employed professionals, proprietors, and farmers) involve self-employment, a characteristic that apparently encourages sons to follow in their fathers' occupation. Part of this occupational inheritance is manifested by a son taking over the family farm, inheriting the family business, or becoming a physician or practicing attorney like his father. One of the consequences of high occupational inheritance is that individuals from different occupational strata encounter restricted access to such occupations. For example, sons of fathers who are not professionals may find entry to medical or law school next to impossible, whereas (perhaps less qualified) sons of professionals may be accorded preferential admission.

The fourth occupational strata with a relatively high rate of inheritance is farm laborer, which is the lowest socioeconomic status occupation. It is interesting to note that the rate of inheritance in this stratum is equal to the inheritance rate for self-employed professionals. However, the rate of self-recruitment for these lowest and highest occupations is only 14.5 per cent, meaning that of every hundred males born to fathers in these occupations, only about fifteen are in the same occupational categories as their fathers; the remaining 85 per cent are mobile to other types of occupations. It is also noteworthy that of the seventeen categories of occupation used by Blau and Duncan, only one—farmers—actually has a high rate of occupational inheritance (82 per cent). All other occupations recruit about 85 per cent or more of their manpower from different occupational strata.

The occupations with the lowest rates of inheritance—that is, those strata that supply about 90 per cent or more of their sons to different occupations—are clerical, sales, the two categories of nonfarm labor, and farm laborers. These occupations constitute the two lowest white-collar strata, the two lowest blue-collar strata, and the lowest farm occupation. Structural changes in the occupational hierarchy and high rates of fertility contribute to the mobility of sons from these strata. This is particularly true among farm laborers—an occupation that, as a consequence of mechaniza-tion and the rapid growth of large corporate farm enterprises, has been declining in terms of its proportion of the labor force and traditionally has had one of the highest fertility rates. Consequently, sons born in these occupational strata have had an above-average opportunity for social mobility to other strata.

The occupations that have been the largest consumers of manpower have been the two lowest white-collar occupations and the three lowest blue-collar strata, although each occupational stratum has recruited no less than 10 per cent of its members from the sons of farmers (which indicates both the high fertility of farmers and the effects of decreasing employment opportunities in this occupation).

The lowest white-collar and the lowest blue-collar strata have been both the highest consumers and suppliers of manpower for other occupations. As Blau and Duncan write of the clerical, retail sales, service, and two categories of nonfarm labor:

> These five occupational strata may be considered distributors of manpower, into which disproportionate numbers move from different origins, and from which disproportionate numbers of sons move to different destinations. The distributing occupations are channels for upward mobility, into which successful sons from lower origins tend to move and from which successful sons tend to move to higher destinations. Simultaneously, they provide a refuge for the downwardly mobile from higher origins . . . thereby enabling unsuccessful sons of nonmanual fathers to maintain their white-collar and unsuccessful sons of manual fathers to find jobs in the urban labor market, respectively. The skidder from a white-collar home, unfamiliar with the working class and possibly threatened by the prospect of becoming part of it, appears to be willing to pay the price of the lesser income offered by the lowest nonmanual occupations to preserve the cherished symbol of the white collar. The skidder from manual homes has probably also little inclination and certainly few qualifications or opportunities to work on a farm.[24]

A complete picture of the structure of inequality involves more than a determination of simple inflow and outflow rates of occupational strata. The permeability of the stratification system pertains to the *relationship* between origin and destination. To reiterate a point, there can be high rates of social mobility and yet low system permeability if those with common origins are mobile to a common destination. Thus, it is necessary to examine the occupational destinations of individuals with common origins or, alternatively, the origins of individuals with common destinations.

The inter- and intragenerational supply and recruitment of manpower for Blau and Duncan's sample of American males is presented in Table 8.6. In each panel of the table, the categories of occupations for destinations are collapsed into upper white collar, which includes the two types of professional occupations (that is, self-employed and salaried); middle white collar, which includes the managers, salesmen, and proprietor strata; lower white collar, which combines clerical and retail sales; upper blue collar, which combines the three strata of craftsmen (that is, skilled labor); middle blue collar, which includes the semiskilled operatives and service occupations; lower blue collar, which includes the unskilled nonfarm labor strata; and farm occupations.

[24] Blau and Duncan, ibid., pp. 41–42.

TABLE 8.6

Flow of Manpower from Origins to Occupational Destinations for a Sample of Males Twenty-five to Sixty-four Years Old.*

	Father's Job (ROWS†) to Son's First Job							Son's First Job (ROWS†) to 1962 Job							Father's Job (ROWS†) to Son's First Job						
	UWC	MWC	LWC	UBC	MBC	LBC	Farm	UWC	MWC	LWC	UBC	MBC	LBC	Farm	UWC	MWC	LWC	UBC	MBC	LBC	Farm
Self-employed professionals	38.1	7.4	22.4	5.8	13.3	3.8	2.8	79.0	9.0	1.5	2.2	0.7	2.5	0.7	48.6	23.8	5.4	6.0	6.0	2.6	2.8
Salaried professionals	30.7	5.8	18.3	10.2	20.7	8.4	2.5	61.0	20.6	5.3	4.0	3.4	0.4	1.1	35.2	23.6	9.3	9.2	15.5	1.6	1.0
Managers	20.1	7.1	26.7	9.0	23.2	9.2	1.6	21.6	49.1	8.9	9.3	4.7	1.8	1.0	26.1	33.5	8.7	13.8	8.0	1.9	0.6
Sales (other)	19.6	15.0	26.1	5.6	20.3	4.9	2.3	9.1	61.2	7.8	5.2	12.1	0.0	0.4	21.7	43.5	8.8	10.1	8.0	0.8	1.3
Proprietors	15.9	13.4	23.5	10.0	22.9	8.3	2.5	7.7	61.9	5.2	4.2	11.6	3.0	3.8	17.4	40.2	9.5	12.6	11.5	1.7	1.5
Clerical	18.4	4.2	26.2	9.5	25.7	10.5	2.0	14.6	30.0	19.4	11.5	14.2	2.8	1.4	25.7	22.2	10.1	15.5	14.0	2.8	1.3
Retail sales	11.5	6.4	31.1	6.4	25.4	11.9	5.0	12.1	34.6	16.7	12.2	16.6	3.0	1.1	14.4	34.4	9.1	12.3	18.5	3.4	2.2
Craftsmen (manufacturing)	6.6	1.4	19.6	15.8	38.6	13.3	2.0	9.6	22.5	4.8	34.3	16.3	4.8	2.3	15.9	17.1	7.8	26.1	21.7	4.1	0.5
Craftsmen (other)	6.6	1.5	19.9	15.6	32.6	14.8	4.8	9.3	18.8	7.5	36.9	16.2	3.1	1.9	12.0	19.6	9.1	24.4	22.0	4.0	1.2
Craftsmen (construction)	5.6	1.4	18.0	19.7	34.0	12.3	6.8	5.9	16.1	3.3	48.2	11.7	4.1	2.9	7.6	18.0	8.7	32.5	18.9	5.4	1.4
Operations (manufacturing)	4.4	1.5	15.0	8.4	48.7	14.7	3.2	6.5	14.3	7.9	24.7	31.1	6.7	2.6	9.6	13.6	7.4	22.7	29.9	7.5	1.4
Operations (other)	5.8	2.6	15.5	9.1	45.3	13.3	4.3	5.5	17.8	5.4	25.0	11.7	5.7	2.8	12.1	14.2	7.7	21.3	28.8	6.3	2.0
Service	4.6	2.9	18.0	11.0	41.2	15.1	5.1	7.6	12.5	6.2	16.0	40.8	8.3	0.9	9.6	16.9	10.9	19.8	30.3	6.0	1.2
Laborers (manufacturing)	3.8	0.1	10.1	6.3	36.4	29.5	8.0	5.8	8.3	7.4	19.7	34.2	14.5	3.3	6.0	9.3	5.1	19.5	36.9	12.9	2.8
Laborers (other)	4.3	0.8	13.8	6.6	35.3	28.7	7.0	5.7	14.5	5.4	22.5	27.6	13.9	3.0	5.3	9.5	10.4	21.6	31.4	13.3	2.0
Farmers	3.5	1.1	6.4	5.7	20.4	11.5	48.0	2.5	8.2	4.2	15.5	17.9	5.0	35.0	4.8	11.3	5.4	18.1	23.6	7.8	20.3
Farm laborers	0.9	0.7	3.5	4.7	20.5	11.4	56.0	1.9	7.9	3.8	17.1	25.5	9.5	26.3	2.1	7.5	4.7	18.8	31.4	12.4	15.1

* Adapted from Blau and Duncan, op. cit., Tables 2.3, 2.4, and 2.2.
† ROWS do not round to 100 per cent because cases with missing data are not reported separately.

From Father's Occupation to Son's First Job

The first panel of the table presents outflow rates (in percentages) of sons from father's occupation to the son's first occupation. Nearly four out of ten sons of self-employed professionals entered the upper white-collar professional strata, compared with three out of ten sons of salaried professionals and two out of ten sons of managers, clerical workers, and the higher category of sales occupations. The percentage of sons entering the highest occupational stratum fell rather consistently as parental stratum declined to where fewer than one out of hundred sons of farm laborers began their occupational careers in the professional stratum. However, each of the white-collar strata was found to supply at least 10 per cent of their sons to professional beginnings. Furthermore, 22 per cent of the sons of independent professionals began their work careers in the lower white-collar occupations, and nearly 14 per cent began in the semiskilled blue-collar jobs. The career starting points of sons of salaried professionals were quite similar to those of independent professionals, although nearly 40 per cent of these sons skidded to blue-collar starting jobs, as compared to 23 per cent of the sons of independent professionals beginning in blue-collar occupations.

Sons of middle white-collar workers were most likely to begin their careers in lower white-collar clerical and sales occupations, although for each stratum about an equal proportion of sons skidded all the way to semiskilled operative occupations. The sons from clerical and retail sales origins were most likely to enter lower white-collar occupations, although about a quarter of the sons entered semiskilled blue-collar jobs. The importance of these lower white-collar occupations as distributors of manpower can be seen by the fact that nearly one in five sons from these strata had career beginnings higher than their origins; about 30 per cent entered occupations in the same stratum as their origins; and nearly 50 per cent experienced downward mobility in entering their first occupation (about 10 per cent to the lowest strata of nonfarm laborers).

The sons of all three categories of craftsmen, which together form the upper blue-collar ranks, had nearly identical patterns of career starting points, although skilled tradesmen in the construction industry had a disproportionate share of the sons entering farm occupations. About one half of the sons of skilled workers were downwardly mobile to their first job. Approximately one third of the sons entered semiskilled operative occupations in manufacturing or elsewhere, and about 15 per cent entered skilled occupations. Another 25 per cent were upwardly mobile to white-collar career starting points. Of those who entered white-collar occupations, the majority began as clerical or sales workers; a few entered the professional ranks; and very few (that is, about one in every hundred sons) became managers, salesmen, or proprietors.

The sons of the semiskilled operative and service occupations were very likely to enter occupations similar to those of their fathers. More than four out of ten sons of middle blue-collar workers began their work careers in operative or service jobs, and approximately 15 per cent experienced downward mobility to blue-collar starting jobs as unskilled laborers. However, more than one out of five sons from these origins skipped over the skilled blue-collar occupations to begin work wearing a white collar and most of these entered the lower white-collar clerical and sales occupations.

Many of the sons of the lowest nonfarm blue-collar strata entered the occupations of their fathers. Nearly three out of ten began work as unskilled laborers and another one third entered the semi skilled occupations. Only about 15 per cent of the sons managed to begin their careers in white-collar occupations and, like the sons of semiskilled workers, most who entered white-collar jobs began in clerical or retail sales occupations. Nevertheless, nearly 60 per cent of the sons were upwardly mobile from their low-status origins to their first jobs.

The farm occupations were clearly the least permeable; at least with respect to entry. No white- or blue-collar stratum contributes more than 8 per cent of their sons to farm occupations whereas, in contrast, farmers and farm laborers contribute 48 and 56 per cent of their sons, respectively. However, the farm occupations were relatively permeable with respect to exit. The majority of sons who did not follow their fathers in farm occupations entered blue-collar jobs—usually semiskilled operative occupations and, to a lesser extent, unskilled occupations as nonfarm laborers. Very few sons were upwardly mobile to the extent that they entered white-collar jobs.

The diverse origins of sons starting their careers in each of the white-collar and blue-collar strata coupled with the diverse destinations of sons born in each strata indicate that the occupational hierarchy in the United States during the first sixty years of the twentieth century was very permeable —at least with respect to an individual's entry into the labor force.

From First Job to Later Job

The second panel of Table 8.6 presents the outflow rates for the intragenerational mobility of sons from their first job to their occupation in 1962. For some individuals in the sample, the occupation held in 1962 was not their "last" job or destination status because many of the sons were still young (that is, less than forty). Nonetheless, this panel of data indicates substantially less downward social mobility than witnessed in the comparison between father's occupation and son's first job.

The highest rate of stability across the work career was exhibited by sons who entered self-employed professional occupations. Nearly four out of five of these sons were still in the upper white-collar professional occupations in 1962, whereas only a little more than three out of five who entered salaried professional occupations remained in similar status occupations in 1962. Twice as many salaried professional starters as independent professional starters skidded to middle white-collar occupations between the time of their entry into the labor market and 1962. However, very few of the professional starters skidded very far down the occupational hierarchy; only 6 per cent of the self-employed professionals and 8 per cent of the salaried professionals were in blue-collar occupations.

Among those beginning work in the middle white-collar occupations, managers were the most likely to be upwardly mobile into professional occupations, whereas about three in five starting in sales or as proprietors remained stable in their work careers. However, between 15 and 20 per cent of the sons starting their careers in middle white-collar positions had skidded into blue-collar employment by 1962. Those who had begun as managers and were subsequently downwardly mobile into blue-collar ranks were in the skilled occupations in 1962, whereas the downwardly mobile salesmen stopped skidding at the middle blue-collar operative jobs and 3 per cent of those starting as proprietors skidded all the way to jobs as unskilled laborers.

Nearly one half of the sons who began their careers in clerical and retail sales occupations were upwardly mobile by 1962. Approximately one third had risen into the middle white-collar jobs as managers, salesmen, or proprietors, but about one in five remained in the same lower white-collar strata. Those who experienced downward mobility (about 30 per cent of the total) ended in middle blue-collar jobs.

The entrants into the upper blue-collar occupations exhibited greater rates of stability than those who entered lower white-collar jobs. About one half of those who entered skilled trades in the construction industry had similar jobs in 1962. Only about one third of those entering skilled occupations in other industries remained in those types of occupations. About 35 per cent of the entrants to skilled-craftsmen types of occupations experienced upward mobility into white-collar occupations. However, very little of this upward mobility was into clerical and retail sales occupations; most of it occurred into the middle white-collar jobs, although about one in ten starters rose to the professional occupations. Only about 20 per cent experienced downward mobility, generally to semiskilled occupations.

With the exception of those entering service occupations, individuals who began their work careers in other middle blue-collar occupations exhibited little tendency to remain in the same type of work. About 25 per cent of those starting as operatives in either manufacturing or other types of enterprises rose to skilled blue-collar occupations, whereas another 30 per cent rose all the way to white-collar status. Most of those who were upwardly mobile to white-collar jobs were employed as managers, salesmen, or proprietors, with fewer than one in ten having attained professional status. The upward mobility patterns for those starting as service workers were similar to those of the operatives, although proportionately smaller, because 41 per cent remained in service occupations.

The individuals who started their careers as unskilled laborers were the most mobile of any occupational strata. More than 85 per cent had different occupations in 1962. However, most of those who were mobile remained in blue-collar occupations—particularly in semiskilled jobs, although approximately 20 per cent of them had become skilled tradesmen by 1962. Very few (only about 20 or 25 per cent) attained white-collar status, generally in the middle white-collar occupations.

Individuals in farm occupations in 1962 came disproportionately from among those who started their careers in such occupations. No nonfarm occupational stratum contributed more than 4 per cent of its starters to farm occupations, whereas 35 and 26 per cent of those in farm occupations in 1962 had begun their careers as farmers or farm laborers, respectively.

From Father's Occupation to Son's Later Job

The analysis of the flow of manpower between son's first job and son's occupation in 1962 again reveals considerable mobility. However, this segment of mobility between generations reveals greater stability and movements of less distance than the segment from father's occupation to son's first job.

The third and final panel in Table 8.6 presents the flow of manpower from father's occupation to son's occupation in 1962. As in the first panel, we find a general decline in the proportion of sons in professional occupations as the father's occupational status decreases. But, again, nearly all occupational strata, with the exception of the two types of unskilled labor and the two farm occupations, contribute about 10 per cent or more of their sons to professional occupations. We also find that as parental status decreases, the proportion of sons in farm occupations increases, although no occupational stratum contributes more than 3 per cent of its sons to farm occupations.

More than 70 per cent of the sons of independent professionals were in professional or middle white-collar occupations in 1962, with about twice as many employed in a professional capacity as in the managers, salesmen, and proprietor strata. Furthermore, only about one in five sons of independent professionals were in blue-collar, particularly semiskilled, occupations.

Sons from the middle white-collar stratum had, by and large, attained occupational positions equivalent to that of their fathers by 1962, although a substantial proportion, particularly of the sons of managers, had risen into the professional strata. Those that were downwardly mobile, about 30 per cent, generally skidded past the lower-status clerical and retail-sales strata for destinations in the skilled and semiskilled blue-collar occupations.

The distributions of occupations held by sons of clerical and retail workers in 1962 are particularly interesting. Historically, these occupations have been characterized by rapid increases in the proportion of the labor force employed and by relatively high fertility rates. It would seem that these two characteristics would contribute to high rates of occupational inheritance. However, out of every ten sons born to fathers in these occupations, half were upwardly mobile, with many of them moving up to the highest occupational strata; only about one in ten remained in the same occupational strata as their fathers; and only between three and four were downwardly mobile, with most of these skidding no farther than semiskilled occupations.

Turning to the sons from the skilled blue-collar strata, between 25 and 30 per cent remained in the same line of work as their fathers, and more than three out of ten rose to white-collar status—often to professional occupations. In contrast, about one in five experienced downward mobility into the semiskilled blue-collar occupations.

Approximately one third of the sons of semiskilled workers were in the same stratum as their fathers. However, fewer than one in ten sons experienced downward mobility into the unskilled nonfarm occupations. The majority of sons from these origins had risen in the occupational hierarchy, with many of them moving all the way up to the middle white-collar strata and about one in ten attaining professional status.

Of all of the blue-collar strata, the unskilled level had the lowest proportion of sons remaining in the same strata as their father. Most of the sons from unskilled nonfarm families experienced upward mobility into the skilled and particularly the semiskilled blue-collar strata. Only about one in five crossed into white-collar status, and these were fairly evenly distributed between the upper-middle, and lower white-collar strata.

Sons of farmers were concentrated primarily in skilled and semiskilled blue-collar occupations, with about an equal percentage remaining on the farm. Fewer than one in five rose to white-collar status, with most of these being in the middle white-collar occupations. The outflow of farmers, as noted, is a consequence of the decline in farming as an important consumer of manpower, coupled with the high fertility rate among farmers.

This analysis of the flow of manpower between father's occupation to son's starting occupation; from son's first occupation to son's occupation in 1962; and from father's occupation to son's 1962 occupation revealed extensive occupational mobility among American males. Upward mobility was more prevalent than downward mobility, and short-distance movements of one or two occupational strata exceeded longer-distance moves of four or five strata. The third panel in Table 8.6 reveals that the lower white-collar strata (consisting of clerical and retail sales occupations) and the lower blue-collar strata (including the two types of unskilled nonfarm labor) had the lowest rates of occupational inheritance. Most of the sons whose origins were in these strata were mobile. Those from lower white-collar origins were generally mobile into higher white-collar strata, with fewer sons experiencing downward mobility into blue-collar status. Similarly, sons with origins in lower blue-collar families were often upwardly mobile into higher blue-collar strata, with fewer sons crossing into white-collar status. Accordingly, for American males from nonfarm origins, the white-collar–blue-collar barrier was real, but relatively permeable.

The Antecedents of Occupational Mobility

A second phase of Blau and Duncan's analysis focused on determining the relative contribution of a number of social-origin variables, including father's occupation, ethnic background, size of family, and size of place of residence as well as son's educational attainment to son's mobility in the occupational hierarchy. The article reprinted here reports some of their findings.

Some Preliminary Findings on Social Stratification in the United States* †

Peter M. Blau and Otis Dudley Duncan

This is a preliminary report from a study of occupational mobility in the United States. The objectives of the study are to describe the patterns of social mobility in some detail, to estimate the influence of various factors on occupational life chances, and to ascertain a few consequences of socio-economic status and mobility, such as their implications for fertility. The present paper reports selected findings pertaining to factors affecting occupational achievement and the chances to move away from one's social origins. In particular, we shall examine the significance for occupational attainment of education, ethnic background, community size, migration, and parental family.

In addition to presenting preliminary substantive findings from our research, this paper also provides an opportunity for illustrating the analytical procedures we have used. The analysis relies to a large extent on the regression

* Reprinted with permission from *Acta Sociologica*, **9**:4–24 (1965).

† We gratefully acknowledge grant number G-16233 from the National Science Foundation, which enabled us to carry out this research.

approach. Two major advantages of this approach which prompted our decision to adopt it are that it is a very efficient method of large-scale data reduction and that it permits, consequently, the simultaneous examination of the interrelations of fairly large numbers of variables, especially if computers are used. Contingency tables containing half a dozen or more variables and many hundreds of cells are too complex to be analyzed by inspection, whereas the regression method permits the analysis of these interrelations. To be sure, a limitation of regression analysis is that it makes restrictive assumptions about linearity and the absence of interaction effects, but the assumptions can be taken into account and hence removed in more complex analytical models. Similar methods we use, such as comparisons of mean scores of occupational status, are complemented by regression analysis to determine not only the gross effects of various factors on socio-economic status but also the net effects with other variables held constant.

Research Procedures

The data for this research were collected by the U.S. Bureau of the Census in March 1962, partly in the course of its regular "Current Population Survey" interview, and partly in a supplementary self-administered questionnaire specifically designed for the purpose of our research. The sample of 20,700 American men between the ages of 20 and 65 represents the 45 million men in this age group who are in the "civilian noninstitutional population," that is, who are neither in the Armed Forces nor in institutions. A subsample of those respondents who failed initially to return the supplementary questionnaire by mail was interviewed and appropriately weighted to make the sample highly representative. The present analysis, however, is confined to men whose fathers were *not* in farming occupations, which excludes a quarter of the total group.[1] In brief, the data derive from a representative sample of the 33 million American men with nonfarm backgrounds between 20 and 65 years old who are not in military service and do not live in institutions.[2]

Respondent's occupation and that of his father when the respondent was 16 years old were transformed into SES (socio-economic status) scores. The score, which ranges from 0 to 96, is based on the proportion of men in a specific occupation ("detailed occupational classification") who were, at least, high school graduates and the proportion reporting an income of over $3,500 in 1949, making adjustments for differences in age distribution between occupations.[3] The multiple correlation between these two predictors—the education and the income of men in an occupation—and the NORC prestige rating[4] for the 45 occupations that could be matched is $+.91$, and the regression equation that expresses this multiple correlation is used to determine the SES scores for all 446 detailed occupations. Respondent's education was transformed into an arbitrary score ranging from 0 to 8 which takes into account the special significance graduation from a given school level has.[5] Whereas socio-economic status and education are assumed to be continuous quantitative variables, no such assumption is made concerning the other factors used in the analysis, which are treated as qualitative attributes in terms of which individuals are classified into discrete categories.

To convey the meaning of the SES scores, the average scores of the conventional major groups of nonfarm occupations are presented below:

Professionals and technicians	75
Managers, proprietors, and officials	57
Sales and clerical occupations	47
Skilled workers and foremen	31
Semiskilled workers	18
Unskilled workers	7

The average difference between two adjacent categories is 13.6. Hence, the finding that an attribute affects the SES score by four or five points implies that, on the average, one third of the men with this attribute are one full step higher in this rank order (for example, are skilled rather than semiskilled workers) than those without this attribute. Fairly small differences in score are, therefore, of substantive significance, and given our large number of cases such small differences also are statistically significant.[6]

Education and Ethnic Background

The over-all correlation between father's and son's occupational status is +.38. This indicates that there is much occupational mobility in the United States; only one seventh of the variance in socio-economic status is attributable to the influence of father's socio-economic status. Nevertheless, this amount of mobility does not seem to be excessive compared to that in other Western countries. To make some rough comparisons, we computed the coefficient of association derived by Carlsson from the index earlier employed by Glass and Rogoff to measure occupational inheritance.[7] Since the Swedish data, which otherwise are most comparable with ours, include persons of farm origins, we did so too in these computations. (The correlation coefficient for the total U.S. population, including men with farm background, is +.42.) Using ten categories of SES scores, this measure of inheritance is 1.51, and using ten occupational categories,[8] as required to make it comparable to the Swedish data, it is 1.95. The same measure applied to the Swedish data divided into ten occupational categories is 1.89 or 2.28, depending on the method used,[9] which implies that there is about as much occupational inheritance in the United States as in Sweden. One of our former associates, R. W. Hodge, has computed age-specific father-son correlations from the British data, using an arbitrary scoring of prestige categories. He finds coefficients varying between .44 and .50 over five age groups. This suggests a slightly higher degree of association between son's and father's status in Britain than in America, although lack of comparability in study design makes one loath to stress this conclusion. Svalastoga's correlations for Denmark are of the same order of magnitude.[10]

To examine the relative importance of social origins and of education for occupational attainments, the (nonfarm background) sample is first divided into five cohorts, providing a control for age (20–24, 25–34, 35–44, 45–54, 55–64). The multiple correlation of education and father's socio-economic status on son's SES increases from +.51 for the youngest group to +.66 for those 25–34 years old and then decreases again to +.59 for the oldest group (Table 1, row 1). This nonmonotonic relationship with age suggests that the influences of social background and of education on a man's career extend beyond its early phases and become increasingly pronounced for some years but that the significance of these factors eventually declines as they recede in time. An alternative explanation of this finding is that the influence of education has become increasingly important since the beginning of this century although a decline may now be under way. There has probably been little change in the significance of father's occupational SES for that of his son in this century.[11] The *beta* coefficients indicate that the net influence of education is at a maximum at about age thirty and then decreases, whereas that of father's SES continues to increase until about age fifty (rows 1a and 1b). Taking these partial regression coefficients in standard form (*beta* coefficients) as indications of the relative significance of the two antecedents, the data also show that the impact on occupational status of education independent of social origin is considerably greater than that of social origin independent of education.[12]

TABLE 1
Correlation analysis: respondent's occupational SES on education and father's SES, for American men with nonfarm backgrounds, age 20 to 64, 1962.

Item	20–24 years	25–34 years	35–44 years	45–54 years	55–64 years
1. Multiple correlations (SES on education and father's SES)	.51	.66	.65	.61	.59
a. *Beta* coefficient, education	.46	.61	.57	.53	.52
b. *Beta* coefficient, father's SES	.09	.12	.15	.16	.13
2. Zero order correlation, SES and father's SES	.29	.37	.40	.38	.34
Components*					
a. Independent of education	.09	.12	.15	.16	.13
b. Mediated through education	.20	.25	.25	.22	.21

* For method of calculation, see O. D. Duncan and R. W. Hodge, "Education and Occupational Mobility: A Regression Analysis," *American Journal of Sociology*, 68 (May, 1963), 629–644.

This finding implies that the influence of father's socio-economic status on son's status is largely mediated in the United States by education. A man's chances of occupation advancement depend on his education (zero-order correlation, +.61), which, in turn, depends to a considerable degree on the socio-economic status of his father (+.41). These relationships can be further clarified by restating them in a slightly different way. Instead of asking how SES is affected by education and by father's SES separately, as we did above, we take now the (zero-order) correlation between father's and son's SES (Table 1, row 2) and ask to which extent this influence of father's SES on son's status is mediated through education (row 2b) and to which extent it is independent of education and thus due to other factors (row 2a). It is apparent from the data that education is the major means by which fathers affect the occupational chances of their sons. It should not be ignored, however, that social origins also have a definite effect on occupational opportunities that has nothing to do with education qualifications.

In Sweden, by contrast to the United States, "differential access to educational facilities as such does not go very far in explaining . . . the correlation between parental and filial status."[13] But in Stockholm, where secondary school education is more prevalent than in the rest of the country, education plays a more prominent role than in other parts of Sweden.[14] Since the educational level in the United States is higher than that in Sweden, the comparison suggests that the expansion of education tends to be accompanied, at least up to a point, by an increase in the significance of education for transmitting socio-economic status from father to son.

Negroes have, of course, far less educational opportunity than whites in the United States. Whereas 18 per cent of the native whites have no more than eight years of schooling, fully 37 per cent of the nonwhites do.[15] The education of the second-generation Americans hardly differs from that of other native whites (21 per cent), but the foreign born are nearly as poorly educated as the Negroes, with 33 per cent not having gone beyond the eight years of elementary school. It is interesting that age affects educational attainment to an even greater extent than race. Among the native whites with native parents, only 8 per cent of the men 20–24 years old have no more than eight years of schooling, as compared with 39 per cent of those 55–64 years old. Among the Negroes, similarly, 22 per cent of the youngest age cohort in contrast to 70 per cent of the oldest one have not gone beyond elementary school. Discrimination notwithstanding, young Negroes in today's nonfarm population are better educated than old whites. Negroes, nevertheless, continue to suffer serious educational handicaps, and these are, moreover, not the only handicaps that impede their occupational opportunities.

To ascertain the impact of various attributes, such as ethnic background, on occupational chances, the following procedure is used. The mean SES score for each age cohort is determined, and so are the deviations from this mean in various subgroups under consideration. Differences between these deviations from the mean indicate the gross effect of the attribute on SES, for example, the gross effect of being a Negro rather than a white with a given education on occupational status. The net effects the same attribute has on SES when father's SES is held constant are derived from a regression equation.[16] These net effects can be considered approximate indications of occupational mobility in the sense that they refer to average occupational achievements of groups whose point of social origin has been standardized. An interesting over-all finding that emerges from our analysis is that controlling for father's occupation reduces the influence of various attributes but hardly ever alters the patterns of influence observed. In other words, the same factors that are associated with differential occupational status are also associated with differential achievements independent of level of origin.

Even when education is held constant, the occupational status of Negroes is far inferior to that of whites in the United States. Twenty independent comparisons between native whites of native parentage and nonwhites can be made in Table 2 (four educational groups in each of the five age cohorts). In all twenty, the score of whites is higher, and the average difference is 12.1, nearly a full step in the rank order of major occupational classes. This is a clear indication of the serious discrimination Negroes with the same educational qualifications as whites suffer in the employment market.[17] Moreover, controlling for father's occupation does not wipe out this difference. All twenty net effects favor the whites, an average of 10.2, notwithstanding the fact that Negroes, due to past discrimination, have much lower social origins than whites. In sum, Negroes are handicapped by having less education and by having lower social origins than whites. But even if these handicaps are controlled statistically—asking, in effect, what the chances of Negroes would be if they had the same education and social origins as whites—the occupational attainments of Negroes are still considerably inferior to those of whites.

Foreign-born Americans and their children, the second-generation Americans, in sharp contrast to Negroes, do not differ in occupational attainments from the native whites of native parentage on the same educational levels. The twenty comparisons of gross effects between native whites of native parentage and native whites of foreign parentage are inconsistent (averaging —1.1), and so are the twenty comparisons between the former and the foreign born (averaging 0.8). The various white ethnic groups in the United States apparently achieve occupational positions commensurate with their education. Whatever occupational discrimination may exist against some of these ethnic groups must be compensated for by other factors since it does not find expression in their over-all occupational chances.

Another perspective on the disadvantaged situation of the American Negro can be gained by examining the rewards he obtains for given educational investments compared to those a white person obtains. The average difference for the five age groups between native whites of native parentage who have some college education and those who have only an elementary school education is 33.0, whereas the corresponding average difference for Negroes is 25.6. In other wards, roughly the same amount of educational investment has one and one third times as much payoff for a white man as for a Negro. The fact that Negroes obtain comparatively little reward for their educational investments, which robs them of incentives to incur these costs, might help explain why Negroes often manifest only weak motivation to pursue their education. The early school leaving that results from this lack of motivation further intensifies the disadvantaged position of the Negro in the labor market.

City Size and Migration

The discussion of the relationships between size of place, migration, and occupational opportunities will concentrate upon the urban areas, since the present analysis is confined to men whose fathers were not in farming occupations. Although data for nonfarm rural areas will be presented too, these must be interpreted with great caution, inasmuch as all the sons of farmers living in

TABLE 2
Ethnic background, education, and occupational SES of American men with nonfarm background, age 20 to 64.

Ethnicity by Education	20–24 years	25–34 years	35–44 years	45–54 years	55–64 years
Grand Mean, All Groups	31.5	41.0	42.6	40.1	40.0
			Gross Effects		
Native white, native parentage					
8 years of schooling or less	−12.9	−18.1	−18.7	−13.8	−10.6
9 to 11 years of schooling	− 8.7	−13.6	−11.1	− 5.6	0.3
High school graduate	0.2	− 3.1	1.7	3.0	8.0
1 year of college or more	8.3	20.1	22.2	19.3	20.9
Native white, foreign parentage					
8 years of schooling or less	−12.9*	−18.0	−18.1	−14.6	− 9.0
9 to 11 years of schooling	2.5*	−11.6	−14.3	− 6.6	− 0.9
High school graduate	4.7	− 3.0	− 0.8	6.4	6.7
1 year of college or more	12.3	21.2	20.3	24.1	21.2
Foreign-born white					
8 years of schooling or less	−12.9*	−15.5*	−19.4	−13.8	−10.8
9 to 11 years of schooling	0.3*	− 9.6*	−12.8*	− 3.0	1.5
High school graduate	1.1*	−13.2*	3.8	− 2.9	4.9
1 year of college or more	5.4*	19.3	12.9	17.0	19.6
Nonwhite					
8 years of schooling or less	−20.3	−25.3	−23.8	−21.0	−19.5
9 to 11 years of schooling	−13.5	−23.4	−20.9	−17.7	−20.6
High school graduate	− 7.5	−19.0	−18.3	−18.3	− 2.8*
1 year of college or more	− 1.4*	9.7	5.4	− 3.9*	8.1*
			*Net Effects**		
Native white, native parentage					
8 years of schooling or less	−12.0	−16.8	−16.8	−12.1	− 9.4
9 to 11 years of schooling	− 8.0	−12.9	−10.4	− 5.6	(−)0.0
High school graduate	0.1	− 3.0	1.3	2.4	6.4
1 year of college or more	7.6	18.9	18.9	16.3	18.9
Native white, foreign parentage					
8 years of schooling or less	−12.2*	−17.2	−15.8	−12.8	− 8.0
9 to 11 years of schooling	2.9*	−10.2	−12.8	− 5.2	− 0.7
High school graduate	4.8	− 2.6	− 0.2	6.3	6.3
1 year of college or more	11.6	20.2	20.2	21.7	20.0
Foreign-born white					
8 years of schooling or less	−12.4*	14.8*	−17.9	−12.1	−10.0
9 to 11 years of schooling	0.5*	−10.6*	−13.2*	− 1.7*	1.7
High school graduate	0.7*	−13.4*	3.8	− 2.6	3.7
1 year of college or more	4.8*	17.5	12.2	15.0	18.3
Nonwhite					
8 years of schooling or less	−18.8	−23.8	−20.6	−18.3	−17.5
9 to 11 years of schooling	−12.1	−21.7	−17.9	−15.4	−19.4
High school graduate	− 6.2	−17.8	−16.5	−16.2	− 4.9*
1 year of college or more	− 0.5*	10.0	6.8	− 1.7*	12.5*

* The cell frequency on which this value is based is less than 100.
** Father's occupational SES held constant.

these areas are excluded from consideration.[18] It should also be remembered that the large number of migrants from farms to cities is not reflected in the data that are now being analyzed.

The findings on size of community reveal few surprises. Table 3 presents the deviations from the mean socio-economic score in each age cohort by city size and by location in the central city or its suburban fringe. People who live in the urban fringe of cities have somewhat higher socio-economic status than those who live in the central cities, and this difference persists if their father's SES is controlled. Of the 15 possible comparisons (three city sizes by five age cohorts), 14 of the gross differences favor the fringe over the central city, an average of 4.1 points, and 12 of the net differences do so, an average of 2.7. The socio-economic status of men who live in suburbs is directly related to the size of the central city, at least for younger men, but the status of the inhabitants of the central cities is not monotonically related to city size.

TABLE 3
Size of place and occupational SES of American men with nonfarm background, age 20 to 64.

Size of Place	20–24 years Central City	20–24 years Urban Fringe	25–34 years Central City	25–34 years Urban Fringe	35–44 years Central City	35–44 years Urban Fringe	45–54 years Central City	45–54 years Urban Fringe	55–64 years Central City	55–64 years Urban Fringe
Grand Mean, All Places	31.5		41.0		42.6		40.1		40.0	
Very large city (over 1 million)	1.8	4.3	−2.2	6.4	−3.7	5.7	−3.5	4.8	−0.5	3.4
Large city (¼–1 million)	1.1	0.0	2.7	5.6	1.2	5.4	3.4	5.8	0.2	4.0
Medium city (50,000–250,000)	−1.6	−1.0	−1.7	2.0	−1.5	3.0	−1.3	5.7	2.3	3.4
Small town (2,500–50,000)	0.0		−1.4		−0.8		−0.6		−0.5	
Rural area (under 2,500)	−3.3		−2.8		−2.4		−4.1		−3.4	
Net Effects										
Very large city	1.9	2.6	−2.0	5.1	−2.6	4.5	−2.4	3.4	−0.1	3.3
Large city	0.5	−1.1	2.0	3.3	1.1	4.0	3.2	5.9	0.1	3.1
Medium city	−1.4	0.3	−0.4	−0.6	−1.8	1.4	−1.0	4.2	1.8	0.7
Small town	0.2		−0.2		−0.9		0.2		−0.8	
Rural area	−2.1		2.2		−1.6		−3.3		−2.6	

Note: No cell frequency is less than 100 and only one—fringe of medium cities for youngest age cohort—is less than 200.

Within the central city, socio-economic status is highest in cities with between one quarter and one million inhabitants. It is somewhat lower in the largest cities of over one million (an average difference of 3.3 points from the former), as well as in the medium cities with 50,000 to 250,000 inhabitants (2.5) and in the small towns with 2,500 to 50,000 inhabitants (2.1). The average socio-economic status in the smallest American towns, however, is still higher than that in rural areas even when form workers and their sons are excluded from the comparison (2.8). All these differences persist in slightly attenuated form when social origins are controlled, as the net effects in Table 3 show. In short, occupational opportunities are poorest in rural areas and best in fairly large cities, and they differ little on the average in the very large cities and those that are medium or small.

The question arises whether this pattern of differences is the result of migration. The answer appears to be that although migration plays a role the basic pattern has not been produced by it. Table 4 presents the data on socio-economic status, again as derivations from the means, by size of present place of residence and by the community where the respondent lived at age 16. The socio-economic status of the nonmigrants—the men who reached adolescence in the same community where they live now—reveals a pattern similar to that previously encountered for the total population. For all five age groups of nonmigrants, as the first row in each section shows, average SES is higher in cities of at least medium size than in small towns (an average difference of 5.2), and it is higher in small towns than in rural areas (3.6), and the same is true for the net differences when father's SES is held constant (4.4 and 2.6). Since all cities with more than 50,000 inhabitants were combined for this analysis, as were the central cities and their urban fringe, it is not possible to determine whether all specific differences observed in the total populations are reflected in parallel differences among nonmigrants. But the evidence does show that the over-all pattern is the same and that migration cannot account for the status differences between fairly large cities and small ones and between the latter and rural regions.

The socio-economic status of urban migrants is clearly superior to that of nonmigrants, though rural migrants are not superior to nonmigrants. In order to isolate the significance of migration as such from that of either living now or having lived previously in a certain environment, nonmigrants will be compared with only those migrants who reside at present in communities of the same size and who also lived as adolescents in communities of about the same size, that is, with those migrants who moved from as well as into communities of approximately the same size. (The cell entries being compared for this analysis are connected by arrows in Table 4.) In all ten comparisons of urban nonmigrants with migrants who came from and are now in the same environment (two city sizes for five age cohorts), the socio-economic status of the migrants is superior, an average of 7.0 (net of father's SES, 5.4). The five comparisons between nonfarm rural migrants and nonmigrants yield no consistent results—two going in one and three in the other direction—and the average difference is very small (0.6; net, 1.3). Migrants within urban areas, then, tend to occupy superior occupational positions and enjoy higher achievements

TABLE 4

Geographic mobility and occupational SES of American men with nonfarm background, age 20 to 64.

A. Gross Effects

Community at Age 16	City over 50,000 and Fringe ("urbanized area")	Town under 50,000 ("other urban")	Rural
	Age and Present Residence		
20 to 24 years (mean, 31.5)			
Same as present	1.3	−2.5	−5.4
Different from present			
Large city & fringe	4.2	5.0*	1.9
Small town	0.6	5.8	
Rural area	−3.0	−3.1	−7.8
25 to 34 years (mean, 41.0)			
Same as present	−1.4	−7.9	−10.7
Different from present			
Large city & fringe	7.6	12.1	3.5
Small town	6.2	7.2	
Rural area	4.3	−7.3	−2.3
35 to 44 years (mean, 42.6)			
Same as present	−0.6	−7.1	−7.1
Different from present			
Large city & fringe	5.7	11.6	2.1
Small town	2.5	2.8	
Rural area	−4.4	−6.2	−9.2
45 to 54 years (mean, 40.1)			
Same as present	0.4	−3.8	−11.7
Different from present			
Large city & fringe	5.7	10.8	1.5
Small town	3.2	2.9	
Rural area	−9.5	1.1*	−7.8
55 to 64 years (mean, 40.0)			
Same as present	2.2	−2.8	−7.4
Different from present			
Large city & fringe	5.0	5.8*	−0.4
Small town	1.1	1.3	
Rural area	−5.5	−4.8*	−12.3

relative to their social origins than their nonmigrant counterparts, but there are no corresponding differences between the migrants within rural areas and the nonmigrants in these areas. These differences cannot be primarily due to the fact that migrants frequently move from smaller to larger communities where occupational opportunities are superior, because the influence of city size has been roughly controlled in this analysis. The inference therefore is that intra-urban migration is selective of men predisposed to occupational success, whereas this is not the case for intra-rural migration.

TABLE 4

Geographic mobility and occupational SES of American men with nonfarm background, age 20 to 64 (continued).

B. *Net Effects*

	Age and Present Residence		
Community at Age 16	City over 50,000 and Fringe ("urbanized area")	Town under 50,000 ("other urban")	*Rural*
20 to 24 years (mean, 31.5)			
Same as present	0.7	−2.0	−4.6
Different from present			
Large city & fringe	2.6	5.2*	2.6
Small town	1.1	5.3	
Rural area	−1.0	−3.3	4.5
25 to 34 years (mean, 41.0)			
Same as present	−1.3	−6.4	−8.3
Different from present			
Large city & fringe	5.4	9.8	1.9
Small town	4.8	8.0	
Rural area	−2.4	−2.9	−0.4
35 to 44 years (mean, 42.6)			
Same as present	−0.7	−6.2	−4.5
Different from present			
Large city & fringe	4.5	9.1	1.1
Small town	1.8	1.4	
Rural area	−1.8	−3.1	−6.9
45 to 54 years (mean, 40.1)			
Same as present	0.8	−3.4	−9.8
Different from present			
Large city & fringe	4.2	6.2	0.4
Small town	2.6	1.9	
Rural area	−7.1	3.4*	−4.8
55 to 64 years (mean, 40.0)			
Same as present	2.5	−2.1	−5.8
Different from present			
Large city & fringe	3.3	5.2*	−0.8
Small town	0.6	−1.1	
Rural area	−3.0	−3.8*	−9.9

* The cell frequency on which this value is based is less than 100.
** The data for migrants to rural areas who come from cities of different sizes have been combined.

We turn now to examine the significance of the change in environment migration produces, which is the very factor we attempted to control in the preceding analysis of the significance of migration itself. What are the implications of the migrant's area of destination for his occupational chances? Regardless of geographical origins, men who move into urban areas tend to achieve higher socio-economic status than those who move into rural areas. Most pronounced is the difference between migrants to small cities and those to rural regions, with nine of ten comparisons indicating a higher SES for the men who moved to small cities, the average difference being 4.2 (and 3.5 if father's SES is held constant).[19] This difference parallels that between nonmigrants in small cities and rural areas. When cities over 50,000 are compared with smaller ones, however, the findings assume quite another pattern. Here point of origin makes a difference, and the situation of migrants differs from that of nonmigrants in the same type of place. Whereas nonmigrants tend to achieve *higher* occupational status in the relatively larger cities than in small ones, the status of migrants from rural areas does not differ consistently in the two localities, and migrants from other urban areas achieve lower status in the larger than in the small cities. Comparison of columns 1 and 2 in Table 4 shows that the SES of nonmigrants is *higher* in the larger than in the smaller cities in five instances out of five, the average difference being +5.2 (net, +4.4), but the SES of migrants from urban areas (rows 2 and 3) is *lower* in the larger than in the smaller cities in nine cases out of ten, the average difference being −2.3 (net, −2.0).

It seems paradoxical that the occupational chances of urban migrants are worse, and those of rural migrants are no better, in larger cities than in smaller ones, while the occupational opportunities of the natives are better in the larger than in the smaller cities. It must be remembered that the urban migrants to larger cities are somewhat superior in socio-economic status to the nonmigrants there, but their superiority is not as great as that of migrants over nonmigrants in small cities. One possible explanation of these findings is that the migrants to larger cities constitute a more heterogeneous group than those to smaller towns, including not only disproportionate numbers with good occupational qualifications but also very many with extremely poor qualifications. Thus the migrants who stream into the large Northern cities from the South can frequently only obtain the least desirable occupational positions, and these migrants take the place at the bottom of the industrial hierarchy that was once occupied by the recent immigrants from Europe. Another reason for the lesser superiority of migrants over nonmigrants in larger cities might be that being raised in large cities gives the natives an advantage in the struggle for occupational success that compensates for some of the other advantages the migrants have. The comparison of men reared in places of different size support this interpretation.

Migrants who lived in larger cities when they were 16 years old tend to be superior in socio-economic status to those raised in smaller cities, and the latter tend to be superior to those who grew up in rural areas (Table 4, rows 2, 3, and 4). Of ten comparisons between migrants coming from larger and those coming from smaller cities, nine show that the former have a higher SES, the average difference being 4.0 (net, 2.9), and of 15 comparisons between migrants raised in small cities and those raised in rural areas, 14 show that the former have higher SES, the average difference being 8.6 (net, 5.5). The same difference is reflected in the finding that the SES of nonmigrants is directly related to the size of their present community, since in the case of nonmigrants the present community is, of course, identical with the place where they lived at age 16. Whether a man is a migrant or not, therefore, and regardless of the size of the community where he now works, the larger the community where he grew up, the better are his chances to achieve occupational success and to move up from the status of his father.

Since growing up in a large city is an occupational advantage, and so is being a migrant to a small city, the highest occupational status is achieved by migrants from larger to small cities, whose status is, on the average, 9.1 points above the mean (net, 7.1 points). One might speculate why men raised in large cities have greater chances of success in their careers. The advantage of the urban over the rural environment is undoubtedly in large part due to the superior educational facilities in the former, but it is questionable whether the superiority of the large-city environment over that in small cities can be attributed to differences in the educational system. It may be that at least part of this superiority is due to the greater sophistication about the labor market and occupational life generally that boys growing up in large cities tend to acquire.

Parental Family

A man's occupational chances are strongly affected by the size of his parents' family. The socio-economic status of men with three or fewer siblings is considerably superior to that of men with four or more siblings. The data in Table 5 permit 20 independent comparisons between men from small and from large families (excluding only children). All 20 indicate that the SES of men from smaller families is superior, the average difference being 8.0. Some of this difference is due to the fact that poorer couples tend to have larger families rather than to the influence of family size on the occupational chances of sons. But even if the former factor is controlled by holding father's socio-economic status constant, the socio-economic status of men from smaller families continues to be higher than that of men from larger families in all 20 comparisons, an average of 5.2 points. This net effect shows that a man's chances of occupational success are impeded by many siblings. Although in strictly economic terms only children must have an advantage over others, since they do not have to share their parents' financial resources with anybody, this economic advantage is not reflected in their careers. Only children do not achieve higher occupational positions than those from small families; the differences between the two groups are inconsistent, and the average approximates zero.

Sibling position as well as number of siblings influences occupational attainments. There are no consistent differences between oldest and youngest children, but the SES of both tends to be superior to that of middle children. Ten independent comparisons can be made between oldest children and middle children with an older brother (two sizes for five age cohorts). Eight of these indicate that the oldest child has a higher status, one that the middle child has, and one reveals no difference. The average difference is 3.7, which is reduced to 2.7 if father's SES is controlled. When youngest children are compared to middle children with an older brother, the youngest are seen

TABLE 5
Parental family and occupational SES of American men with nonfarm background, age 20 to 64.

Sibling Position and Number of Siblings	20–24 years	25–34 years	35–44 years	45–54 years	55–64 years
Grand Mean	31.5	41.0	42.6	40.1	40.0
Gross Effects					
1. Only child, no siblings	5.1	6.0	4.1	7.0	3.0
2. Oldest, 1 to 3 siblings	3.6	6.4	6.1	4.7	7.0
3. Oldest, 4 or more siblings	−2.1	−6.0	−6.0	−4.8	−0.3
4. Youngest, 1 to 3 siblings	5.3	3.6	6.5	5.3	5.6
5. Youngest, 4 or more siblings	−2.3	−2.4	−2.5	−2.3	−1.6
6. Middle, 2–3 s's, no older brother	−2.1	0.6	4.7	0.3	10.2
7. Middle, 2–3 s's, older brother	−2.3	−0.8	3.7	1.5	−0.1
8. Middle, 4+ s's, no older brother	−7.3	−4.3	−8.2	−4.8	−5.4
9. Middle, 4+ s's, older brother	−6.3	−7.6	−7.5	−3.6	−5.1
Net Effects*					
1. Only child, no siblings	3.8	3.9	2.9	4.2	3.0
2. Oldest, 1 to 3 siblings	2.6	4.0	4.2	2.6	4.4
3. Oldest, 4 or more siblings	−1.8	−4.5	−4.0	−3.1	0.8
4. Youngest, 1 to 3 siblings	4.4	2.3	4.0	3.5	4.6
5. Youngest, 4 or more siblings	0.1	−0.4	0.7	−0.6	−0.2
6. Middle, 2–3 s's, no older brother	−3.0	−0.1	3.8	0.3	8.4
7. Middle, 2–3 s's, older brother	−2.3	−0.5	1.9	1.1	−0.7
8. Middle, 4+ s's, no older brother	−5.6	−2.6	−7.1	−4.6	−3.8
9. Middle, 4+ s's, older brother	−4.5	−5.1	−5.3	−1.9	−4.5
Residual Effects**					
1. Only child, no siblings	1.5	−1.2	−1.3	0.5	−0.9
2. Oldest, 1 to 3 siblings	1.0	1.0	1.4	0.5	1.3
3. Oldest, 4 or more siblings	0.3	−0.3	0.2	−0.8	1.7
4. Youngest, 1 to 3 siblings	2.4	−0.3	0.6	0.6	1.4
5. Youngest, 4 or more siblings	0.3	0.9	2.4	−2.5	0.5
6. Middle, 2–3 s's, no older brother	−2.7	0.5	2.0	−1.0	6.5
7. Middle, 2–3 s's, older brother	−3.4	−0.8	1.8	1.5	−1.2
8. Middle, 4+ s's, no older brother	−3.3	0.5	−3.2	−0.2	−1.1
9. Middle, 4+ s's, older brother	−1.0	0.0	−1.7	0.2	−1.7

Note: No cell frequency is less than 100 and only one—youngest in large families for cohort 20–24 years—is less than 200.
* Father's occupational SES held constant.
** First job, education, father's occupational SES, ethnic classification, region and place of birth and residence, and geographic mobility held constant.

to have superior SES in all ten cases, the average difference being 4.3, and this difference persists if father's SES is controlled (net, 4.0). (Comparisons with middle children without an older brother yield essentially the same results.) Both oldest and youngest children gain advantages from their positions compared to middle children, but perhaps for different reasons. The fact that the occupational advantages of oldest children depend in part on the socio-economic status of their fathers while those of youngest children do not suggests that the latter are due to socio-psychological rather than economic factors. It may be that the occupational success of youngest children is primarily due to the fact that their education pre-empts the economic resources of their parents.

Middle children with and without an older brother have been separated in order to examine the implications of having an older brother for occupational chances. The significance of an older brother for careers appears to be slight and confined to small families. Four of the five comparisons in small families (Table 5, rows 6 and 7) indicate that middle children without an older brother have higher SES than those with one, with an average difference of +2.3, but four of the five comparisons in large families go in the opposite direction and the average difference is zero. If father's SES is controlled, the difference in small families is +2.0 and that in large ones is —0.5. Having no older brother is a slight advantage for middle children in small families but not in large ones.

The bottom third of Table 5 presents the residual effects of size of parental family and sibling position when not only father's SES but also a number of other factors are controlled, namely, respondent's education, his first job, his ethnic background, the region where he was born and where he lives at present, the size of his place of birth and of his present community, and migration status. It is evident from the table that the residual effects of parental family on socio-economic status that remain after all these conditions have been held constant are small. This does not mean, however, that the effects of number of siblings and sibling position previously observed were spurious, because the factors that are now being controlled are not independent of a man's parental family. Some of these control factors are directly determined by the family into which a man is born, such as his ethnic affiliation and the area where he grows up, and others are strongly affected by the size of his family and his position in it, such as his education and his first job. The reduction in effects produced by the introduction of these controls indicates, by and large, the degree to which the initial effects of parental family were mediated by various social and economic conditions, for example, the training and experience a man obtained and the opportunities existing in the area where he was raised. If the initial (gross) effects are little reduced by introducing the controls, it suggests that they are not primarily due to the economic advantages children gain from their families, directly or indirectly, but to other, socio-psychological forces in the family.

Whereas the gross effects on SES of sibling position are considerably smaller than those of sib size, the former persist to a greater degree than the latter when economic conditions are controlled. Instituting these controls reduces the impact of family size on SES very much, it reduces the influence of sibling position a great deal, though not as much, and it reduces the interaction effect of having no older brother in small families hardly at all. The average gross difference in SES between men from small and from large families of 8.0 points is reduced to a residual average difference of merely 1.1 points in Table 5. In contrast to this decrease to one seventh of the original difference, instituting controls decreases the effects of sibling position on SES considerably less, only to about one third of their original size, from 4.3 to 1.3 for youngest (vs. middle) and from 3.7 to 1.3 for oldest (vs. middle) children. The case is more extreme for the interaction effect of having no older brother and family size on SES. The gross differences in SES between middle children with no older brother and those with an older brother are +2.3 in small families and 0.0 in large ones, and the residual differences are +1.5 in small and —0.6 in large families. Hence, the difference between these differences, which indicates the interaction effect, is virtually not affected by introducing controls, being 2.3 originally and still 2.1 for the residuals. Although the residual effects are very small, the reduction in gross differences effected by introducing controls varies so greatly that we are tempted to hazard some interpretations based on these variations.

The superior occupational achievements of children from small families are largely accounted for by the better economic conditions in which they find themselves compared to children from large families. The superior occupational achievements of oldest and youngest children relative to those of middle children, on the other hand, seem to be due to a combination of economic and psychological factors. The distinctive position the oldest and the youngest child occupy in the family may not only have the result that parents devote disproportionate resources to their training but also make it likely that these children receive more social and emotional support from other members of the family than do middle children. (Since the residual effects for oldest and for youngest child do not differ, we had to modify here an interpretation advanced earlier that distinguished the situation of the youngest from that of the oldest.)

The occupational advantages middle children without older brothers have in small families but not in large ones are apparently not due to economic factors. A possible explanation of this interaction effect is that an older brother is more likely to be the oldest child in a small than in a large family, and oldest children occupy, as we have seen, privileged positions, which means that not having a brother who is an oldest child is an advantage. One might also speculate whether older sisters are protective and supportive of younger brothers and thereby strengthen their potential for subsequent occupational success. If older sisters actually have such a beneficial influence on their younger brothers, it would explain the observed interaction effect, because the middle child without an older brother necessarily has an older sister, and the middle child with an older brother in a small family is unlikely to have also an older sister but in a large family he is likely to have also an older sister.

Conclusions

We have illustrated our procedures as well as some preliminary findings from our research in this paper. The complexity of the analysis required when several factors influence occupational success has undoubtedly become evident. Since the condensed discussion may well have been difficult to follow at various points, it might be useful to summarize in conclusion the main substantive findings.

There is much intergenerational occupational mobility in the United States, though probably not much more than in other Western countries such as Sweden and Britain. The correlation between father's and son's SES is +.38. The influence of father's on son's status is largely mediated through education, in apparent contrast to the situation in some other countries, but socio-economic origins also influence career chances independent of education.

It hardly comes as a surprise that racial discrimination in the United States is reflected in the Negro's inferior chances of occupational success, although the extent to which Negroes with the same amount of education as whites remain behind in the struggle for desirable occupations is striking. Negroes receive much less occupational return for their educational investments than whites do, and their consequent lesser incentive to acquire an education further disadvantages them in the labor market. What may be surprising, however, is that white ethnic minorities, on the average, appear to have as good occupational chances as the majority group. At least, the occupational achievements of foreign-born and second-generation Americans are no worse than those of native whites of native parentage with the same amount of education.

Urban migrants are more likely to occupy desirable occupational positions and to have moved up from the socio-economic status of their fathers than nonmigrants. Migration to urban areas brings occupational success more often than migration to rural areas (for the nonfarm population here under consideration), and migration from urban areas to small cities is particularly advantageous. The larger the place where a migrant grew up, the greater are the chances of his occupational success, regardless of the type of place where he ends up working. Indeed, for nonmigrants as well as migrants, there is a direct correlation between the size of the place where a man was reared and his occupational achievement.

Size of parental family and sibling position affect careers. The occupational attainments of men with many siblings, with whom they had to share parental resources, are inferior to those of men with few siblings, but only children do not achieve higher socio-economic positions than men from small families. Oldest and youngest children tend to have more successful careers than middle ones. In small families, though not in large ones, finally, having no older brothers appears to give a middle child a slight advantage in the struggle for occupational success, which suggests that older sisters improve future life chances.

NOTES

1. We plan, of course, to analyze the farm population in the future, with particular attention to the patterns of geographical and occupational mobility into urban sectors.
2. All frequencies in the original tables, from which the analytical tables presented in this report are derived, refer to the estimated actual population in the United States in the given categories, reported in 1000's. The sampling ratio is, on the average, 1:2,173. To obtain the approximate numbers of actual cases from whom data were collected, therefore, the numbers reported in 1000's should be divided by 2.2.
3. See Otis Dudley Duncan, "A Socio-Economic Index for All Occupations" in Albert J. Reiss, Jr, *Occupations and Social Status*, New York: Free Press, 1961. (This score was derived from the 1950 U.S. Census of Population, not from our sample.)

4. National Opinion Research Center, *Jobs and Occupations*, Opinion News, vol. 9 (1947), pp. 3–13.
5. Education is scored by the following system, which takes into account the special significance of graduation from one of the three main levels of schooling:

    0   No school
    1   Elementary, 1 to 4 years
    2   Elementary, 5 to 7 years
    3   Elementary, 8 years
    4   High school, 1 to 3 years.
    5   High school, 4 years
    6   College, 1 to 3 years
    7   College, 4 years
    8   Graduate school, 1 year or more

6. The complex nature of the weighted sample makes it difficult to determine levels of statistical significance accurately, but the following conservative estimates may serve as an approximate guide: All differences between specific pairs of cells of 1.5 or more are significant on the .05 level unless the reported number in one of the two cells involved in the comparison is less than 200. All those differences of 2.0 and above are significant unless one of the reported frequencies is less than 100. Any difference of 5.0 or more is significant. When nearly all of several independent comparisons are in the same direction, the chance that an average difference of a given size is not statistically significant is further reduced. Cells where the reported number is less than 100 are indicated by an asterisk in the tables.
7. Gösta Carlsson, *Social Mobility and Class Structure*, Lund: Gleerup, 1958, pp. 74–75.
8. The ten occupational categories are the six previously reported in the text, except that clerical and sales occupations are divided, service occupations are separately shown, and two categories of farm occupations are added, farmers and farm managers, and farm laborers.
9. Ibid., p. 114.
10. Kaare Svalastoga, *Prestige, Class and Mobility*, Copenhagen: Gyldendal, 1959, p. 351.
11. Although we plan to investigate the problem of estimating time trends more thoroughly in the future, a re-analysis of Rogoff's data for the city of Indianapolis by Duncan indicates that there is no change in the father-son correlation between 1910 and 1940.
12. Since the index used to score the status of an occupation is based on the amount of education and the amount of income that prevailed in the occupation, it is necessarily related to education to some degree. Experimentation with an alternative index of occupational SES, not based explicitly on education levels, however, shows that the results are not dependent on the specific form of SES index used here.
13. Carlsson, op. cit., p. 135.
14. Ibid., pp. 135–136.
15. Our data actually refer to "nonwhites" but 92 per cent of all nonwhites in the United States are Negroes.
16. For an explanation of the statistical model used, see Otis Dudley Duncan, *Farm Background and Differential Fertility*, paper presented to the Population Association of America at its June 1964 annual meeting. For a published discussion, see T. P. Hill, *An Analysis of the Distribution of Wages and Salaries in Great Britain*, Econometrics, vol. 27 (July 1959), pp. 355–381.
17. It should be noted that some of the difference between Negroes and whites, though hardly all of it, may be due to the fact that holding constant the amount of education for the two groups does actually not hold constant their educational qualifications, since many of the schools to which Negroes go are inferior to those whites attend. Moreover, our broad categories do not even hold the amount of education fully constant, since, given the lower educational attainments of Negroes, there are undoubtedly fewer Negroes than whites near the upper end of the distribution within each category; for example, within the category, "one year of college or more," the proportion of college graduates is slightly smaller for Negroes than for whites.
18. Since the criterion of nonfarm background is whether a man designated his father's occupation as being in farming, not whether he lives on a farm, there are a few farm residents in this nonfarm population. Wherever possible, these have been excluded from this analysis, but this was not possible in all cases. However, the numbers involved are so small that it is unlikely that these farm residents affect the results substantially.
19. Since only one value for migrants from the two urban to rural areas is given, the unweighted average of the two values for the migrants to small towns from large cities and those from small towns was used in computing the differences. In case of the youngest age group, for instance, 1.9 was subtracted from 5.4 (the average of 5.8 and 5.0).

During the twentieth century, years of formal education completed has become the single most important factor affecting an individual's point of entry into the labor market[25] and subsequent career attainment.[26] Father's occupation has continued to be an important factor partly because of the relationship between parent's status and offspring's educational attainments. While in high school, for example, the sons of fathers in white-collar occupations have been about 50 per cent more likely to plan on going to college than have been the sons of blue-collar workers.[27] And this class difference remains in effect even after they reach college. Students with middle-class backgrounds have been more likely than their working-class counterparts to graduate—even when native ability, past school performance, and financial resources are the same.[28]

Father's occupational position also is correlated with a number of other factors affecting sons' school attainments and aspirations. For example, the sons of higher-status fathers are more likely to live in the neighborhoods in which educational accomplishments are more highly valued. They are, therefore, more likely to associate with friends who plan to attend college, and this exerts a strong influence on their own plans, regardless of status level.[29] C. Norman Alexander and Ernest Q. Campbell report, for example, that more than 95 per cent of high school students of the highest-status parents plan to go to college if their best friends do too.[30] However, when best friends do not plan on college, then it is planned by less than two thirds of similar-status boys. At the other status extreme, less than 10 per cent plan to go to college when their best friends do not; but, even among seniors of the lowest-standing fathers about one half plan to go to college when their best friends do also.

In sum, all of the evidence presented shows that the father's occupational position exerts multiple influences—both direct and indirect--·on the son's educational attainments. Given the increasing relationship between educational and occupational attainments, greater mobility opportunities in

[25] Robert M. Hauser and David L. Featherman, "Trends in the Occupational Mobility of U.S. Men, 1962–1970," *American Sociological Review*, **38**:302–310 (June 1973).

[26] Otis Dudley Duncan and Robert W. Hodge, "Education and Occupational Mobility," *American Journal of Sociology*, **68**:629–644 (May 1963).

[27] Irving Krauss, "Sources of Educational Aspirations Among Working Class Youth," *American Sociological Review*, **29**:867–879 (Dec. 1964).

[28] Bruce K. Eckland, "Social Class and College Graduation: "Some Misconceptions Connected," *American Journal of Sociology*, **70**:36–50 (July 1964).

[29] Apart from differences in status levels associated with neighborhoods, the norms of communities, per se, do not seem to exert an independent influence on boys' aspirations, although they do independently influence many girls to a limited extent. See William H. Sewell and J. Michael Armer, "Neighborhood Context and College Plans," *American Sociological Review*, **31**:159–168 (April 1966).

[30] C. Norman Alexander and Ernest Q. Campbell, "Peer Influences on Adolescent Academic Aspirations and Attainments," *American Sociological Review*, **29**:568–575 (Aug. 1964).

American society require continuing efforts at reducing the relationship between father's position and son's education. Until this relationship is reduced, education's role as a filter into the occupational system will continue to be influenced toward perpetuating socio-economic differences from generation to generation.

9 Persistent Obstacles to Social Mobility

Ascription and Social Placement

Ascribed characteristics—such as race, religion, age, sex, and ethnicity—can function very effectively as means of placement into divisions of labor. At one time or another they have served this function in virtually every society, sometimes with great legitimacy and sometimes not.

Ascription effectively limits the pool of persons who are considered either eligible or appropriate for certain types of tasks, such as picking cotton or keeping house. All ascribed characteristics, however, imply at least two positions that stand in complementary relationship to each other: black and white, young and old, male and female. Each would be meaningless as a social position without its complement, and divisions of labor are frequently based on their coordination. Thus, females tend the house while males earn a living, blacks pick cotton and whites sell it.

Much of the socialization of young people in any society is oriented to the *matching* of ascribed characteristics with socially approved tasks. This matching process is manifested in infant toys, resonates in educational institutions, and is reinforced continually by the mass media. Ascription-related socialization is so pervasive that, despite its arbitrariness, many people confuse it with "human nature" and view compliance with the matching process as a moral obligation. The internalization of expectations appropriate to one's ascribed position is also functional for social order. Associated with ascribed statuses are normative and behavioral expectations regarding persons in complementary positions. Efforts to change the matching of tasks with ascribed characteristics therefore possess a revolutionary quality, in a sociological sense; that is, fundamental social patterns are challenged.

Thus far we have discussed the social consequences of ascribed characteristics as though they uniformly possessed a great deal of legitimacy. Without question, many people do accept them and consider them to be morally binding. Many others accept what they perceive as arbitrary but consensual social definitions and learn to live with them. Still others dedicate their lives to attempts to change the social definitions. Without a minimal degree of voluntary acceptance though, ascription could not function effectively as a basis for functional differentiation—even if acceptance is viewed as the result of an exercise in power. Theodore D. Kemper, for example, has proposed that in every case one complementary ascriptive position has power over another: whites over blacks, Protestants over Catholics, and so on. It has been expedient, he argues, for groups who enjoy exclusive privileges to maintain their relative advantages by convincing the subordinated parties to accept lesser rewards as legitimate, without overt struggle.[1]

This view provides an important insight that we will consider shortly, but it overlooks the degree to which persons in the subordinate category socialize each other into the dominant view after it once becomes the legitimate view. Mothers, for example, have historically limited the occupational and educational aspirations of their daughters. Thus, the continuation of such patterns may not be dependent on differential power or the dominant group's control over socialization processes.

The explanatory emphasis on socialization and differential power also can lead to an exaggeration of the degree to which the subordinate category comes to accept the dominant view as legitimate. Sheer compliance does not necessarily indicate a belief in legitimacy. An individual's perception of probable rewards and punishments, or naked fear, also can be sufficient to produce compliance. In this regard, Helen Hacker has described the similarities with which blacks and women historically have learned to display deference in accommodating to dominant groups. Her observations can be extended easily, however, to Indians, the elderly, and other subordinated groups as well. From this perspective, they all have accommodated historically by attempting to conceal their true feelings. Interaction then becomes a game of trying to outwit men folks or white folks or young folks.[2]

---

[1] Theodore D. Kemper, "On the Nature and Purpose of Ascription," *American Sociological Review*, **39**:844–853 (Dec. 1974).

[2] Helen Hacker, "Women As a Minority Group," *Social Forces*, **30**:56–68 (1951).

On the other hand, the analysis of power raises the important insight that ascription serves as a basis not only for horizontal differentiation, but for vertical rankings as well. In other words, the tasks performed by all complementary positions are not accorded equal amounts of prestige in the larger society. Such differences are clearly reflected in the remark of the woman who, when asked what she does, replies: "I am just a housewife."

Recognition of the stratification-linked aspects of ascription has been part of the consciousness-raising experiences of many subordinated groups. Their awareness of a sense of deprivation has led to social movements aimed at changing traditional power relationships within ascribed categories. Black power, woman power, Indian power, and so on, are all ready examples.

In a preceding chapter we viewed two important aspects of the American Dream as involving a moral obligation to strive for higher positions and an assumption that such efforts could be successful. Viewed in this context, it can be seen that ascriptive statuses have led frequently to the exclusion of certain categories of people from the Dream. Their exclusion historically has been the result of both systematic discrimination from outside their ranks and their own internalization of ascriptively matched expectations for themselves.

This internalization frequently resulted in feelings that to compete in the "mainstream" of American life was inappropriate for persons like themselves. Correspondingly, they pursued low-status jobs that offered no *opportunity* for social mobility: posing for pictures in tribal headgear, working as maids and janitors, and so on. Many lacked family precedents that might have served to stimulate higher aspirations. Furthermore, many families viewed the very existence of serious mobility aspirations as the hopes of fools and discouraged them. Relatives, friends, teachers, and the mass media all subtly rewarded limited aspirations as a sign that one had learned his or her appropriate place. At the same time these limited aspirations were conventionally approved because they symbolically reaffirmed the continuation of a traditional division of labor.

Under such circumstances, where rewards are extremely diffuse, many members of subordinated groups historically internalized the traditional values. (In some respects, of course, they were not members of groups because the subordinated categories lacked sufficient solidarity and self-awareness to be considered groups.)

Obviously, however, many persons did not view the ascribed social definitions as legitimate and did not internalize them; but, nevertheless, they did not overtly fight the system. They posed in their Indian clothes or scrubbed floors because they perceived no other alternatives as open to someone with their ascribed characteristics.

In many societies, lineage, or birthright, has been an extremely important ascribed status, with important consequences both for actual mobility and mobility aspirations. Prior to the relatively recent emphasis on a "culture of poverty," however, most sociologists have tended to minimize the direct effects of "hereditary" transmission of status in the United States.[3] In the following reading, persistent differences in class-related values are examined in relation to both the social structure and opportunities for mobility.

[3] See, for example, Dennis H. Wrong, "Inequality and Stratification," *Canadian Review of Sociology and Anthropology*, **1**:1–13 (1964).

Aspiration and Poverty*

Ephraim H. Mizruchi

During the past several decades, a great deal of research and theoretical interest has been generated in relation to Emile Durkheim's concept of anomie. Of even greater interest to American sociologists, however, has been Robert K. Merton's concept of anomie which was formulated in his widely cited essay, "Social Structure and Anomie."[1] Studies in the areas of suicide, crime, and delinquency, to suggest only a few categories, have attempted to utilize this concept empirically, focusing on it as an explanatory device.[2] Leo Srole's anomia scale was developed as an index to Durkheim's anomie and has been used to assess Merton's theory.[3]

A careful examination of Merton's concept of anomie suggests that his emphasis is different from Durkheim's and that this difference leads to varying hypotheses. Merton's conception of anomie is one of a condition in society in which there is a disjunction between socially mandated goals and the means by which these goals are pursued. This disjunction is reflected in the great emphasis which is placed on success goals in American society and the lack of similar emphasis on legitimate means for the attainment of success. Furthermore, since access to the legitimate means for the attainment of success is differentially distributed, there is differential utilization of illegitimate means. It follows, then, that the lower the social class position, the less the access to legitimate means and the greater the tendency to deviant behavior. Thus, crime and delinquency rates could reasonably be expected to increase as social class declines.

* Revision of paper published in *The Sociological Quarterly*, **8**:439–446 (Autumn 1967). Paper originally read at the annual meeting of the Upstate New York Sociological Society, Ithaca, May 15, 1965. Support for the over-all research, of which this is a part, under National Institute of Mental Health Grant M6413 (A), is hereby acknowledged. I thank S. M. Miller, Delmar Palm, and Alex Inkeles for their comments on an earlier draft of this paper. Detailed description of the over-all study and methodology will be found in the writer's *Success and Opportunity* (New York: Free Press, 1964).

Durkheim did indeed discuss the problem of the disjunction between means and ends in his study, *Suicide*.[4] However, the emphasis in his theory of anomie was on the unrealizable goals which characterized periods of prosperity and upward mobility. The greatest effect of anomie was experienced not by those in poverty but by the more affluent in society. According to Durkheim, poverty is a restraining force in relation to anomie. It is the lifting of the limitations on aspirations which reflects Durkheim's major concern with anomie rather than the utilization of illegitimate means for the attainment of given ends. In Durkheim's own words,

> Poverty protects against suicide because it is a restraint in itself. No matter how one acts, desires have to depend upon resources to some extent; actual possessions are partly the criterion of those aspired to. So the less one has the less he is tempted to extend the range of his needs indefinitely. Lack of power, compelling moderation, accustoms man to it while nothing excites envy if no one has superfluity. Wealth, on the other hand, by the power it bestows, deceives us into believing that we depend on ourselves only. Reducing the resistance we encounter from objects, it suggests the possibility of unlimited success against them. The less limited one feels, the more intolerable all limitation appears. Not without reason, therefore, have so many religions dwelt on the advantages and moral value of poverty. It is actually the best school for teaching self-restraint. Forcing us to constant self-discipline, it prepares us to accept collective discipline with equanimity, while wealth, exalting the individual, may always arouse the spirit of rebellion which is the very source of immorality. This, of course, is no reason why humanity should not improve its material condition. But though the moral danger involved in every growth of prosperity is not irremediable, it should not be forgotten.[5]

That this difference in emphasis between Durkheim and Merton significantly affects our sociological perspective is reflected in the following quotation from Ely Chinoy's widely cited study dealing with Merton's conceptualization of anomie.

> Only in the occasional instances of men who could be defined in Marx's terms as *Lumpenproletariat* or in W. L. Warner's terms as "lower class" could one find workers who had totally rejected American success values. (No such workers were interviewed, although several were pointed out or identified.) But this solution to the problems imposed on workers by the disparity between their goals [Chinoy's assumption] and achievements on the one hand and the tradition of opportunity on the other was in effect no solution. Such men offered no alternative value to replace those which they had rejected: they were in a state of anomie.[6]

The Merton theory, at least in part since its focus is on means rather than ends, assumes relatively uniform aspirations across the class structure and a greater impact of anomie on the relatively lower classes. The theory, however, largely ignores observations made not only by Durkheim but by Veblen and

Marx, among others, regarding the relatively low levels of aspiration which characterizes those at the lowest levels of the class structure, and it ignores certain qualitative differences within and between the classes.[7]

Thorstein Veblen, in his *Theory of the Leisure Class*, wrote of a conservatism[8] which characterized the lowest segment of the class structure. Karl Marx and Friedrich Engels in *The Communist Manifesto* were similarly aware of the passivity of many in the lower reaches of the class structure in their acrimonious characterization of the *Lumpenproletariat* as "that passive social scum." [9] And Durkheim, as we noted earlier, described the indigent as having limited aspirations.

Albert B. Wolfe, whose concern was in part with social change, took note of this process and described it as "the conservatism of the necessitous condition."

> The propensity to fear any alteration in the status quo is widely diffused. It is to be found even in those lowest classes who possess no property, who enter into no contractual relations which will do them appreciable harm if they are broken, and who are devoid of elements of prestige. These classes can hardly be said to have vested interests, yet they not infrequently act as if they cherished a vested right to their poverty and dependence. . . . It is a well-known and significant fact that the lower the standard of living, the more depressed in physical health, and the more fatalistically contented people are, the harder it is to assure their interest in their own betterment or to get them to put forth any effort or to take any risk to that end.[10]

Indeed, recent observation, contrary to what seems to have been generally assumed, suggests that rebelliousness is not a characteristic of those who are most needy and oppressed. Ralf Dahrendorf points out that revolutions occur after "need and oppression have reached an extreme point . . . and . . . the lethargy given with it superseded." [11] Dahrendorf's observations are based on his study of recent Eastern European revolts. Recent efforts to motivate Negroes to rebel as part of the civil rights movement also indicate that subordinate groups often resist change. Similarly, Pedro Martinez is conspicuous because he is, as an activist, a deviant.[12]

More directly to the point of our concern with aspiration and poverty is Allison Davis's description of the perspectives of the "underprivileged worker."

> The actual daily pressure of five to ten hungry stomachs to fill, backs to clothe, and feet to cover forces the working-class parent to reduce his ambitions to the level of subsistence; to lower his sights as far as long-term planning and studying for better jobs and for finer skills are concerned; to narrow, limit, and shorten his goals with regard to the care, nutrition, education, and careers of his children.
>
> This terrible pressure for physical survival means that the *child* in the average working-class family does not learn the "ambition," the drive for high skills, and for educational achievement that the middle-class child learns in his family. The working-class individual usually does not learn

to respond to these strong incentives and to seek these difficult goals, because they have been submerged in his family life by the daily battle for food, shelter, and the preservation of the family. In this sense, ambition and the drive to attain the higher skills are a kind of luxury. They require *physical security*; only when one knows where his next month's food and shelter will come from, can he and his children afford to go in for the long-term education and training, the endless search for opportunities, and the tedious apple-polishing that the attainment of higher skills and occupational status require.[13]

Strong emphasis on security, as an integral factor inhibiting aspiration in segments of the lower class, is noted by Herbert Hyman in an analysis of opinion-poll data,[14] and in a cross-national survey Alex Inkeles described the strong emphasis on security associated with the values of workers in several European countries.

At the same time, we note that there are certain attitudes which position in the occupational hierarchy does not seem to influence. For example, all occupational groups agree on the relative ranking of the status or desirability of different jobs. And they seem to agree in favoring job security at less pay over a better-paying but less secure job. Yet in the latter realm we discover an interesting fact. *When we add the special ingredient of a promise of success, promotion or advancement, we trigger a special propensity to risking in those in more esteemed occupations, whereas those in the manual classes remain unmoved and stick to security.*[15]

Still more recently Inkeles has noted:

The fear of risk-taking does indeed go with extreme poverty. We have noted it very markedly in our recent work with Pakistani peasants, and we see it now as a large factor in their apparent unwillingness to adopt changes [modernization]. For them a mere "mistake" can mean starvation.[16]

Methodology

In a very recent study which attempts to assess Merton's theory, an effort was made to test empirically the hypothesis that the desire to "get ahead" in American society is uniformly distributed throughout the class structure.

In order to throw light on the nature of the relationships between aspirations and social class and their bearing on Merton's theory of anomie, we undertook a study in an upstate New York city (population approximately 16,000). A subsample of 183 adult respondents who were included in a large, systematic sample taken in 1958 were reinterviewed in 1960 along with 44 others who were used as replacements in the sampling processes. Graduate and undergraduate students, trained and supervised by the writer, administered a one-hour precoded interview on a range of value items, demographic characteristics, and behavioral indices.

The interview schedule evolved sixty-two open-end interviews taken by the writer in two villages in western New York State in 1956, which were coded. The code was used as a precode in 1958, revised in a study in 1959, and refined in 1960. In addition, items used by other researchers in similar studies were included.

Finally, hypotheses were tested using IBM data-processing techniques and parametric and nonparametric statistics (where applicable).

Class and Aspiration

Although, as we reported earlier,[17] "getting ahead" appears to be an important value in the sample selected for analysis and, furthermore, even though success is defined differently by the various classes, there is little apparent willingness to take risks to attain these goals.

Using the Gallup poll question selected by both Hyman and Inkeles, for example, elicited the distribution shown in Table 1. As the data indicate, there is an association between social class, as measured by Hollingshead's two-factor index of social position, and occupational choice. The selection of an occupation with low income and high security increases from 34 per cent in classes 1 and 2 combined to 84 per cent in class 5. Chi-square = 37.4, with 6 degrees of freedom, and P is less than .001.

TABLE 1
Social Class and Type of Occupational Choice
(in percentages)*

	Class (ISP)				Totals	
Occupational Type	1 and 2	3	4	5	Percentage	N
High income, high risk	10	32	16	8	16	33
Moderate income, moderate risk	56	19	19	8	21	45
Low income, high security	34	49	65	84	63	135
Totals						
Percentage	100	100	100	100	100	
N	30	37	82	64		213

* Chi-square = 37.4, 6 d.f., P < .001.

A datum which is more directly related to the problem of success aspiration is the result obtained from replies to another item in our interviews. Our respondents were asked, "Do you think a man should run risks to better himself, or should he be content with what he has?" The distribution is presented in Table 2. As the data indicate, the proportion of respondents who feel that "men should be content" increases as social position declines, thus supporting the observations of Hyman, Inkeles, and Wolfe. In short, lower valuation on risk taking among lower-class categories appears to be a characteristic of diverse societies, and the existence of the pattern lends stronger support to Durkheim's observations when compared with Merton's hypothesis.

TABLE 2
Social Class and Valuation of Risk Taking
(in percentages)*

Opinion	Class				Totals	
	1 and 2	3	4	5	Percentage	N
Men should take risks	93	82	68	64	74	156
Men should be content	7	18	32	36	26	54
Totals						
Percentage	100	100	100	100	100	
N	32	45	80	36		210

* Chi-square = 11.9, 3 d.f., $P < .01$.

Discussion

What we are suggesting here is that there is a significant segment of those in the relatively lower social classes who either do not aspire to changing their socioeconomic condition or who, if they do desire change, display an unwillingness to take risks to bring about this change.[18] What remains for us to suggest, in this brief statement, is (1) what the source is of this aspirational conservatism; (2) what some of its consequences are for those who adhere to this pattern; and (3) of what significance this pattern is in terms of sociological theory.

Limits to aspiration and risk taking would appear to be a result of sociological and sociopsychological processes. Obstacles to movement up the so-called ladder of opportunity are both internal and external with respect to given social classes, and these obstacles would seem to play a role in conditioning the nonmobile to an attitude of risk-avoidance.

As we have suggested elsewhere,[19] there is outright discrimination against lower status groups by those who are in relatively higher class categories. Indeed, it is this process which *is* stratification. In addition, those in the same class position tend to discourage others from moving ahead. This, too, has been documented in a number of studies.[20] In addition to the frustrations resulting directly from group efforts to block social mobility, there is the indirect effect of seeing oneself as one who has not achieved a measure of the "success" associated with the American Dream and who, furthermore, is not even in the process of achieving it! As the Lynds suggested years ago, we must note the effect on the lower classes of "the major constraints of inactivity due to recurrent unemployment and to being 'bottom dog' in a culture which habitually stresses and glorifies the traits and possessions of its 'top dogs.' "[21]

Thus, according to a number of observers, there are both direct and indirect effects associated with relatively low status in contemporary societies. In more sociological terms, we must note that in addition to a condition in which there is little aspiration to begin with, the withdrawal of aspiration for those who *do* aspire operates to mitigate the potential strains inherent in the mobility process and, as a result, proclivity to the effects of anomie. Thus, the effect of sudden change and immobility is greatest on those whose aspirations are highest.[22]

In short, we would hold that aspirational conservatism represents both adaptation to a social condition in which there is a discrepancy between the goals of the larger society, that is, "success," and the limited means available as well as a more chronic condition characteristic of many societies rather than "retreatism" in relation to the American Dream.

Thus, our analysis clearly suggests that (1) more clarity regarding the differences between Merton's and Durkheim's concepts of anomie would be desirable; (2) our conception of lower-class social processes may well require overhauling;[23] and (3) although Merton's theory does, at given points in the social structure, provide insight and understanding of these processes, contemporary sociology needs a continued assessment of the theory's strengths and weaknesses in juxtaposition to the Durkheim theory.

Must we assume that only one theory is necessary to explain a given set of phenomena—for example, deviant behavior? Can a field afford several theories which may be utilized in attempting to understand diverse aspects of the same general phenomenon? It is our position that sociology can and should direct itself to developing *parallel* theories in given content areas rather than monolithic ones. Thus the immediate theoretical problem *is not simply a matter of middle-range* as against highly generalized theories. It is one of developing typologies and classifying processes of behavior along with corresponding theoretical formulations. The current state of sociology can well tolerate both Merton's and Durkheim's theories of anomie so long as we maintain a proper perspective in relation to each.

NOTES

1. *Social Theory and Social Structure*, rev. ed. (New York: Free Press, 1957).
2. Most influential from Merton's point of view is the study by Richard A. Cloward and Lloyd E. Ohlin, *Delinquency and Opportunity* (New York: Free Press, 1960).
3. "Social Integration and Certain Corollaries: An Exploratory Study," *American Sociological Review*, **21**:712–715 (Dec. 1956); cf. also Wendell Bell, "Anomie, Social Isolation, and the Class Structure," *Sociometry*, **20**:105–116 (June 1957); Ephraim H. Mizruchi, "Social Structure and Anomia in a Small City," *American Sociological Review*, **25**:645–654 (Oct. 1960); Mizruchi, *Success and Opportunity*, loc. cit.
4. Ed. by George Simpson, trans. Irving Spaulding and George Simpson (New York: Free Press, 1951).
5. Ibid., p. 254.
6. Ely Chinoy, *Automobile Workers and the American Dream* (New York: Doubleday, 1955), pp. 127–128.
7. Cf., for example, S. M. Miller and Frank Riessman, "The Working-Class Subculture: A New View," *Social Problems*, **9**:86–97 (Summer 1961).
8. New York: Modern Library edition, n.d. p. 204. Cf. also Louis Schneider, *The Freudian Psychology*. New York: Basic Books and Thorstein Veblen's *Social Theory* (New York; King's Crown Press, 1948), pp. 209–212.
9. In V. F. Calverton, ed., *The Making of Society* (New York: Modern Library, 1955), p. 351.
10. Albert B. Wolfe, *Conservatism, Radicalism, and Scientific Method* (New York: Macmillan, 1923), pp. 63–64.
11. Ralf Dahrendorf, *Class and Class Conflict in Industrial Society* (Stanford, Calif.: Stanford University Press, 1959), p. 132.
12. Oscar Lewis, *Pedro Martinez* (New York: Random, 1964).

13. Allison Davis, "The Motivation of the Underprivileged Worker," in W. F. Whyte, ed., *Industry and Society* (New York: McGraw Hill, 1946), p. 89. In this context, compare also Louis Schneider and Sverre Lysgaard, "The Deferred Gratification Pattern," *American Sociological Review*, **18**:142–149 (April 1953); and, more recently, Murray Straus, "Deferred Gratification, Social Class, and the Achievement Syndrome," *American Sociological Review*, **27**:326–335 (June 1962). Peter Munch (in a personal communication) has suggested that there is an implicit assumption in Davis's statement that if "physical security" were attained, middle-class aspirations would spontaneously emerge. We agree with Munch that this is doubtful. Note also the last sentence in the quotation from Inkeles here.
14. Herbert Hyman, "The Value Systems of Different Classes," in Reinhard Bendix and Seymour Martin Lipset, eds., *Class Status, and Power* (New York: Free Press, 1953), pp. 426–442.
15. Alex Inkeles, "Industrial Man: The Relation of Status to Experience, Perception, and Value," *American Journal of Sociology*, **65**:12–13 (July 1960). Italics supplied.
16. Personal communication, January 21, 1964.
17. Mizruchi, *Success and Opportunity*, loc. cit.
18. Our value position here is explicit. A "higher" standard of living in terms of material goods, improved medical care, and educational opportunity is, we assume, the goal of change in this case.
19. Mizruchi, *Success and Opportunity*, op. cit., Chap. 6.
20. William F. Whyte, Jr., *Street Corner Society* (Chicago: U. of Chicago, 1943); B. Spinley, *The Deprived and the Privileged* (New York: Humanities Press, 1953); and Herbert Gans, *The Urban Villagers* (New York: Free Press, 1962).
21. Robert and Helen Lynd, *Middletown in Transition* (New York: Harcourt, 1937), p. 427.
22. Mizruchi, *Success and Opportunity*, op. cit., Chap. 5.
23. Cf. Miller and Riessman, loc. cit.

Women and Blacks

Recently, as we have previously noted, there have been a number of social movements that have attempted to readjust power relationships with ascribed categories. Their goals have been the opening of channels of mobility to the ascribed categories that previously were excluded and the transformation of collective self-images—that is, a redefinition of the applicability of the American Dream to the ascribed categories. With increasing efforts to attain mobility, however, subordinated groups have come to realize that their own values are only the first of several barriers. Even in the face of equal rights legislation, they have encountered systematic discrimination all along the way. The discrimination has been both personal and intentional and institutional and unintentional—but, nonetheless, discriminatory in that its effects on all categories of persons are not equal.

Women, for example, hold a disproportionate number of the lowest-ranking professional positions in a wide variety of organizational contexts. Thus, even when they have been able to hurdle the educational and organizational entry barriers, they still have found themselves in the lowest-ranking positions.[4] ("All our girls start in the typing pool.") One concrete illustration of this type of ascribed role distribution is provided by the results of a

[4] Randall Collins, "A Conflict Theory of Sexual Stratification," *Social Problems*, **19**:1002–1016 (1971).

survey of women and minority faculty ranks in graduate sociology departments. Changes in their distribution between 1970 and 1974 are presented
in Table 9-1.[5]

TABLE 9.1
Changes, in per cent, 1970–1974

Rank	% Women	% Black
Professor	1.6	.6
Associate professor	3.5	1.1
Assistant professor	10.7	2.5
Instructor–lecturer	23.4	3.9

It can be noted from Table 9-1 that the lower the rank involved, the greater
the increase in the per cent of women or the per cent of blacks in the
position between 1970 and 1974.

A still more formidable situation is confronted by many people who
simultaneously possess two (or more) ascriptive statuses, both of which
can be targets of discrimination. Examples of such "multiple negatives"
include Polish Jews, elderly Indians, and black females. In the following
paper, Epstein analyzes the barriers that have to be confronted by black
women in route to professional careers.

[5] Table 9.1 is prepared from data presented by Joan R. Harris, "Women and
Minorities in Sociology," *ASA Footnotes* (Jan. 1975), p. 3.

Positive Effects of the Multiple Negative: Explaining the Success of Black Professional Women[*][1]

Cynthia Fuchs Epstein

Despite American society's myth and credo of equality and open mobility,
the decision-making elites and elite professions have long remained clublike
sanctuaries for those of like kind (Goode 1957; Merton, Reader, and Kendall
1957; Hughes 1962; Hall 1948; Epstein 1970b, p. 968).

To be Jewish, black, foreign born, or a woman have all been bases for
exclusion from law, medicine, engineering, science, the supergrades of the
civil service, architecture, banking, and even journalism. Only a few in the
professions find that good can come from being born of the wrong sex, race,

* Reprinted with permission from *American Journal of Sociology*, **78**:912–935 (Jan., 1973).

religion, or ethnic group. This is a report on a set of these deviants who possess at least two—and often more—statuses deemed to be "wrong." It attempts to analyze why they nevertheless were successful in the occupational world.

In the exchange system of American society, women's sex status and blacks' racial status have typically cost them prestigious and remunerative jobs because society did not evaluate them as being high in either capacity or potential. Those who did succeed had to be brighter, more talented, and more specialized than white males in a comparable labor pool, whom the society ranked higher. Thus, they paid more for the same benefits (or "goods"), if they were permitted to acquire them at all.

Where categories of persons have more than one of these negative statuses, there often tends to be a cumulative negative effect. The costs of having several negatively evaluated statuses are very high and lead to social bankruptcy when people simply cannot muster the resources to pay them. This effect has been elsewhere conceptualized as "cumulative disadvantage" and has explained the poor representation of blacks (among others) in skilled occupations. Black women, for example, because of their two negatively evaluated statuses, are situated at the very bottom of the occupational pyramid.

Indeed, the status set which includes being black and being a woman has been one of the most cumulatively limiting.

These ascribed sex (female) and race (black) statuses are dominant;[2] they are visible and immutable and impose severe limits on individuals' capacities to alter the dimensions of their world and the attitudes of others toward them. In the elite professions, blacks and women have been considered inappropriate and undervalued, and as a result they have constituted only a tiny proportion of the prestigious professionals.[3] Not only have they been prevented from working in the elite professions, but the few who do manage to become professionals tend to work in the less remunerative and prestigious subfields (Epstein 1970c. p. 163).

Women typically have jobs which rank lower than men at every class level, and, contrary to some current misconceptions about the existence of a black matriarchy, black women are most typically at the very bottom of the occupational pyramid. They earn less than white women who, in turn, make less than men, white or black.[4] This economic distribution is constant for every category of worker, including professionals, with the sole exception of domestic workers. Although black women earn less, they are also much more apt to work than white women of the same age and education (Bureau of the Census, *Current Population Reports*, P-60, no. 75 [1970], table 50, p. 113).[5]

Yet there are black women who have achieved success in the popular definition of the term, becoming professionals of high prestige and acquiring high incomes as well. For them the effect of status sets with two immutable negatively evaluated statuses—the sex status of female and the race status of black—did not result in negative consequences but formed a positive matrix for a meaningful career.

This paper is based on interviews with a sample of 31 such women who achieved occupational success in the prestigious male-dominated professions and occupations of law, medicine, dentistry, university teaching, journalism, and public relations.[6]

Studying these successful black professional women we located three major patterns resulting from the interaction between statuses which accounted for their success. They may be outlined as follows:

1. Focusing on one of the negatively valued statuses canceled the negative effect of the other. (That is, raised its "worth." For example, in a white professional milieu, a black woman is viewed as lacking the "womanly" occupational deficiencies of white women—for example, seeking a husband —and the black woman's sex status is given a higher evaluation.)

2. Two statuses in combination create a new status (for example, the hyphenated status of black-woman-lawyer) which may have no established "price" because it is unique. In this situation, the person has a better bargaining position in setting his or her own worth. This pattern may also place the person in the role of a "stranger," outside the normal exchange system and able to exact a higher than usual price.

3. Because the "stranger" is outside the normal opportunity structure, he or she can choose (or may be forced to choose) an alternate life-style. This choice was made by many black women forced to enter the occupational world because of economic need, and, in turn, it created selective barriers which insulated the women from diversions from occupational success and from ghetto culture, thus strengthening ambition and motivation.

In the sections which follow, we will locate black professional women among other professionals to demonstrate their very special position in the social structure and further illustrate the process by which they were able to "make it" in American society.

Black Women in the Professions

Like the pattern for whites over 25, black women currently in the labor force have had more median years of schooling than black men, and more of them have been high school graduates. Furthermore, although black men in college now exceed black women, more black women over 25 are college graduates than are men in this age group (U.S. Department of Commerce, *Statistical Abstract 1968* [1968], table 156, p. 110; *Statistical Abstract 1970* [1970], table 157, p. 109; data derived from the *U.S. Census of the Population: 1960*, vol. 1, and *Current Population Reports*, ser. P-20, nos. 169, 194). Their educational advantage accounts partly for their greater access to professional jobs, and a significantly higher proportion of black women than men hold professional jobs—60 per cent of the total numbers of blacks holding such jobs—as reported by the 1960 census (Bureau of the Census, *1960 Subject Reports. Occupational Characteristics*, PC(2) and 7A, table 3, p. 21). Of all employed black women, 7 per cent were professionals, in contrast to 3 per cent of all employed black men (Ginzberg and Hiestand 1966, p. 210).

Like all American college women, black women are often steered into teaching and nursing careers. Black college women generally have taken

B.A. degrees in education[7] and found employment in the segregated school systems of the South (Ginzberg and Hiestand 1966, p. 216). Although the census has always counted teachers as professionals, teaching has always ranked low in occupational prestige,[8] and black men, like white men, did not enter teaching in any numbers.[9]

There are no census figures on the total number of graduate and professional degrees earned by black men and women,[10] and seemingly contradictory figures appear in the sources available. A study of Negro colleges— where the majority of blacks have earned their graduate degrees (Blake 1971, p. 746)—shows that black women earned 60 per cent of the graduate and professional degrees awarded in 1964–1965 (United Negro College Fund 1964–1965, appendix I). However, a Ford Foundation study (1970) of all black Ph.D. holders in 1967–1968 (p. 3) indicated that of a 50 per cent sample of the total, only 21 per cent were women. Another source covering black colleges for the same period as the UNCF report (1964) lists more women than men earning M.A.'s (799 as compared with 651; probably a majority were education degrees) but more men than women earning Ph.D.'s (five men and two women) (Ploski 1967, p. 527).[11]

If one compares the proportion of black women with black men in those professions higher in prestige than teaching, we find a more traditional picture. More black men than women are editors, doctors, lawyers, scientists, and college teachers (Bureau of the Census, *1960 Subject Reports. Occupational Characteristics*, PC (2)-7A, table 3, p. 21). Furthermore, they consistently have higher median incomes than do the women in these professions. (Bureau of the Census, *1960 Subject Reports. Occupational Characteristics*, PC (2)-7A, table 25, p. 296; table 26, p. 316).[12]

But relative to their male colleagues, black career women have done better than their white sisters; they constitute a larger proportion of the black professional community than women in the white professional world. Only 7 per cent of white physicians are women, but 9.6 per cent of black doctors are women; black women make up 8 per cent of black lawyers but white women constitute only 3 per cent of all white lawyers. Black women approach real equality with black men in the social sciences—they are 34 per cent of all blacks in the profession—although the absolute numbers are small (data derived from same Bureau of the Census 1960 as indicated above).

In most professional groups, black women constitute a larger proportion of women than black men do among males in these groups (U.S. Bureau of the Census, *1960 Subject Reports. Occupational Characteristics*, PC (2)-7A, table 3, p. 21). In terms of earnings they are also far more equal to white women than black men are to white men. In fact, black women accountants, musicians, professional nurses, and social workers exceeded their white female colleagues in earnings, according to the 1960 census (U.S. Bureau of the Census, *1960 Subject Reports. Occupational Characteristics*, PC (2)-7A, table 25, p. 296; table 26, p. 316).

However, one cannot ignore the fact that for all professions the absolute numbers of blacks are small, and the numbers of black women are so tiny that they may go unreported and unanalyzed. In the 1960 census, only 220 black women lawyers and about 370 black women social scientists were counted. No doubt there have been increases in all fields, but this remains conjectural in view of the fact that the proportion of all women in the professions has remained fairly static over the past 40 years (Epstein 1960*b*).

Black Women Have Greater Access

It is believed that in some sectors, probably as professionals in white firms, hospitals, and communities, black women have done better than black men. Historically, black women have had more access to white society than black men and have had opportunities to learn the "ropes" of the white world. Because they were desired as house servants, nursemaids, and sexual partners, black women often became intimates of whites, learning their values and habits. They could be intimates because as women they were not only powerless but were never regarded as potentially powerful, an attribute which has its analogue in their admission to the male-dominated professions.

Although it is difficult, if not impossible, to document the sense of threat with which white male professionals react to the thought of black men as colleagues, it is clear that black men and women perceive this reaction as a barrier to them. It was a common feeling among the black women in this study that this perceived threat was not as great for them. Being a woman reduced the effect of the racial taboo.

On the other hand, black women are found in professions and occupations known to be difficult for white women to penetrate. Because these women are black they are perhaps not perceived as women; they may be regarded as more "serious" professionals than white women; they may not be viewed as sexual objects nor be seen as out to get a husband. The stereotypes attached to the so-called feminine mind, emotions, or physiology may not seem easily transferable to black women, for whom there seem to be fewer stereotypes in the context of the professionally trained.

We have concentrated on several themes: (1) the special conditions which created for these women an image of self and an achievement value structure, (2) the problems attached to playing out traditional, idealized female dependency roles; and (3) the reinforcing components of the work situation.

Woman As Doer

Although the situation of the black woman is in many ways unique, many of the problems she faces are also experienced by other groups of women with negatively evaluated statuses. The mechanisms she uses to cope with strain are mirrored in their experiences as well. But perhaps more than the others, the black woman has been the subject of myths and misinterpretations often applied to behavior of minority group members (see Hyman 1969; Mack 1971).

The most pernicious of the popular stereotypes about the black woman holds that a black matriarchy exists and is a key factor in the social disorganization of the Negro family and the "irresponsibility" of the male as provider and authority. It is a perfect example of the "damned if you do, damned if you don't" syndrome (Merton 1957, p. 480).

Although a greater proportion of black women than white women work, and a greater proportion are the heads of families, the assumption that these factors have an independent negative effect has been challenged. The great majority of black families are intact families and, although a higher proportion of black wives work than do white wives, the typical pattern of black family life is an equalitarian one rather than one of wife-mother dominance. The strong mother figure is prevalent in the black family, but as Ladner (1971) has recently pointed out, strength is not the same as dominance. There have been many instances of strong mother figures in American history (immigrant mothers and pioneer mothers) who have been idealized as women who made it possible for their families to endure in punishing situations. Somehow, these other women were subjected to a different set of norms in contexts in which work was considered appropriate, in which running the shop, sitting at the cash register, or administering the farm was not viewed as masculine or, worse "castrating" behavior. Sometimes the work was done side by side with husband, sometimes alone because of his incapacity or unavailability. Only the rich could afford to keep their women unoccupied and unhelpful.[13]

The analogue of the immigrant woman probably fits the black woman's situation best, for she also was aware that the men in her family might not be able to provide for it entirely. Sharing or assuming work obligations were real expectations, and enough women did so to become models for generations to come. Both this study of black women professionals and my earlier study of women lawyers, many of whom came from immigrant families, showed that these women had in their lives models of mother-provider figures[14]—a mother or grandmother who, as a domestic worker or proprietor of a small store, or as a seamstress and, later, teacher and suffragette, generated a positive image of woman as doer, not as a passive and dependent person. The mother-provider figure appeared not in the absence of a father but often as the figure who worked with a father in a family business or who shared the economic burden by working at another enterprise. In fact, the mother-provider as heroine is a common image in many of these case studies because the activity of these women was so positively experienced and cherished.

The following description of a mother, offered by a woman physician in the study, is typical: "My mother was not the stronger of my parents but she was the more aggressive, always planning and suggesting ideas to improve the family's situation. A dressmaker by trade, she would slip out to do domestic work by the day when times got hard, often not telling my father about it. He was a bricklayer and carpenter but had trouble finding work because he was unable to get union membership."

Most of this sample of black women came from intact families. What was important was that their mothers, forced to work, canceled the "female effect" of motivation and offered an alternative model of adult women to that of the larger white culture. The black women interviewed showed a strong maternal influence; of the 30 interviewed, only four said their mothers had never worked (and one of these "nonworking" mothers had 13 children). Even more unusual was the fact that many of the mothers had been professionals or semiprofessionals. Seven had been teachers, one a college professor, two were nurses, and one a physician. This heritage is unique for any population of women, including professional women, whose mothers are more likely to have worked.

Middle-Class Values

Most women interviewed in this study came from families which stressed middle-class values, whether or not their incomes permitted middle-class amenities. I have already noted the high proportion of mothers who held professional jobs, and although far fewer of the fathers' jobs ranked high (five of the 30), the fathers all had occupational talents and skills. Generally the fathers held a variety of jobs which defy ordinary classification because, though not middle-class jobs by white standards (for example, as truckers and post office employees), they were at the time good opportunities for blacks.

The Special Case of the West Indians

Considering the size of its population in the United States, an unusually large proportion of my sample (one-third) is West Indian, and this helps account for the high level of aspiration found in the sample. It is generally believed that black professionals are of West Indian extraction in far greater proportion than could be expected by chance.[15] The situation of the black women of this group is illustrative of the "positive" effect of holding two or more negative statuses.

The experience of West Indians in the United States is different from that of other blacks because they face double discrimination—from the larger society for being black and from the black community for being foreign.[16] West Indian children are often persecuted and taunted as "monkey chasers." Their way of speech identifies them to other blacks as foreigners, and they experience the same kind of ostracism as white immigrants who bear visible negatively valued statuses. But, as a group, West Indians are known to have a sense of pride, to value education, and be characterized by Protestant Ethic strivings. Although the assimilation of second-generation immigrants into the main culture is common, and they may have difficulty maintaining their values in the context of competing views of work and study in the ghetto, being a West Indian black does create a circumscribed set of possibilities and insulation from the larger society, black and white. Marginality to black society (as immigrants) and to white society (as blacks) means an absence of diversion from the group's goals and competing values. Because they are isolated and the young women are segregated by their parents even more than the men,[17] the threat of the street and the illegitimate opportunity structure is cut off. At the same time, West Indian youth receive a heavy dose of achievement input from parents and their extended-kinlike community.[18] Many prominent West Indians referred repeatedly to their British training in thrift and self-esteem, to the importance given by their elders to education, to respect for adults, and at the same time, to the importance of being "spunky."

Self-Confidence

Black women seem to have acquired a sense of confidence in their competence and ability. Interviews with these black professional women revealed a strong feeling of self-assurance. Further support comes from Fichter's study of graduates from predominantly black colleges, which indicates that college-educated black women have more confidence in their abilities than a comparable group of white women graduates (1964, p. 12; table 5.17, p. 92).

Asked by Fichter if they thought they had personalities suitable to a career as business executives, 49 per cent of the white women interviewed but 74 per cent of the black women thought they did (1964, table 5.18, p. 93).

This high degree of self-confidence may result from their special condition of having gone to college, a very special event in the black community. Their self-confidence is probably reinforced as they overcome each obstacle on the way to the top.

Education and Its Structure

It is commonly believed that a greater premium is placed on the higher education of girls than boys in the black community.[19] Until recently the greater number of black women college graduates have supported this assumption. This view and the statistics supporting it have their origins in the structure of discrimination; even with college degrees, black men could not penetrate the high-ranking occupations, while black women graduates could always go into schoolteaching. Thus it has been suggested that contrary to the pattern believed to be true of underprivileged white families, in which male children got preference if not all could be sent to college, in the black family the female child would get preference.

However, the number of black men in college has grown steadily in the past decade and by 1963 surpassed the number of black women students. Further, if one measures the proportion of women among blacks in professions other than teaching, it is not true that more girls get professional training than men. Only 9.6 per cent of black doctors are women (again a higher percentage than in the white community, where only 7 per cent of doctors are women). Certainly black families, like many white immigrant families in the past, could not afford sex discrimination when they needed the contribution of any family member who showed promise. As one dentist of West Indian extraction put it: "Girls or boys—whoever had the brains to get education was the one pushed to do it and encouraged."

Although white families support the notion of college education for girls, they are somewhat ambivalent about encouraging them to go beyond the B.A., viewing professional training as a waste, detrimental to marriage chances, or simply inappropriate for a woman (Epstein 1970c, p. 62). Not a single black woman in the study reported opposition from her family on the matter of professional training; many referred to their parents' attitudes in the same terms as the dentist quoted above, and with the intensity characterized by a physician: "From the time you could speak you were given to understand that your primary interest in life was to get the best education you could, the best job you could. There was no other way!"

Where the parents could, they paid for the education of their daughters, often at the cost of years of savings and great personal sacrifice. Most of the women interviewed received at least a small amount of financial help from their parents and supplemented the costs of education by working while in school or through scholarship aid.

The black woman's education is considered a real investment in her future. She could not expect, like a white woman, to put her husband through college in order to enjoy a life of leisure on her husband's achievement and income. She knows, too, that a stable marriage is much more problematical as she moves up in educational status.

Of the black women college graduates studied by Noble, 90 per cent said that "preparing for a vocation" was first in a list of reasons for going to college (1956, p. 46, table 16). These responses followed a pattern reported in two earlier studies (Johnson 1938; Cuthbert 1942). And it should be noted that, far more than for the black man, a college education radically improves the income potential of the black woman; her median income is even higher than that of white women with college degrees (*The Social and Economic Status of Negroes in the United States, 1970*, table 102, p. 125, and table 25, p. 34).

In general, black women are more concerned with the economic rewards of work than are white women (Shea, Spitz, and Zeller 1970, p. 215).

Furthermore, the economic necessity expected by black women indicates a canceling of female occupational role stereotypes. The black women interviewed were not bound by conventional stereotypes of the professions deemed suitable "for a woman"; instead, they weighed the real advantages and disadvantages of the occupation. Although my earlier study of white women lawyers found that some of their parents had tried to deter them from that male-dominated occupation, the black women interviewed for this project reported their parents not only encouraged them but a number had suggested they try law or medicine. One woman who wanted to be a nurse was persuaded by her mother to become a physician.

Professional Schools

Most of the women interviewed were educated at white schools, a number of them having gone to private white elementary schools, to white colleges (79 per cent), and to white professional schools (70 per cent). A little more than half of the physicians went to white medical schools (and most of these attended the very top schools—Yale and Columbia, for example), and the rest went to predominantly Negro schools.[20] This is extremely unusual because the great majority of black doctors have always been educated in black medical schools.

No figures exist on the proportion of male and female black students admitted to white medical schools, and one can only suppose that black women had as hard a time getting admitted as any women or any blacks. A few of the doctors interviewed, however, felt that they had a slight edge over both groups—again the interaction effect of their two negative statuses; their uniqueness made their admission more likely. None, however, could say exactly why they thought this was true. One commented: "I think that being both black and female may have been an asset, in a peculiar sense, both in getting into medical school and subsequently."

Being black attenuated the effect of feminine roles in the university setting. Dating was difficult because there were so few black men; furthermore, being a specially selected female meant a high commitment to scholarship. The girls who went to all-white schools were good students, and most reported they had virtually no social life.

Marriage

For most women, getting married and becoming a mother are still the most salient decisions in the setting of a life course. These decisions usually follow a fairly certain pattern and serve as limits on the acquisition of other statuses, especially occupational ones. But marriage is not by any means a certainty for black women, and for those who do marry being a wife may not offer the security to replace a career.

The factors which result in the educated black woman's contingent marital status derive from the marginal position of blacks in American society and from their inability to conform to a number of norms in the family setting which are rooted in patriarchial-focused values. The black male's marginality makes it doubtful he will acquire a professional career; whatever the level of occupation he attains, he will have difficulty in providing a middle-class lifestyle on his income alone. The educated black woman thus is unlikely to find a mate of similar social rank and education, and it is doubtful she can expect to play the traditional middle-class housewife role played by educated white women.

Lacking the usual guarantee that Prince Charming will come equipped with a good profession and a suburban home, or will come at all, the educated black girl is prepared in both subtle and direct ways to adapt if the dream should fail. The women in our sample reported that their parents did not push them toward marriage, and though they generally married late if they married at all (one-third had not), they did not feel anxious about being unmarried.[21] Although there is some change today, most white girls have internalized enormous pressures to marry and marry early. Not only do black women probably invest less in the good-life-through-marriage dream, there is evidence that a great proportion feel they can do without it.

Bell (1971, p. 254) suggests that "marriage has limited importance to black women at all educational levels" and that it is also possible that "if education were held constant at all levels, black women would show a greater rejection of marriage than would white women." At lower-class levels it is clear that the rejection of marriage comes because it is perceived as unreliable, and at upper-class levels because of the small pool of eligible men and the competition for husbands.

Although the white college-educated woman is strongly deterred from focus on a career when she marries (though she may work), the black woman who marries a black college-educated man cannot consider withdrawing from the marketplace. She knows that her husband's education is no guarantee of his financial success. It has been clearly established that the discrepancy in income between white and black male college graduates is wider than the gap between incomes of those who are less well educated (Sheppard and Striner 1966, p. 24). Educated black women, like other black women who seem able to trim their expectations to the realities of their lives, know they will have to share the financial responsibilities for a middle-class standard of living. One-half of the college-educated black women studied by Fichter (1964, p. 81) said they preferred to combine their family role with an occupational role. This made them twice as likely as Southern white women or the comparable group of other white women in a national NORC sample to select a combination of marriage, child rearing, and employment.

It seems probable, too, that black women view careers differently than white women who expect to combine marriage and career. White women like to view their work as supplemental to the husband's. They tend not to think of their work as a career growing out of their own life aims. Black women tend less to view their work as a "hanger-on" activity. One gets the feeling in interviews with them that the quality of their lives is determined by their own endeavor and is less a response to their husband's occupation situation. Perhaps this is a function of their relatively high self-confidence. White women lawyers I studied who practiced with their husbands typically referred to their work as "helping their husbands" and not in terms of a real career (Epstein 1971). Of course, black women have less opportunity to reason so circuitously. They are not in any structure where they could work for a husband. None of the lawyers had lawyer husbands, and only one of the doctors had a husband who was a physician. All of the doctors made more money than their husbands. There was almost no occupational homogamy and very little occupational-rank homogamy between husbands and wives, contrary to the marriage pattern for white women professionals, in which occupational homogamy is exceptionally strong.[22]

Our respondents, following a pattern common to other educated black women,[23] often married down occupationally. Although some white women in my study of lawyers had husbands who earned less than they did, they appeared more threatened by this situation than the black women studied. Some of the white women, faced with developing careers, checked them to assure they would have lower-ranking, lower-paying jobs than their husbands.[24] Black women also consider checking their career progress for this reason, but feel the costs are too great. Although the white woman usually can withdraw from her profession and continue to live at the same economic standard, the black woman who does so pulls the family to a lower standard of living. If the black woman acts like a woman occupationally, she is failing as a mother in helping her family.

The negative rank differential present in most marriages of black professional women has an important effect on their commitment to career. Although black women are probably as hopeful as white women for a long and happy life with their husbands, they face the reality of a higher probability of marital breakup. Divorce and separation rates for blacks are higher than for whites,[25] and their remarriage rates are lower. Although rates of dissolution for black women professionals are the lowest of any category of black women workers, they are still higher than those for white women in similar jobs (Udry 1968, p. 577). Eight of the 24 women we studied who had ever been married had been divorced.

Caroline Bird suggests that black professional women's deviant place in the structure of marriage expectations "frees" them: "Negro career women are freer than white career women not to marry, to marry outside their race or class. . . . They are . . . much less bound than white women by the role duties most frequently cited as universal and inescapable limitations on the career aspirations of all women forever" (1969, p. 38). Whether or not they are free, it is certainly true that their lack of a safe haven in marriage gives them independence, motivation, and perhaps more reinforcement of self-confidence than the white woman who may retreat to full-time marriage at the first feeling of fear or insecurity as a professional.

Motherhood

Although getting married may determine whether or not a woman takes her career seriously, it is the demands on her as a mother and how she deals with those demands which become most important in her ability to focus on career.

Having children is costly for a family not only because of what it takes to feed, clothe, and educate them, but because typically the wife leaves the labor force—and her income—for long periods to care for them. And for black families it has been imperative that both wife and husband work to maintain their hold on a middle-class life-style.

Although blacks generally exceed the fertility pattern of whites, the fertility rates of upper-class Negro families are the lowest of any group (Moynihan 1965, p. 758).[26] Noble's study of Negro women college graduates found that although the majority of her sample married, more than 40 per cent were childless and 38 per cent had only one child (1957, p. 17). Of the 24 ever-married women in my study, 17 had children and seven did not. Of those who had children, more than half had two or more. Strikingly, all of those with two or more children were upper-income professionals—an editor, a lawyer, a dentist, and a half-dozen physicians. The sample's only mother of five is a practicing M.D.

Though black women who have careers can be assumed to reduce demands made on them by having fewer children than their white counterparts, it is more interesting to see the ways in which they handle their role demands as mothers and the unique aspects of the black social structure which help them do so.

The black mothers interviewed seemed far less anxious about their children than whites. They did not insist that it was their sole responsibility to care for their children, nor did they fear that their absence from home during the children's early years would be harmful to their psychic and physical growth. They seemed freer to accept help from relatives (particularly grandparents, who often volunteered it), to leave the children for long periods, and even to let the children accompany them to work if that became necessary. Hill (1971) suggests that black families are generally more adaptable to absorbing new members—other relatives' children, grandchildren, or grandparents —and that often the "new" older members play important roles in caring for young children while the mother works (p. 5).

Black women, whether of Southern or of West Indian origin, share an extended family tradition in which "others" can routinely perform tasks which middle-class white society would see as exclusively the responsibility of the husband and wife. This aspect of the black social structure meshes neatly with the needs of the black professional woman; it makes it possible for her to continue studies or career after having children, and makes combined motherhood and career a rational decision to be made on its merits.

Careers

The occupational spread of the 31 women interviewed ranged from physicians (12, including four psychiatrists), to lawyers (eight), dentists (two), a university professor, three journalists, and several in public relations work, business management, and top administrative posts in social services (One was in library science, a "woman's field" except in administration; this woman was in charge of a noted collection.) We excluded nursing, social work, and teaching, which are not only women's fields but are low in prestige and considered professions almost solely by the United States census.

An early decision to go into professional work was characteristic of most of the women in the sample. They share this history with male professionals of both sexes (Rogoff 1957, p. 111) and with other black women professionals (Ostlund 1957; Brazziel 1960). Considering the years of preparation, both in terms of anticipatory socialization and formal educational requirements, early deciders have an advantage over those who choose late.

Blacks, however, suffer from having fewer real models in their decision matrix, although doctors (in particular) and lawyers have always been held in high esteem in the black community. Until recently, physician was the highest status occupation a black person could hold, but the absolute number has been, and remains, small. In 1956 New York City had only 305 black physicians, the largest number of any city in the country, and in 1960 the total census figure for the United States was 5,038, of whom 487 were women.[27]

In contrast to the strong family encouragement of professional careers already noted, most black women recall, as do white women, being urged by primary and high school teachers and guidance counselors to go into schoolteaching or social work. This advice was based on their racial and sex statuses, although black men, too, are sometimes directed into these occupations because of the barriers they face in the more prestigious professions. But the significant messages for them were from their parents, who were encouraging them to be whatever they wanted and who did not raise objections to their trying a white, male profession.

Eight of the physicians went to "white" medical schools (NYU, New York Medical College, Boston University, Philadelphia Women's) or to elite white schools (Columbia's Physicians and Surgeons and Yale).

Despite their educational credentials, most of the doctors work in the black community. Elite medical careers require not only degrees from good schools but a status sequence of internships at elite training hospitals which are hard for any black to get, and which most of the women did not get, or which they did not seek because they felt their chances were nonexistent. None of the women who went to a black medical school was able to work within the medical "establishment," although a few had some contact with it under new programs pairing private teaching hospitals with municipal hospitals.

The lawyers interviewed went exclusively to white law schools; four to Columbia, one to the University of Michigan, two to NYU, and one to Brooklyn Law School, a lower-ranking school with an evening program. Two of the lawyers who achieved elite establishment careers did so after a top-rank legal education during which they had performed at the top of their class. Following another typical route for the ethnic minorities, the Brooklyn Law School graduate achieved a high-ranking position within the city government. Nearly all of the women interviewed found, regardless of educational attainment, that some professional gates were simply locked. It was one thing to get admitted to school, another to find a job.

Like blacks and women, following the negative effect of holding "inappropriate statuses," they tended to go into protected work settings. Most of the doctors and lawyers started in salaried jobs—no government work and clinics—where getting clients was not an immediate problem. Many of the doctors took residencies in municipal hospitals and went directly onto the staffs of these same hospitals or into clinics in the black community. Some of the psychiatrists later mixed private practice with their institutional jobs, but only one could be said to have a truly full-time private practice. It was not only the closed opportunity structure which led these women into clinics and municipal hospitals, but also their sense of service and duty to the black community. Later, some with research interests were able to work in private hospitals within the structure of new programs.

Six of the doctors interviewed were on the staff of Harlem Hospital (the hospital has 15 women physicians, a few of whom are white). This was partially the result of sampling by referral and partially because Harlem Hospital is one of the few U.S. hospitals that has any number of black physicians. It is unique in that women doctors are heads of three departments. All of the women interviewed were specialists. In 1952, out of 33,000 medical specialists, only 190 were Negroes (*Negroes in Medicine* [1952], p. 6, cited in Lopate [1968]). With the exception of three (one of whom had done breakthrough research on the "kidney machine") all were in specialties which historically have been relatively open to women and blacks: four were psychiatrists, two were pediatricians, one was in community medicine, and one in dermatology. A few now in psychiatry had been practicing pediatricians. One can see that their specialization and superior training placed them high on the eligibility list. Most black physicians have not had top-rank educations; more than four-fifths of black physicians were graduated from Meharry Medical College and Howard University (Altman 1969, p. 38). The fact that they claimed to work very hard and the somewhat greater tolerance of black men to women's participation in the professions made it possible for black women to get better posts than most white women can aspire to.

The lawyers followed the pattern of protected salaried positions to a lesser degree than the doctors. Three had their own practices, and two had become public figures. One was salaried but had attained the superelite position of partnership in a Wall Street firm. One was the first woman assistant district attorney in New York, and another was moving from a poverty program into private practice. All had been affected by the social changes in attitudes toward racial discrimination in New York; all were exceptionally attractive or outstanding in some way, all were highly articulate; all had solid educational credentials. With one exception, all worked in the white world. All felt that being black and women gave them additional possibilities that they might not have had as only women or as only black. The lawyers' extremely unique status combination made them highly visible, and in the law, where performance is quite open to the scrutiny of peers, news of one's excellence spreads quickly.

Women lawyers interviewed in my previous study emphasized their need to be better than others so that no one could use incompetence or lack of devotion to work against them. Black women professionals also stressed this motivating factor and were even more passionate about it. Their need to prove themselves and be the best was often tied in with self-consciousness about their visibility and their sense of responsibility for others of their race and sex. These remarks were typical:

> Being a black woman . . . . It's made me fight harder. . . . I think probably one of the strengths of being black or being a black woman is that if you have the native material you really do learn to fight and try to accomplish and all the rest. If I had been white, with the same abilities, I'm not so sure the drive would have been the same.
>
> Women have some advantages as trial lawyers, for one thing they are well remembered, or remembered, well or not, depends on how they perform. The judge is not as likely to forget them if he has ever seen them before, because we women are in the minority. And, of course, for a Negro woman, she is very likely to be remembered. It is always a help, not to be forgotten.

Some of the younger women were well aware of today's emphasis on having women and blacks in hospitals, firms, corporations, and schools. Most spoke of it with irony, but with an air of confidence and a sense that they deserved whatever benefits came out of the new social awareness. Some recognized they were useful because an employer could kill two birds with one stone by hiring a black woman; one said pithily: "I'm a show woman and a show nigger, all for one salary." Some older women felt they had been accepted in their professional work because being a Negro woman was not as bad as being a Negro man. About a third said they believed Negro men were "a threat" to white men or alluded to that belief as if it were well known to all, and that a black woman constituted less of a threat.

Whether or not this is true (and certainly, no data are available on it), the belief may act to discourage black men from seeking entry into white domains and encourage the black woman because she thinks she has more of a chance. Black women doctors and dentists who worked with white patients (one had almost a totally white practice) felt that because most of their patients were children, and therefore brought in by mothers, no "male threat" was operative in their relationship.[28]

Black women probably get "straighter" treatment in white professional setting than do white women. For one thing, white men do not as often see black professional women as romantic partners, or feel the black woman is out "to catch" one of them as a husband, and therefore respect their serious intent. In black settings, the black professional women report suspicious views of their competence and career involvement similar to those encountered by white women in white male settings, but the fact that the working woman is a more familiar image to the black man, and the "woman as doer" is more familiar to him (as it is for the woman), means that attitudes are more tempered.

Black women professionals also seem to have higher regard for each other than white women professionals. I encountered far less self-hatred among them than among the white women lawyers interviewed earlier. The latter shared the (male) negative stereotypes of women lawyers as excessively aggressive and masculine. The black women interviewed seemed to have a more matter-of-fact attitude toward their sister professionals; they never indicated doubts about the competence of other women, and some said they favored women as colleagues because they were more reliable and more willing to work than the men they knew. Few white women professionals favored other women professionals.

These phenomena in the professional world, which grow out of black women's unique position, probably reinforce their self-confidence and act to motivate them toward a career line similar to that of the white male. However, given the limits imposed by the current social structure, only the most extraordinary black women, those who are intellectually gifted and personally attractive, can make it. The fact that some do indicates that an enormous amount of energy in the social system must be directed to keeping others out.

The chance to become professionals developed out of a structure which narrowed their choices, made them visible and unique. For these few, the effects of living in a world otherwise beset with limits fed their determination and made them feel the only road to survival lay in occupational success. For those without the special support of family and personal networks of these women, and without their extraordinary ability to drive ahead, the limits of the occupational structure could only be defeating, even to those with ability. The self-maintaining mechanisms of the present stratification system within the professions clearly operate to keep the participation of certain persons low in spite of their possible intellectual contributions. Ironically for this small sample of black women, the effect of mechanisms within the larger stratification system (which operate to keep blacks and women down) served to reinforce their commitment to careers which would be normally closed to them, and by defining them as superunique, made it possible for some to rise within the professional structures. It has become clear that the elaborate filtering system which keeps elite spheres clear of alien groups is costly and self-defeating. It is rare that those who do push through emerge unscathed by the passage. Those who fall on the way are lost to the greater society. But the mechanisms which contribute to the status quo are often not consciously known even by those who participate in their exercise, and only by analyzing the various structural nexus in which they occur can they be isolated and evaluated for what they are.

NOTES

1. This is publication A-662 of the Bureau of Applied Social Research, Columbia University. It is a revision of a paper presented at the Annual Meeting of the American Sociological Association, 1971, in Denver, Colorado, and was prepared with the support of grants from the Research Foundation of the City University of New York, no. 1079 and grant no. 91-34-68-26 from the Manpower Administration, U.S. Department of Labor. The author is indebted to Diana Polise for help in its preparation and to Florence Levinsohn and Howard Epstein for editorial suggestions. Critical issues were raised by William J. Goode, Gladys G. Handy, Jacqueline J. Jackson, Robert K. Merton, and Lauren Seiler (some resolved, others not).

2. According to Robert K. Merton, statuses are dominant when they determine the other statuses one is likely to acquire (see Epstein 1970c, p. 92). Part of this analysis (as that in my earlier work [1970b, 1970c] draws on Robert K. Merton's conceptualization of the dynamics of status sets, part of which is found in *Social Theory and Social Structure* (1957, pp. 368–384), and much of which has been presented in lectures at Columbia University and is as yet unpublished (see footnotes in Epstein 1970b, p. 966).

3. In 1960, blacks constituted 1.3 per cent of all lawyers, and the proportion of women in law was 3.4 per cent.

4. Median earnings of full-time year-round workers were reported as follows for 1967: Negro women—$3,194; white women—$4,279; Negro men—$4,777; white men—$7,396 (U.S. Bureau of Census, *Current Population Reports*, ser. P-60, no. 60, table 7, p. 39). Although figures went up in 1970 the relationship remained the same (U.S. Bureau of Census, *Current Population Reports*, ser. P-60, no. 75, table 45, pp. 97–98).

5. In 1968, 49 per cent of Negro women were in the work force compared with 40 per cent of white women (Brimmer 1971, p. 550).

6. Because no lists exist of black women in any of these professions, there was no way to systematically sample the universe of black women professionals. Instead, respondents were obtained by referral from friends and colleagues. Because of the extremely small absolute number of black women in these fields, and because the study was limited to the New York area, a great deal of time was spent simply trying to find subjects.

7. In predominantly Negro colleges and universities, for the years 1961–1964 the proportion of women students majoring in elementary education was 24.4 per cent as compared with 6.4 per cent of the men (McGrath 1965, p. 80). The field of education alone accounted for 38 per cent of all bachelor's degrees earned by women in 1967. Education also accounted for 51 per cent of the master's and 29 per cent of the doctor's degrees earned by women in 1967 (*Handbook of Women Workers 1969*, pp. 192–193); 53.5 per cent of black women in the "Professional, Technical & Kindred Workers" category in the U.S. census were elementary (43.1 per cent) and secondary (10.4 per cent), school teachers (Ginsberg and Hiestand 1966, p. 215).

8. Teaching ranked thirty-sixth in the NORC study of occupational prestige in 1947 and rose to twenty-sixth place in 1963, still placing it far below medicine, law, banking, college teaching, etc.

9. Black men have gone into teaching to a somewhat greater degree than white men but not nearly to the extent of the women. Of professional men, 11.9 per cent were elementary school teachers and 13.1 per cent were secondary school teachers; the absolute numbers being considerably smaller as well, as the adjacent table indicates:

**Percentage of Negro Professional, Technical and Kindred Census
Category Who Were Teachers, by Sex, 1960**

Teachers	Men		Women	
	Number	*%*	*Number*	*%*
Elementary	13,451	11.9	75,695	43.1
Secondary	14,828	13.1	18,194	10.4

Source: Ginsberg and Hiestand 1966, pp. 110, 215.

10. Statistics on doctorate production of blacks can only be based on the number of graduate degrees produced by the predominantly black colleges and by estimates of the number of blacks in the integrated colleges. Statistics are unavailable because of fair educational practices laws. The absolute number of black doctorates ever held is small, estimated by Horace Mann Bond (1966) at 2,485 (comprising those awarded 1866–1962) (Ginsberg and Hiestand 1966, p. 564). The Ford Foundation study cited herein found 2,280 current holders of Ph.D. degrees in 1967–1968.

11. Although the Ford study included education doctorates, we suppose that the high figure for women graduates in black institutions is probably due to the high proportion of education doctorates awarded by Negro institutions when compared with the range of doctorates awarded by white institutions. This is probably due to perennial fiscal problems and inability to fund programs in the hard sciences until quite recently.

12. If one uses nonwhite categories (which, for the general population, is 92 per cent black) to get figures for blacks in the professions, a misleading impression will result. Certain professions (see n. 15) have almost equal numbers of blacks and other nonwhites, such as Chinese, Japanese, etc.

13. The managerial ability of women throughout history has been understated. Although women have always worked in agrarian societies and at the lower strata in all societies, upper-class women have assumed economic roles in a variety of circumstances. Women of rank managed estates in France and England in the absence of male heirs or when men went off to war.

14. In my sample of women lawyers, nearly all of whom were white, 20 per cent had mothers who were or had been engaged in professional occupations, nine of whom were teachers. Thirty per cent never worked (Epstein 1968, p. 96). In Rita Stafford's larger study of women in *Who's Who*, 11.5 per cent of the mothers of lawyers were in a profession and close to 70 per cent were housewives (Epstein 1968, p. 236).

15. West Indians have contributed disproportionately to the current Negro leadership, including Stokely Carmichael, Lincoln Linch, Roy Inniss, and other accomplished people. Glazer and Moynihan (1963) assert that in the 1930s foreign-born persons were to make up as much as one-third of the Negro professional population, especially physicians, dentists, and lawyers. We can assume these foreign born were predominantly West Indian. This seems to hold true today if one examines the proportion of foreign-born nonwhites in the professions. Almost one-half of the nonwhite male college instructors, presidents, and so on, were listed as foreign born in the 1960 census, about 20 per cent of the natural scientists, about 40 per cent of the doctors, but only a tiny percentage, 0.8, of the lawyers. This also holds true for black women with almost 11 per cent of the nonwhite female college faculty being foreign born, 26 per cent of the natural scientists, 60 per cent of the doctors, and no lawyers listed (U.S. Bureau of Census 1963, vol. 2, PC [2]-7A, table 8, pp. 114–115). And the census figures do not include the large numbers of professionals who were born here of West Indian parentage. Although the nonwhite population is 92 per cent black, and the category in the census data is often taken to mean "mostly black," one must be wary of the percentages for certain professions because tiny numbers of blacks are often matched in number by other non-whites, such as Chinese. This can be seen in the table on the following page.

16. Cruse (1967, p. 121) suggests that native (New York) Negroes frowned on West Indians mainly because the islanders presented a threat of competition for jobs available to blacks. The West Indian influx into New York in the 1920s coincided with the great migration of Negroes from the South. However, he does note the severe antipathy of native blacks to West Indians because of their alleged "uppity" manner.

17. One women commented: "I was not only protected; I was overprotected. West Indians are real Victorians regarding the behavior of their girls."

Number of Negro and Other Nonwhites in Selected Occupations,
United States, 1960

	Negroes	*Other Nonwhites*
College president, professor, instructor	5,910	2,794
Chemists	1,799	1,115
Physicians, surgeons	5,038	5,007
Lawyers, judges	2,440	530

Source: U.S. Census of the Population, vol. 2, 1960 Subject Reports, Occupational Characteristics, PC (2)-7A, table 3, pp. 21–22.

18. The isolation and special character of the black West Indian have probably emphasized a sense of community bolstered by mutual benevolent associations (also known as "meetings" and "hands") which are often church associated. Members have pooled resources to meet mortgage payments on homes, appraised property, and in other ways have acted as pseudokin groups in assisting talented youngsters with college scholarships. Often these groups had a geographic base and were Jamaican, or Trinidadian, and so on. Paule Marshall's *Brown Girl, Brownstones* (1959) is a vivid portrait of a Barbadian community in Brooklyn, focusing on a young girl growing up, her hard-working mother, and the influence of a Barbadian community organization in reinforcing work, ownership, and scholarship norms.

19. See, for example, Silberman's assertion about the black woman: "Her hatred of men reflects itself in the way she brings up her own children; the sons can fend for themselves but the daughters must be prepared so that they will not have to go through what she has gone through" (1964, p. 119). And Cogan's statement: "In the Negro family the oldest girl is most protected and most often encouraged to go on with her education" (1968, p. 11).

20. Seventy per cent of Negro medical students in 1955–1956 attended black medical schools as opposed to only 30 per cent who attended white medical schools (Reitzes 1958, p. 28).

21. But generally women in the male-dominated professions marry late and a substantial proportion are unmarried (see Epstein 1970a, p. 905).

22. Compared by race, marriages tend to be homogamous—husbands and wives coming from similar social, religious, ethnic, and educational background. Within this general similarity, there is some tendency for men to marry a little below their own level, so that they are slightly hypogamous while their wives tend to be slightly hypergamous. The reverse tends to be true for blacks; women tend to marry below their own level (Bernard 1966, p. 90).

23. Noble reported that more than 50 per cent of the husbands of college-educated black women in her study were employed in occupations of lower socioeconomic level than those of the wives. In more than 60 per cent of this study's cases in which wives reported on their husband's education, the man had a lower level of education than his wife. Noble reports low levels of response for both these items in her questionnaire (1956, p. 51).

24. Perhaps this is a manifestation of the ambivalence women feel toward success. Matina Horner's work suggests that most women will explore their intellectual potential only when they do not need to compete—least of all with men. They feel success is unladylike and that men will be put off by it (1969, p. 62).

25. Black women appear more likely to encounter marital discord than whites. In 1970, 19 per cent of all black women who at some time had been married were either divorced or separated as contrasted with 6 per cent of white women who had been married (*New York Times,* July 26, 1971, p. 1).

26. Although there are no data for fertility of women by their own occupation, the percentage of nonwhite wives of professional men who were childless in 1950 was 33 per cent (Whelpton, Campbell, and Patterson 1966, p. 153).

27. Michel Richard figured that by interviewing 98 black physicians in New York in 1965 he had a sample of about 28 per cent of all black doctors in New York City, using an estimate of 355 for 1965 (1969, p. 21). By doing a little creative statistical calculation, we figured that using the national percentage of black women doctors (9.6 per cent of black doctors) would mean that there are about 28 black women doctors in New York. We interviewed 12, which would be about 40 per cent if one allowed for a general increase in the total number of black doctors by 1968–1969, when most of these interviews were done.

28. William J. Goode suggests (personal communication) a general psychodynamic interpretation–that perhaps there is such a cultural emphasis on the fragility of the male ego that the typical traditional male professional may, indeed, play it safe in choosing his colleagues (certainly in choosing someone to act in an authority position over him, as a patient does when he chooses a doctor). The black woman professional may not only face less resistance from a white women client (she might prefer a male doctor but certainly would choose a black woman over a black male doctor) but she herself might be willing to challenge the professional setting to a greater extent in attempting to enter the white establishment than the black man because, being a woman, she is not so sensitive to the fear of "losing face" (the woman in American society not being socialized to think she has much face to lose, anyway).

REFERENCES

Altman, Lawrence K. 1969. "Funds Urged to Attract Negro Doctors." *New York Times,* October 5, 1969.

Bailyn, Lotte. 1964. "Notes on the Role of Choice in the Psychology of Professional Women." *Daedalus* **93** (Spring): 700–710.

Bell, Robert R. 1971. "The Related Importance of Mother-Wife Roles among Black Lower-Class Women." In *The Black Family: Essays and Studies,* edited by Robert Staples. Belmont, Calif.: Wadsworth.

Bernard, Jessie. 1966. *Marriage and Family among Negroes.* Englewood Cliffs, N.J.: Prentice-Hall.

Bird, Caroline. 1969. "Black Womanpower." *New York Magazine* **2** (March): 35–42.

Blake, Elias, Jr. 1971. "Future Leadership Roles for Predominantly Black Colleges and Universities in American Higher Education." *Daedalus* **100** (Summer): 745–71.

Bond, Horace Mann. 1966. "The Negro Scholar and Professional in America." In *American Negro Reference Book,* edited by John P. Davis. Englewood Cliffs, N.J.: Prentice-Hall.

Brazziel, William F., Jr. 1960. "Occupational Choice in the Negro College." *Personnel and Guidance* **39**:739–742.

Brimmer, Andrew. 1971. "Economic Outlook and the Future of the Negro College." *Daedalus* **100** (Summer): 539–572.

Cogan, Lee. 1968. *Negroes for Medicine.* Baltimore: Johns Hopkins Press.

Cruse, Harold. 1967. *The Crisis of the Negro Intellectual.* New York: Apollo Editions.

Cuthbert, Marion. 1942. "Education and Marginality." Ph.D. dissertation, Teachers College, Columbia University.

Epstein, Cynthia F. 1968. "Women and Professional Careers: The Case of the Woman Lawyer." Ph.D. dissertation, Columbia University.

———. 1970a. "Current and Emerging Occupation-centered Feminine Life-Career Patterns and Trends." *Annals of the New York Academy of Science* **175**:898–909.

———. 1970b. "Encountering the Male Establishment." *American Journal of Sociology* **75**:965–982.

———. 1970c. *Woman's Place: Options and Limits of Professional Careers.* Berkeley: University of California Press.

———. 1971. "Law Partners and Marital Partners: Strains and Solutions in the Dual-Career Family Enterprise." *Human Relations* **24** (December 1971): 549–564.

———. Forthcoming. *The Woman Lawyer.* Chicago: University of Chicago Press.

Fichter, Joseph H. 1964. *Graduates of Predominantly Negro Colleges—Class of 1964.* Public Health Services Publication, no. 1571. Washington, D.C.: Government Printing Office.

Ford Foundation. 1970. *The Black American Doctorate.* New York: Office of Reports, 320 E. 42 St.

Ginzberg, Eli, and Dale L. Hiestand. 1966. "Employment Patterns of Negro Men and Women." In *American Negro Reference Book,* edited by John P. Davis. Englewood Cliffs, N.J.: Prentice-Hall.

Glazer, Nathan, and Daniel Patrick Moynihan. 1963. *Beyond the Melting Pot.* Cambridge, Mass.: Harvard University Press and M.I.T. Press.

Goode, William J. 1957. "Community within a Community: The Professions." *American Sociological Review* **22**:195–200.

Hall, Oswald. 1948. "The Stages of a Medical Career." *American Journal of Sociology* **53**:327–336.

Hill, Robert. 1971. "Strengths of the Black Family." Mimeographed. Washington, D.C.: National Urban League.

Horner, Matina. 1969. "A Bright Woman Is Caught in a Double Bind." *Psychology Today* **3** (November): 36, 62 ff.

Hughes, Everett C. 1962. "What Other." In *Human Behavior and Social Processes,* edited by Arnold Rose. Boston: Houghton Mifflin.

Hyman, Herbert. 1969. "Black, Matriarchy, Reconsidered." *Public Opinion Quarterly* **33** (Fall): 346–347.

Johnson, Charles S. 1938. *The Negro College Graduate.* Chapel Hill: University of North Carolina Press.

Ladner, Joyce. 1971. *Tomorrow's Tomorrow.* New York: Doubleday.

Lopate, Carol. 1968. *Women in Medicine.* Baltimore: Johns Hopkins Press.

McGrath, Earl. 1965. *The Predominantly Negro Colleges and Universities in Transition.* New York: Teachers College, Columbia University.

Mack, Delores E. 1971. "Where the Black Matriarchy Theorists Went Wrong." *Psychology Today* **4** (January): 24, 87 ff.

Marshall, Paule. 1959. *Brown Girl, Brownstones.* New York: Random House.

Merton, Robert K. 1957. *Social Theory and Social Structure.* Glencoe, Ill.: Free Press.

Merton, Robert K., George Reader, and Patricia Kendall. 1957. *The Student Physician.* Cambridge, Mass.: Harvard University Press.

Moynihan, Daniel Patrick. 1965. "Employment, Income and the Ordeal of the Negro Family." *Daedalus* **94** (Fall): 745–770.

Noble, Jeanne L. 1956. *The Negro Women's College Education.* New York: Stratford.

———. 1957. "Negro Women Today and Their Education." *Journal of Negro Education* **26** (Winter): 15–21.

Ostlund, Leonard A. 1957. "Occupational Choice Patterns of Negro College Women." *Journal of Negro Education* **26** (Winter): 86–91.

Ploski, H. 1967. *The Negro Almanac.* New York: Bellwether.

Reitzes, Dietrich C. 1958. *Negroes and Medicine.* Cambridge, Mass.: Harvard University Press.

Richard, Michel. 1969. "Ideology of Negro Physicians: A Test of Mobility and Status Crystallization Theory." *Social Problems* **17**:20–29.

Rogoff, Natalie. 1957. "Decision to Study Medicine." In *The Student Physician,* edited by Robert K. Merton, George Reader, and Patricia Kendall. Cambridge, Mass.: Harvard University Press.

Shea, John, Ruth S. Spitz, and Frederick A. Zeller. 1970. *Dual Careers: A Longitudinal Study of Labor Market Experience of Women.* Vol. 1. Columbus: Center for Human Resources Research, Ohio State University.

Sheppard, Harold L., and Herbert E. Striner. 1966. *Civil Rights, Employment, and the Social Status of American Negroes.* Report of the U.S. Commission on Civil Rights. Washington, D.C.: Government Printing Office.

Silberman, Charles. 1964. *Crisis in Black and White.* New York: Random House.

Udry, J. Richard. 1968. "Marital Instability by Race, Sex, Education, Occupation, and Income, Using 1960 Census Data." In *Selected Studies in Marriage and the Family,* edited by Robert F. Winch and Louis W. Goodman. New York: Holt, Rinehart & Winston.

United Negro College Fund. 1964–1965. "Statistical Information, UNCF Office of Development and Educational Services." Report of member institutions of UNCF. New York: United Negro College Fund.

U.S., Bureau of the Census. 1963. *1960 Subject Reports. Occupational Characteristics.* Final Report PC (2)–7A. Washington, D.C. Government Printing Office.

———. 1967. *Current Population Reports.* Series P-60, No. 60. Washington, D.C.: Government Printing Office.

———. 1970. *Current Population Reports.* Series P-60, No. 75. Washington, D.C.: Government Printing Office.

U.S., Department of Commerce. 1968. *Statistical Abstract, 1968.* Washington, D.C.: Government Printing Office.

———. 1969. *Changing Characteristics of the Negro Population.* Washington, D.C.: Government Printing Office.

———. 1970. *Statistical Abstract, 1970.* Washington, D.C.: Government Printing Office.

U.S., Department of Commerce and Department of Labor. 1970. *The Social and Economic Status of Negroes in the United States, 1970.* BLS Report No. 394, and Current Population Reports, Series P-23, No. 38. Washington, D.C.: Government Printing Office.

U.S., Department of Labor. 1967. *Negro Women in the Population and the Labor Force.* Washington, D.C.: Government Printing Office.

————. 1970. *Handbook of Women Workers 1969.* Women's Bureau Bulletin No. 294. Washington, D.C.: Government Printing Office.
Whelpton, Pascal K., Arthur A. Campbell, and John E. Patterson. 1966. *Fertility and Family Planning in the United States.* Princeton, N.J.: Princeton University Press.

Historical Precedents

Thus far in this chapter our emphasis has been largely on current patterns of ascriptively blocked mobility. However, the processes of exclusion and of providing only minimal (that is, token) entrance, has a long history both in the United States and in many other parts of the world. Our attention turns now to an examination of some of these historical processes. American society always has been characterized by structured social inequalities. The legal basis for the establishment of the United States emerged out of a number of compromises that were intended to protect not only varying regional interests in the former British Colonies but class and caste interests as well. Thus, from the very beginning, the Jeffersonian principles that were directed, among other things, to the establishment of a structure to insure "life, liberty and the pursuit of happiness" were understood as normative ideals rather than expectations for concrete behavior. The conspicuous maintenance of the most rigid form of structured social subordination, slavery, is evidence enough that the framers of the Constitution of the United States did not intend to tamper with the organized inequities of privilege from which they personally derived benefit.

Rigid structures for group subordination were not peculiar to the relationship between white Anglo-Saxons and black Africans in the Northern Hemisphere. The Spanish and Portuguese who invaded, explored, and colonized South and Central America, enslaved thousands of Indians and also forced them to work for the benefit of those in foreign lands.[6] Thus, in contrast to the black slaves whose labor contributed to support the expansion of the larger society in which they lived, the Indian slave's efforts were directed to a system that took resources from the land and, as in most colonial relations, stripped the society's potential for long-range growth.

[6] Although the *encomienda* system was not normatively a system of slavery, it tended, on the whole, to be little more in the way of personal freedoms and mobility. Throughout the sixteenth and seventeenth centuries debate continued and decrees were written establishing and abolishing the system, as threats to the colonial system were differentially perceived. In this context see the documents compiled by A. C. Wilgus, ed., *Readings in Latin American Civilization* (New York: Barnes & Noble, 1946). More important, for the contemporary situation, however, is the fact that although color differences are important in South America, a caste system comparable to that in the United States has not emerged. Cf., for example, Donald Pierson, *Negroes in Brazil* (Chicago: U. of Chicago, 1942). On the origins of ethnic and racial stratification, see Donald L. Noel, "A Theory of the Origin of Ethnic Stratification," *Social Problems*, **16**:157–172 (Fall 1968).

The society of the United States of America was one that intended to be independent of foreign exploitation and European influences. The social structure that emerged was indeed different from the ones from which its members came.

Although ascriptive criteria were formally rejected as legitimate bases for social differentiation, the stratification structures that evolved paid homage to the characteristics of those who were most closely related, ethnically and socially, to the British. Thus, the earliest leaders of the new nation shared the same religious, educational, and social-class characteristics as their English cousins. That they shared similar values is, probably, for the most part, true. The American Revolution was not simply fought over differences in ideals or status, but over differential power and wealth as well. The leaders of the new nation effected a transfer of privilege from the British crown to themselves, and the stratification arrangements that emerged insured that the most influential positions remained in the hands of those most like the British. This was true whether one considers Massachusetts merchants or Virginia gentlemen farmers.

Even though a good deal is made of the opportunity for social mobility during the early decades of the growth of the nation, a class and caste system was in the making that reinforced the privileges of those of British and Northern European descent. As the Irish, German, Central and East Europeans, Jews, and Italians emigrated to the United States, relatively few were admitted into the highest ranks. Immigrant groups bettered their social circumstances *en masse,* but entry into the highest strata was closed to those who, even though they may have acquired the wealth and social graces of the ensconced classes, maintained their ethnic identities.

With regard to Jews, for example, note the following comment by Baltzell in discussing the *Social Register* list of 1905:

> the exclusion of (Jacob H.) Schiff was presumably due to the fact that he was a Jew, and Jews constituted a group somewhat apart; the fashionable clubs were almost exclusively gentile; and the "Social Register" was virtually a gentile register.[7]

Jacob Schiff's grandson, however, who married a gentile member of the elite, is listed in the 1940 *Social Register* and *Who's Who*. Thus, entry into elite groups, we suggest, is associated with abandoning ethnic identity. This process functions to maintain the status quo because it is only *individuals* who, after identity change, enter the highest strata—that is, it is

---

[7] E. Digby Baltzell, " 'Who's Who in America' and 'The Social Register,' " in *Class Status and Power,* Reinhard Bendix and Seymour Martin Lipset, ed. (New York: Free Press, 1966), p. 269.

opened to individuals qua individuals, not as members of a subordinated group.

Essentially the same process has operated in Great Britain, as reflected in Benjamin Disraeli's conversion to Christianity in order to become prime minister; and in Germany, by Felix Mendelssohn's conversion (by his father), who realized that many channels of social mobility in Germany were closed to Jews.

Groups that are set apart and denied access to associations based either on class, status, or power (in Weber's sense) tend to form what have been referred to as parallel classes—that is, vertically stratified classes that coexist horizontally with each other. It may be more accurate, however, to refer to them as quasi castes.

Quasi Castes in American Society

The American social context within which the caste concept historically has applied most conspicuously is to relationships between blacks and whites. Unlike the caste system of India, which was normatively legitimate, color-caste relations in the United States are a social reality that runs counter to fundamental, albeit abstract, values of American society. An interesting way to approach this assumption about quasi caste relations in the United States is to juxtapose characteristics of black-white relations in American society with some of the salient characteristics of Indian castes.

That castelike relations within the United States are changing can hardly be denied. For example, laws against black-white intermarriage, which until recently helped to support endogamous patterns, have been struck down by the courts. Job ceilings, to further illustrate progress, have at least formally been raised. What remains less clear is the degree to which the quasi caste model continues to be applicable.

If we could assume that achievement criteria operated relatively evenly across social relationships in occupation, kin, and other contexts, the view of American social stratification as simply horizontal would be adequate to understanding the processes of social mobility in the United States. However, such an assumption oversimplifies the empirical realities. Ascriptive criteria not only influence social distance in informal ways, but also provide bases for organized, persistent patterns of exclusion of identifiable ethnic subgroups from important spheres of life. Thus, as we have suggested, endogamous marriage and other forms of relationships is the rule rather than the exception in interethnic as well as black-white relations.

As previously noted, the quasi caste model closely resembles what Hollingshead and associates have termed "parallel class structures." They

TABLE 9.2

Traditional Caste and Quasi Caste Relations in India and the United States

	Indian Castes* (Formal)	Black-White Relations in the U.S.† (Informal)	Interethnic and Interreligious Relations in the U.S.‡ (Informal)
Heredity membership, fixed for life.	Yes	Yes	Yes (if identity is retained)
Endogamous marriage.	Yes	Yes	Yes
Contact with other castes is limited by restrictions such as touching, associating with, dining with, or eating food cooked by outsiders.	Yes	Yes (Except for eating food cooked by lower caste, breast feeding of infants, etc.)	Yes (degree of intimacy varies)
Consciousness of membership is emphasized by caste name, by identification of the individual in the eyes of the community, by his conformity to peculiar customs of his caste and by his subjugation to government by his caste.	Yes	Yes	Yes
The caste is united by a common traditional occupation, or belief in a common racial or tribal origin, by adherence to a common religious sect, or by some other common peculiarity.	Yes	Yes	Yes
The relative prestige of the different castes in any locality is well established and jealously guarded.	Yes	Yes	Yes (amorphous)

* Kingsley Davis, The Population of India and Pakistan, Princeton: Princeton University, (1951), p. 162.

† Compiled from a number of studies. The classic in this case is John Dollard, Caste and Class in a Southern Town (New York: Doubleday Anchor Books, 1957).

‡ Edward O. Laumann, "The Social Structure of Religious and Ethnoreligious Groups," American Sociological Review, **34**:182–197 (April 1969); and A. B. Hollingshead et al., "Trends in Social Stratification," American Sociological Review, **17**:685–686 (1952).

described New Haven as "differentiated *vertically* along racial, ethnic, and religious lines, and each of these vertical cleavages, in turn, is differentiated horizontally by a series of strata or classes that are encompassed within it." [8] One of the clearest examples of such parallel class structures is the existence in the community of seven different Junior Leagues, each for an appropriate group of upper-class young females.

> The top ranking organization is the New Haven Junior League which draws its membership from "Old Yankee" Protestant families whose daughters have been educated in private schools. The Catholic Charity League is next in rank and age—its membership is drawn from Irish-American families. In addition to this organization there are Italian and Polish Junior Leagues within the Catholic division of the society. The Swedish and Danish Junior Leagues are for properly connected young women in these ethnic groups, but they are Protestant. Then, too, the upper-class Jewish families have their Junior League. The Negroes have a Junior League for their top-drawer young women. This principle of parallel structures for a given class level, by religious, ethnic, and racial groups, proliferates throughout the community.[9]

These patterns are not so dramatically different from patterns that persist in many American communities, particularly in the eastern United States. As communities increase in size to where there is sufficient differentiation and identification by ethnic or racial groups, organized patterns of inclusive and exclusive relations emerge.

That the quasi caste pattern is changing can be readily observed. In what ways and at what levels is still another matter. In the East change has occurred at some conspicuous levels but the inner quasi caste circles remain closed. A series of articles dealing with "society" in various cities, published by *The New York Times,* describes Boston relations as more open than before World War II. Members of all ethnic groups work together on matters of civic concern. But intimate social relationships maintain an endogamous character. Even though the Boston debutants list now includes some Irish, Italian, and Slavic names, "In general, Boston society has come to be made up of an increasing number of concentric circles. The inner circle remains impregnable. Admission is by inheritance or tradition." [10] The New York context appears to be less caste-like near the top and more differentiated, ethnically and racially, at the lower rungs of the stratification ladder. The "international set," including social leaders whose positions grow out of high positions in commerce, industry, and international rela-

[8] A. B. Hollingshead, et al., "Trends in Social Stratification," *American Sociological Review,* **17**:685–686 (1952).

[9] Ibid.

[10] John H. Fenton, "Cabots and Howells of Boston Society Are Less Isolated—To a Degree," *New York Times,* 28 January, 1957, p. 25.

tions (including United Nations personages), at a conspicuous level *seem* to have severed the bonds of endogamous relationships. At the top, however, remnants of the highest stratum of the prewar years still maintain exclusive relations. "But despite the brilliance of the international set, the old guard still 'has its friends' and some of its precincts are still impenetrable—or nearly so. . . . The influence of the old guard is still potent and its contribution to culture and generality is immeasurable." [11] Descendants of the early Dutch "are found on the boards of leading civic and charitable institutions." [12] Along with the descendants of British settlers the Dutch form the backbone of the old guard.

The changes largely are superficial, however, as revealed in the following quotation:

> The city's great religious groups—47 per cent of its people are of Roman Catholic background, 26 per cent Jewish, and 22 per cent Protestant—have learned to work together and to play together.[13]

What is superficial and ephemeral about the purported inclusiveness of interethnic, interreligious, and interracial relationships is that even though particular individuals may be associating more frequently with one another, structures that enhance castelike relations persist. Thus, so long as private clubs, private schools, fraternities, and sororities remain socially segregated *in principle,* and they remain socially *preferred* by higher-caste groups, the caste and quasi caste character of social relationships will persist beyond the current generation.

[11] Russell Edwards, "Gilt and Glitter of New York Society Yield to the Alchemy of Time and Economics," *New York Times,* 4 March, 1957, p. 29.

[12] Ibid.

[13] Ibid.

10 Social Stratification and Social Mobility in Comparative Perspective

Cultural Similarities and Differences

In order to view structured social inequality and social mobility in a broader and more encompassing perspective, it is necessary to extend our analysis across societies. However, before proceeding, a word of caution is in order. In comparing social structure as well as the rate and extent of social mobility in different societies, we are crossing cultural lines that are considerably less clear than the geographic boundaries that separate nation-states. These cultural differences will manifest themselves as (1) differences in the extent to which social norms prescribe and stress achievement and mobility, (2) diverse criteria for evaluating success and failure, and (3) different social meanings and definitions of social mobility. Such differences are important obstacles in any comparative research or analysis.

To a degree, the experience, or "phenomenology," of social stratification and mobility are unique to a given society.[1] Nonetheless, comparable

---

[1] To assess the comparability of experiences, feelings, and the like would require extensive ethnographical studies in every society we wanted to compare. Such data are not generally available; and where they are, they will not be emphasized here because our primary emphasis is on the comparison of social structure and the equality of opportunity as manifested in rates of social mobility.

social structures can be identified in different societies and patterned changes in these structures can be associated with certain common antecedents and consequences, including changes in values and norms and other components of culture. Thus, in spite of the caution made earlier, social structure and culture are not independent phenomena. Rather, as Weber's classic analysis of the *Protestant Ethic and the Spirit of Capitalism* has shown, cultural (that is, religious) values have an important impact on social structure[2] and, conversely, as scholars in the area of the sociology of knowledge are quick to add, social structure is an important determinant of cultural values and ideas.[3] The reciprocal relationship between culture and social structure is particularly evident in the association between technological development (that is, industrialization) and changes in occupational values. As societies industrialize, there is a corresponding development of "modern" occupational values in virtually every cultural context in which industrialization occurs. In turn, the development of modern occupational values facilitates continuing social structural changes including, for example, changes in the structure and role of the family and, perhaps most importantly, continued urbanization and industrialization.[4]

Industrialization and Cultural Values

Lenski's analysis of the distributive systems in primitive and modern societies indicated the important role of technology for the structure of social inequality.[5] It is more than a coincidence that industrialization, the organization and appplication of technology, is one of the most commonly emphasized social structural variables in comparative research. One of the classic theoretical statements underlying this emphasis has been offered by Kingsley Davis.[6] In preindustrial societies, Davis argued, social position is ascribed, determined by one's location in a kinship system. Such ascription is further reinforced by cultural values, which emphasize an orientation to tradition. Part of this tradition is that sons are expected to follow in their

[2] Max Weber, *The Protestant Ethnic and the Spirit of Capitalism*, trans. Talcott Parsons (New York: Scribners, 1958).

[3] See, for example, Gunter Remmling, *Road to Suspicion* (Englewood Cliffs, N.J.: Prentice Hall, 1967).

[4] Reinhard Bendix, "Industrialization, Ideologies, and Social Structure," *American Sociological Review*, 26:616–623 (1959); W. W. Rostow, "The Takeoff into Self-sustained Growth," *The Economic Journal*, 64:25–48 (1956); Wilbert E. Moore and Arnold S. Feldman, eds., *Labor Commitment and Social Change in Developing Areas* (New York: Social Science Research Council, 1960).

[5] Gerhard E. Lenski, *Power and Privilege: A Theory of Social Stratification* (New York: McGraw Hill, 1966).

[6] Kingsley Davis, "The Role of Class Mobility in Economic Development," *Population Review*, 6 (October, 1962).

father's occupational footsteps. With industrialization, however, the emphasis on tradition is weakened, ascribed status based on kinship becomes increasingly less salient, and there is a greater probability of intergenerational movement.

Upon close inspection, two distinct propositions may be identified in the theory offered by Davis and others. There is, first, the hypothesis that rates of mobility vary directly in relation to degree of industrialization. The second assertion is that variation in rates of mobility can be explained best by the changes in value orientations that are generated by industrialization. It is apparent that the second hypothesis rests on the first. A consistent relationship between mobility and industrialization must be demonstrated before the relationship can be (causally) attributed to industrialized values. Viewed conversely, failure to confirm the first hypothesis precludes confirmation of the second. Our initial attention will, therefore, be directed at the former.

One limited, but very important, aspect of this proposition concerns mobility into the ranks of high-status, or elite, groups. Robert Marsh has studied this type of movement in two samples: one a preindustrial society, the other a highly industrial society. The first contained approximately 1,000 government officials in China, between 1831 and 1879. The industrial sample, taken from a study by Robert Perrucci, consisted of about 2,500 contemporary American engineers, many of whom were high-ranking officials of large organizations.[7]

This approach raises some immediate questions concerning the comparability of the two groups. They are most alike, Marsh states, in their means of entry into an elite group. All of the engineers held degrees from the same university and all of the officials held degrees from the same government examination system. Furthermore, it would be difficult to find two more comparable groups. Current American government officials would not be more comparable, for example, because their nineteenth-century Chinese counterparts had relatively greater prestige.[8]

Marsh first analyzed both groups with respect to intergenerational mobility. This entailed noting the status level of fathers of persons in both types of elite groups and then comparing the distributions of the fathers'

---

[7] Robert Marsh, "Values, Demand and Social Mobility," *American Sociological Review*, **28**:565–575 (Aug. 1963). Cf. also, Robert Perrucci and Graham Kinloch, "Sponsored and Contest Mobility Among College Graduates," *Social Forces,* 36–45 (Sept. 1969); and Robert Perruci, "The Significance of Intra-Occupational Mobility: Some Methodological and Theoretical Notes, Together with a Case Study of Engineers," *American Sociological Review,* **26**:874–883 (Dec. 1961).

[8] In addition, the persons included in both samples were divided into three subcategories to permit more precise comparisons of relatively elite groups. For example, the highest American group consisted of engineers who had become company presidents and vice-presidents. They were compared to the highest-ranking Chinese officials.

status. The results show a more evenly distributed pattern of fathers' status for the engineers than the officials. Specifically, almost three fourths of the Chinese officials were sons of the highest-status fathers in their society, compared to 40 per cent of the American engineers. Thus, as expected, mobility into elite groups appears to be more open in industrial than in preindustrial society.

Marsh then compared the two groups with respect to career advancement—that is, the relationship between the position of origin in the organization and the position eventually attained. In both groups, the influence of family background (as indicated by fathers' status) is found to be minimal. In other words, although movement into the elite group is affected by fathers' status, this influence virtually terminates after recruitment occurs (and this is true in both groups).

This similarity in intragenerational patterns among American engineers and Chinese officials is surprising, and it is emphasized by Marsh who states:

> This finding must not be dismissed as "obvious." In a preindustrial society like China, with a high degree of kinship solidarity, especially at the elite level, it has often been held or implied that advancement would vary with family background, regardless of similarities in education and in career seniority. But this is not the case.[9]

In sum, fathers' status is shown to exert a rather small, and approximately equal, effect on promotion within elite groups both in the contemporary United States and in nineteenth-century China. Initial recruitment, however, is affected more in the preindustrial than in the industrial sample. Thus, the hypothesis initially presented corncerning industrialization—values—mobility may be substantially true, at least intergenerationally. However, when Marsh held structurally forced mobility constant, the two societies were seen to be substantially more alike; that is, the greater intergenerational openness of the contemporary United States was due primarily to forced demands, and therefore, not to achievement-oriented values.

To pursue this finding further, Marsh subsequently took a larger sample of societies, varying greatly in their degree of industrialization. For each of the thirty-two societies included, three measures were obtained:

1. degree of industrialization
2. elite demand (that is, structurally forced mobility into elite positions)
3. elite mobility (that is, the total amount of upward intergenerational mobility into elite positions)

---

[9] Marsh, op. cit., p. 571. However, the study by Perrucci and Kinloch, loc. cit., shows that advancement in higher-level occupational categories is indirectly influenced by family social position.

The correlations among all three measures are direct and strong. They are interpreted by Marsh as indicating that industrialization produces both elite demand and elite mobility. However, the strongest relationship ($r = .95$) is between elite demand and elite mobility. Thus, virtually all of the variation in amounts of elite mobility is due to structural modification, or demand.

The conclusion suggested by these findings supports the first proposition, which viewed intergenerational differences in elite mobility as due to industrialization. With respect to the second proposition, however, even though achievement values may be strongest in industrial societies, the increased rate of mobility in such societies does not appear to be a consequence of these values. In diagram form, the relationships indicated are as follows:

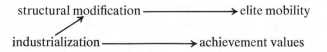

Let us reflect on these findings for a moment. If increased openness, at least with respect to elites, is due to changes in demand rather than values, what about motivational factors? That is, while industrialization is creating occupational opportunities people must be willing to fill these new positions. However, commitment to traditional values could inhibit this process of occupational transition. Thus, the question of motivation leads us to focus on how changes in occupational prestige intervene in the relationship between industrialization and comparative intergenerational mobility.

James R. Wood and Eugene A. Weinstein have examined the preceding issues in a study of Uruguay.[10] They began by questioning whether the new jobs created by industrialization would be evaluated according to traditional values or whether industrialization would first produce a new set of evaluative criteria. If the former, then occupational prestige hierarchies would be a barrier to further industrialization and mobility. Because of great variations in its cities, Uruguay presents an excellent country in which to examine these relationsihps. It contains a number of small, rural, and somewhat isolated cities in which little industrialization has occurred. The seaport capital of Montevideo, by contrast, is an industrialized city of a million persons. There are also several intermediate types. This investigation was carried out in seven cities, varying from the most to the least industrialized.

In terms of its traditional culture, Uruguay is representative of traditional Spanish culture. This entails a disdain for manual labor of any kind,

---

[10] James R. Wood and Eugene A. Weinstein, "Industrialization in Uruguay," *American Journal of Sociology*, **72**:47–57 (July 1966).

and an orientation toward noneconomic "self-improvement": for example, a cultivated use of leisure, an emphasis on nonutilitarian intellectual development, and like sentiments. By contrast to the orientations toward hard work and economic profit that are generally associated with industrialization, the traditional Uruguayan values would seem to present a barrier to industrialization.

To focus on this possibility, the investigators distributed almost five hundred questionnaires to students in the seven Uruguayan cities. All were finishing their final year in secondary schools, after which nearly all were going to enter the labor market. Thus, questions asking them to choose occupations they considered desirable were highly relevant. Specifically, they were presented with thirty paired occupations: one modern, one traditional. Each student was then given a score indicating his relative preference for either traditional or modern occupations. In addition, the investigators administered an attitude scale dealing with acceptance of traditional values: willingness to work with hands, importance of leisure, and the like.

The results showed that in communities with higher concentrations of factories (that is, more industrialized) the students' selections were more likely to involve the modern rather than traditional occupations. However, there was virtually no correlation between industrialization of the community and the students' affirmation of traditional values.

There is an apparent contradiction in these results that makes them very interesting. The traditional cultural values—the broad evaluative categories—did not vary in response to industrialization, but the evaluation of specific occupations did. Wood and Weinstein resolve the apparent contradiction by proposing that occupational evaluations change in response to exposure. As students and others observe the rewards of persons in modern occupations—factory workers, for example—their evaluations of the specific occupations change. Cultural values, however, change at a slower rate.

L. F. Liss provides us with a study of occupational choice in a modern industrialized nation, the USSR. In it he notes the importance of "conceptions about the occupational spectrum and the demands which the chosen occupation makes on those engaged in it," as well as the importance of social-origin factors.

ɔ

The Social Conditioning of
Occupational Choice*†

L. F. Liss

The choice of an occupation requiring a corresponding level of education is a complex and protracted social process which can be divided into the following main stages:

The *preliminary stage* involves the formation of occupational plans. This is the period in which occupational interests and inclinations arise and develop, and having become consolidated in the course of their development, are transformed into a definite occupational focus which forms the area of occupational preference. This is the foundation on which the choice of a future occupation is made. It is during this stage that an orientation toward a definite activity and the mode of life associated with it is developed. When it is a matter of selecting the first occupation, this stage corresponds, as a rule, to the training period in general-education schools.

The *stage of adopting and implementing* the decision is characterized by the fact that the individual, having made a choice, then attempts to implement it by gaining admission to an appropriate educational institution. During this stage an important role is played by the individual's perception of his interests, inclinations, and actual abilities, as well as by his conceptions about the occupational spectrum and the demands which the chosen occupation makes on those engaged in it and the chosen educational institution makes on its students. Not only does the individual choose an occupation at this stage, but the occupation selects the individual (the selection system in admissions to specialized educational institutions).

The *stage of occupational training* consolidates the previously apparent occupational interests and inclinations on the basis of a fuller conception of the content of the chosen specialty acquired in the process of training. Occupational knowledge, skills, habits, and value orientations are developed during this period. The process of selection continues simultaneously—those who change their occupational interests leave the educational institution, as do those who show an inability to study there.

In the formation of an occupational direction, the general social conditions of the socialist society create a common foundation in the form of the corresponding value orientations. As numerous studies have shown,[1] the orientations which are most characteristic of Soviet youth are associated with essential matters—the content of the future occupation and the individual's relation to society, his yearning to be useful to society. Among university applicants this is a yearning to understand and discover the new: a yearning

* From Tartuskii Gosudarstvennyi Universitet, *Materialy konferentsii "Kommunisticheskoe vospitanie studenchestva,"* Tartu, 1971, pp. 137–150.
† Reprinted with permission from *International Journal of Sociology*, **3**: 275–288 (Spring–Summer, 1973), published by International Arts and Science Press, Inc., White Plains, New York 10603.

339

for labor that is creative and useful to society, and that is connected with an interest in the chosen sphere of knowledge, and that is based on the conception of the scholar as a creator, a discoverer, whose activity is among the most useful for society. The predominance of these values reflects the shared world outlook of Soviet youth, its high moral aspirations, and that romantic elevation which is characteristic of young people.

It is against this background, and under the influence of both common and specific social circumstances (which still differ substantially under socialism), that the area of occupational preference is developed and becomes the basis on which the concrete choice is made. Given the variety of channels through which the individual is connected with society (school, out-of-school institutions, the system of mass communications) and its strata and groups (through family, friends, neighbors, etc.), the specific character of the individual (socially determined on the basis of native characteristics) predetermines the variety of types of behavior even within similar social circumstances of individual development. Among university applicants, formation of the area of occupational preference and the concrete choice are influenced by such factors as the study of particular subjects at school, the reading of books, journals, and newspapers; various personal contacts (with friends, teachers, specialists); activities in specialized classes and schools, in various clubs; participation in olympiads, etc.

Study of the composition of applicants' families and of their places of settlement shows the connection between social origins and the formation of occupational orientations. Although individuals from the most varied strata and groups of our society aspire to gain admission to the University,* the applicants' parents are mostly employed in primarily mental work[2] (64–66 per cent of the men and 63–66 per cent of the women) and are characterized by a high educational level (65–67 per cent of the men and 58–60 per cent of the women have a higher, secondary-specialized, or secondary-general education). The most sizable groups among the men are engineering-technical personnel, executives of enterprises or their structural subdivisions, personnel in the sciences and in education, as well as industrial workers. Among women the major groups are personnel in the sciences and education, engineering-technical personnel, medical personnel, and planning and accounting workers.

Although the occupations and educational levels of the parents are closely connected, a clearer picture of the character of the families and their connections with different social strata is obtained by considering family structure with regard to both parents (see Table 1).

Families which include specialists with higher or secondary specialized education predominate (60–66 per cent). In a third of the families the parents are employed in primarily manual labor. Families from different places of settlement have different characteristics with respect to occupation and, especially, education. Thus, while higher education predominates among applicants' families from large cities in which both parents are employed in

* The data and general discussion are based on Liss's studies of applicants and students at Novosibirsk State University.

TABLE 1
Family Structure of Applicants to Novosibirsk State University, 1970,
by Education of Parents (in per cent of total)

		Education of Mothers							
		H	*SS*	*SG*	*IS*	*P*	*Total*	*Single Fathers*	*Total, Fathers*
	H	18.3	7.3	2.2	1.7	0.5	30.0	0.3	30.3
Education	SS	3.6	9.1	2.5	5.4	1.0	21.6	0.1	21.7
of	SG	0.4	1.0	1.5	2.0	0.6	5.5	0.2	5.7
fathers	IS	1.0	3.5	1.1	8.0	3.6	17.2	0.2	17.4
	P	0.3	1.0	0.7	2.8	6.3	11.1	0.5	11.6
Total		23.6	21.9	8.0	19.9	12.0	85.4	1.3	86.7
Single mothers		3.2	3.8	0.8	3.2	2.3	13.3		
Total, mothers		26.8	25.7	8.8	23.1	14.3	98.7		

Note: Education groups are: H—higher education; SS—secondary specialized; SG—secondary general; IS—incomplete secondary; P—primary or less.

mental work requiring either a higher or secondary specialized education, secondary education is predominant among analogous rural families. We should note an essential stability in the distribution of different types of families over the last five years (both with respect to occupation and education), which means a stability in the orientation toward a university education for youth among the various social strata which they represent.

The distinctive nature of the University applicants' families, as an index of the influence of a social stratum on the formation of occupational orientations, is clearly revealed when we compare these families with the social structure of society (according to data from the All-Union Population Census of 1959 for the RSFSR).[3]

We take the age group closest to the age of the bulk of applicants' parents, and also the families of secondary school graduates (using 1966 data from V. N. Shubkin's study of the Novosibirsk Region). The general results reveal considerably more individuals employed in skilled mental work among families of secondary school graduates compared to the employed population as a whole, and the same is true of University applicants' families compared to the families of secondary school graduates.[4] Moreover, the relative shares of different groups of occupations among applicants' parents vary unevenly compared to the employed population as a whole. The proportion of agricultural workers is particularly low compared to other groups of workers, while the proportion of personnel in science and education and engineering-technical personnel is high compared to other groups employed in primarily mental work. The same tendency is revealed in the dynamics of educational levels. While among urban males from the corresponding groups of the whole population, 6.3 per cent have a higher education and 11.5 per cent have a secondary specialized education, among parents of secondary school graduates the figures are 20.0 per cent and 12.0 per cent respectively, and among applicants' parents they are 39.9 per cent and 23.0 per cent. The comparable figures for urban females are, for higher education, 6.4 per cent, 13.4 per cent, and 26.9 per cent, and for secondary education—12.8 per cent, 9.0 per cent, and 23.0 per cent.

University applicants come from different regions of the country, but the bulk are from Siberia and the Far East. Large cities (with a population of 100,000 or more) are the most typical places of settlement, accounting for 56–60 per cent of the applicants, while villages account for 15–18 per cent (these types of settlements comprise 34 per cent and 39 per cent, respectively, of the population of the RSFSR, and 33 per cent and 37 per cent, respectively, of the population of Siberia and the Far East).[5]

Given the differences in the composition of applicants' families from areas of different degrees of urbanization, it must be recognized that the formation of occupational objectives by young people is connected with both the character of the family and the area of residence. Both of these factors are, so to speak, superimposed on each other, and ultimately determine the specific features of behavior.

Although the applicants for the various specialties have much in common as regards their social origins, which affects their integrating attraction to the scientific sphere, certain specialties are chosen by applicants who have distinctive features with respect to both the composition of their families and the extent to which they come from different types of settlements. All of the data show that the orientation of different strata to the education of their children, as well as the occupational focus of youth from different social strata, vary depending on the sphere and character of labor, the level of education, and the nature of the place of settlement which is specific to the given social stratum.

This tendency may be observed in the evaluation of the attractiveness of occupations by graduates of secondary schools from different social strata,[6] in their career plans, in the differing composition of applicants to the individual higher educational institutions, and indirectly—in the differing social composition of students at individual higher schools and technicums.[7] Thus, studies conducted in Novosibirsk Region show that at technicums, during the last five years, workers and their children comprised 62–65 per cent of the students, and employees and their children—22–24 per cent. At higher schools the corresponding figures were 40–42 per cent and 49–52 per cent. Moreover, the social composition of the students at specific higher educational institutions and technicums varies depending on the kind of specialized training offered. During this period, for example, workers and their children comprised 19–28 per cent of the students at the University, 28–40 per cent at the Medical Institute, 37–47 per cent at the Electrical Engineering Institute, and 55–63 per cent at the Institute for Railroad Engineers.

Thus, the specific nature of applicants' social origins observed in our study of University applicants reflects objectively existing tendencies in society for the formation of young people's occupational goals to be connected with the character of the social stratum from which they derive. This connection is revealed both at the level of general plans (to continue one's education) and particular ones (the choice of a specific occupational direction). It must be emphasized that there is no social exclusiveness in the formation of occupational inclinations of youth under socialism, that the occupational goals of youth from the different strata are varied. But the very fact of belonging to a certain social stratum, the greater familiarity with the kind of employment typical for its members, and the greater opportunity for assimilating its mode of behavior, create the conditions for developing the kind of occupational orientation which is more typical for this stratum. To the extent that the impact of the social stratum is exercised against the back-ground of many other influences operating through the schools, the mass communication media, and various personal contacts, it manifests itself as a tendency toward a high degree of preference for a definite group of occupations.

Both the sex and age of the individual have a certain impact on the choice of occupation. Data covering the last nine years show that physics is most popular among male applicants—40–53 per cent seek admission to physics departments, followed by 13–21 per cent who apply for mathematics and 10–14 per cent who aspire to applied mathematics. Chemistry, geology, and history each account for 5–8 per cent, economic cybernetics for 4–6 per cent, biology for 3–5 per cent, and linguistics for 0.3–0.7 per cent. Girls are distributed more evenly among the various specialties: 15–20 per cent seek admission to chemistry departments, while the figures for mathematics, biology, economic cybernetics, and history are 11–16 per cent in each case; 7–11 per cent apply for physics; applied mathematics and linguistics each account for 7–9 per cent; and geology attracts 3–4 per cent. The consequence is a clear division of all University specialties into "primarily male"—physics, geology, applied mathematics, and mathematics (with the shares of male applicants accounting for 86–90 per cent, 67–72 per cent, 67–69 per cent and 57–64 per cent, respectively)—and "primarily female"—chemistry, history, economic cybernetics, biology, linguistics (with the shares of female appli-cants accounting for 71–76 per cent in 1962–1965 and 59–62 per cent in 1967–1970,* 62–66 per cent, 71–75 per cent, 66–74 per cent, and 89–94 per cent, respectively).

The relationship between the applicants' sex and the preference for par-ticular specialties may also be observed among applicants at more homoge-neous technical higher educational institutions.[8] Analysis of applicants' ques-tionnaires shows that the selective attitudes of boys and girls toward different kinds of activities emerge at an early school age, and continue during the period of intensive formation of interests and inclinations. All this testifies to the existence in society of certain stereotypes of occupational preference according to sex, which is confirmed by differences in the ratings of occupa-tions by secondary school graduates and teachers, and by the actual feminiza-tion of a number of occupations in whole branches of the economy. Under

---

* These figures, for 1962–1965 and 1967–1970, presumably apply to chemistry. The ones which follow presumably apply to history, economic cybernetics, biology, and linguistics, in that order, and are for the whole period 1962–1970.

current conditions these stereotypes are not always connected with the essence of the occupation itself, and apparently they have deep historical-psychological causes which call for special study. At the same time, the attitudes of boys and girls toward individual specialties are not completely static, and are subject to change as a result of purposeful activity. But stereotyped preferences are so deep that the process of change is proceeding slowly and, apparently, has a definite limit.

A study of the age composition of applicants shows that in recent years they have become younger (this has also been noted in other studies).[9] Most are 17–18 years old and have completed secondary school in the year of enrollment or in the preceding year. Although this is the general tendency, there are some differences in age composition among individual specialties. One consequence of the "youthful" composition of the applicants is that their life experience is limited (to schooling in most cases), and the same is also true with respect to the channels through which they are connected with society. This also applies to those who have worked after completing secondary school, 75 per cent of whom worked for no more than a year. Although this year, spent in new surroundings, has not passed without leaving any mark at all, we can hardly say that there has been any important change in the applicants' social status compared with that of their families, or that they have assimilated new value orientations and norms of behavior. Therefore, in appraising the social composition of applicants and students at higher schools, it is not enough to study only their own social position just prior to admission, without considering the social position of their families.

Thus, the formation of occupational orientations is determined through different channels of influence which are connected with both general and specific social circumstances. Within this framework the individual himself is an active participant in the ongoing process. As analysis of questionnaires, school references and other materials shows, he strives to express the interests which have emerged in the form of some kind of activity—a search for and reading of literature, club activities, participation in olympiads, conversations with specialists, heightened attention to the particular subjects in school, etc. Perception of his own abilities in performing these activities also has an impact on the consolidation of his occupational orientation. An indicator of abilities is success in those kinds of activities, accessible to young people, which are connected in some way with the chosen occupation. The role of external factors in this situation consists in providing greater or lesser opportunities for involvement in these activities.

Analysis shows that in selecting a specific higher educational institution and a specialty within it, the applicants consider, directly or indirectly, many factors: the geographic location and character of the institution; the peculiarities of its operation; whether it includes specialties which interest them, or related specialties; the economy's need for specialists in those areas (which is reflected in the institution's admissions plans); the intensity of competition and associated factors; and the difficulty of admission associated with the institutions's examination requirements.

When we consider differences in the occupational aspirations of boys and girls, differences in the social composition of applicants for the individual specialties, and so on, we can conclude that the attractiveness of a specialty is determined both by societal needs for the corresponding specialists, as well as by the nature and intensity of the interest in it on the part of boys and girls, and of youth from different social strata. The role of interest is particularly evident in heightened striving for certain specialties despite the unfavorable situation created by the high degree of competition for them. Thus, the prestige of occupations is formed on the basis of societal needs as these are refracted through societal, group, and individual interests. The resulting contradiction between societal and individual interests is resolved by means of competitive selection of the most deserving, prepared, and capable individuals who have passed their entrance examinations. This kind of selection process, although it basically satisfies the needs of society (which is interested in the most qualified performance of every occupational activity) and the interests of particular individuals (who are interested in the realization of their creative potentials in the kind of activity for which they are most suited), nonetheless contains certain contradictions. The social character of the contradictions arising in the process of competitive selection requires special study. Here we shall examine some of those connected with the influence of the personal qualities and social characteristics of applicants on the results of University entrance examinations. Performance on entrance examinations is an indicator of the possibility of attaining one's occupational choice at the stage of admission to a higher school.

In the case of difficult entrance examinations whose emphasis is predominantly on subjects in the physics-mathematics cycle, boys do significantly better than girls (this divergence already begins with the mathematics results). The influence of the degree of interest and purposefulness may be observed in the fact that among physics applicants whose secondary school references directly or indirectly noted an interest in subjects in the physics-mathematics cycle, one out of every two passed the examinations, while among the others it was only one out of every six. Moreover, the closer the content of the examination subjects to the specific features of a specialty, the less the impact of different social factors. The influence of levels of ability is shown indirectly in the fact that among a homogeneous group of youth from large Siberian cities, the examination results in mathematics were distributed in accordance with their secondary school performance in this subject.

Examination results are also connected with the social position of applicants' parents. Among those who come from families in which both parents are employed in highly skilled mental work, 59 per cent passed the examinations, while 55 per cent did so where the parents are in less skilled mental work, and 39 per cent where the parents are in primarily manual labor. The examination results are most clearly differentiated with respect to the educational level of the family (see Table 2).

A more detailed analysis shows that the greater or lesser role of the family is also connected with the degree of urbanization of the place of residence (which affects the character of the family and the school), the sex of the applicant, and the nature of the specialty. The more the applicant is oriented to a

Table 2
Results of Entrance Examinations, Novosibirsk State University,
1967, 1968, 1970
Depending on Educational Level of Applicants' Parents,
Where Both Parents Have Same Educational Level
(Per Cent Passing Examinations)

		Education of Parents			
Year	Higher	Secondary Specialized	Secondary General	Incomplete Secondary	Primary or Less
1967	57	41	37	28	23
1968	66	54	43	48	38
1970	71	50	42	36	33

specialty and the closer the connection between the examination and the specialty, the less the influence of the family on examination results, and vice versa. The role of the family's educational level is not only explained by the fact that is determines how favorable or unfavorable the circumstances and atmosphere will be to development, and the intensity of the orientation to inherit this educational level, but also by the fact that this characteristic synthesizes in itself the influence of a number of others: the parents' employment status, the family's place of residence, etc. It is as though the family's education contains within itself the essence of the specific social circumstances of the individual's development, and this strengthens its differentiating function.

Although in statistical terms the applicants' examination results are distributed in accordance with their secondary school performance, the differences in the quality of schools is reflected in the fact that even among applicants who received the highest ratings in their graduation certificates we find the whole gamut of examination grades (including unsatisfactory grades). The best results were obtained by those who had been in specialized classes and schools (specializing in mathematics or physics-mathematics). The greater the demands made on entering students, the closer the connection between the place of residence and examination results. Applicants from large cities show better results than those from rural areas (54 per cent and 46 per cent, respectively, of these groups passed the examinations).*

All this material shows the dependence of University entrance examination results on both the applicants' personal characteristics and individual orientations and the specific social circumstances of their development.

The degree of success in studies at higher schools is also connected with both the students' personal qualities and their social origins. Study of data for the University that cover a number of years shows the dual nature of this connection: on the one hand, the connection is with the earlier conditions of

---

* It is not clear whether the figures refer to the relative shares of these two groups in the total number who passed the examinations, or the proportion of individuals in each group who passed the examinations. The latter seems more likely.

development of the student, and on the other—with the results of the University entrance examinations. Thus, while one-third of the workers' children who were admitted during 1966–1968 dropped out, and one-quarter of employees' children did so (the chief reason for dropping out was manifest or latent failure in studies), among those who received the highest grades on entrance examinations only one-fifth dropped out, and among those who received lower grades, two-fifths dropped out. This testifies to the fact that the social circumstances of the individual's earlier development leave their mark on his success at the higher school to the degree that they are reflected in the extent of his preparation for higher education.

Thus, the social conditioning of occupational choice may be observed at all the main stages of this process. While at the stage of formation of occupational orientations it is primarily connected with the existence of certain models of behavior among the different social strata and groups, at the stage of implementation of occupational choice and during the period of occupational training the primary factors are the differences in the cultural levels of these groups and in the quality of the educational system and the character of different places of settlement, all of which, in combination, create more or less favorable external conditions for the development of young people.

NOTES

1. Our material was obtained in studying applicants and students at Novosibirsk State University.
2. Our classification of employments is based on that used in the All-Union Population Census of 1959.
3. *Itogi Vsesoiuznoi perepisi naseleniia 1959 g. RSFSR,* Moscow, 1963.
4. L. F. Liss, "On the Stability of the Characteristics and Specific Features of the Social Origins of University Applicants," *Sotsial 'noe prognozirovanie v oblasti obrazovaniia,* Novosibirsk, 1969.
5. *Narodnoe khoziaistvo RSFSR v 1967. Statisticheskii ezhegodnik,* Moscow, 1967.
6. See V. V. Vodzinskaia, "Orientations Toward Occupations," *Molodezh' i trud,* Moscow, 1970; *Kolichestvennye metody v sotsiologicheskikh issledovaniiakh,* Novosibirsk, 1964.
7. See V. V. Vodzinskaia, "On the Problem of the Social Conditioning of Occupational Choice," *Chelovek i obshchestvo,* II, Leningrad, 1967; O. I. Zotova, A. G. Ashkinazi, and Iu. P. Kovalenko. *O nekotorykh sotsiologicheskikh aspektakh vybora professii vypuskni-kami srednykh shkol,* Moscow, 1970; M. N. Rutkevich and F. R. Filippov, *Sotsial'nye peremeshcheniia,* Moscow, 1970; *Effektivnost' podgotovki spetsialistov,* Kaunas, 1969.
8. L. T. Pesochina, "Some Generalized Characteristics of a Higher Educational Institution and Its Structural Subdivisions," *Materialy seminara po programmirovannomu obycheniiu i nauchnoi organizatsii uchebnogo protsessa,* No. 4, Novosibirsk, 1968.
9. See B. Rubin and Iu. Kolesnikov, *Student glazami sotsiologa,* Rostov State University Publishing House, 1968; M. N. Rutkevich and L. I. Sennikova, "On the Social Composition of the Student Body in the USSR and Its Changing Tendencies," *Sotsial'nye razlichiia i ikh preodolenie,* Sverdlovsk, 1969.

The general conclusion that emerges is that industrialization increases the exposure of young persons to well paying modern jobs. Their evaluations of the occupations change accordingly, producing a modern type of occupational prestige hierarchy. This resolves the motivational problem raised earlier. Broad cultural values seem much more resistant to change; however, evidence from other countries indicates that they do eventually change. In Japanese cities, for example, industrialization probably has been more pervasive and of longer duration than in Uruguayan cities. Correspondingly, studies indicate that quite different cultural values coexist in Japan. In the more industrial urban centers, industrial values predominate; but traditional values remain quite salient in rural sectors.[11]

Industrialization and the Hierarchy of Occupational Prestige

The studies thus far reviewed suggest that industrialization leads to a modern occupational-prestige hierarchy. This was initially supported as an explicit cross-cultural hypothesis by Alex Inkeles and Peter H. Rossi.[12] They selected six countries: the United States, Great Britain, the USSR, Japan, New Zealand, and West Germany. The data on occupational prestige were taken from various surveys conducted in each of the countries in about 1950. The surveys included between about one thousand and three thousand respondents, but they differed substantially in their procedures. Nevertheless, the results are interesting, if only tentative.

For the occupations that could be identified as comparable, the correlations between their ranking in the various countries ranged from .83 (New Zealand and the USSR) to .97 (Great Britain and Germany). The average correlation was quite high, approximately .90, indicating a substantial degree of agreement in occupational prestige in all the countries, despite the disparities in the research designs.

To give the reader a little more familiarity with the nature of this research, several occupations are presented in the following table along with their rank in the various countries.[13]

Occupation	U.S.	Germany	Great Britain	New Zealand	Japan
Physician (doctor or medical officer)	1.5	2.0	1.0	1.0	5.0
Company director (factory manager)	9.0	4.0	2.0	2.0	4.0
Schoolteacher	16.0	9.0	10.0	10.0	12.0
Machine operator	28.5	18.0	21.0	20.0	22.0

[11] David M. Lewis and Archibald O. Haller, "Rural Urban Differences," *Rural Sociology*, **29**:324–329 (Sept. 1964).

[12] Alex Inkeles and Peter H. Rossi, "National Comparisons of Occupational Prestige," *American Journal of Sociology*, **61**:329–339 (June 1956).

[13] Rank is based on an occupation's location among the occupations compared by Inkeles and Rossi, ibid. Apparent discrepancies are sometimes due to unequal numbers of occupations representing various countries. For this reason, ranking in the USSR is excluded from this table.

Inkeles and Rossi concluded their study by emphasizing the observed similarities: "there is a relatively invariable hierarchy of prestige associated with the industrial system."[14] Furthermore, they proposed, when differences in prestige between nations do occur, they are probably the result of variations in degree of industrialization. Conceptually, this is an argument for the structuralist position, asserting that an industrial system of production generates its own prestige values, with traditional culture patterns seen as exerting little influence.

Their conclusions seem to be in general accord with their findings—despite the methodological problems noted—except for the homogeneity of their sample. That is, all six of the societies studied by Inkeles and Rossi were relatively highly industrialized. Such societies, it may be argued, probably also share features in common other than industrialization. Perhaps, therefore, their similarities in occupational prestige should not be attributed primarily to industrialization.

In order to assess the preceding possibility, Hodge and his associates focused on comparative prestige judgments in a broader, less homogeneous sample of societies.[15] Specifically, they studied twenty-three countries, including the six utilized by Inkeles and Rossi and other highly industrialized societies (for example, Canada and the Netherlands). However, the sample also included a variety of less industrialized countries, such as the Belgian Congo and India.

In addition to correlating the ratings of specific occupations in these varied nations, the researchers also examined the comparisons among blue-collar, white-collar, and all nonfarm occupations. This latter analysis followed from their assumption that cultural differences might account for specific variations in occupational ratings and that these might be obscured unless one focused on specific categories:

> Cultural variation may act to produce inversions among occupations within a narrow range of prestige positions. Thus, disagreement in the relative ratings accorded to such functionaries as priests, high government officials, scientists and businessmen . . . may be the major consequence of cultural differences. . . . But we can hardly expect that cultural traditions will produce inversions of dominant functionaries and blue collar workers. . . .[16]

Furthermore, when the similarity between all occupations is examined, the resultant correlations are probably influenced by the extreme occupations; that is, some occupations are always very high, whereas others are always

[14] Ibid., p. 339.
[15] Robert W. Hodge, Donald J. Treiman, and Peter H. Rossi, "A Comparative Study of Occupational Prestige," in *Class, Status and Power*, Reinhard Bendix and Seymour Martin Lipset, ed. (New York: Free Press, 1966).
[16] Ibid., pp. 311–312.

very low. Therefore, when a strong correlation coefficient results, it may obscure inconsistences among middle-scoring occupations.

Their findings, even within specific categories, however, continue to indicate very strong intersocietal similarities. Among all nonfarm occupations in the twenty-three varied countries for which they had data, the average over-all blue-collar occupations is somewhat lower, .83. They conclude the following:

> Major institutional complexes serving central societal needs which exist in all societies, and the common bureaucratic hierarchy imposed by the nation state, act to insure . . . similarity between nations in the white-collar prestige hierarchy . . . but these factors cannot be expected to induce a corresponding degree of prestige similarity at the blue-collar level. However, the fundamental conclusion that wide differences in cultural traditions . . . are insufficient to produce major inversions in the occupational-prestige hierarchy is not altered by these findings, since even the lower average within blue-collar titles is still sizeable.[17]

Perhaps surprisingly, the investigators have noted that these strong similarities persist even when societies that differ vastly in level of industrialization are compared. This suggests modification of the earlier Inkeles-Rossi conclusion that emphasized industrialization as generating consistent occupational values. Rather, these similarities are produced, they now conclude, by similarities in more fundamental structural organization. Essentially, they conceptually differentiate between societies according to degree of complexity. This pushes us toward a dichotomous view of "primitive" societies, on the one hand, and "modern" ones on the other. The former are characterized by a general lack of social differentiation. The specialization common to modern societies, regardless (within limits) of their degree of industrialization, produces needs for control and coordination, as well as values that uniformly emphasize health, education, and the like. These needs and values, in turn, result in uniform occupational-prestige hierarchies.

Other studies also support this emphasis on societal complexity. Within largely preindustrial societies, for example, the development of an autonomous and specialized political system has been found to be associated primarily with differentiation, or elaboration, of the division of labor.[18]

Economically oriented theories of societal development, despite their popularity, do not seem as able to account for the observed patterns. Generally, these theories view rates of economic development as the crucial independent variable—that is, as best able to explain variations in political

---

[17] Ibid., p. 318.

[18] Mark Abrahamson, "The Correlates of Political Complexity," *American Sociological Review*, **34**:690–701 (Oct. 1969). See also Robert M. Marsh, *Comparative Sociology* (New York: Harcourt, 1967).

development, occupational prestige, or the like. However, in the study of political complexity, degree of economic development of societies was found to be of virtually no (independent) predictive value. Furthermore, Hodge et al., observed marked discrepancies in levels of Gross National Product (a frequently used index of economic development) in Western and non-Western nations. However, similarities in occupational prestige were not markedly affected by these differences in levels of GNP.

In sum, the results indicate that societal complexity is the structural variable that best accounts for similarities in occupational prestige. This supports the structuralist as opposed to the culturalist viewpoint in comparative analysis. As Hodge and his associates conclude: "wide differences in cultural traditions, institutional forms, and levels of living are insufficient to produce major inversions in the occupational-prestige hierarchy."[19]

Viewed in a general way, this emphasis on societal complexity is not all contradictory to our earlier emphasis on industrialization. Complexity is the more inclusive phenomenon. Industrialization may be largely equated with the high end of the complexity continuum. In other words, the general relationship is between degree of societal complexity and comparability of occupational prestige.

Industrialization and Social Mobility

The process of industrialization, which is a fundamental aspect of increasing societal complexity, creates increased opportunities for social mobility. Phillips Cutright has explored the relationship between intergenerational mobility and degree of industrial development.[20] To measure degree of industrial development, Cutright used a number of factors, including level of technological development, literacy rates, rural-urban population ratios, and family size, while measuring the extent of social mobility in terms of occupational inheritance controlling for structural changes. The measure of mobility that Cutright developed (Q) would be 1.0 if all of the observed mobility in a society were a consequence of structural changes (that is, demand mobility).

The combined-item index of industrialization was very highly correlated with international variations in rates of occupational inheritance. Specifically, the index accounted for more than three fourths of the variations in inheritance ($r = .88$, $r^2 = .77$). Furthermore, Cutright was also able to demonstrate that structural modifications rather than value changes

[19] Hodge, et al., op. cit., p. 318.
[20] Phillips Cutright, "Occupational Inheritance: A Cross-National Analysis," *American Journal of Sociology,* **73**:400–416 (Jan. 1968).

were the mechanism through which industrialization affected mobility. This was shown by correlating total mobility from all sources in each society with structural modifications. The resultant correlation is an almost perfect .96, providing further support for the assertion that changes in cultural values are, like mobility, a reaction to industrialization rather than an antecedent to mobility.

The *Q* values obtained in the sampled countries varied from .61 to .90, indicating that when structural changes were held constant all the societies were more closed than open—that is, inheritance exceeded movement. Despite this similarity, however, there were substantial intersocietal differences. The figures are presented in the following table with each of the thirteen nations arranged in increasing order of inheritance.

**Variations
in Occupational Inheritance***

Nation	Q Values
Great Britain	.614
Netherlands	.684
United States	.685
Denmark	.689
Norway	.709
Sweden	.735
France	.759
Japan	.768
West Germany	.777
Yugoslavia	.846
Italy	.878
Finland	.883
Hungary	.904

* Figures ibid., p. 412.

To persons in the United States it is probably surprising not to see their country at the very top of the list. Compared to most of the included countries, the United States is, of course, relatively open. It and the Netherlands are about equal in inheritance, and second only to Great Britain. The high rate of nonstructural movement in Great Britain is not surprising in light of other studies, however. In comparing the fathers of sons in various elite groups, for example, high-status fathers have been found to be more common in the United States than in England.[21] In other words, there is less inheritance of elite positions in England than in the United States.

In order to further clarify the role of values, Cutright subsequently examined the discrepancies between the total amounts of mobility observed

[21] Joel Gerstl and Robert Perrucci, "Educational Channels and Elite Mobility: "A Comparative Analysis," *Sociology of Education*, **38**:224–232 (Spring, 1965).

in each society and the amount that would be predicted by structural modifications. Given the previously reported correlation of .96 between total and structural mobility, the over-all magnitude of discrepancies will necessarily be small. However, in some societies there was slightly more mobility than would have been predicted, for example, Yugoslavia), and there was slightly less in others (for example, Finland).

In the United States the amount of observed mobility was virtually identical to the amount predicted. The discrepancy is .005. Only in France was the correspondence between observed and predicted closer together; discrepancy = .002. The conclusion that follows again is that the relatively high rate of intergenerational mobility in the United States is best explained by relatively great structural opportunities for mobility rather than by highly equalitarian values. Whether the values are, in fact, highly equalitarian is another question. What the results indicate is that these values—regardless of their intensity—are not of great causal importance to social mobility. This also does not mean, by implication, that variations in the internationalization of achievement values will not explain mobility differences *within* a society. Such values, as held by individuals, are associated with interasociety variations. However, intersocietal differences must be explained more by changes in structure than values.

Thus far the discussion of mobility in industrial societies has focused exclusively on rates of mobility. As noted in previous chapters, it is also important to consider the distance of the mobility. That is, is movement restricted to adjacent strata or does movement occur across a wider range of the stratification hierarchy? The following article by Thomas Fox and S. M. Miller accomplishes such an analysis.

Intra-Country Variations*
Occupational Stratification and Mobility[1]

Thomas Fox and S. M. Miller

The Study of Social Mobility

The sociological study of social mobility is almost exclusively concerned with occupational mobility. Changes in the distribution of citizenship rights or in social acceptance are not likely to be in the forefront of study of social mobility. Within the investigation of occupational social mobility, primary emphasis is on ranking occupations by prestige levels rather than by indicators of skill, income, or span of control. Occupational prestige indicators, based on surveys of attitudes of a national cross section, are assumed to be adequate summaries of the other dimensions of job positions. The emphasis in present day studies is still chiefly on intergenerational mobility (the relation of son's occupation to father's) rather than on intragenerational mobility (the course of job movement in one individual's career) or of stratum mobility (the movement of one stratum relative to other strata along the relevant dimensions). Thus, the definition of social mobility and the indicators employed to measure it provide only a limited slice of the phenomena commonly regarded as social mobility by other social scientists.[2]

In making comparisons among nations, a leap of courage must be made. Many of the difficulties of individual studies are compounded in comparative perspective. Some national studies are of poor technical quality, but we have no choice of substitutes if we wish to include a particular nation in a comparison. Time periods differ in various studies; occupational titles and ratings are not fully comparable. Consequently, it is important to recognize that *any comparisons are at best only approximations.*

The usual comparison in mobility studies is the movement of sons of manual families into nonmanual occupations.[3] The concern is with vertical mobility, though downward mobility from nonmanual strata into manual strata has been widely neglected. Cross-national studies of manual–nonmanual mobility make the heroic assumption that the manual–nonmanual divide has equal importance in all nations at all times. This assumption is obviously untrue but it is difficult to make comparisons without it. The manual–nonmanual comparison also suffers from a neglect of intra-stratum mobility, for example, the movement from unskilled to skilled; from the lower levels of the middle class to elite positions. This kind of movement can be substantial and important but is not caught when the manual–nonmanual divide is the focus of attention.

A number of technical problems intrude in international comparisons. The number of strata employed in a study affects the amount of mobility: the

---

* Published by permission of Transaction, Inc. from *Studies in Comparative International Development*, Vol. 1, No. 1, Copyright © 1965, by Transaction, Inc.

more strata, the more mobility. Therefore, for comparative purposes it is necessary to compress categories into a similar number of groupings. This technical need encourages the utilization of manual–nonmanual compressions. Another difficulty is that while we speak of a sons' generation and of a fathers' generation, we do not in actuality have such pure categories. There are fathers and sons in each occupational category but we treat our data as though each could be factored out.

A number of different types of comparisons are possible with the same data. Movement can be viewed from different perspectives and it is easy to become dizzy with perspectives and over-produce results. In the standard mobility matrix, the rows represent the outflow: "What is the occupational distribution of sons born of fathers in a given stratum?" This type of analysis is the usual one. But we can look across the principal diagonal of the matrix and note the degree of inheritance by sons of fathers' occupations. The columns provide inflow data: "What are the social origins of individuals presently in a given occupational stratum?" Now, the same sons are involved in outflow and inflow analyses; the difference is in what base they are related to in computing rates or percentages. For example, an outflow analysis can show that of 1,000 nonmanual sons 250, or 25 per cent, move into manual strata. From the point of view of manual strata which are larger than the non-manual strata say, 2,500 sons, the extent of inflow is only 10 per cent. The same movement can have different implications from varying perspectives.

Despite myriad difficulties, comparative studies of social mobility have endured. Sorokin, in his classical study of *Social Mobility in 1927* amassed a great deal of data but it was not subjected to careful, systematic analysis. Yet, his work was prescient in many ways. For almost two decades comparatively little work was done that referred to nations as a whole. David Glass and Theodore Geiger, in their own work and in the work they fostered in the Research Sub-Committee on Social Stratification and Social Mobility, emphasized in the fifties national studies executed with similar concerns and well-developed methodologies. As a result, we now have many more studies of national rates of social mobility. Seymour Martin Lipset and his collaborators, Reinhard Bendix, Hans Zetterberg and Natalie Rogoff Ramsoy, attempted to make sense out of the array of national mobility data by suggesting a basic similarity in the rates of advanced industrial nations. Miller, in his appraisal of the data, emphasized the neglect of downward mobility in most generalizations about mobility, the varied contours of mobility, (for example, knowledge of manual–nonmanual movement is not revealing about manual–elite movement), and the value of developing typologies of mobility. The work of Peter Blau and Otis Dudley Duncan in making a careful analysis of mobility patterns in the United States based on fresh data in a comparative perspective, may have great significance. At the moment, though, there seems to be a standstill in developing international comparisons of mobility.

The present paper illustrates a few of the various ways of utilizing mobility data. It does not question the international comparability of the data but attempts to improve comparability by restricting analysis to four nations. The concern is with both outflow and inflow. Its particular contribution is that it

introduces a new measure which facilitates statements comparing the degree
of equality and inequality of mobility among nations.

The Manual-Nonmanual Dichotomy

The conventional profile of social mobility is projected by the manual–nonmanual dichotomy. Table 1 presents profiles for the four nations by way of
passage into (inflow mobility) and away from (outflow mobility) the manual
and nonmanual strata. Our analysis encompasses both upward and downward
mobility in contrast to the more frequent solitary emphasis on upward
mobility.[4] Manual inflow and nonmanual outflow illustrate *downward* mobility for sons of nonmanual origins from two points of views—the manual
stratum and the nonmanual stratum. Conversely, manual outflow and nonmanual inflow record the *upward* mobility of sons of manual origin into the
nonmanual stratum. The importance of qualifying statements about mobility
rates by specifying a particular point of reference (inflow or outflow for a
particular stratum) is exemplified by studying Table 1.

Beginning with the data on outflow mobility we see that in Great Britain
the rate of outflow is greater for the nonmanual stratum than for the manual.
Downward movement is greater than upward movement: this description also
applies to Japan and the Netherlands but not the United States where upward
mobility predominates.

TABLE 1
**Comparative Manual and Nonmanual Inflow and Outflow
Mobility (in percentages)**

Nation	Manual Mobility		Nonmanual Mobility	
	Inflow	*Outflow*	*Inflow*	*Outflow*
Great Britain	24.83	24.73	42 01	42.14
Japan	12 43	23.70	48.00	29 66
Netherlands	18.73	19.77	44.84	43.20
United States	18.06	30.38	32.49	19.55

Source: Data sources for computations are D. V. Glass
et. al., Social Mobility in Britain (London: Routledge and
Kegan Paul, Inc., 1954), p. 183; Special tabulations of Johan-
nes van Tulder based on the Survey of the Institute for Social
Research in the Netherlands; Sigeki Nishihira, "Cross-
National Comparative Study on Social Stratification and Social
Mobility," (Japan), *Annals of the Institute of Statistical
Mathematics*, Vol. VIII, No. 3, 1957, p. 187; Richard Centers,
"Occupational Mobility of Urban Occupational Strata,"
American Sociological Review, Vol. XIII, No. 2, April, 1948,
p. 138 (limited to sons of urban whites). These social mobility
matrices are given in appendix of S. M. Miller, "Comparative
Social Mobility," *Current Sociology*, Vol. IX, No. 1, 1960,
pp. 1 ff. (Note: in Center's data for the U.S. as cited by
Miller above, categories VIII [farm owners or managers] and
IX [farm tenant or laborers] which appear only in the sons'
generation have been omitted.)

A comparison of the nations on the outflow indicators shows that the United States has the highest rate of upward movement, for example, manual to nonmanual. It also has the lowest rate of downward movement from the nonmanual stratum. Great Britain has the most downward movement and is second in terms of upward mobility.

Downward mobility may be more indicative of social fluidity than upward mobility. To illustrate, we are well aware that the process of industrialization has been associated with a decline in the size of the manual stratum, relative to the nonmanual—a phenomenon contributing to upward intergenerational mobility. Downward movement on the other hand may be evidence that sons are not always entitled to their fathers' social position as heir apparent but must be able in their own right or suffer displacement by more capable individuals from lower social strata.[5] If this argument is valid, then the social structures of Great Britain and the Netherlands are less congealed in some respects than in the United States and Japan—contrary to popular opinion.

The inflow patterns pertain to mobility into a stratum. All four nations are characterized by more heterogeneity of social origins in the nonmanual stratum than in the manual. Heterogeneity is measured by the extent to which sons born into another stratum become members of a given stratum. With Herrington C. Bryce, we have elsewhere dealt in depth with the concepts of heterogeneity–homogeneity that are used here.[6] Britain has the highest heterogeneity in the manual stratum as we would expect from its nonmanual pattern of outflow. But the Netherlands with a similar percentage of nonmanual outflow has less heterogeneity in the manual stratum. Even though nonmanual outflow is high in the Netherlands, its compositional effect on Dutch manual inflow is less than in Great Britain because of the relatively larger proportion of manual sons in the Netherlands.

Japan and the United States are similar in their changing occupational patterns. Japan has a lower rate of movement out of the manual stratum than the United States but an even higher degree of nonmanual heterogeneity: almost half the nonmanual workers originated in manual families. The United States has an expanding nonmanual stratum which absorbs many from manual homes and, as the nonmanual outflow figure (19 per cent) shows, has the highest level of inheritance of the nonmanual strata.

The data for Great Britain and the Netherlands show little change in the contours of the occupational structure between generations: a contour map which *only approximates* reality is presented in Table 2. In the British manual stratum (Table 1), about 25 per cent are of nonmanual backgrounds, "replacing" the 25 per cent born in manual families who have moved up into nonmanual occupations. The corresponding Dutch occupational interchange is about 19 per cent. The inference is that a virtual exchange of social position occurred between the manual sons moving up and an equal *absolute* number of nonmanual sons moving down.

As we have seen, the nonmanual strata are characterized by higher rates of both inflow and outflow mobility than the manual strata in these countries. Interestingly without a deep-seated change in the occupational distributions

TABLE 2
Percentage Distribution of Strata by Fathers' Generation and Sons' Generation

	Great Britain		Japan		Netherlands		United States	
	Fathers'	Sons'	Fathers'	Sons'	Fathers'	Sons'	Fathers'	Sons'
Nonmanual	37.11	37.02	26.74	36.17	29.98	30.87	43.97	52.40
Manual	62.89	62.98	73.26	63.82	70.02	69.13	56.03	47.60
Total	100.00	100.00	100.00	99.99	100.00	100.00	100.00	100.00
Elite	7.98	7.49	11.15	11.74	7.18	11.08	8.92	16.86
Middle class	29.13	29.52	15.59	24.45	22.80	19.79	35.04	35.54
Skilled	38.74	33.91	8.52	12.06	32.65	34.22	29.59	19.50
Semiskilled	13.09	16.95	4.02	7.50	26.41	27.39	20.16	20.33
Unskilled	11.06	12.12	60.72	44.26	10.96	7.52	6.28	7.77
Total	100.00	100.00	100.00	100.01	100.00	100.00	99.99	100.00

Source: See Table 1.

among generations, Great Britain and the Netherlands have considerable interchange among social strata. For Japan and the United States, the relative growth of the nonmanual stratum (see Table 2) can account for much of the observed upward mobility. But in Britain and the Netherlands with relatively constant occupational distributions, technological or demand induced mobility fails to explain the fluidity of their respective social structures.

The lower portion of Table 2 pictures changes in occupational structures between generations in greater detail. The elite and middle class were formerly subsumed under the nonmanual category; the skilled, semiskilled, and unskilled collectively composed the manual stratum.

In Great Britain, little change is evident in the sizes of either the elite or middle-class groups—little mobility can be attributed to variations in the relative number of positions within the nonmanual stratum. However the structure within the manual category has altered between generations. The data suggested a decrease in the level of manual skills: the relative size of the skilled substratum has diminished while the semiskilled and unskilled groups have expanded in the sons' generation.

Japan shows little change in the relative size of elites between generations, but a large increase in the middle class. The quality of the manual stratum has shifted upward; the proportion of unskilled declined while both the skilled and semiskilled proportions have increased. Use of the manual classification blankets considerable intra-stratum mobility due to structural changes over time.

The compositional change within the Dutch nonmanual stratum is unusual. Here we note that the relative size of the elite increases, but accompanied by a shrinking middle class. (The other countries portray, at minimum, a moderate middle-class expansion.) Within the manual category, the qualitative trend parallels that in Japan; the unskilled proportion diminishes while that of the skilled and semiskilled increases.

The trend for the elite in the United States shows a large increase, but little change for the middle class. A sharp decline is evident for the skilled group. The semiskilled and unskilled substrata have moderate increments in proportions in the sons' generation. Over half the sons are in the nonmanual stratum, which, as in Japan, is characterized by a large increase in the relative number of nonmanual positions between generations.

Skilled, Semiskilled, and Unskilled Outflow into the Nonmanual Stratum

Table 3 breaks down the manual stratum into integral parts, skilled, semiskilled, and unskilled, for a closer look at the sources of upward mobility into the nonmanual category.

TABLE 3
Outflow of Sons of Skilled, Semiskilled, and Unskilled Origins into the Nonmanual Stratum (in percentages)

Social Origin	Great Britain	Japan	Netherlands	United States
Skilled	29.08	30.19	26.92	38.55
Semiskilled	18.78	29.33	14.79	21.31
Unskilled	16.54	22.42	10.47	21.05

Source: See Table 1.

In Great Britain, the chances of sons of skilled workers entering the nonmanual stratum are less than two times that of semiskilled sons. Unskilled sons have the greatest disadvantage for such movement but not strikingly less than the semiskilled. The data for the Netherlands and the United States roughly parallels that of the British case: all three nations are characterized by a large gap between the skilled and semiskilled components of the manual stratum with a relatively smaller gap between the semi-skilled and unskilled substrata.

In Japan there is little difference between the skilled and semiskilled movement into nonmanual occupations although intuitively one would expect the skilled to enjoy a relative advantage over the unskilled for upward mobility; both have considerably better opportunities than the unskilled.

Great Britain, the Netherlands and Japan have quite similar percentages of skilled sons entering the nonmanual stratum, but considerably less than in the United States. Inter-country similarities are less pronounced as we turn to the semiskilled and unskilled groups. Semiskilled outflow in Japan is greater than skilled outflow in the Netherlands and has an 8-percentage-point edge on United States semiskilled outflow, which in turn is less than 3 points greater than Great Britain and almost 7 points over the Netherlands. Unskilled outflow is similar in Japan and the United States, followed at some distance by Great Britain, and at a much larger interval by the Netherlands.

This table demonstrates the importance of compositional effects. Despite the highest rate of overall manual movement into the nonmanual stratum, the United States ranks but second in terms of semiskilled and unskilled movement into the top stratum. The United States overall manual rank as highest is primarily due to a considerably larger degree of skilled outflow than that observed in the other nations, and to the numerical importance of the skilled component within the manual stratum.

Sources of Nonmanual Heterogeneity

Table 4 shows the contribution of skilled, semiskilled and unskilled mobility in the composition of the nonmanual stratum. We are now looking at the sources of heterogeneity in social origins among the nonmanual occupations.

TABLE 4
Sources of Nonmanual Heterogeneity (in percentages)

Social Origin	Great Britain	Japan	Netherlands	United States
Skilled	30.42	7.11	28.47	21.77
Semiskilled	6.64	3.26	12.65	8.20
Unskilled	4.94	37.63	3.71	2.52
Total nonmanual inflow	42.00	48.00	44.83	32.49

Source: See Table 1.

In Great Britain, almost three-quarters of the heterogeneity of the non-manual stratum is due to the mobility of sons of skilled workers. The semi-skilled contribution to nonmanual heterogeneity is slightly higher than the unskilled, but considerably less than the skilled. In the Netherlands, the entry of skilled sons accounts for somewhat less than two-thirds of the nonmanual heterogeneity; the semiskilled sons are decidedly more important than the unskilled. Two-thirds of United States nonmanual heterogeneity is due to the movement of skilled sons; semiskilled sons are three times as numerous in the nonmanual stratum as are unskilled. Japan is an anomaly: unskilled sons are the predominant source of nonmanual heterogeneity. This is largely but not fully due to the high percentage of the Japanese labor force which is classified as unskilled. Except for Japan, the skilled category is the greatest contributor to nonmanual heterogeneity. Movement of the semiskilled is greatest in the Netherlands and the United States.

Elite and Middle-Class Movement into the Manual Stratum

A breakdown of the nonmanual stratum into the elite and middle class permits a closer look at the sources of manual heterogeneity. Taking the outflow mobility dimension first, Table 5 gives the percentages of *downward* elite and middle-class mobility.

The United States and Great Britain have low rates of elite outflow. The low figure for the United States was anticipated from prior observations where we noted nonmanual inheritance to be high. Given the extremely high rate of nonmanual outflow in Great Britain (42.1 per cent), a much greater rate of elite outflow would be expected if this substream is almost as congealed as in the United States. Elite inheritance is lowest in Japan and is similar to the Netherlands in terms of elite outflow.

TABLE 5
Outflow of Sons of Elite and Middle-Class Origins into the Manual Stratum
(in percentages)

Social Origin	Great Britain	Japan	Netherlands	United States
Elite	17.92	26.92	24.26	14.81
Middle class	47.62	31.62	49.16	20.75

Source: See Table 1.

Middle-class outflow in Great Britain and the Netherlands are similar and high, 50 per cent higher than in Japan and more than double that of the United States. The difference between elite and middle-class outflow rates into the manual stratum is greatest in Great Britain, lowest in Japan.

Table 6 shows the impact on manual heterogeneity by the *downwardly* mobile sons of elite and middle-class origins. For all countries the elite contribution to the composition of the manual stratum is relatively small, less than 5 per cent (less than 3 per cent if Japan is excepted). Most of the heterogeneity results from the downward movement of the middle-class origins. Middle-class origins in the manual stratum account for over 20 per cent of the sons in this category in Great Britain and over 15 per cent for the other countries. The four nations each have a noticeable middle-class origin effect on the composition of the manual stratum but elite representation is almost nil.

TABLE 6
Sources of Manual Heterogeneity (in percentages)

Social Origin	Great Britain	Japan	Netherlands	United States
Elite	2.27	4.70	2.52	2.78
Middle class	22 56	15.28	16.22	15.28
Total manual inflow	24.83	18.06	18.74	18.06

Source: See Table 1.

Intra-country Equality of Mobility Opportunity

Within each country, the distribution of opportunities of sons of other social origins entering any given stratum can be studied with the aid of Feldmesser's index of equality of opportunity.[7] This index takes the proportion of sons remaining in their stratum of origin (for example, nonmanual sons of nonmanual fathers) in each country as 100. The proportions of sons of other origins entering the given stratum are expressed as ratios to 100. If the proportions or frequencies of sons of all social origins entering any given stratum are equal, all ratios will have the value of 100. In other words, this index examines the proportional representation of all social strata in any given stratum. The further any ratio is from 100, the less opportunity that group has for entering any given stratum than do the sons who inherit the status.

Table 7 presents the indices of intra-country equality of opportunity for the elite, middle class, skilled, semiskilled, and unskilled strata for each of the four nations.

TABLE 7
Indices of Equality of Opportunity for Entry into Elite, Middle-Class, Skilled, Semiskilled, and Unskilled Strata

Equality of opportunity for:

Elite	Great Britain	Japan	Netherlands	United States
Elite	100	100	100	100
Middle class	19	39	22	37
Skilled	7	21	20	22
Semiskilled	3	17	6	6
Unskilled	2	18	5	9
$\bar{X}$	26.2	39.0	30.6	34.8
Middle Class				
Middle class	100	100	100	100
Elite	88	65	57	51
Skilled	61	41	41	45
Semiskilled	39	43	29	31
Unskilled	36	29	20	27
$\bar{X}$	64.8	55.6	49.4	50.8
Skilled				
Skilled	100	100	100	100
Semiskilled	84	53	64	70
Unskilled	80	18	62	56
Middle class	76	20	68	28
Elite	29	20	39	27
$\bar{X}$	73.8	42.2	66.6	56.2
Semiskilled				
Semiskilled	100	100	100	100
Unskilled	75	23	89	47
Skilled	54	50	46	47
Middle class	36	29	31	21
Elite	16	25	13	8
$\bar{X}$	56.2	45.4	55.8	44.6
Unskilled				
Unskilled	100	100	100	100
Semiskilled	57	33	48	27
Skilled	48	19	28	18
Middle class	23	24	18	6
Elite	7	18	3	5
$\bar{X}$	47.0	38.8	39.4	31.2

Equality of Opportunity in Entering the Elite and Middle-Class Strata

In Great Britain, sons of middle-class fathers enjoy a distinct advantage over sons of skilled, semiskilled, and unskilled in securing membership in the elite stratum. The middle-class sons have almost three times the opportunities of the semiskilled sons (19/7) of entering the elite, six times the opportunities of the semiskilled (19/3), and nine times the chances of the unskilled (19/2). But the son of an elite father has the best opportunity to become an elite himself—his chances are five times greater than for the son of a middle-class father (100/19) and fifty times that for the son of an unskilled father (100/2). Thus equality of opportunity for movement into the elite category appears extremely limited in Great Britain.

The son of a middle-class father in Japan enjoys almost twice the opportunity of a skilled son (39/21) for gaining admission to elite status, and only slightly more than twice the advantages of the semiskilled and unskilled (respectively, 39/17 and 39/18). Japanese sons of middle-class origins are more than one-third of the way toward achieving elite entry equality with the sons of elite fathers (100/39).

In the Netherlands, sons of middle-class origins have very little advantage over the sons of skilled origins in securing elite status, their chances are almost equal (22/20). But skilled and middle-class sons have considerably better chances of entering the elite than the semiskilled or unskilled sons. The close proximity of the opportunities of the middle-class and skilled for elite entry suggest, as a possibility, that these groups are more closely related to each other than to the elite category.

Turning now to the United States, we find that here, as in Japan, the sons of middle-class fathers have traveled more than a third of the route leading to equality of opportunity with sons of elite fathers (100/37). Middle-class advantage over offspring of the skilled exists but is less than double the chances of the latter (37/22). The son of a skilled father has almost four times the opportunity of a semiskilled to reach the elite stratum (22/6). (Although the index for equality of opportunity for entry into the elite in the United States is greater for the unskilled than for the semiskilled, its validity may be questioned and perhaps attributed to weaknesses in the original study.)

An average value for the index is given below the last stratum for equality of opportunity of movement into the elite (and for each strata below) but can only be compared within countries, not between them. The data in Table 7 then, do not say that equality of opportunity is greatest in Japan and least in Great Britain.

Equality of Opportunity in Entering the Skilled, Semiskilled, and Unskilled Strata

One of the most striking findings, with the exception of Japan, is that the averages of the indices of equality of opportunity are largest within each country for entry into the skilled stratum, not the middle class, which might be expected. Lloyd Reynolds has recently argued (with respect to the manual stratum) that there is a tendency for the skilled category to become more of a closed group, with the opportunities of movement from unskilled and semi-skilled occupations into the skilled stratum declining.[8] Although our data are not appropriate for directly questioning this hypothesis, our calculations for Great Britain, Netherlands and the United States show that the skilled stratum is *the group* in which equality of opportunity is the greatest.

Turning to the other end of the social spectrum from the elites—the unskilled—we find an interesting pattern in the USA. The USA shows a relatively lower degree of equality of access to this occupational substratum than do the other nations. At this end of the occupational ladder, low access has different implications than it does at the other end. At the high end, it shows the inability of those below the elite to overcome the barriers. For at the low end, it represents the pooling of the unskilled, their low ability to leave and the relative invulnerability of the higher strata to such drastic falls in position.[9]

Inter-country Equality of Opportunity

Feldmesser's index of equality of opportunity for each of the four nations can be made directly comparable by selecting the proportion of occupational inheritance within any given country as the base of the index for each stratum. This measure, developed by Fox, gives the inter-country equality of opportunity indices for all countries, relative to the nation selected as the base. Great Britain has been used as the base nation for this paper. If the index for, say, elite inheritance is above 100 in the United States, occupational inheritance would be greater in the United States than in Great Britain with the difference between the respective index values indicating how much greater. (The values of the comparative indices for the base-country Great Britain in Table 8 are the same as in Table 7).

Elite Stratum Comparisons

Table 8 clearly shows that the ability of sons of elite fathers to inherit their fathers' socioeconomic status is greatest in the United States, 24 per cent greater than in Great Britain. The proportion of elite inheritance is second greatest in the Netherlands—least in Japan. Middle-class and skilled sons in the United States also have better chances of becoming elites than their counterparts in the other three nations. The USA has high inheritance and high accessibility. The middle class in Japan has almost double the opportunity of the British middle class of gaining elite membership and 30 per cent better than the Netherlands middle class. Skilled opportunity for elite entry in the Netherlands is about three and one-half that of the skilled in Great Britain—one and one-fourth that in Japan. The Japanese semiskilled and unskilled have the advantage over their contemporaries in Great Britain, the Netherlands, and the United States in terms of their chances of becoming elites—almost the opportunities of the middle class in Great Britain.

Strikingly, the averages of the indices for elite entry show opportunity to be greatest in the United States (more than one and a half that in Great Britain), followed at some distance by the Netherlands, then Japan and Great Britain. When we examined the intra-country equality of opportunity in Table 7 (within countries), Japan had the highest rate of intra-country elite equality, followed by the United States. This means that in Japan, there is less difference

TABLE 8
Comparative Indices of Equality of Opportunity for Entry into Elite, Middle-Class,
Skilled, Semiskilled and Unskilled Strata (Base = Great Britain)

Equality of opportunity for:

Elite	Great Britain	Japan	Netherlands	United States
Elite	100	86	119	124
Middle class	19	34	26	46
Skilled	7	18	24	27
Semiskilled	3	15	7	7
Unskilled	2	15	6	12
$\bar{X}$	26.2	33.6	36.4	43.2

Middle class

Middle class	100	143	92	137
Elite	88	93	53	70
Skilled	61	59	38	62
Semiskilled	39	61	27	42
Unskilled	36	42	18	37
$\bar{X}$	64.8	79.6	45.6	69.6

Skilled

Skilled	100	111	112	81
Semiskilled	84	59	72	56
Unskilled	80	19	69	45
Middle class	76	22	77	22
Elite	29	22	43	23
$\bar{X}$	73.8	46.6	74.6	45.4

Semiskilled

Semiskilled	100	81	148	144
Unskilled	75	19	132	67
Skilled	54	40	69	68
Middle class	36	23	45	30
Elite	16	20	19	12
$\bar{X}$	56.2	36.6	82.6	64.2

Unskilled

Unskilled	100	233	74	144
Semiskilled	57	78	35	39
Skilled	48	44	21	26
Middle class	23	56	14	9
Elite	7	42	2	7
$\bar{X}$	47.0	90.6	29.2	45.0

between the proportions of various strata entering the elite and the proportion of elite inheritance. But in the United States (with its expanding elite) the *actual* proportions of the different strata entering the elite are greater than those in Japan. In other words, relatively larger proportions of non-elite and elite origin sons tend to become members of the elite stratum in the United States than in Japan.

Middle-Class Comparisons

Middle-class stratum inheritance is proportionally highest in Japan, then the United States, both with a degree of middle-class inheritance at least 35 per cent greater than in Great Britain. The Netherlands has the lowest proportion of inheritance. Sons of elite fathers have the highest relative chance of falling into the middle class in Japan and England. This might be expected since elite inheritance was lowest in Japan and England, therefore, relatively more sons of elites experience downward mobility of one step to the middle class.

Strikingly, although United States elite inheritance was the highest, then closely followed by the Netherlands, United States sons of elite fathers have considerably greater relative likelihood of entering the middle class than in the Netherlands.

There is little difference between the proportion of skilled entering the middle class in the United States and Great Britain, with Japan in close proximity. But much less opportunity for skilled movement into the middle class exists in the Netherlands.

Semiskilled and unskilled opportunity for middle-class movement is greatest in Japan and the United States, then Great Britain. The opportunity for unskilled entry into the middle class in Japan is about two and a half times as great as in the Netherlands.

Skilled Comparisons

When the focus of attention shifts to comparison of equality of opportunity for entry into the skilled category, the United States loses much of its former prominence, showing considerably less skilled inheritance that the base-country Great Britain and the other two nations. Dutch skilled inheritance is slightly greater than Japan; both are about 10 per cent greater than in Great Britain. The proportion of semiskilled entering the skilled category is highest in Great Britain, strangely enough, with this holding also for sons of unskilled origins. In the Netherlands, the opportunity of semiskilled and unskilled movement into the skilled stratum is considerably less than in Great Britain but well above that in the United States and Japan. Japanese sons of semiskilled fathers have but a slight advantage over those in the United States. The Japanese unskilled are the most disadvantaged, having but about one-half the chances of the United States unskilled to enter the skilled stratum and one-third the Dutch unskilled chances. The unskilled in Great Britain have four times the proportion of sons in the skilled categories as in Japan.

Over all, averages of the indices show the chance to become a member of the skilled stratum is highest in the Netherlands and Great Britain, with both countries ranking well above Japan and the United States.

Semiskilled Comparisons

The Netherlands and the United States have considerably greater semiskilled inheritance than Great Britain. In turn, Japan has about 20 per cent less than Great Britain. The proportion of unskilled entering the semiskilled stratum in the Netherlands is double that in the United States, less than twice that in Great Britain. Skilled and unskilled chances for semiskilled stratum entry are about equal in the United States. The middle classes and elites are less represented in the semiskilled stratum.

Unskilled Comparisons

Unskilled socioeconomic inheritance in Japan is two and one-third that in Great Britain—significantly greater than in the United States, the second highest nation on unskilled inheritance. Dutch unskilled inheritance is but about one-half that in the United States. Japanese unskilled inheritance of such astronomical proportions is in part explained by the tremendous size of this group in the Japanese social structure. But the most astounding index value for the unskilled stratum occurs for the elite chance in Japan of becoming a member of the unskilled. Elite entry into the unskilled in Japan is six times greater than in the United States and Great Britain, twenty times that in the Netherlands. The unskilled entry values in Japan for skilled, middle-class and elite movement are similar within a limited range, whereas the spread between these social strata is considerably greater for the other three countries. In the case of Great Britain, we find, however, that the proportion of the skilled entering the unskilled is somewhat greater than in Japan, but around twice that in the United States and Netherlands.

Conclusions?   We wish that we could offer a concise and parsimonious explanation of the variations in the rates of social mobility both within and between the countries. But we cannot. The following fragmentary observations are substitutes for all-encompassing empirical generalizations or explanatory theorems.

There are a host of different ways of measuring mobility. And mobility has many varied contours. Mobility statements, as we have said elsewhere,[10] must be specific—indicative of a particular frame of reference, for example, only manual into nonmanual; or the degree of heterogeneity of the elite substratum. As a corollary, patterns of mobility seem to differ in different parts of the class structure. A statement of accessibility to elite status is inadequate for describing (let alone understanding) accessibility to the unskilled stratum. Inheritance and accessibility are different dimensions of similar phenomena.

Aware of the pitfalls inherent in mobility analysis, we still find it a fruitful area of research. We think it can be further extended, as we plan to do, attempting to see under what conditions of social mobility, political stability is greatest. If political scientists and others would give us indicators of political stability, it would be helpful.

Mobility analysis is not an "open sesame" to understanding everything —studies of fertility have shown this. We think American sociologists have a dreadful predilection to explain *everything* in terms of status panic or reward, instability or stability. This status concern may be more revealing about sociologists than about societies! But we believe that the study of social mobility, especially if broadly conceived, gives us a picture, though not complete, of changes taking place in sociooccupational patterns. And it gives snapshots of different periods of time, which if used judiciously, should be illuminating.

NOTES

1. This study has been supported by Project 6-25-124 of the National Science Foundation.
2. Cf. S. M. Miller, "Comparative Social Mobility: A Trend Report," *Current Sociology*, Vol. IX, No. 1, 1960, pp. 1–5.
3. We are interchangeably and loosely using terms like stratum, occupations, and categories.
4. Cf. Seymour Martin Lipset and Reinhard Bendix, *Social Mobility in Industrial Society* (Berkeley: University of California Press, 1959).
5. But the possibility of downward mobility by choice can not be denied. In this case the son simply prefers an occupation and "way-of-life" that differs from that of his "origin."
6. Herrington C. Bryce, S. M. Miller, and Thomas Fox, "The Heterogeneity of Social Classes in Industrial Societies: A Study in Social Mobility," paper presented at the Spring meetings of the Eastern Sociological Associations, New York City, April, 1963.
7. Robert A. Feldmesser, *Aspects of Social Mobility in the Soviet Union* (unpublished Ph.D. thesis, Harvard University, 1955), pp. 223–225.
8. Lloyd G. Reynolds, "Economics of Labor," p. 277 in Howard S. Ellis, ed., *A Survey of Contemporary Economics* (Philadelphia: American Economic-Assoc., Blakiston Co., 1948), pp. 255–287.
9. Cf. Lipset and Bendix, op. cit., pp. 57–58 and 64–68.
10. Miller, op. cit., p. 5; Bryce, Miller, and Fox, loc. cit.

Industrialization and the Convergence of Stratification Systems

An important theme pervading much of the comparative research is that the process of industrialization leads to a "standardization" or uniformity, of social structure across societies.[22] Institutional arrangements, including the structure of social inequality, are viewed as converging toward a common form as a consequence of forces inherent in industrialization.

Involved in this convergence of stratification systems are changes in three fundamental aspects of social inequality. First, there is increased social differentiation, particularly in terms of "functional differentiation," or division of labor, which is coupled with the growing importance of multiple dimensions of "rank differentiation." Specifically, advancing technology and its application gives rise to a wide range of new and very specialized occupations, particularly in the skilled and semi-skilled manual and in the clerical and managerial categories. Furthermore, the occupations that emerge require greater skill and training and command greater rewards such as income and prestige. As a result, education and training become increasingly important as filters into the occupational hierarchy.

Secondly, industrialization, presumably because of increasing emphasis on production and achievement, leads to a greater correspondence between occupational performance, training, and rewards. In other words, industrialization creates pressures toward equilibration[23]—that is, the tendency

[22] Alex Inkeles, "Social Stratification in the Modernization of Russia," in *The Transformation of Russian Society*, Cyril E. Black, ed. (Cambridge: Harvard U., 1960).

[23] See the discussion of status equilibration and status consistency in Chapter 6.

for individuals and groups to occupy relatively consistently ranked positions across the multiple dimensions of social stratification.

Thirdly, industrialization leads to an increase in the rate of social mobility. A substantial part of this increase is a consequence of the pro-liferation of occupations in the middle of the stratification hierarchy (that is, demand mobility) although, presumably, there is also an increase in voluntary circulation as a consequence of a greater emphasis on achievement values.

The convergence hypothesis views industrialization as a process that overrides other factors, such as cultural differences or differences in political systems, that may make for divergence between stratification systems. In this respect, the view that industrialization leads to convergence is subject to many of the same kinds of criticisms as those directed toward Marx's theory, for example, that it is deterministic. Furthermore, political ideology permeates the convergence hypothesis just as ideology permeated the crit-icisms of Marx. For instance, the Soviet sociologists M. N. Rutkevich and F. R. Filippov assert that the idea of convergence between Western and socialist stratification systems is "bourgeoisie sociology," and that attempts to show the socialist countries as having a social hierarchy in the Western sense of the word are "slanderous in nature and are widely used by impe-rialist propaganda in the ideological struggle against socialist countries.[24]

Despite the ideological assertion of Soviet sociologists, the Soviet Union and other socialist societies are stratified, and in many ways that closely resemble Western capitalist and postcapitalist countries. However, there is an important difference between socialist and capitalist societies that does undermine the logic of the argument that industrialization, or increasing complexity, per se causes a convergence of stratification systems. This difference stems from the fact that the stratification system of socialist countries is a direct product of government decisions and control over the economy. In the Soviet Union, for example, wages are set, individual in-comes are determined, and production quotas are fixed not by free market forces of supply and demand, but rather by government decree. In this respect the economy is totally planned and exists within the political order. Consequently, market forces have only indirect effects on the structure of inequality.

In contrast, Western capitalist and postcapitalist societies exhibit considerably less concentration of political power and the stratification system, particularly the distribution of the labor force, reflects the market forces of supply and demand. Nonetheless, government actions impact the

[24] M. N. Rutkevich and F. R. Filippov, "Principles of the Marxist Approach to Social Structure and Social Mobility," *International Journal of Sociology*, **3**:237 (Spring, Summer 1973).

stratification system via legislation (that is, civil rights legislation that mandates equal employment opportunities for women and minorities) and, most dramatically, as an employer. In the United States, for instance, approximately 16 per cent of the labor force is employed by federal, state, or local government, many in white-collar bureaucratic jobs. Furthermore, the economies of contemporary Western industrial nations do not operate in a laissez faire environment. Rather, the economy is "managed" and the stratification system affected by government fiscal and monetary policies that redistribute income via progressive taxation (that is, the graduated income tax) and transfer payments (that is, social security, old-age assistance, welfare payments, and the like) and regulate the demand for goods and services by controlling the supply of money in the hands of consumers and lenders.

John H. Goldthorpe summarizes these differences:

> It is then not too much to say that in Soviet society hierarchical differentiation is an instrument of the regime. To a significant degree stratification is organized in order to suit the political needs of the regime; and, as these needs change, so too may the particular structure of inequality. In other words, the Soviet system of stratification is characterized by an important element of "deliberateness," and it is this which basically distinguishes it from the Western system, in spite of the many apparent similarities. In the industrial societies of the West, one could say, the action of the state sets limits to the extent of social inequalities which derive basically from the operation of a market economy: in Soviet society the pattern of inequality also results in part from "market" forces, but in this case these are subordinated to political control up to the limits set by the requirements of the industrial system. For this reason, one may conclude, Soviet society is not, in the same way as Western society, *class* stratified.[25]

As Goldthorpe points out, if these arguments are correct,

> it becomes difficult to see how one can formulate *any* general and comprehensive propositions concerning stratification change as part of a "logic" of industrial development. For the essential assumption involved in such propositions—that of some necessary "primacy" of the economic system over the political—is no longer a reliable one. It has to be recognized, rather, that stratification systems are not to be understood as mere "reflections" of a certain level of technology and industrial organization but are shaped by a range of other factors, important among which may be that of purposive

[25] John H. Goldthorpe, "Social Stratification in Industrial Society," in *Structured Social Inequality*, Celia S. Heller, ed. (New York: Macmillan, 1968), p. 463.

political action; and further, that the importance of this latter factor in societies in which political power is highly concentrated is such as to create a distinctive type of stratification which is difficult even to discuss in terms of concepts developed in a Western, capitalist context.[26]

The Future of Mobility in the United States

The great observed importance of industrialization as an antecedent to mobility raises an interesting question with respect to the future of mobility in the United States. The greatest acceleration in rates of industrialization probably have occurred already in this country. New technological innovations and more automation will surely occur. But their relative effects—in terms of degree of industrialization—will be less than those that have occurred previously. Can we therefore expect a relative decline in rates of intergenerational mobility?

To be more specific, a high percentage of the structural modification in preceding decades has involved the displacement of farmers and manual laborers. While the percentage of the labor force engaged in these occupations may continue to be reduced toward some hypothetical minimum, the rate of decline will necessarily be smaller. In terms of the conceptual dichotomy we have been following, then, rates of mobility should become increasingly dependent on societal values. Thus, voluntary circulation may ultimately account for more of the total mobility than structural modification.

A comparison of the United States and Australia, presented by Leonard Broom and F. Lancaster Jones, is illustrative of this forecast.[27] There are two important reasons for having selected Australia. First, it is a relatively unique country in that it has traditionally had large-scale agricultural industrialization. There has, therefore, been little recent agricultural to industrial-urban movement of the labor force. Secondly, Australia has long been considered highly equalitarian in orientation. Can this result in a higher than expected rate of intergenerational mobility?

The United States and Australia were compared according to amount and type of mobility. This involved breaking down total observed mobility into a structurally forced and a voluntary circulation component. Expected rates of mobility also were calculated, based on the assumption that there would be no occupational inheritance in the society. Finally, observed and expected rates were examined for discrepancies. The resultant statistical summary of mobility in the two societies is presented in the following table.

---

[26] Ibid., pp. 464–465.
[27] Leonard Broom and F. Lancaster Jones, "Father-To-Son Mobility: Australia in Comparative Perspective," *American Journal of Sociology,* **74**:333–342 (Jan. 1969).

	Country	
Characteristic	Australia	United States
Total observed mobility	42%	49%
Structural mobility	10	23
Circulation mobility	32	26
Expected mobility	62	64
Deviation: observed-expected	−20	−15

Examination of the figures indicates that there is somewhat more (observed) mobility in the United States, but that there is a greater deviation between observed and expected mobility in Australia. This reversal of standing occurs because substantially less of the mobility in Australia is structurally forced. Thus, viewed in terms of the possibilities of intergenerational mobility, the equalitarian values of Australia result in a relatively higher rate of mobility. This finding quite possibly foretells a future in which values rather than structures will be of paramount importance.

Summary and Conclusion

THE UNITED STATES IN HISTORICAL AND COMPARATIVE PERSPECTIVE. In the preceding chapters we have examined mobility in the United States from a variety of perspectives. Historically, the first decades of the twentieth century were seen to be a period of relatively little movement. Despite dramatic rags to riches tales, the vast majority of persons moved little up the social ladder: either with respect to where they began or where their fathers finished. The alarming notes of some sociologists during the 1930s and 1940s that urban-industrial work was reducing mobility were rejected, however, as pre-twentieth-century America did not seem to offer substantial opportunities either.

Although the costs of World War II were great in every respect, it did mark a time of change in the mobility patterns of the United States. Like all wars it was, of course, unsettling for millions of persons; it probably predisposed many to pursue opportunities they would not otherwise have sought. This was especially true with respect to education. Correspondingly, there was an increase in the degree to which education was becoming the vehicle to occupational attainments. The result has been increasing mobility from World War II to the present. However, father's occupational (and related) standings continue to exert a substantial impact on son's educational attainments. So, despite the openness of the occupational structure with respect to education, the educational structure has not been sufficiently open to provide an escape hatch for the majority of our ghetto dwellers.

The postwar upsurge in mobility was seen to be primarily the result of structural modifications. High-prestige jobs were expanding while low-prestige jobs were declining—both as the result of industrialization. More equalitarian values, if they did indeed result, were a consequence rather than a cause.

Viewed comparatively, rates of mobility in the United States were observed to be relatively high, largely due to the high rate of structurally induced, forced demand. In trying to glimpse the future though, our guess about postindustrial mobility patterns is that they will reflect increasingly the intensity of equalitarian values as structural modifications occur with declining impact.

Subject Index

Name Index

Abbott, L., 232–233
Abegglen, J. C., 149, 160, 228
Abrahamson, M., 27, 36, 100, 113–121, 350
Acker, J., 211
Adams, S., 149, 154
Alexander, C. N., 293
Altman, L. K., 319, 325
Anderson, C. A., 148, 153, 154
Anderson, D. H., 145, 155, 261
Anton, T. J., 153, 154
Armer, J. M., 293
Aron, R., 81, 88
Auber, J. F., 59

Baltzell, E. D., 328
Barber, B., 4, 151, 154, 185
Barber, E., 4
Barnes, H. E., 6, 7
Bauman, K. E., 60–61
Becker, H., 6, 7
Bell, D., 149, 154, 228
Bell, R. R., 315, 325
Bell, W., 304
Bendix, R., 52, 73–88, 146, 149, 153, 154, 186, 194, 214, 253, 305, 334, 349, 368
Benoit-Smullyan, E., 55–58
Bergel, E., 15, 153, 154
Berle, A., Jr., 145, 154
Bernard, J., 324, 325
Berry, K., 67, 69
Beshers, J., 9–11, 250
Billewicz, W. Z., 207
Bingham, A. M., 145, 154
Bird, C., 317, 325
Black, C. E., 368
Blalock, H. M., 71
Blau, P. M., 43, 45, 153, 154, 207,

219–220, 260, 264–269, 275–292
Blauner, R., 39, 44
Bloch, M., 85–86, 88
Bogue, D. J., 130
Bok, D. C., 38, 44
Bond, H. M., 323, 325
Borkenau, F., 91
Boskoff, A., 143, 152, 153, 154
Bottomore, T. B., 7, 145, 154
Bradburn, N. M., 39, 44
Brand, H., 150, 154
Brazziel, W. F., Jr., 317, 325
Bressler, M., 207
Briefs, G., 145, 154
Brinton, C., 41, 44
Bronfenbrenner, U., 244
Broom, L., 43, 44, 251, 371
Brunner, O., 84, 88
Bryce, H. C., 357, 368
Buchanan, W., 40, 44
Buckley, W., 107, 111, 147, 153, 154
Burgess, E. W., 129–131
Burke, P. J., 61

Calverton, V. F., 304
Campbell, A. A., 324, 326
Campbell, E. Q., 293
Cantril, H., 40, 44
Caplovitz, D., 39, 44
Carlsson, G., 277, 292
Cayton, H., 136, 147, 155
Centers, R., 36, 171, 172, 251, 263, 356
Chambliss, W. J., 59, 67–68
Chapin, F. S., 189
Chinoy, E., 299, 304
Cloward, R. A., 304
Cohn, W., 148, 155